Iron Curtain Trail

German-German Border Trail

Along the "Green Belt" from Lübeck to Hof

An original *bikeline*-cycling guide

VERLAG**ESTERBAUER**

bikeline®-Cycling Guide
Iron Curtain Trail 3
German-German Border Trail
© 2019, **Verlag Esterbauer GmbH**
A-3751 Rodingersdorf, Hauptstr. 31
Tel.: +43/2983/28982-0, Fax: -500
E-Mail: bikeline@esterbauer.com
www.esterbauer.com
1st edition 2019
ISBN: 978-3-85000-790-0
Please quote edition and ISBN number in all correspondence!

Translation: Marie and Chris Lines
We wish to thank all the people who contributed to the production of this book.

The *bikeline*-Team: Birgit Albrecht-Walzer, Katharina Amon-Schneider, Sabine Bacher-Baumgartner, Beatrix Bauer, Michael Binder, Veronika Bock, Petra Bruckmüller, Roland Esterbauer, Dagmar Güldenpfennig, Martina Kreindl, Nora Ludolph, Gregor Münch, Karin Neichsner, Carmen Paradeiser, Sabrina Pusch, Claudia Retzer, Petra Schartner, Sonja Schleifer, Isabella Tillich, Christian Thoren, Martin Trippmacher, Carina Winkelhofer, Martin Wischin, Wolfgang Zangerl

Cover photos: Michael Cramer (large photo on the right), Hötensleben Border Monument; Jürgen Ritter (small ones on the left), The "Bridge of Unity" to Vacha (1986/2006)

Photo credits: Atelier Blume: 37284 Waldkappel: 128; DDR-Fotoarchiv Marco Bertram: 46, 48, 136; Dieter Hertwig: 40; Dirk Eisermann: 20; Hans Arndt: 94; Hans-Georg Schwedhelm: 116; Henning Meyer: 94; H.-L. Vogt: 140; Jürgen Ritter: 15, 44, 51, 84, 90, 96, 122, 134, 166, 180, 181; Marco Bertram: 28, 44, 50, 52, 54, 64, 80, 88, 89, 98, 102, 104, 106, 107, 108, 112, 113, 114, 117, 136, 138, 139, 146, 148, 149, 150, 152, 154, 156, 158, 176, 183, 184; Martin Kozàk: 22; Michael Cramer: 21, 26, 34, 36, 61, 62, 66, 68, 84, 92, 182, 182; Sabine Wittkopf: 65; Stadtinformation Boizenburg/Elbe: 43; Stephan v. Dassel: 19; Stiftung Aufarbeitung: 28, 104, 137, 162; Stiftung Aufarbeitung/Uwe Gerig: 56, 58, 106, 110, 121, 167, 172; Tourismus Coburg: 164; Tourismus GmbH Ilsenburg, Andreas Lander: 101; Tourismus- und Veranstaltungsbetrieb der Lucas-Cranach-Stadt Kronach, Dr. Otmar Fugmann: 168; Tourist-Information Eschwege, J. Riedl: 126; Touristinformation Fladungen: 144; Tourist-Information Tann (Rhön): 140; Trägerverbund Burg Lenzen e. V.: 42, 58

Cartography created with *axpand*
(www.axes-systems.com)

911wzmib

bikeline

Preface

To live, breathe and experience history in its purest form – that is the goal of the "European Iron Curtain trail". From the Barents Sea to the Black Sea, this guide traces the history of the Cold War and takes you along the Western border of the old Warsaw Pact countries across Europe. The route does not just embody European culture, history and sustainable tourism, but also provides cyclists who are interested in history with some spectacularly beautiful and varied landscapes and unique habitats in the European Green Belt, which one is sure to find along the border strip.

This volume describes the 1,100-kilometre-long part from Lübeck to Hof, where the borders of Saxony, Bavaria and the Czech Republic meet.

Maps, route descriptions, extensive historical background information, references to the cultural and tourist offering of each region as well as practical travel and accommodation advice make this cycling guide a truly valuable companion on your journey to discovering the route along the former Iron Curtain.

map legend

Cycling routes (Radrouten)

Main cycle route, low motor traffic
(Hauptroute, wenig KFZ-Verkehr)
- ▬▬▬▬ Paved surface (asphaltiert)
- ▬ ▬ ▬ Unpaved surface (nicht asphaltiert)
- ▪▪▪▪▪ Bad surface (schlecht befahrbar)

Main cycle route, without motor traffic / cycle path
(Hauptroute, autofrei / Radweg)
- ▬▬▬▬ Paved surface (asphaltiert)
- ▬ ▬ ▬ Unpaved surface (nicht asphaltiert)
- ▪▪▪▪▪ Bad surface (schlecht befahrbar)

Excursion or alternative cycle route, low motor traffic
(Ausflug od. Variante, wenig KFZ-Verkehr)
- ▬▬▬▬ Paved surface (asphaltiert)
- ▬ ▬ ▬ Unpaved surface (nicht asphaltiert)
- ▪▪▪▪▪ Bad surface (schlecht befahrbar)

Excursion or alternative route, without motor traffic / cycle path
(Ausflug od. Variante, autofrei / Radweg)
- ▬▬▬▬ Paved surface (asphaltiert)
- ▬ ▬ ▬ Unpaved surface (nicht asphaltiert)
- ▪▪▪▪▪ Bad surface (schlecht befahrbar)

Other cycle routes (Sonstiges)
- ▬▬▬▬ Other cycle route (sonstige Radroute)

- ●●●●● Cycle route with significant motor traffic (verkehrsreiche Radroute)
- ▬▬▬▬ Cobbled street (Kopfsteinpflaster)
- ▬▬▬▬ Cne-way connection (Einbahnführung)
- ⚓▬▬ Ferry connection (Fahrverbindung)
- ▬▬▬▬ Road surface unknown (unbekannter Belag)
- ▬▬▬▬ Tunnel (Tunnel)
- ▬▬▬▬ Dismounting recommended (Schiebestrecke)
- ▬▬▬▬ Train connection (Zugverbindung)
- ○○○○○○ Planned cycle path (Radweg in Planung)
- ✕✕✕✕✕✕ Closed cycle path (Radweg gesperrt)
- ▬▬▬▬ Cycle lane (Radfahrstreifen)
- ▬▬▬▬ Cycle path along road (straßenbegleitender Radweg)
- ✕▬✕▬✕ Road closed to cyclists (Straße für Radfahrer gesperrt)
- ⇨ Described direction (Beschriebene Fahrtrichtung)
- ⑤ Waypoint (Wegpunkt)

Gradient / Distance (Steigungen / Entfernungen)
- ➤ Steep gradient, uphill (starke Steigung)
- ➤ Light gradient, uphill (leichte bis mittlere Steigung)
- ⌐2,4¬ Distance in km, rounded (Entfernung in Kilometern, gerundet)

Important cycling information (Radinformationen)

- 🔧 Bike workshop* (Fahrradwerkstatt*)
- 🚲 Bike rental* (Fahrradvermietung*)
- 🚲 Covered bike stands* (überdachter Abstellplatz*)
- 🚲 Lockable bike stands* (abschließbarer Abstellplatz*)
- 🔋 E-bike charging station (E-Bike Ladestation)
- ℹ Information board* (Infotafel*)
- ⚠ Dangerous section (Gefahrenstelle)
- ⚠ Read text carefully (Text beachten)
- ⬛ Stairs (Treppe)
- 🚴 Bicycle must be carried! (Tragestrecke)
- ✕ Constriction, bottleneck* (Engstelle*)
- ○¹⁷ Nodal point (Knotenpunktnummer der Wegweisung)
- ⬜ Town or city map (Stadt- /Ortsplan)

Symbols only in the city maps (Nur in Ortsplänen)
- 🅿 Garage* (Parkhaus*)
- 🎭 Theatre* (theater*)
- ✉ Post office* (Post*)
- 🅰 Pharmacy* (Apotheke*)
- 🅷 Hospital* (Krankenhaus*)
- 🄵 Fire brigade* (Feuerwehr*)
- 🛡 Police* (Polizei*)

* Selection (* Auswahl)

Scale 1 : 85.000
1 cm ≙ 850 m

0 1 2 3 4 5 6 7 8 9 10 11 12 13 14 15 km

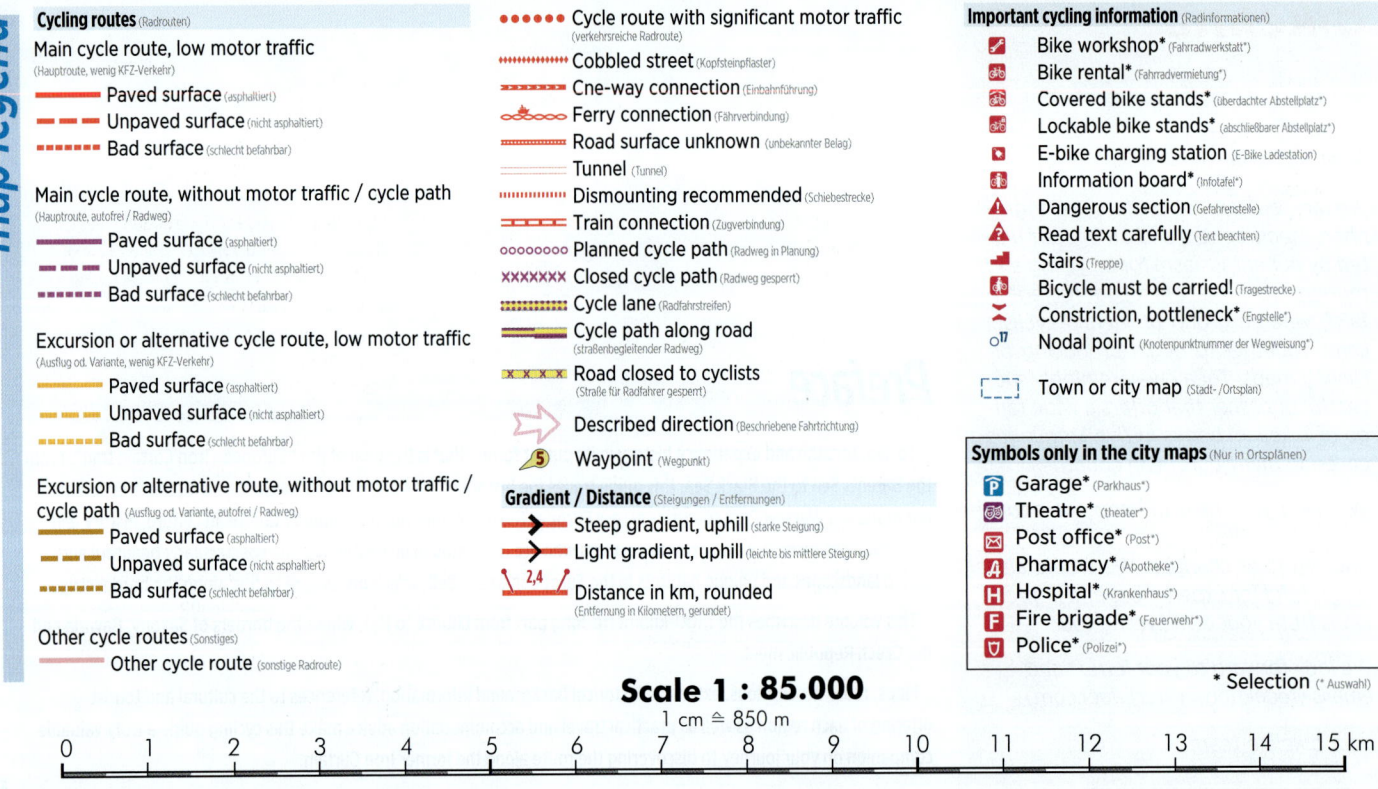

Sights of interest / Facilities (Sehenswertes / Einrichtungen)

- Church; Chapel (Kirche; Kapelle)
- Monastery/Convent (Kloster)
- Synagogue; Mosque (Synagoge; Moschee)
- Palace, Castle; Ruin (Schloss, Burg; Ruine)
- Tower; Lighthouse (Turm; Leuchtturm)
- Watermill; Windmill (Wassermühle; Windmühle)
- Power station (Kraftwerk)
- Mine; Cave (Bergwerk; Höhle)
- Airport, Monument (Flughafen, Denkmal)
- Other sight of interest (sonstige Sehenswürdigkeit)
- Museum (Museum)
- Excavations; Roman site (Ausgrabungen; röm. Objekte)
- Zoo; Nature info (Tierpark; Naturpark-Information)
- Nature reserve/Monument (Naturpark, -denkmal)
- Natural sight of interest (sonstige Natursehenswürdigkeit)
- Panoramic view* (Aussichtspunkt*)
- Tourist information; Restaurant (Tourist-Info; Gasthaus)
- Hotel, Guesthouse; Youth hostel (Hotel, Pension; Jugendherberge)
- Campground; Simple tent site* (Camping-; Lagerplatz*)
- Shopping facility*; Kiosk* (Einkaufsmöglichkeit*; Kiosk*)
- Picnic tables*; Covered stand* (Rastplatz*; Unterstand*)
- Outdoor pool; Indoor pool (Freibad; Hallenbad)
- Natural pool; Thermal baths/Waterpark (Naturbad; Thermal-/Erlebnisbad*)
- Drinking fountain*; Parking lot* (Brunnen*; Parkplatz*)
- **Schönern** Picturesque town (Sehenswertes Ortsbild)
- Facilities available (Einrichtung im Ort vorhanden)

Topographic information (Topographische Informationen)

- Church; Chapel (Kirche; Kapelle)
- Monastery/Convent (Kloster)
- Synagogue; Mosque (Synagoge; Moschee)
- Palace, Castle; Ruin (Schloss, Burg; Ruine)
- Tower; Lighthouse (Turm; Leuchtturm)
- Watermill; Windmill (Wassermühle; Windmühle)
- Power station, Solar power station (Kraftwerk)
- Mine; Cave (Bergwerk; Höhle)
- Monument; Burial mound (Denkmal; Hügelgrab)
- Airport; Airfield (Flughafen; Flugplatz)
- Windturbine (Windkraftanlage)
- TV/Radio tower (Funk- und Fernsehanlage)
- Transformer station (Umspannwerk, Trafostation)
- Wayside cross; Boundary stone (Wegkreuz; Grenzstein)
- Playing field, Stadium (Sportplatz, Stadion)
- Golf course; Tennis courts (Golfplatz; Tennisplatz)
- Boat landing; Sluice/lock (Schiffsanleger; Schleuse)
- Natural spring; Wastewater treatment plant (Quelle; Kläranlage)
- International border crossing (Staatsgrenze; Übergang)
- State border (Landesgrenze)
- District border (Kreis-, Bezirksgrenze)
- Nature reserve, National park (Naturschutzgebiet, Naturpark, Nationalpark)
- Prohibited zone (Truppenübungsplatz, Sperrgebiet)
- Contour line 100m/50m (Höhenlinie 100m/50m)
- UTM-grid (2 km-grid) (UTM-Gitter)

- Motorway/Freeway; Expressway (Autobahn; Schnellstr.)
- Highway (Fernverkehrsstraße)
- Main road (Hauptstraße)
- Secondary main road (untergeordnete Hauptstraße)
- Secondary road; Access road (Nebenstraße; Fahrweg)
- Track; Ferry (Weg; Fähre)
- Road planned/under construction (geplant/in Bau)
- Railway/station; S-train station (Eisenbahn/Bahnhof; S-Bahnhof)
- Railway disused; planned (Eisenbahn stillgelegt; geplant)
- Narrow gauge railway (Schmalspurbahn)
- Mountain railway; Cable car (Bergbahn; Seilbahn)
- Forest; Park (Wald; Parkanlage)
- Marsh/Bog; Heath (Sumpf; Heide)
- Vineyards; Allotment gardens* (Weinbau; Gärten*)
- Quarry; Open cast mine* (Steinbruch, Tagebau*)
- Cemetery; Dunes/Beach (Friedhof; Düne, Strand)
- Tidal flats; Glacier (Watt; Gletscher)
- Rock; Cliff; Scree (Felsen; Geröll)
- Greenhouse; Plantation (Gewächshäuser, Plantage)
- Commercial/Industrial area (Gewerbe-, Industriegebiet)
- Urban area; Public building (Siedlung; öffentl. Gebäude)
- Defensive wall/Wall (Stadtmauer, Mauer)
- Embankment, Dike (Damm, Deich)
- Canal (Kanal)
- River/Dam/Lake (Fluss/Staumauer/See)

Content

5   Preface

6   map legend

8   The author

10 German History after 1945

19 German-German Border Trail

24 About this book

25 **From Lübeck**
    to Schnackenburg/Wittenberge   227 km

63 **From Schnackenburg/Wittenberge**
    to Bad Harzburg/Ilsenburg   257 km

100 **From Bad Harzburg/Ilsenburg**
    to Fladungen/Fulda   331 km

145 **From Fladungen/Fulda**
    to the Czech Republik border   308 km

186 Overnight accommodation and bike service list

200 Thanks

200 Geographical Index

The author

Michael Cramer was born on 16 June 1949 in Gevelsberg, Westphalia and attended the Reichenbach grammar school in Ennepetal. He studied music, sports and education in Mainz from 1969-74. From 1975-95 he taught at a grammar school in Berlin-Neukölln.

From 1989-2004 he served as transport spokesman for The Greens in the Berlin House of Representatives. Alongside his work as an MP he took several teaching positions relating to transport and urban policy at the Otto Suhr Institute of the Free University of Berlin.

Michael Cramer was a member of the European Parliament and represented the GREENS/EFA group in the Committee on Transport and Tourism from 2004-2019, where he also served as a chairman from 2014 to 2017. He also continues to pursue several journalistic activities through publications in journals and books.

Three key events from his youth acted as the catalyst for his intensive study of the German-German history. The first was in 1961 when the Wall was built and he went on his first holiday without his parents to the North Sea resort of St. Peter Ording. There, he did not just marvel at the beach sailors but was also able to listen to the legendary 80-year-old Count Luckner (1881–1966), who was said to be able to tear telephone books apart as well as bend and flatten 5-Mark coins with his bare hands.

Whilst on holiday he read a newspaper with the headline: "Berlin Wall – is this the start of World War III?" At once he remembered the stories his parents and teachers had told him about the war period and grew increasingly anxious that he too, might live to experience such terrible times.

Two years later he journeyed with his football club TuS Ennepetal to West Berlin and played against BFC Südring. Whilst there he ate his first curried sausage - which did not yet exist in West-Germany - played for the first time Mini-Golf in the Hasenheide – which back then was not possible in Ennepetal - and drank his first Fassbrause lemonade – something that cannot be found today in West-Germany. His aunt gave him a camera for the trip and the first pictures he took were of the Wall at Bernauer Straße.

www.michael-cramer.eu

Every time he returned to Berlin thereafter, he went to Bernauer Straße and recorded how the Wall changed. Initially, only the windows were bricked up on the ground and the first floor. A short while later, however, the windows on the other floors were also bricked up. Eventually, the houses that stretched to the first floor were replaced by the "modern" Wall.

A year later he read his first book on politics: "Child of the revolution" by Wolfgang Leonhard (1921-2014), who in 1935, as a child of Communist parents, fled from Nazi Germany with his mother, Susanne Leonhard, to seek refuge in the Soviet Union. After a

short time, however, his mother was arrested and exiled to a labour camp in Siberia. Her son Wolfgang was brought up as a "socialist" in children's homes and boarding schools. As a committed communist, he was part of the "Ulbricht Group", which after the war was sent from the Soviet Union to live in occupied Germany.

From July 1945 to September 1947 Wolfgang Leonhard worked for the Central Committee of the Communist Party (from 1946 known as the SED) and was active in the department of "agitation and propaganda" and also taught from 1947-49 history at the Karl Marx SED school in Kleinmachnow. In 1948, Wilhelm Pieck, the man who would later become GDR president, helped him rescue his mother from Siberia and bring her to Germany. Susanne Leonhard (1895-1984) first lived in East Berlin and then in the spring of 1949, moved to West-Germany. She was arrested by US intelligence CIC (Counter Intelligence Corps) and detained until April 1950. As a committed anti-Stalinist socialist, she declined to work for the US as a spy. In 1956 she published the book "Stolen Life. The fate of a political emigrant in the Soviet Union". In 1949, her son Wolfgang broke with Stalinism, fled via Prague to the "non-aligned" Yugoslavia and has been living in the Federal Republic of Germany since the 1950's.

After studying in Mainz and as an active "Germany politician", Michael Cramer moved to Berlin (West) in 1974 and confirmed the frequently quoted observation: "Either you pack your bags and leave Berlin after six months or you stay and live in Berlin forever." He stayed.

In the summer of 1989 he cycled for the first time along the 160 km long "patrol route" around West Berlin, which had been created by the Western Allies behind the Wall. Back then it was impossible to get lost because you just stayed on the West Berlin side and followed the Wall. Then the Wall fell and he was able to repeat this tour around the Wall in the spring of 1990 on the patrol road between the front wall and the hinterland wall. It was during one of such cycling rides that the idea for cycling trips centred around the Berlin Wall was born.

However, it took another ten years until he could realise his vision. After the fall of the Wall, the slogan in Berlin was: "The Wall must go". The responsibility for this task fell upon the shoulders of the GDR border guards who were in charge until 2 October 1990 and who carried this out with typical Prussian-Socialist thoroughness. It was only in those parts where district councils, organisations or individuals intervened that parts of the Wall were left standing.

On the 40th anniversary of the Wall, Michael Cramer returned to his original idea and in the summer of 2001, organised public "Wall-forays". The Senate and House of Representatives of Berlin decided to protect the remaining Wall by making it a listed monument, added signposting to the Berlin Wall, made it bike-friendly and put up a memorial stele dedicated to the last fugitive shot there, Chris Gueffroy. These measures were completed in 2007.

The book "Berlin Wall Trail" was first published in 2001 by the Esterbauer publishing house, and detailed a route of 160 kilometres along the former border to West Berlin. It was presented by Volker Hassemer, who had served for many years as the Berlin Senator for Urban Development and Environmental Protection. The book has since been revised several times and was also printed in English for the first time in 2003.

The book "German-German Border Trail" first appeared in the summer of 2007 - in English in 2008 - and was presented at the European House in Berlin by Wolfgang Thierse, the then President of the German Bundestag (1998-2005). He quoted the former President of the European Commission, Jacques Delors (1985-1995), with his statement: "The European Union is like a bicycle. If you stop riding it, it will fall over."

The three volumes of the "Europa-Radweg Eiserner Vorhang" were published in 2009 and as the "Iron Curtain Trail" in English in 2010. They were also presented in the European House in Berlin by Hans-Gert Pöttering, the then President of the European Parliament (2007-2009). The revised version of the southern part from Hof to Szeged with a unified scale of 1:85,000 was published in 2014 - in English in 2017 - and presented by the EU Commissioner for Regional Development, Johannes Hahn, in the European House in Vienna.

In 2019, on the 30th anniversary of the fall of both the Berlin Wall and the Iron Curtain in Europe, the updated versions of the entire section from the Barents Sea to the Black Sea were completed. The number of books increased from three to five and an improved scale was also added. These books are available in German as well as English.

Michael Cramer has been navigating his way around Berlin without a car since 1979. He uses his bike as well as buses, trains and taxis and prefers soft tourism when on holiday. This is why he was able to experience many of the Velo Routes in the USA – in 2004 his "San Francisco Bay Trail" was published, a 750-kilometre-long bike trail around the bay of San Francisco – as well as Switzerland, Austria, France and Germany.

German History after 1945

The history of the German-German border does not begin with the building of the Wall on 13 August 1961, but with Hitler seizing power on 30 January 1933, and with the beginning of the Second World War on 1 September 1939, as the German Army marched into Poland. Had Nazi-Germany not started the Second World War, Germany would not have been occupied or divided.

Already during the war, the Allies decided that they would divide Germany into zones of occupation after its defeat, which were to be administered by the three victorious powers, the USA, Great Britain and the Soviet Union – France was only added to this group at the Yalta Conference in February 1945.

Despite their different ideologies the anti-Hitler coalition was able, after the unconditional surrender of the German Wehrmacht, to agree on the indictment of the leading Nazi prisoners in Nuremberg.

The Nuremberg Trial

The three allied parties, USA, Great Britain and the Soviet Union, agreed to bring the main war criminals to justice. France was also given a place at the tribunal. The public hearing against Hermann Göring, Rudolf Heß, Joachim von Ribbentrop, Wilhelm Keitel, Ernst Kaltenbrunner, Hjalmar Schacht, Albert Speer and others took place before the International Military Tribunal in the Palace of Justice of the City of Nuremberg and began on 20 November 1945.

On 30 September and 1 October 1946, 12 of the 24 defendants were sentenced to death in the first trial after almost a year of hearing evidence. Hermann Göring eluded his sentence by killing himself with a cyanide capsule shortly before his execution was scheduled to take place, despite being under strict watch. Due to the beginning of the Cold War, joint trials by the victorious powers no longer took place. The subsequent Nuremberg trials were then conducted by the American military courts alone.

The trial protocols were published by the American government in the years 1949-1953. However, despite this fact, they remained largely unknown in Germany in the 1950s. Ralph Giordano (1923-2014) described the ignoral of the Nuremberg Trials as part of a major collective repression and as the "second guilt of the Germans".

The Auschwitz trials

It was not until the early 1960s that German jurisdictions began to deal with National Socialist crimes. The first proceedings were the three Auschwitz trials against those responsible for crimes relating to the Auschwitz extermination camp. The first took place from 1963-65 in Frankfurt am Main. It is above all thanks to the efforts of Hessian Attorney General Fritz Bauer that these trials took place in the face of strong resistance from local politicians and the

Germany in its borders of 1937

German Reich border 1937
National borders 1970
State borders in Germany
Oder-Neisse line

Allied zones of occupation
American
British
French
Soviet

FRG since 1949
GDR since 1949

Former eastern parts of German Reich and Danzig
Under Soviet administration
Under Polish administration

Saarland
French customs and economic area since 1946
*Berlin administered by four occupying powers

judiciary. "When I left my office, I entered enemy territory," he said when describing the time. No wonder then, that he preferred working with the Israeli secret service "Mossad" to arrest the SS-Obersturmbannführer Adolf Eichmann, who had gone into hiding in Argentina, so that he would have to stand trial in Jerusalem rather than Germany.

The descriptions of the unspeakable suffering of prisoners who had survived caused consternation and bewilderment to the listening audience. The defendants showed no remorse and excused themselves by stating that they had only been following orders. They outright rejected any personal responsibility for their actions. In the trial, however, it was demonstrated there had always been room for personal conduct, and that no SS man was punished with death if he did not carry out the extermination orders. The first sentences were pronounced in 1965 and were lifelong prison sentences.

The testimonies of 318 witnesses were recorded on tape and saved from destruction by Hesse's Justice Minister Lauritz Lauritzen (SPD). Almost fifty years later, they were processed by employees of the Fritz Bauer Institute in Frankfurt and made available on the Internet. The Frankfurt Auschwitz trials were addressed by Peter Weiss in 1965 in his play "Die Ermittlung" and in 2014 in the film drama "Im Labyrinth des Schweigens" by Giulio Ricciarelli.

The Potsdam Conference

At the Potsdam Conference on 2 August 1945, the victorious powers agreed to treat Germany as an economic entity and to rule it without regard to the zones and sectors into which it had been divided. Germany – also the former capital Berlin – was divided into American, British, French and Soviet zones. The borders were to be treated as administrative lines and were called "demarcation lines". However, with the former Allies increasingly drifting apart, the character of the demarcation line changed between the three Western zones on the one side and the Eastern zone on the other.

Winston Churchill, who failed to get elected again as British Prime Minister after the war, had already stated in his famous speech in Fulton, Missouri, on 5 March 1946, that a part of Europe had disappeared behind an "Iron Curtain" and that Europe was divided. The Cold War had begun.

In the Soviet zone of occupation certain reforms were instituted: there was a reform of land ownership, companies were nationalised, reparations were obtained and the German Communist Party (KPD) was forcibly united with the Social Democrats (SPD) to form the Socialist Unity Party of Germany (SED). A vote by SPD members on 31 March 1946 in West Berlin whereby 82.6 % voted "against the immediate merger of both workers' parties" was ignored.

From 1947 the Soviets reinforced the development of the zonal border by erecting road blocks and barbed-wire obstacles at various points. At the same time the differences in the economic performances of the zones intensified because the Western zones had been profiting from the Marshall Plan since 1947 and the demarcation lines were losing their significance.

The final break was caused by the currency reform in the West, instituted on 21 June 1948. This was used by the Soviets to block off West Berlin.

BERLIN

Berlin during the time of the wall

Berlin-Blockade 1948-49

The blockade lasted from 24 June 1948 until 11 May 1949. The three Western sectors of Berlin were fed and received heating material with the help of airplanes, via the so-called "Airlift". The Berliners called many of the planes "Raisin Bombers", because of the pilot's propensity to throw sweets, chewing gum and raisins to the children. One of these planes can be seen today at the German Technical Museum in Berlin (Möckern Bridge). During this time, 72 pilots lost their lives. Following this event, history books in the East never spoke of a blockade but only about a "self-blockade", which had

been provoked by the West-Allies. The "Airlift" was called an "instrument of imperialist strife for profit and aggression", the end of which had been a "triumph of compromise policies" and a result of the "persistent and constant endeavours for peace by the Soviet Union".

On 23 May 1949, the "Federal Republic of Germany" with its temporary capital Bonn, was announced through the adoption of the "German Constitutional Law" (Grundgesetz). Its "rival", the German Democratic Republic, was established on 7 October 1949. The demarcation line not only became the border between two states, but also a border between two systems, between the power blocs fighting the "Cold War". However, despite the border being increasingly fortified and regulated by the Soviets, it could at this time nevertheless still be crossed.

Stalin Note 1952

On 10 March 1952, the deputy Soviet foreign minister André Gromyko gave a so-called "Stalin-Note" to the representatives of the other Allies occupying Germany, with proposals for solving the "German problem". He proposed a four-power conference, which would conclude with a peace treaty for Germany. He also proposed that the Oder-Neisse border be recognised and that the Allies should withdraw all their troops.

Konrad Adenauer, chancellor of the Federal Republic, judged the note as just another diversion from the integration of the Federal Republic into the Western System: "I have always conducted my politics from the assumption that the goal of Soviet Russia is to make the integration of Europe impossible by neutralising Germany [...] and to get the USA out of Europe this way; additionally, to use the Cold War to bring Germany,

the Federal Republic and Europe into the Soviet sphere of power." Adenauer therefore wished to continue negotiations with the Western Allies "as if the note did not exist".

His policies were not wholly supported by his cabinet. The Minister for All-German Affairs, Jakob Kaiser (CDU) for example supported the idea of a neutral Germany as a bridge between East and West. Kaiser demanded publicly that the Soviet proposals be examined carefully so that no opportunity for a reunification of Germany would be excluded.

Among the publicists it was Paul Sethe, co-publisher of the newspaper "Frankfurter Allgemeine Zeitung" (FAZ) in the early 1950s, who criticised Adenauer´s non-consideration of Stalin´s offer the most. Due to his fierce criticism of Adenauer´s Western politics, Sethe was excluded from the publisher circle of the FAZ in 1955. In a passionate Bundestag debate on 23/24 January 1958, which lasted almost 17 hours, chancellor Adenauer, who had the absolute majority in parliament, was criticised for having missed a unique opportunity. Thomas Dehler (FDP), who had been Adenauer´s federal minister of justice until 1953, said: "Everybody knows that we are talking about German unity and reunification, but that we are not seriously striving towards it." He also said that in 1952 a soviet "offer" had been on the table and that the chancellor had done everything "to prevent the reunification". The SPD-parliamentarian and former CDU minister of the interior Gustav Heinemann, who had resigned at the end of 1950 due to the chancellor "acting on his own" with regards to the question about Germany´s defence systems, criticised Adenauer´s understanding of the Stalin-Note and recited all the missed chances "to reach a reunification by discussing the questions of state security": "For me, it is the historical

culpability of the CDU that until 1954 has acted so carelessly and has failed to capitalise on the possibilities that we now regrettably do not have anymore." His attack on Adenauer culminated in him asking openly if he did not "want to resign now" in order to make way for "other people", who "can do what is necessary in a credible manner".

SPD and FDP unsettled the government and the CDU like never before. In a radio address on 29 January, Adenauer gave reasons for why he had not answered straight away in 1952 and warned about "the creation of myths, which confuses the minds and has the potential of throwing a whole nation into misfortune".

Even today, historians are divided into followers of the "offer-thesis" and the "propaganda-thesis" and debate whether or not a great chance of reunification was missed and what the goals of Stalin's note were. They, however, all agree that the Stalin notes – there were all together four notes – were a direct reaction to the Treaty of the European Defence Community, which was about to be signed, and which, in the last instance, would have led to West Germany being rearmed. One of Stalin's goals was to prevent West-Germany from becoming a member of the EVG. In the end, however, the EVG was not created. After suffering an incredible defeat in Indochina, the French Parliament rejected the EVG with a large majority on 30 August 1954.

Germany – United Fatherland

The German Democratic Republic first dropped the demand for Germany`s reunification toward the beginning of the 1970s, as Erich Honecker, when he became leader of the GDR in 1971, propagated the "Two-State-Theory". It sounded very

different in the GDR's National Anthem of November 5th, 1949, when it, with words by Johannes R. Becher and music by Hanns Eisler began with the words:

Resurrected from the ruins,
Facing the future,
Let us serve you for good
Germany, United Fatherland.

The anthem was not changed, but from the beginning of the 1970s until the end of the GDR, the text was not officially sung. Only the melody by Eisler was played. At the "working visit" of the SED-Secretary-General Erich Honecker on 7 September 1987 at chancellor Helmut Kohl´s residence in Bonn, both national anthems were played without their lyrics. While the Berlin newspaper "tageszeitung" headed their front page: "Travel permission for Honecker", the FAZ commented on the fact that the lines "Unity and justice and freedom for the German Fatherland" and "Germany, United Fatherland" had been left out in both hymns: "Is the protocol not merciful that it does not oblige the Germans that have gathered here together, to pay lip-service to their unity at this demonstration of their separation, and therefore not force them to endure the bitter feeling of self-mockery?" The sentence of the GDR anthem in question was only played again in the GDR parliament when prime minister Hans Modrow presented his concept "For Germany, United Fatherland" on 1 February 1990. With this, also the last SED-government decided in favour of a reunited Germany.

The GDR in the first post war years

The Treaty on Germany that the Federal Republic concluded in 1952 with the western powers was reason enough for the SED leadership to close the zonal borders and establish strict border controls. On 26 May 1952, the GDR Council of Ministers ordered the construction of stronger border defences. The border area consisted of a 10 m wide control strip directly at the border, which was not to be trespassed, another 500 m wide 'protection' strip, and finally a 5-kilometre-wide control zone. The streets and roads in the GDR were closed with red-white barriers and patrolled; the residents of the area were given special passes and visitors had to have a special permit. In the first three years of the GDR, from 1949 until 1952, 675,000 people fled the regime, so that the border was continually 'improved' to prevent people from voting with their feet'.

Operation "Vermin"

In 1952 the regime forced thousands of people who had been living in the border areas into the hinterland – the regime itself called it "Operation Ungeziefer", (Operation Vermin), which shows how indifferent the SED ideologists were towards the Nazi barbarity. The time in which humans had been decreed by the Nazis as 'vermin' and also killed was not that long ago. From the end of May until the beginning of June 1952, more than 8,000 GDR citizens were forcibly resettled from the 5-kilometre zone, as they were declared as "unreliable elements". In Streufdorf there was some resistance to these measures - the only one before 17 June 1953 - but it was swiftly defeated by the military. Over the years, the German-German border systems were perfected, until it became virtually impossible to flee from East Germany to the West.

The dissatisfaction in the GDR grew after the 2nd SED party conference in July 1952, where the "Building of Socialism" was

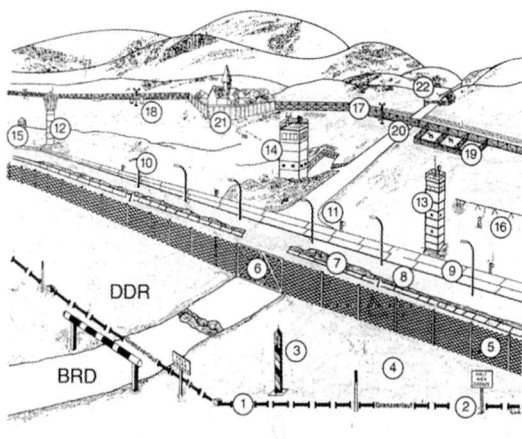

DDR-Grenzsicherungsanlagen (Schema, ab etwa 1984)

1 Grenzverlauf mit Grenzsteinen
2 Grenzpfahl, teilweise mit Hinweisschild „Landesgrenze"
3 DDR-Grenzsäule schwarz-rot-gold mit Hoheitszeichen
4 „Vorgelagertes Hoheitsgebiet" der DDR
5 Grenzzaun-I
6 Gassentor
7 Kfz-Sperrgraben
8 Kontrollstreifen K-6
9 Kolonnenweg
10 Lichttrasse
11 Ruf- und Sprechsäule
12 Beobachtungsturm BT-11 (runde Bauweise, Durchmesser 1 m)
13 Beobachtungsturm BT-11 (quadratische Bauweise 2x2 m)
14 Führungsstelle
15 Beobachtungsbunker
16 Hundelaufanlage
17 Grenzsignal- und Sperrzaun-II
18 Stromverteilungs- und Schalteinrichtung für den GSSZ-II
19 Hunde-Freilaufanlage
20 Signalzauntor
21 Betonsperrmauer
22 Kontrollpunkt an den Zufahrtsstraßen ins Grenzgebiet

Border protection system of the GDR

adopted. This meant a concentration of financial and economic resources on heavy industry and away from the daily provision of the population and also the - due to ideological reasons - forced transfer of the Soviet system to the GDR. Agriculture was collectivised, the church was attacked and independent entrepreneurs, workers and business people were embattled. These measures did not just result in a bad supply-crisis but also in a growing number of political prisoners (70,000) and a drastically rising escape movement (300,000 fugitives in the first six months of 1953).

The revolt on 17 June 1953

This revolt against the GDR leadership resulted from the intention to increase the production quotas of the workers without increasing their wages ("norm increase"). The SED slogan: "First work more, then live better" caused outrage among the construction workers. According to what we know now, about one million people in 700 communities of the GDR participated in the wide-spread rebellion during the "Five Days In June" (novel by Stefan Heym, whose book was only allowed to be published in the GDR in 1989). There were strikes, demonstrations and public and state buildings were stormed. The main demands of the demonstrators were highly political and - for the GDR-revolutionary:

• Free and secret elections in the whole of Germany
• Lifting of the zonal borders and a peace treaty for the whole of Germany
• Freedom for all political prisoners

The rebellion in Berlin on 17 June 1953 was put down by Soviet tanks. The SED leadership, which had already devised evacuation plans 'if the counter-revolution wins' (Erich Honecker), would never have been able to hold on to power by itself. The 3,000 arrests by Soviet troops were followed by 10,000 arrests by GDR officers, at least 2,300 of which were sentenced. Soviet ad hoc tribunals executed 18 people. Four were sentenced to death by the GDR courts, those sentences against Erna Dorn and Ernst Jennerich were also carried out. Between 60 and 80 people were killed on the streets and squares and during demonstrations or storming public buildings. 10 to 15 SED officials and police or security employees also died.

The revolt of 17 June 1953 was spontaneous – it surprised not only the secret services in the East, but also in the West. In the GDR it was officially declared a "fascist putsch", which had been prepared for a long time and then carried out by the Western secret services. Until the demise of the GDR, this revolt was the epitome of a threat for the government from its own people and as such provided the reasons to establish an extensive system of spying, for intimidation and imprisonment of the people.

In the West, 17 June was celebrated as the "Day of German Unity" from 1954. Whereas in the first years, hundreds of thousands of people commemorated how Soviet tanks had put down the rebellion, the day was later taken over by the conservative part of the population as "their" day, something which the Left had no real answer to. In the final years before the fall of the Wall, the day was seen as more of a holiday than a day of remembrance.

Fugitives and Emergency Relief Camps

After 17 June 1953, many of the GDR citizens, who were unhappy with the conditions and circumstances in the GDR, used the way through West Berlin in order to escape the GDR. They also needed a special permit for a visit from East-Berlin; however, it was impossible to completely control this. Until the Wall was built, it was still possible to move around the four-sector-city relatively freely. For example, it was easy to get from East- to West-Berlin with an U-Bahn or S-Bahn ticket; from there, one could easily take a flight to the Western parts of the Federal Republic.

It was not unusual to live in one sector of Berlin and work in another. For example, Berlin Senator Kurt Neubauer, also a member of the SPD-group in the German Bundestag, lived in Friedrichshain, the Soviet sector of Berlin, until the Wall was built. In the Bundestag he represented the West-Berlin City Parliament, which lay in Schöneberg in the American sector.

"Khrushchev Ultimatum 1958"

In order to stop the flow of fugitives, the Soviet Union tried to change the status of Berlin in its favour with the "Khrushchev Ultimatum" in 1958. The USSR demanded the Western Allies leave Berlin. The attempt failed, however, and the flow of fugitives, the 'voting with feet' continued. Until the Wall was built, about four million people fled from the GDR.

The Building of the Wall and "Operation Cornflower" 1961

Unwilling to grant political rights of freedom and incapable of solving the economic problems, the leadership of the GDR and the USSR came up with a grotesque idea: On 13 August 1961, they began to build a wall around Berlin`s Western sectors so that nobody could escape to West Berlin anymore. At the same time, they forced the development and re-enforcement of the border between the Federal Republic and the GDR, through their "Operation Strengthening", also known as "Operation Cornflower". During this phase, more

than 12,000 people were forcibly removed from their homes in the border region and moved to places further inland; many communities were broken up or even completely razed to the ground. The cross-border traffic was reduced to six railway lines and five road crossings. The harassments at the border crossings increased, so that West-Berliners often had to spend hours waiting, even if they simply wanted to go on a weekend trip to West-Germany. This situation only ended with the new "East politics" of Chancellor Willy Brandt, which led to the signing of the "Basic Treaty" (Grundlagenvertrag) between the two German states in 1972.

Not only did many young people leave Berlin for West-Germany, but also many of the remaining big corporations. West-Berlin was now hanging on the "drip of West-Germany", which contributed 52% of the West-Berlin city budget. In order to prevent the city from draining altogether, the public sector was artificially bloated and companies and individuals received high tax breaks. For their service in the walled-in city, workers and other employees received a so-called "Berlin supplement", which was an extra 8% added to their wages. The locals called it a "Zitterprämie", or "shiver bonus".

After the wall had been put up, the whole inner-German border was re-enforced and became nearly impenetrable due to the installation of land mines, vehicle ditches (after 1966), 39,000 automatic shooting devices (after 1970), and a second, 1,281-kilometre-long hinterland fence with optical and acoustic signals (after 1973).

When the West-German government under Helmut Kohl granted the GDR a loan of one billion Marks in 1983, facilitated by Franz Josef Strauß (1915 - 1988), it made the grant conditional upon the removal of the 60,000 split mines (SM-70)

and over one million land mines. That, however, did not make crossing the border any easier, as the GDR authorities simply moved their safety and control measures further back from the border so that escape attempts were not hindered by the West-German border officials anymore.

Change through rapprochement

During and especially after the grand coalition of 1966-69, a new "Germany policy" was put into effect in West-Berlin. The goal of Willy Brandt`s "de-escalation politics" (1969-74) was to improve relations between East and West with long-lasting effect through treaties. He believed that if the two German states approached each other, the conflict between East and West could be defused. Many treaties were negotiated, signed, ratified and became operational: with the USSR a treaty of non-aggression in 1970, another one which recognised the Oder-Neisse line as the de facto "inviolable" western border of the People's Republic of Poland, subject to a change within the framework of a peace settlement of Poland, and the Basic Treaty of 1972, with the GDR – all of these and others contributed to better relations between the communist states and the Federal Republic. They also permitted both German states to become members of the UN. Contacts between individuals became easier. The Soviet Union guaranteed access to West-Berlin and accepted its close political ties with the Federal Republic..

The CSCE-Process

The Conference for Security and Cooperation in Europe (CSCE) took place on 3 July 1973 in Helsinki. The USA, the Soviet Union and all European states except Albania took part. The new German "East policy" of Chancellor Willy Brandt had

Border near Görsdorf (Thuringia), 1984/2006

provided the basis for the conference. At the end, the Treaty of Helsinki was signed on 1 August 1975.

The conference aimed to help the Eastern and Western blocs in Europe establish better relations. For the East, this meant the recognition of the borders as agreed after the Second World War and a stronger economic exchange with the West. In return, the East had to make concessions with regards to human rights, which the civil rights movements in the Eastern bloc could rely on: The GDR not only agreed to grant the right "that everyone is free to leave every country, including his own, and he may also to return", but it also promised to guarantee this right and to ensure that it was being granted.

Trading of political prisoners

A total of 33,000 prisoners were ransomed between the time the Wall was built and the fall of the Wall, and 215,000 family members and those wishing to leave received permission to leave the country. In addition, 150 agents from opposing secret services were exchanged. Because of its precarious economic situation, the SED was forced by domestic pressure from the Bonn government to trade "humanity for cash".

In 1963, the first 20 prisoners were released, plus just as many children - for the equivalent of three railcars of potash fertilizer. For a while, only goods were delivered as part of the trade. It was only later that payment was made, with prices rising rapidly from DM 40,000 to almost DM 100,000 for one prisoner. A total of DM 3.4 billion was paid to the GDR.

Rebellions in the Soviet bloc

The rebellion of 17 June 1953 in the GDR was the first in the Soviet bloc since the end of the war. It was followed

13

IRON CURTAIN TRAIL

by demonstrations in Poznan in June 1956, the revolution in Hungary in October 1956, the Prague Spring in 1968 in Czechoslovakia, the workers' revolt in Poland in 1970, and the Charta 77 in Czechoslovakia in 1977 as well as the beginning of the Solidarnosc movement in Poland in 1980. The fall of the Berlin Wall on 9 November 1989 and the end of the Iron Curtain in Europe were prepared by a long list of previous events, such as the activities of the Solidarnosc trade union in Poland, the successful turn towards the West by the Hungarians, the struggle of the independence movements known as the "Singing Revolution" in the Baltic states, the "Velvet Revolution" in Czechoslovakia, the increasingly strong opposition movement in the GDR and not least also the Foreign Ministers Gyula Horn and Alois Mock taking-down the barbed wire on the border between Hungary and Austria on 27 June 1989.

The 9th November

This day represents numerous turning points and impactful events in Germany history.

On 9 November 1848 Robert Blum, the Leipzig representative of the Paulskirchen Constitution was executed. He died in the name of freedom and his sentence captured rather well the Zeitgeist in 1989: "In a way, which the world has never seen before, the people in German have created their revolution. With only a few exceptions, they did not resort to violence."

On 9 November 1918, Philipp Scheidemann proclaimed the end of the empire after the end of the Second World War and proclaimed the republic.

On November 9, 1923, Adolf Hitler attempted - in vain - to seize state power by marching to the Feldherrnhalle in Munich.

November 9, 1938 is the 'night of the broken glass'. During this and the following nights, 270 synagogues and 7,500 Jewish shops burned down. At least 91 people were murdered, countless were beaten up. 30,000 Jewish men and youth were deported to the concentration camps of Buchenwald, Dachau and Sachsenhausen, where they were abused and many of them killed. After that, almost all Jewish organizations were dissolved and the Jewish press was banned.

The fall of the Berlin Wall on 9 November 1989 ended the division of Germany and marked the end of the GDR. This made the reunification of the two German states possible, which began with the help of a treaty on 3 October 1990.

The Treaty of Unification

After the first and last free elections of the GDR parliament on 18 March 1990, a grand coalition government between the CDU and the SPD was formed under the leadership of Lothar

de Maizière (CDU). On 30 April the Bundestag and the freely elected GDR-Volkskammer convened in their first joint session. On 20 September 1990, both parliaments voted for the Treaty of Unification and with that for the GDR´s accession to the Grundgesetz (German Constitution).

The Two-Plus-Four Treaty

The post-war period came to an end on 12 September 1990 with the signing in Moscow of the "Treaty on the Final Settlement of Germany" between the two German governments and the four Allied Powers and the withdrawal of Allied troops from Germany in the summer of 1994. It also clarified that the defeated Germany was not, as was the case in the Treaty of Versailles after the First World War, to have oppressive payments imposed upon it by the victorious powers. The possible reparations had been postponed in 1953 under the London Debt Agreement to the point in time of a peace treaty which, at that time, seemed very far away. When the situation changed suddenly in 1990, the Allies accepted the Two-Plus-Four Treaty proposed by Germany - without any reparations. Because the GDR had to pay high reparations to the Soviet Union until 1953, it bore almost the entire reparations burden on its own.

In addition, the final recognition of the Oder-Neisse border sealed the loss of the eastern territories, limited the number of the armed forces to a maximum of 370,000, and reaffirmed the renunciation of nuclear, biological and chemical weapons.

The final sentence in the preamble of the German Constitution – "The entire German people are required to complete the unity and freedom of Germany in free self-determination" - could now be deleted.

Segments of the Wall in the UN-garden in New York, 2003

On 4 October 1990, one day after the GDR's accession to the Federal Republic, the first all-German Bundestag met in the Reichstag building in Berlin, to which the People's Chamber sent 144 MPs. The first all-German elections took place on December 2, 1990, in which Chancellor Helmut Kohl with his CDU/CSU/FDP majority was able to assert himself.

On 4 October 1990, one day after the GDR had joined the Federal Republic, the first joint session of the all-German Bundestag took place in the Reichstags-building in Berlin, to which the Volkskammer sent 144 members. The first all-German elections took place on 2 December 1990. Chancellor Helmut Kohl, with his CDU/CSU/FDP, was able to obtain a majority.

Trials of the perpetrators

Trials were held against the former East German border guards and those responsible for giving the orders to kill East-German fugitives. 139 people lost their lives at the Berlin Wall and 327 people fell victim to the GDR border regime at the inner-German border outside Berlin.

The Berlin authorities had issued a warrant for Erich Honecker´s arrest on 1 December 1990, who had been disempowered as the head of the GDR since 18 October 1989. However, before he was captured, the Soviets secretly flew him to Moscow from a military hospital in Beelitz (near Berlin) in March 1991. After much diplomatic wrangling, the Russian government under Boris Yeltsin finally decided to extradite him. He subsequently found asylum in the Chilean embassy, but he was put under pressure from Moscow to leave it on 29 July 1992 and answer to the Berlin authorities´ indictment concerning 49 counts of manslaughter.

On 12 November 1992 the trial began against the members of the GDR´s National Defence Committee. Honecker acknowledged his political responsibility for the Wall victims, but refused to accept any "legal or moral guilt" for those killed. When he was diagnosed with cancer, the Berlin Constitutional Court decided on 12 January 1993 that the trial had to be halted as it would otherwise constitute a breach of human rights. Honecker then settled in Chile, where he eventually died on 29 May 1994.

The trial against the other GDR leaders for the manslaughter of 66 GDR-fugitives started on 13 November 1995. Those on trial for the deadly shots on Michael-Horst Schmidt (20), Michael Bittner (25), Lutz Schmidt (24) and Chris Gueffroy

(20) were Egon Krenz, Günter Schabowski and Günther Kleiber. All three defendants pleaded not guilty.

Günter Schabowski had supported Krenz throughout the trial and had developed a strategy with him to place the main responsibility onto Honecker, Mielke and the Ministry for State Security. Additionally, as the chief editor of the SED-newspaper "New Germany", he had supported the SED-policies for years. It was therefore no wonder that he could hardly get a word in at the big demonstration on Alexander Square (4.11.1989) over the crowd´s loud whistles and shouts.

However, he was the only one who accepted a 'moral guilt' at his trial and who asked for forgiveness from the victims' families. He did not support the "legal construction" that he was guilty of manslaughter, however. In response to this, all three defendants declared that they had not had the power to make the border regime more humane – as only the Soviet leaders could have decided such matters. This contradicts the note from 10 June 1988, however, in which Gorbachev expressed his opinion to the GDR-leaders: "Only the GDR as a sovereign state can decide who secures its border."

The Federal Court in Leipzig (BGH) upheld the sentences of all three defendants on 8 November 1999. Egon Krenz was sentenced to six and a half years´ for four cases of manslaughter and Kleiber and Schabowski to three years´ of imprisonment each. The judgment states that they were "indirect perpetrators" and therefore politically and criminally responsible for the shootings of the fugitives. The accused border guards had previously already been given sentences on parole.

The fight over Wall real estate

When the GDR government erected the Wall in 1961 it threw many inhabitants in the border area out of their homes; some received damages, some however, did not.

According to GDR law, the expropriated owners had a right to get their property rights restored, because § 9 of the Border Law from 25 March 1982 states: "Property no longer necessary for protecting the State Border is to be given back to the owner, legal proprietor or other users."

In the Treaty of Unity between the GDR and the FRG from 6 September 1990, the principle of "return before payment of damages" was established. It was, however, not to be applied to the areas that had been taken away to construct the Wall and other border facilities. Allegedly, the return of the real estate to their previous owners had been 'forgotten'.

The debate about the properties along the Wall lasted a long time. The return "without ifs and buts" finally failed in the German Bundestag due to resistance from the CDU/CSU. According to the solution put forward by the Bundestag, the former owners could buy back their former properties for 25% of their value, "as long as the State [did] not require the properties for important public purposes nor had a public interest in selling them to third parties." If that was the case, the former proprietors had the right to receive 75% of the value of the real estate. The properties in Berlin and the areas along the German-German border were handed over to the newly founded Bundesländer.

The question about the German capital

Although article 2 of the Treaty of Unity stated that Berlin was to be the German capital, it also stated that the decision about where the parliament and the government have their headquarters would only be made after German unity had been restored. On 20 June 1991, the Bundestag passed the "Resolution for Completing the German Unity" by a small majority (338:320 and with it decided that the parliament (Bundestag) and government were to move from Bonn to Berlin.

On 7 September 1999, the 50th anniversary of its first session, the Bundestag began its parliamentary work in the Berlin Reichstag building with a new glass dome, designed by Sir Norman Foster. The same day the government also moved to Berlin – Chancellor Gerhard Schröder first worked in the former building of the East German State Council, until he and his government moved to the new Chancellery - designed by Axel Schultes and Charlotte Frank - in the Spree-curve on 2 May 2001.

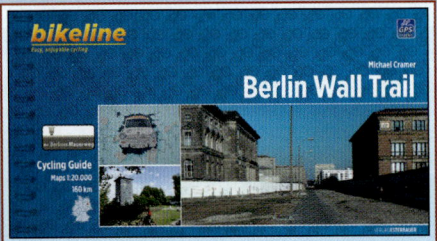

Berlin Wall Trail
212 p., 1 : 20,000, **ISBN:** 978-3-85000-458-9, **€ 13,90**

German-German Border Trail

Cycling tour on the Berlin Wall Trail

The Iron Curtain divided the continent into East and West and extended from the Barents Sea through Europe to the Black Sea - a distance of 10,000 kilometres. Until the Peaceful Revolutions in Eastern Europe, it was the physical and ideological border between two mutually hostile blocs. It did not just divide many neighbouring states, but also divided Germany into East and West. Few things remain of the former death strip today. The few relics that are still there remind us of our past but thankfully no longer separate us.

From death strip to natural habitat

The former 1,400-kilometre-long death strip with its 3,000-kilometre-long fences, 730-kilometre-long vehicle ditches, 830 watchtowers, floodlit corridors, walls and bunkers has been almost completely dismantled. Only the eastern colonnade paths with the perforated slabs still remind us of this time. In just a few more years time, it will only be possible to recognise the former border strip by its lower tree growth. Today, more than a quarter of a century after the fall of the Berlin Wall and the Iron Curtain in Europe, there is not much to see of the former German-German border.

Remembering the Wall

The question of what to do with the border facilities was widely debated after the fall of the Wall. Most people wanted the Wall to disappear completely – for political as well as moral reasons. However, a small minority tried to see the bigger picture and look further ahead into the future and actually campaigned to keep the Wall preserved. They were private individuals, representatives of monument preservation committees and citizens´ initiatives – thanks to them, the last traces of this historical period have not disappeared.

One of those in favour of preserving parts of the Wall was Willy Brandt, who was the Mayor of Berlin at the time the Wall went up. The former chancellor was awarded the Nobel Peace Prize on 20 October 1971 for his "East politics" and "peace politics". He told the people who had gathered in front of the Schöneberger City Hall (city hall to West-Berlin during the time of Berlin`s division), just one day after the fall of the Wall: "We should save a piece of this horrible structure [...] to remind us of this historical monster. Just like we consciously decided after heated debates to keep the ruins of the Memorial Church."

The former "Green" Senator for City Planning and Environmental Protection, Michaele Schreyer – later EU-Commissioner (1999 – 2004) – also overrode all objections of her SPD coalition partner and the opposition and placed - as the Senator in charge of these matters - the Wall segment at the Niederkirchnerstraße on the list of protected landmarks. At the time people strongly opposed her actions. Today, everyone is grateful that some authentic parts of the Wall have been kept at this site.

Berlin Wall Trail

Memories must be made visible! We know that the border was interpreted completely contrary by the official politics of both German states. The SED termed it an "anti-fascist protective wall". For the West it symbolised a prison and the lack of freedom in the socialist regime.

Visible memories already exist with the "Berlin Wall Trail". On 10 May 2001, the Berlin House of Representatives approved the motion initiated by the author and submitted by the parliamentary group Bündnis 90/Die Grünen, thus calling on the Senate to designate a cycle and hiking trail along the former border. In the summer of 2001, about 1,000 people took part in the author's "Mauerstreifzüge" (wall forays). It was also a result of the positive media reports that on the occasion of the 40th anniversary of the construction of the Wall, the Red-Green Senate, which was in power from 16 June 2001 to 17 January 2002, decided to put almost all remaining parts of the Wall under monument protection and to design the entire course in a bike-friendly way.

The Berlin Wall Trail has also been signposted in recent years, with the signs being placed exactly at the height of the Wall of 3.60 metres. It is a great combination of history workshop and bike tourism, of leisure, nature and culture. Above all, the inner-city section between Bernauer Straße

Border Opening Potsdamer Platz (12.11.1989)

and Oberbaumbrücke is so informative and steeped in history that it is not only great for cycling but it also takes you on a fascinating historical-political journey.

To compliment the various stops along the former Wall, the "Berlin Wall History Mile" was launched, a permanent exhibition with artistic designs of the crossings in four languages (German, English, French, Russian), with about 30 panels detailing the history of the division of Berlin, the Wall construction and when it came down. Photographs and short texts describe events that took place at each location. The "Berlin Wall Trail" became part of Berlin's tourism program and is the first project that combines soft tourism and city tourism. In Berlin you can really experience history, politics, nature and culture.

German-German Border Trail

It was not just Berlin that was divided for decades, it was Germany, too. The memory of the present 1,400-kilometre inner-German border strip must be preserved. With this in mind, on 30 June 2004, the coalition parties of the SPD and Bündnis 90/Die Grünen brought forward the motion in the German Bundestag (DS 15/3454) to convert the former death strip into an ecological habitat. They argued that it should be developed for sustainable tourism and for the "European Green Belt" along the "Iron Curtain". The German Bundestag voted unanimously in favour of these plans in December of 2004.

The "German-German Border Trail" along the "Green Belt" takes you from Lübeck to the German-Czech border at Hof, with numerous rivers and lakes along the way and covers not just the elevation of the Harz mountains but also the Thuringian Forest. There are many monuments and border museums to discover, as well as some remaining watchtowers.

The Green Belt

The Green Belt, which was initiated by the "Federation for environmental and nature protection in Germany" (BUND), is the transformation from death strip into a thriving natural habitat.

The route passes through several national parks, each with a variety of interesting flora and fauna and combines a beautiful assortment of unique landscapes that have remained largely untouched due to their remote border location and the former restriction zones. It also connects numerous memorials, museums and open-air facilities, which remind us of Europe's division and how it was overcome by the Peaceful Revolutions in East Central Europe.

In the restriction zone, agricultural use was mostly prohibited, therefore no tractors, fertilisers or herbicides were used there. From an ecological perspective, this was a positive development.

Today you can find 150 nature reserves in the Green Belt, numerous flora and fauna, the three biosphere reserves Schaalsee, Elbaue and Rhön and also the Harz National Park. It is roughly 1,400 km long and is between 50 and 200 m wide. The area covers almost 18,000 ha, 85% of the landscape is wild, almost 30% is under natural protection and 38% is registered as habitats for flora and fauna.

In order to protect the former inner-German border, which serves as a habitat for more than 2,000 endangered animals and plant species, the BUND announced a fundraiser. In the four pilot regions Salzwedel, Eichsfeld, Sonneberg and Großen Bruch, it has so far bought over 200 hectares. This was made possible by more than 8,000 donations. More information on this project can be found at www.dasgrueneband.info.

The European Iron Curtain Trail

It wasn't just Berlin and Germany that were also divided for decades, but also Europe itself: the "Iron Curtain" stretched from the Barents Sea at the Norwegian-Russian border all the way down to the Black Sea at the Turkish-Bulgarian border. Today, it does not divide us anymore. It is a symbol of a common and pan-European past in a now reunited Europe. This is another reason why in th autumn 0f 2005 the European Parliament decided to add the Iron Curtain Trail in its report regarding "New perspectives and new challenges for sustainable European tourism". A large majority from across all Member States and from all political groups voted in favour of my proposal, which called on the Commission and the Member States to "implement the 'Iron Curtain Trail' initiative [...] in order to promote European identity".

The trail traverses many national parks with interesting flora and fauna and connects many unique landscapes which, because they were either within or close to the border areas, are nearly untouched. The trail also connects numerous monuments, museums and open-air sites, which remind us of the history of the division of Europe and how it was overcome via the peaceful revolutions in Eastern and Central Europe.

The Austrian publishing house Esterbauer-Verlag has published a bike tour guide in five volumes in German and English about the 10,000-kilometre-long Iron Curtain Trail.

Twenty countries are participating in this project, including 15 EU Member States. Starting at the Barents Sea, the hiking and biking trail extends along the western border of the former Warsaw Pact countries to the Black Sea. You begin by cycling along the Norwegian-Russian and Finnish-Russian border until you reach the Baltic Sea and continue along the shoreline of Russia, Estonia, Latvia, Lithuania, Kaliningrad, Poland and the former GDR. The route from the Priwall peninsula at Travemünde to the Saxon-Bavarian-Czech border triangle follows the former inner-German border strip. It then leads over the elevations of the Bohemian Forest, past Moravia and the Slovak capital Bratislava, and here, one must cross the Danube. The route takes you along the southern border of Hungary, across Slovenia and Croatia. Between Romania and Serbia, it largely follows the course of the Danube, then continues through Bulgaria, Macedonia, Greece and Turkey and ends on the Bulgarian-Turkish Black Sea coast.

As in the Berlin Wall Trail and the German-German Border Trail, it is also possible along the Iron Curtain Trail to use the paved former patrol roads of the border troops. The trail still requires some work in quite a few countries and regions, but in many parts it is already well signposted and developed.

The route proposal

Of course, there are many alternative routes to get around the "Green Belt" by bike. Whether cycling on the Western or Eastern side, closer to or further away from the border, or taking former patrol roads with perforated paving slabs or asphalt, the proposed route has been chosen according to the following five criteria:

- as close as possible to the former border,
- on as comfortable a path as possible,
- avoiding roads with heavy traffic,
- integrating historical monuments,
- crossing the former border frequently.

The suggested route is to be understood as a "work in progress". It should go without saying that the local people know more about their area, and there is always the possibility of construction works. And sometimes, of course, a detour is suggested to take in a nearby tourist attraction. This has been done sparingly, however, because otherwise the whole route would become very long. With this in mind, the author and the publisher hope the readership of this book will take this into account, but are nonetheless pleased to accept suggestions and improvements bearing in mind the criteria mentioned above.

Acknowledgements

The revision of the five parts of the "Iron Curtain Trail" would not have been possible without the support I received from many people and institutions. Therefore, I would like to thank very much the Austrian publisher Roland Esterbauer and his team,

Segments of the Wall at the European Parliament in Brussels, 2006

who have been supporting the project from the beginning and who have implemented my ideas so professionally.

As for the "Berlin Wall Trail", I was also able to cycle and provide descriptions for this part of the "Iron Curtain Trail" myself.

For the coordination of the project as well as the editing of the books I was greatly supported by Philipp Cerny, Alexander Kaas Elias, Constantin Lehnert, Jens Müller, Sara Ott, Nils Peters, Erdmute Safranski and Justyna Wladarz, whom I would also like to thank very much. And of course, many thanks to Marie and Chris Lines, who have translated the text into English.

I would like to pay special thanks to the European initiative European Green Belt (www.greenbelt.eu), which together with conservationists from the Central and Eastern European countries brought the project "Green Belt" to life - now one of the most successful and at the same time one of the most symbolic European projects.

Václav Havel · Marianne Birthler · Lech Wałęsa

On 23 September 2014 a "Memorandum of Understanding" was signed in Slavonice by Gabriel Schwaderer for the European Green Belt Initiative, Daniel Mourek for the European Cyclists´ Federation and Michael Cramer for the European Parliament, with the aim to protect the Green Belt and enable cycling in it.

As part of both projects, the signing institutions undertook to support sustainable tourism, the protection and preservation of the special flora and fauna as well as the awareness of the history and culture. They are unified in their conviction that these goals can only be reached together with the population. Sustainable tourism in particular strengthens the local economy which is also supported by improving the existing infrastructure.

I would then like to thank Jürgen Ritter, who took countless photos on his walks along the inner-German border in 1984, and who 22 years later documented from the same photographic perspective how the death strip had changed into a living space. The photos provided by him are a valuable contribution to this book.

I would also like to thank Mikhail Gorbachev, who was elected as the Secretary General of the Communist Party of the Soviet Union in March 1985 with a majority of only one vote - something very unusual. The former President of the Soviet Union is today the president of the Green Cross International (GCI). With this, the significance of the "Green Belt" for the protection of the natural environment and its value as a symbol of unification between East and West is also recognised internationally.

And last but not least, I would like to thank Marianne Birthler, Vaclav Havel (1936-2011) and Lech Wałęsa, who are serving as patrons of the "Iron Curtain Trail".

History workshop live

Nearly 30 years have passed since the fall of the Iron Curtain in Europe. In Wilhelm von Humboldt's words: We know that "only those who know their past have a future", which is why we have to first deal with the past. Therefore, we maintain with gratitude the memory of the Peaceful Revolutions in Eastern and Central Europe in order not to forget the decades of division on our continent. This bike trail is a great combination of history workshop and bike tourism, of leisure, nature and culture. It shows that the former terrible border strip between East and West Germany, the so-called death strip, is today a living ecological monument as a large biotope network, and therefore a unique reminder of the division of Germany and how it was overcome.

On 18 April 2008, the transport ministers of the German federal states issued the so-called "Brocken Declaration" in which they advocated the erection of commemorative plaques on important roads crossing the former inner-German border. They are intended to commemorate the opening of the border and the fall of the "Iron Curtain".

The 1,100-kilometre-long "German-German Border Trail" is divided into more than 40 parts, the beginning and end of each part are, wherever possible, located at a railway station. Bicycles can be taken on all regional and some long-distance trains in Germany.

With all this in mind, I wish you great pleasure along your journey of exploring European history, politics, nature and culture.

Michael Cramer

About this book

This cycling guide contains all the information required for a cycling tour along the Iron Curtain Trail: precise maps, detailed route descriptions, accommodation options and the most important practical information about tourist attractions and sights worth seeing.

And all that information comes with our bike line pledge: The route described in this book has been tested and evaluated in person by the author! To assure that the book is as up-to-date as possible, we welcome corrections submitted by readers and local officials or businesses. We cannot, however, always check and confirm such changes before a deadline.

The maps

The detailed maps are at scale of 1:85,000 (1 centimetre = 850 metres). Apart from the exact route, the maps also provide information on the nature of the surface (solid or unsurfaced), gradients (light or strong) and distances as well as cultural, touristic and gastronomic facilities along the route.

However, even the most accurate maps cannot replace a look at the description of the route. Please note that the recommended main route is always indicated in red and purple, with variants and detours in orange. The exact significance of the individual symbols is given in the legend on pages 6 and 7.

Route altitude profile

The route altitude profile in the introduction provides a graphic depiction of elevations along the route, the total length, and the location of larger towns and cities along the way. Additionally, a detailed altitude profile is provided

at the beginning of each section which shows many of the smaller centres along the way. The latitude profiles do not show every individual small hill and dip, but only the major changes in elevation. On the detail maps smaller gradients are shown by arrows that point uphill.

The text

The maps are supplemented by a written text that describes the route starting in Prague and proceeding down the Vltava and Elbe rivers to Magdeburg. Key phrases about the route description are indicated with the ⟶ symbol.

Many distinctive or important positions along the route are marked as waypoints with consecutive numbers **1**, **2**, **3**, ... and, to help with navigation, are to be found with the same symbol in the maps.

The description of the main route is also interrupted by passages describing alternative and excursion routes. These are printed in orange colour.

TIPP Text printed in purple indicates that you must make a decision about how your tour shall continue. For instance, there may be an alternative route that is not included in the tour description, or a turn-off to another location.

AUSFLUG These also indicate excursion suggestions, interesting sights or recreational facilities that are not directly on the main route.

Furthermore, the names of important **villages**, towns and cities are printed in bold type. If a location or community has important points of interest, addresses, telephone numbers and opening times are listed under the headline with the name of the place.

Descriptions of the larger towns and cities, as well as historic, cultural and natural landmarks help round out the travel experience. These paragraphs are printed in italics to distinguish them from the route description.

Opening hours - Categories

- ⊙ Opening hours
- 24 freely accessible
- 7d daily
- ⊜ frequently (5-6 days/week)
- ⊝ average (3-4 days/week)
- ⊙ rare (up to 2 days/week)
- ⊘ after tel. request

This information is valid during the cycling season and serves as a guide. The daily opening hours can be found via the web link.

Weblink

In the location data block at the respective tourist entry there is a six-digit number and a letter combination after the @ symbol (e.g. @ abc123). Entering this weblink ID on our website www.esterbauer.com will take you directly to the corresponding website and thus replace the tedious entry of long web addresses..

Accommodation and service directory

On the last pages of this cycle tour book you will find a list of overnight accommodations in almost every place along the route, from simple campsites to 5-star hotels. You will also find extensive information about bike workshops and bike rental stations.

From Lübeck to Schnackenburg/Wittenberge

227 km

Holstentor in Lübeck

Lübeck is easily accessible by train and has a lot to offer both historically and culturally. Lübeck is also the birthplace of Willy Brandt, who was born here on 18 December 1913. Three Nobel Prize winners once lived in this city: Thomas Mann, Willy Brandt and Günter Grass.

Hansestadt Lübeck

prefix: 0451

- Tourist-Information, Holstentorpl. 1, ✆ 8899700, @ lbg213
- CitySchifffahrt (Passenger shipping City), Wallstr. 17, ✆ 2963424, ✆ 0177/2287888. City, channel and harbour round-trips, @ mit835
- Könemann Schifffahrt (Könemann Passenger shipping), An der Untertrave, ✆ 2801635. Trips to Travemünde, @ yec375

- Hanse (Passenger shipping Hanse), ✆ 0163/5475773. Trips to Travemünde, @ kcp252
- Quandt-Linie (Passenger shipping Quandt-line), Willy-Brandt-Allee, Pier Quandt line, ✆ 77799, @ ntg675
- Wakenitz-Schifffahrt (Wakenitz Passenger shipping), Moltkestr., ✆ 793885, @ dub287
- Europäisches Hansemuseum (European Hanseatic Museum), An der Untertrave 1, ✆ 148222 ☜ Museum about the rise and fall of the Hanseatic League. @ rmb564
- Museumsquartier St. Annen (St. Anne's Museum Quarter), St.-Annen-Str. 15, ✆ 1224137 ☜ The Quartier combines the history, art and present of the Hanseatic city. @ dpm758
- Buddenbrookhaus, Mengstr. 4, ✆ 1224240 ☜ This house is dedicated to the brothers Thomas and Heinrich Mann and was turned into a literary monument thanks to the Nobel-Prize-winning novel "The Buddenbrooks" by Thomas Mann. @ myl251
- Günter-Grass-Haus (Günter Grass-House), Glockengießerstr. 21, ✆ 1224230 ☜ Here you can see works of the Nobel Prize winner in Literatur Günter Grass, @ fnv571
- Holstentormuseum, Holstentorpl., ✆ 1224129 ☜ City history Museum, @ dif427
- Museumshafen (Museum harbour), Willy-Brandt-Allee 35, ✆ 4008399, @ xpw856
- TheaterFigurenMuseum (Museum of Theatre Puppets), Kolk 14, ✆ 78626, @ eqh587
- Willy-Brandt-Haus (Willy-Brandt-House), Königstr. 21, ✆ 1224250. Exhibition about the life and legacy of the Federal Chancelor and Nobel Peace Prize laureate Willy Brandt. @ ltp746
- Museum Behnhaus Drägerhaus, Königstr. 9-11, ✆ 1224148 ☜ You can see an interesting exhibition on art from the 19th and 20th

century in these two lovingly restored merchant houses from the 18th century. @ rbx355
- Museum für Natur und Umwelt (Museum of Nature and Environ-ment), Musterbahn 8, ✆ 1224122 ☜, @ tem644
- Dom (Cathedral), Mühlendamm 2-6, ✆ 74704. Heinrich der Löwe ordered the construction of Lübeck Cathedral in 1173. 70 years later, the red brick church, which has two 115-metre-tall towers, was in-augurated. Just like the Church of St. Mary and Petri Church, the Cathedral was also badly damaged during the Second World War. The city began its reconstruction in 1960. The numerous art treasu-res are well worth a visit. @ ass641
- Katharinenkirche (Church of St. Catherine), Königstr., ✆ 1224137. The Church of St. Catherine also dates back to the 13th century. The western façade of the former church is decorated with figurines by the famous artist Ernst Barlach. Today, the building is used for ex-hibitions. @ twh641
- St. Aegidien (Aegidien Church), Aegidienstr. 75, ✆ 705622. The Aegidien Church was built in the 14th century.
- St. Jakobi (Jakobi Church), Jakobikirchhof 3, ✆ 308010. The Jakobi Church is the church of seafarers. A memorial plaque is dedicated to the sunken Lübeck ships as well as to one of the lifeboats of the Pamir. This training sailing boat sunk in 1957 just off the Azores. Only six seamen survived this disaster. Unlike the Church of St. Mary, the Jakobi Church remained undamaged throughout the Second World War. You can therefore still see the original altar and organ.
- St. Petri (Petri Church), Petrikirchhof, ✆ 397730. The restoration works on the church, which was badly damaged during the Second World War, were finished in 1987. You can enjoy wonderful views over the old town from the platform of the church tower. @ fbb657

Marienkirche (Church of St. Mary), Schüsselbuden 13, ☎ 397700. The Church was built between 1250 and 1350. There are three anecdotes connected with this church which relate to two stony figurines and the stone in front of the main church portal. In the interior of the church you can admire the astronomical clock. It displayed the date and time for 376 years until 1942 when the church was hit by bombs. During this attack, the big church bells were also destroyed. Their remains can still be seen. With the help of donations, the Lübeck watchmaker Paul Behrend was able to reconstructed the clock.

MUK (Music and Concress Centre), Willy-Brandt-Allee 10, ☎ 79040, @ ytt767

Historische Altstadt (Historical old town). In 1987 Lübeck old town was listed as a UNESCO World Heritage Site and included in the list of the "Cultural and Natural Heritage of the World".

Holstentor, Holstentorpl. The Holstentor is the city's main landmark. Originally used as a battle stronghold, with room for more than 30 cannons, visitors today are greeted by the inscription on the gate: "Concordia Domi Foris Pax" ("inside unity, outside peace").

Rathaus (Townhall), Breite Str. 62. The external façade of the town hall with its gold-plated spires and the detailed coat-of-arms depictions has remained unchanged. However, a large part of the building which was constructed in the 13th century, was significantly changed during the last few centuries.

Heiligen-Geist-Hospital, Koberg 11. The hospital, which was built between 1276 and 1286 is the oldest remaining hospital in Germany. From 1517 until 1970 it was used as a care home and the elderly people living there were provided rooms that were only around 4 square metres in size.

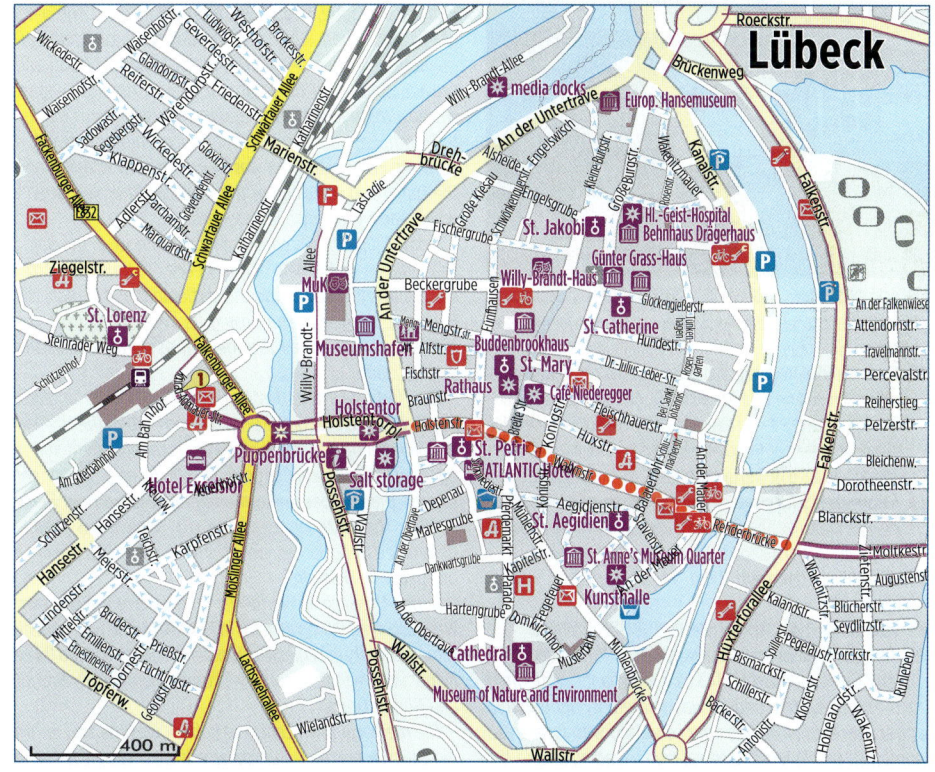

Lübeck

Border Documentation Center in Lübeck-Schlutup

❋ **Café Niederegger**, Breite Str. 89, ✆ 5301126. Café Niederegger with marzipan-lounge. This café put Lübeck on the map for marzipan. @ lxp467

❋ **Puppenbrücke**. The bridge Puppenbrücke is decorated with seven different limestone figurines from 1778. Among them is Mercury, the God of merchants and commerce, which is very befitting to the character of the city. Ironically, he shows his bare naked "Achter-steven" ("stern post") to the merchants coming in by boat.

❋ **Salzspeicher (Salt storage)**, Wallstr. The salt storage is located very near the Holstentor. This was used to store the salt from Lüneburger Heide and to later transport it by sea, mainly to Scandinavia.

✉ **Altstadtbad Krähenteich (Lido)**, An der Mauer 51, ✆ 3970650, @ ebq685

✉ **Falkenwiese (Lido)**, Wakenitzufer 1b, ✆ 794315, @ lnm786

✉ **Zentralbad (Indoor pool)**, Schmiedestr. 1-3, ✆ 7025821, @ xlc867

Lübeck was founded in 1143 as a merchants' settlement for the north-eastern trade. It was granted city rights in 1158 under the reign of Heinrich der Löwe and with it received numerous privileges. The city played a leading part in the Hanseatic League, which was founded in 1266. The aims of this association, which in its heyday had more than 200 member cities, were, among others, to secure trade and provide support in times of war. The Hanseatic League, whose arms reached from Flanders to Russia, from Cologne to Stockholm, was the most important economic network in northern Europe. Its fleet was bigger than the English and the Dutch and consisted of the so-called "Hansekoggen", which had a capacity of 100 tonnes.

From 1370, Lübeck cemented its dominance in the Baltic Sea region with the help of the "Peace of Stralsund". After the discovery voyages and the settlement in America, the Hanseatic League started losing its importance from the 16th century onwards. The trade centres shifted to England and Holland.

The Thirty-Year War passed the city by. Under Napoleon it was declared part of the Empire even though the city had remained neutral. Lübeck received its independent status back with the Vienna Congress in 1815. As an independent county, the city became a member of the German Reich in 1871. The Nazis annexed the city, which was mainly dominated by social democrats, into the Prussian province of Schleswig-Holstein.

During the Second World War, one third of the old town was destroyed during air raids in 1942. After the war, Lübeck remained a city in Schleswig-Holstein. It has produced three Nobel Prize winners, namely Thomas Mann, Willy Brandt and Günter Grass.

The medieval town centre of Lübeck was the first entire old town in northern Europe which was recognised as a UNESCO World Heritage Site in 1987. This obligates the city to ensure extensive monument protection. This was another contributing reason as to why in 1995 it was decided to completely ban cars from the old town.

As a former border city along the German-German border, the economic development in Lübeck suffered during the Cold War. Since the end of the GDR, the city has become very attractive again, due to its mixture of important past and vivid present. Additionally, it profits from the increased trade in the Baltic Sea region and it has the biggest ferry port in Europe. Today, Lübeck has 215,000 inhabitants. From the main station you can take direct trains to Hamburg and Kiel.

Monument "Unity of the Nation"

On the administration building next to St. Mary's Church you will find a double sign with the article from the German

The barricaded Brandenburger Straße in Lübeck, 1985

Constitutional Law about reunification which was erected in 1975. After the fall of the wall, the date "October 3, 1990" and the words "The goal is reached" were added to the monument. Since 1994 the left side reads: "From August 13, 1961, the Berlin Wall separated the nation but the German Constitutional law obliges, October 3, 1990". The right side reads: "The entire German folk remains requested to strive towards the unity and freedom of Germany under free will. The goal is reached."

From Lübeck to Ratzeburg   28 km

1 From the **main station** in Lübeck, cycle over Konrad-Adenauer-Straße to **Lindenplatz** and from there over **Puppenbrücke** to **Holstentor**. Via **Holstenstraße**, **Kohlmarkt** and **Wahmstraße** cycle on the **Rehderbrücke bridge**, which is available for bicycles and taxis, over the Trave to **Moltkestraße**. On the **Moltke bridge** cross the Wakenitz. **2** Then turn right onto **Elsässer Straße**. At **Danziger Straße** turn right onto the cycle path to the river bank, where you keep right and cycle along the Wakenitz, known as the "Amazon of the North". Behind the Kaninchenbergweg turn right and immediately left again and before the tracks you will come across another cycle path, into which you turn right. Cycle parallel to the tracks, pass under them, cross the Wakenitz on a bridge and turn left behind the bridge onto an unpaved cycle and hiking path.

3 Follow the Landgraben until you reach the **Drägerweg**, where you turn left, cross the Landgraben and reach the Wakenitz, where you turn right. At **Müggenbusch** we recommend a detour of about 1 kilometre to the Bundespolizei-

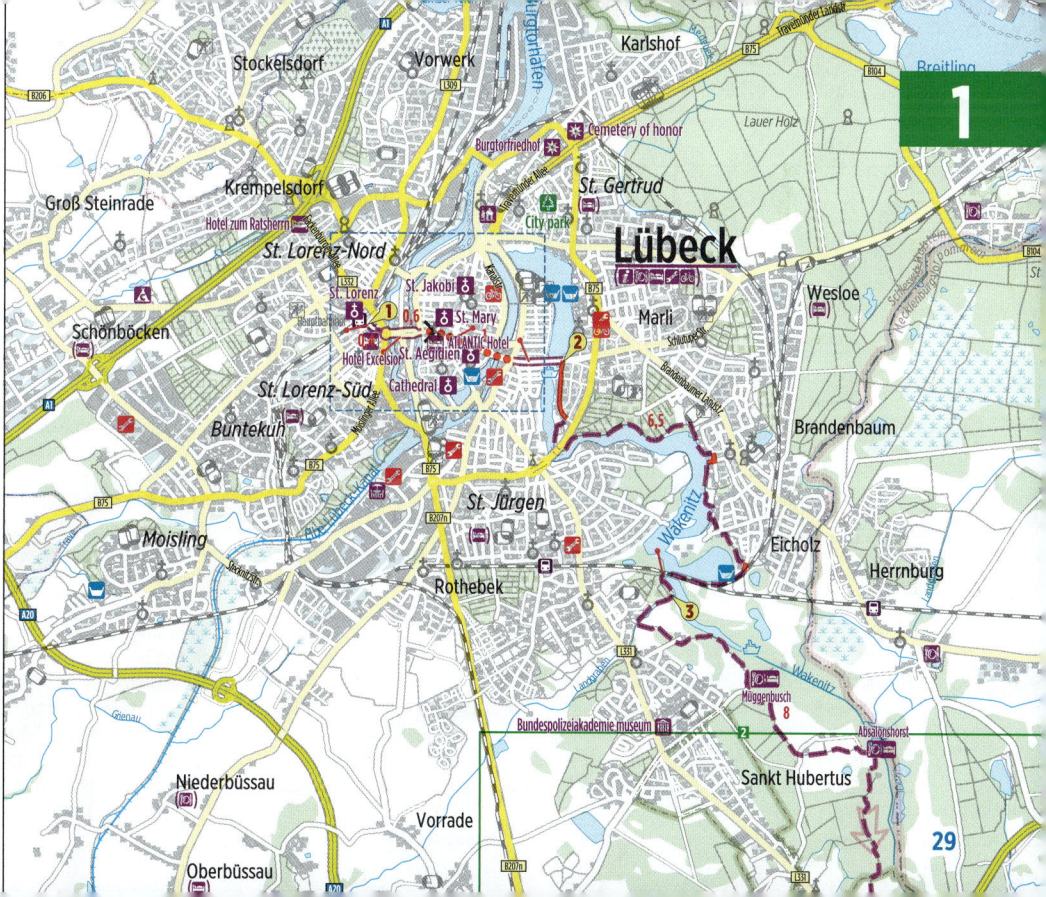

akademie museum in Lübecker Ratzeburger Landstraße 4. As the museum is not open to the public, please call (✆ 0451-1203-1081).

Along the Wakenitz you come to **Groß Grönau**, where you turn left onto the **Drägerweg**, pass under the motorway, where you can make a detour to the village of Lenschow. **4** Continue until you reach the **Ziegelhorst**, into which you turn left. Then immediately turn right into the forest path, which meets the **Rothenhusener Weg**, where you turn left and cross the Wakenitz.

Wakenitz

Wakenitz became known as the "Amazon of the North" not least because of its rows of trees, which are called gallery forests in the tropics. In 1291 the people of Lübeck bought the canal from Lake Ratzeburg and dammed it for their mills and breweries.

South of Lübeck the Wakenitz was the German-German border. After 1990 parts of the eastern shore were placed under nature protection and nine years later areas on the western shore followed, leading to the fantastic development of flora and fauna.

After the woods which obscure the Ratzeburger lake, turn right onto the asphalted bicycle path to **Wiesenstraße** and continue until you reach Utecht.

Utecht

You are better off travelling on the pavement in Utecht due to the cobblestone streets. At the end of town, continue in the direction of Campow. In **Campow** continue straight ahead towards Römnitz.

TIPP The cycle trail south of Campow is merely a dirt road. It is however, good to travel on and offers a view of Lake Ratzeburg.

After the branch to Hoheleuchte, the road is paved again. Keep right and continue on the "**RRW 9**".

INS ZENTRUM Those wishing to cycle to Ratzeburg – 7 kilometres to the market place – can turn right in Bäk in the direction of Römnitz. In Ratzeburg you will find the "Seehof" restaurant and hotel (✆ 04541/860101) which is located directly by the lake. There is a trail from Römnitz along the water to the B 208, which turns to the right and continues on a separate cycle trail to the market place in Ratzeburg.

Ratzeburg
prefix: 04541

🅸 **Tourist-Information**, Unter den Linden 1, ✆ 8000886, @ lio872

⛴ **Personenschifffahrt (Passenger shipping)**, Schlosswiese 6, ✆ 7900, @ sqo576

🏛 **A.-Paul-Weber-Museum**, Domhof 5, ✆ 860720
ⓔ You will find the works of A. P. Weber who

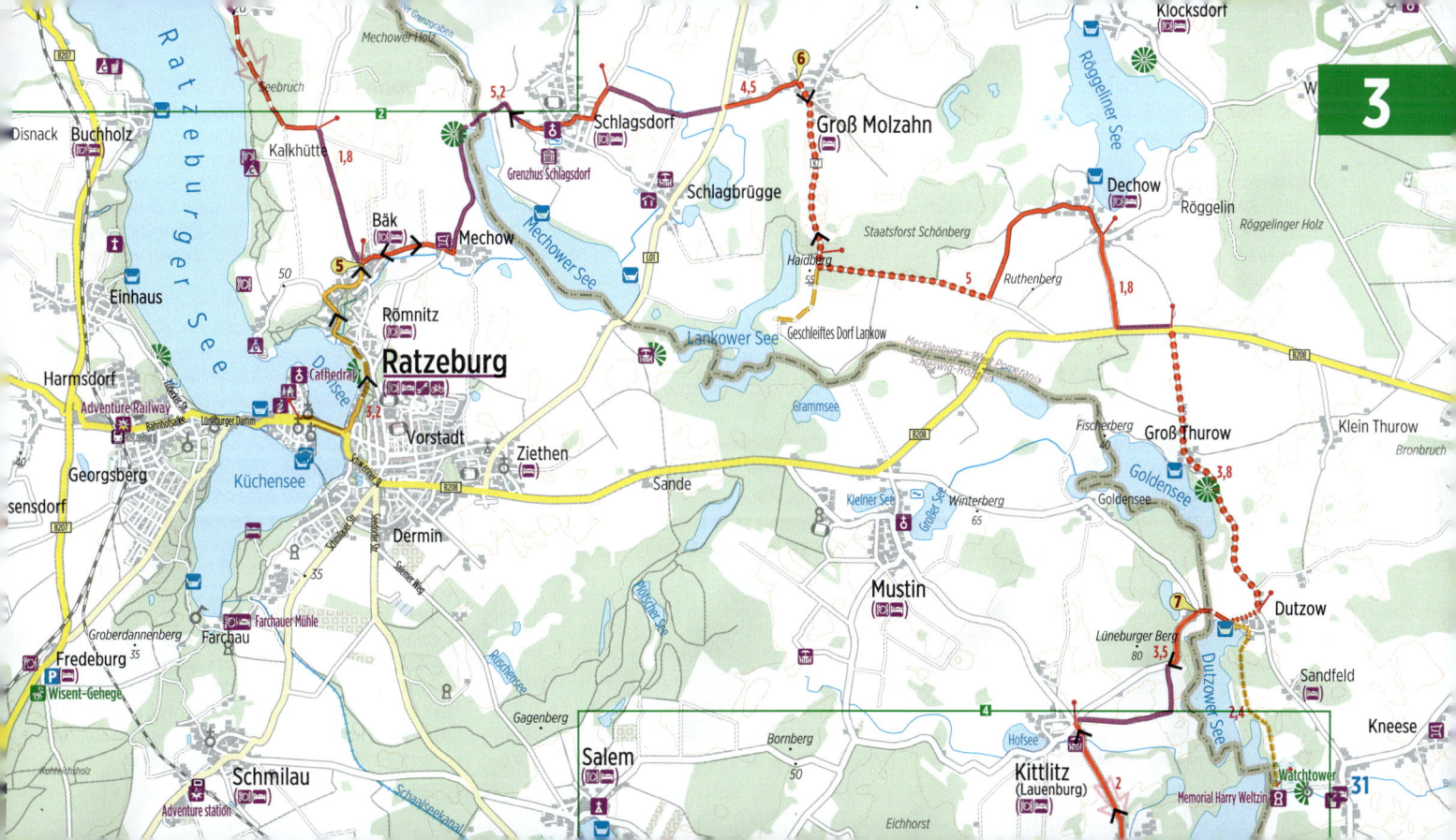

passed away in 1980 and was famous for his graphical work. @ fhj276

🏛 **Ernst-Barlach-Museum**, Barlachpl. 3, ☎ 3789 ⊜ Here you will find the works of the famous painter and sculptor, Ernst Barlach (1870-1938), who spent his youth in Ratzeburg. @ ehh553

🏛 **Kreismuseum (Local Museum)**, Domhof 12, ☎ 86070 ⊜ Former manor of the Dukes of Mecklenburg from the year 1764. Exhibitions on the history of the city and local and natural history. Also worth viewing is the valuable stucco in the Rococo hall. @ mki274

⛪ **Ratzeburger Dom (Cathedral)**, Domhof 35. In the years 1154-1220, Henry the Lion had the Cathedral of Ratzeburg built. It is a Romanic brick building with a carved Renaissance pulpit worth visiting, a relief in the altar wing and a grand cloister with a ribbed vault. In the courtyard of the cloister you will find the work „Beggar on Crutches" from Ernst Barlach.

🛶 **Aqua Siwa**, Fischerstr., ☎ 4822, @ ixk764

The climatic spa Ratzeburg with a population of 13,000, is on an island and surrounded by four different lakes: the Küchensee, Stadtsee, Domsee and the long Lake Ratzeburg. „Racesburg" was first mentioned in a document which was issued in Worms in 1062.

The name probably originated from the Slavic Prince Ratibor, who was called „Ratse" and resided in a ring-fort. In the 11th century, Ratzeburg was the site of many conflicts between Christians and Slavs. Henry the Lion feoffed Count Heinrich of Bodwide with the fortification in the 12th century.

After the fall of Henry the Lion, Ratzeburg and Lauenburg were under Ascanian rule whereby the two cities formed the Duchy of Lauenburg. After the Ascanian House died off, a larger fortification was built by the House of Luneburg-

Celle. Since the Danish King Christian V. saw a violation of the „Peace of Westphalia" therein, he had the city levelled in 1693. The city was then rebuilt in the style of a Baroque geometric construction.

In the beginning of the 19th century, Ratzeburg suffered from poverty and was under alternating rulers until the city was issued to the Danes in the Vienna Congress of 1815. The fortification was torn down and Ratzeburg became part of Prussia in 1865. The area on the old town island around the cathedral was a Mecklenburg exclave in the Schleswig-Holstein Ratze castle until 1937.

The city was not destroyed during World War II. Due to the inflow of fugitives, the population after the war grew to 12,000.

There are various restaurants and overnight accommodation in Ratzeburg. Trains travel from the train station to Luneburg and Lübeck.

From the market place in Ratzeburg to the main route at Mechower Holz is a good 5 km. ▮EINSTIEG

From the market place in Ratzeburg, continue until you reach the B 208 and turn left right after the bridge at the "Eiscafé Bruhn" in the Bäker Weg. The dead-end continues as a cycle trail. At the next fork in the road, take the middle road and continue through hilly terrain. At the end of the forest, turn right into Mühlenweg, which leads to Ratzeburger Straße, into which you turn left and you will reach Bäk.

The main route follows the **Hoheleuchte road**, at the end of which you turn right and reach the car-free **Neuhofer Weg**. **5** In **Bäk** turn left into **Mechower Straße**, which becomes **Bäker road**. In **Mechow** turn left onto **Schlagsdorfer way**, cycle to the shore of Mechower lake, which back in the day completely belonged to the GDR and which the villagers could see but not enter. Indeed, bathing was forbidden here for 40 years.

In the northwest of the lake there is an observation tower. In 2012, twelve information boards were erected around the lake as "border parcours", which displayed the local aspect of German-German history. Via the **Mechower Grenzgraben** and the **Aalkistenweg** you come to the **Moorweg**, which you turn right onto. On it you reach Schlagsdorf, where the Grenzhus is located at the corner of Neubauernweg

Grenzhus Schlagsdorf

The Grenzhus is found in the border town of Schlagsdorf, Neubauernweg 1, in the northern area of the biosphere reserve Schaalsee and has various exhibitions on the German-German border spread across three levels. The exhibitions on the uppermost level frequently change. The restaurant offers many regional delicacies to try.

On an outdoor area the size of a football field, a section of the GDR border installations has been reconstructed with original parts. These include a metal fence, a trench to stop cars from getting past, a dog run free facility, an observation bunker, and watchtowers with a concrete barrier wall. Opening times: Mon-Fri 10-16.30, Sat, Sun 10-18.00.

Coming from the museum, turn right and then left onto the **Hauptstraße**., follow the signposts through the village, then turn right and after crossing the L 01 you will reach **Groß Molzahn**.

6 There you turn right onto **Thurower Straße**. When the road beds around to the left, continue straight ahead and you will get to the part on the lakeshore, where the village of Lankow was once situated.

The razed village of Lankow

The village of Lankow in the former GDR restricted military zone had to give way to the development of the German-German border in 1979. In order to remind the passing visitor of these past times, a commemorative stone with the name and dates of the village as well as an information panel with old photos and historical data about Lankow has been put up.

The main route follows **Thurower Street** and then turns left towards Dechow, one of the charmingly restored villages in the Schaalsee Biosphere Reserve. A visit to the Dairy is highly recommended.

Gadebusch Agreement

The "Barber-Lyashchenko Agreement" was a British-Soviet territorial exchange

which was agreed upon in November 1945. To prevent the Mecklenburg cathedral peninsula of Ratzeburg from becoming a Russian exclave, the British encouraged the communities of Römnitz together with Hohenleuchte, Bäk, Ziethen with Wietingsbek and Mechow to join the British sector. In return, the municipalities of Dechow and Thurow as well as the exclaves in the east of the Schaalsee from Bernstorf to Hakendorf, Stintenburg Hütte, Lassahn, Stintenburg and up to Techin then belonged to the Soviet sector. This exchange of territories was not reversed in 1990.

Follow the **Dorfstraße** until you reach the **B 208**, where you turn left, and take the cycle path that accompanies the road. Turn right a short while later onto **Kneeserstraße** to Zarrentin, 30 kilometres away.

The road is a very charming, typically West Mecklenburg route. After Groß Thurow you will soon reach the village of Dutzow, where you turn right onto the historic cobblestone road leading to Rosenhagen.

The bridge over the border stream

This bridge is somewhat of a curiosity, not least because it was put up in December 1989 as a provisional bridge during the general euphoria of the Wall coming down by the

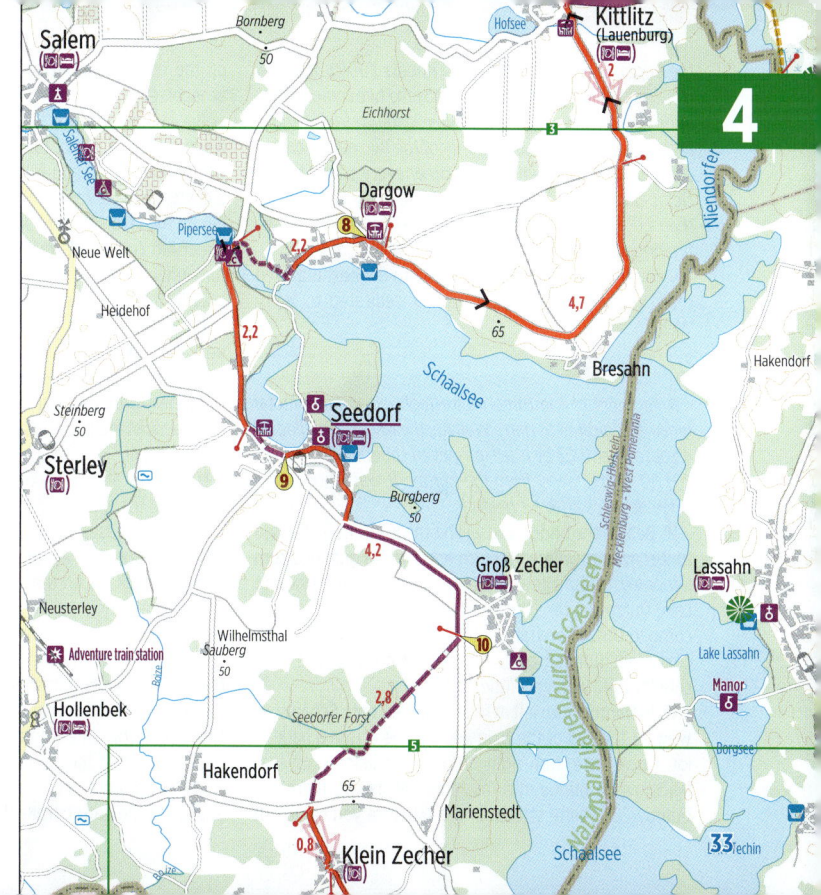

fire brigades of *Kittlitz (FRG)* and *Kneese (GDR)*. The final construction was jointly carried out by the two communities in 1993 in the face of considerable resistance from various authorities. It shows the solidarity of the two neighbouring communities, which invite each other every year on the 3 October to a large celebration. In 2014, for example, more than 1,000 guests swayed to the brass music of the two fire brigades.

If you turn left before the bridge onto the next unpaved road, you will come to a memorial dedicated to Harry Weltzin.

Harry Weltzin

A segment of the three-metre-high expandable metal fence is dedicated to Harry Weltzin, the last victim killed on 4 September 1983 by a self-propelled shooting facility (SM 70) 50 metres away from the border. It was inaugurated three decades after his death.

7 Behind the bridge you will hit the **K 1** from Goldensee to Kittlitz, into where you turn left. After a gradient, turn left onto the asphalted farm road. After a beautiful view of Lake Dutzower, take the next right and in **Kittlitz** you will come to **Dutzowerstraße**, into where you turn left. At the crossroads turn left again onto **Niendorferstraße**, a wide country road with very little traffic.

8 In **Dargow** turn left at the fire station onto **Schaalsee-weg**. At the end of the road you'll come across a parking lot. Once there, turn right onto an asphalted path that leads over a bridge into the forest. At its end there is a bumpy 200 metre stretch of road, before you come out

on the county road at the car park at Pipersee and turn left. When you arrive in **Seedorf**, turn left onto the **Hauptstraße**. **9** Then, turn left onto **Dorfstraße**, which you follow - past a church, a place for bathing and an inn by the lake - until you reach the street **Am Zuckerhut**, into which you turn left.

Cycle upon the newly built cycle path along a country road for the next 2 km. A detour to Groß Zecher is not only worthwhile because of its culinary offerings, but also to visit the classicist manor house with its nostalgic flair.

10 Shortly after Groß Zecher, turn right onto the asphalted forest road, which later ceases to become asphalted. After the right bend it is asphalted again and you will reach Zecher after crossing the K 44 on the village road Klein Zecher. Once there, cycle straight along the Zarrentiner Weg. Shortly before the border the asphalt stops and you'll cycle through the forest on some historical, yet bumpy cobblestones. At the entrance to the forest you can see how fast the forest has grown since the opening of the border. In this part of the "death strip" one crosses one of the few sections of the patrol paths that has been preserved for the longest time **11** In Zarrentin, continue straight onto **Töpferstrasse** and follow the **Hauptstraße** through the town to **Pahlhuus**.

Watchtower at the Schlagsdorf border museum

Zarrentin

prefix: 038851

ℹ️ Tourismus-Information, Hauptstr. 15, ☎ 333435, @ exi161

⚓ Personenschifffahrt Schaalseetour (Boat excursions Schaalseetour), Heegenring 14, ☎ 25311, @ lcx515

🏛 Kloster und Heimatmuseum (Cloister and Regional Museum), Kirchpl. 8, ☎ 838510 ☻ The cloister was founded in 1246 by Countess Audacia and her son. A Cistercian convent for the daughters of the Mecklenburg princes and the Patrician families of Lübeck. It was dissolved in 1552 and was then put to many different uses, for example as a brewery, an administrative seat and as a hostel. It is currently being renovated for use as a cultural centre. @ yyu183

St. Petrus und St. Paulus (St. Peter and St. Paul), Kirchpl. The present gothic church was built in the 15th century.

Informationszentrum Biosphärenreservat Schaalsee PAHLHUUS (Information centre biosphere reserve Schaalsee), Wittenburger Chausee 13, ☎ 3020 ☻ Comprises 309 km² of biosphere reserve with untouched fauna and flora. Numerous rare plants such as sundew or cotton grass thrive here and several endangered animals such as the sea eagle or the otter can also be observed. @ uir417

✉ Strandbad am Schaalsee (Resort on Lake Schaal), Am See

Zarrentin is a small town with a population of approx. 4,600 in the municipal Ludwigslust in Mecklenburg-Western Pomerania. The city is the home of the so-called „Pahlhuus"

– the information centre of the biosphere reserve Schaalsee.

The town of Zarrentin was officially mentioned for the first time in 1194, first settlers to the region date back to 7500 B. C. The name "Zarnethin" indicates a Slavic background: It could be connected to the God „Czernebog", whom the Slavs worshiped. The area could also have served as a ritual or a sacrificial place.

The cloister at Lake Schaal was donated to the town by the Countess Audicia of Schwerin in 1246. After this, a Cistercian convent existed in the direct vicinity of Zarrentin until 1552. Duke Johann Albrecht I secularised the church during the reformation and the cloister became property of the Duke.

The town severely suffered during the Thirty-Year War. In 1775, it was nearly completely destroyed by fire, since there were very few fire-fighters available. Zarrentin was also a theatre of war in the Napoleonic Wars.

In the 19th century, the population of Zarrentin nearly doubled. In 1896, the town's connectivity to the outside areas was boosted with the railroad Hagenow Land – Neumünster, which led to numerous companies moving to the area. In 1911, the so-called Strangendamm was built,

which directly connected Zarrentin with the Strangen peninsula. In 1938, Zarrentin was granted city rights since it had a population of more than 2,000.

On July 1, 1945, the city was added to the Soviet Occupational Zone. In the times of the GDR, Zarrentin was part of the restriction zone on the inner German border. The residents suffered under the strict regulations. A windmill which was built in the middle of the 19th century was also torn down. In November of 1982, the Hamburg-Berlin motorway was completed and a large border crossing was constructed by Zarrentin. This was removed again after the reunification.

Today, the Schaalsee motorway service is located on the site, in the „MEGA-Park Valluhn/Gallin" - the largest commercial and logistics area in Mecklenburg. It is so large that its administration has even built its own privately financed motorway access.

Bridge house at Lake Schaal

After the GDR, the family of the resistance fighter Albrecht Graf von Bernstorff, who was murdered by the SS in 1945 and who belonged to the "Mecklenburg nobility", received a large part of land back from the Stintenburg County estate. His great-nephew, Johann Hartwig, renovated the old

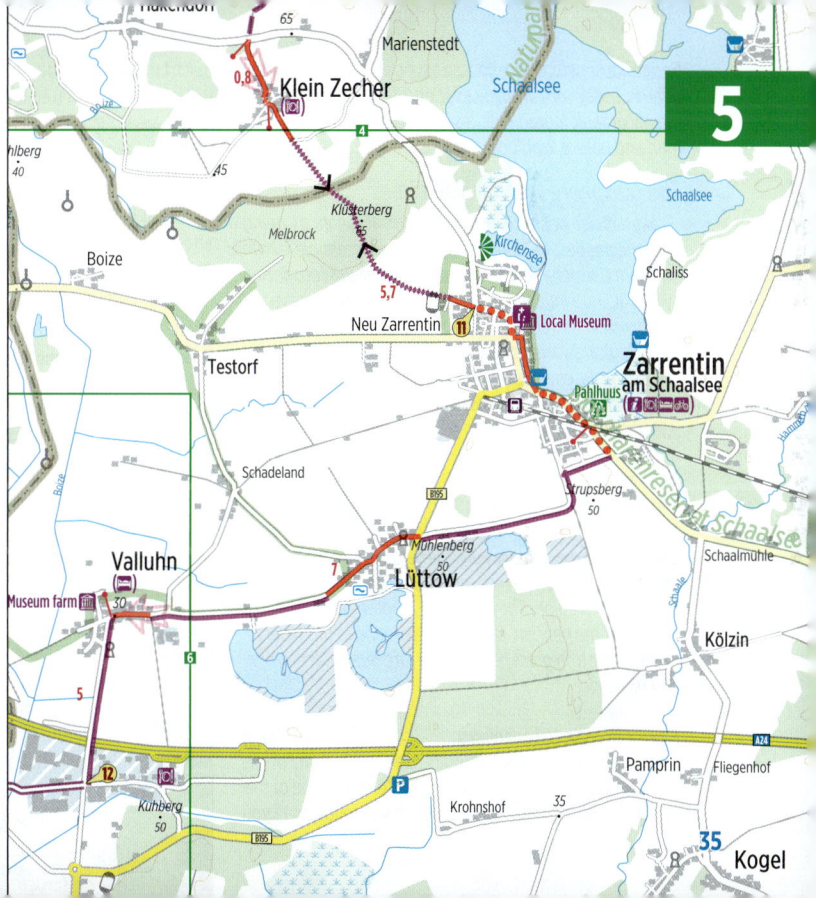

bridge house, which once housed a special unit of GDR border guards. Today you can enjoy a variety of regional dishes with mainly organic ingredients. It symbolises a bridge between man and nature, tradition and modernity, East and West.

The biosphere reserve Schaalsee

Lake Schaal was a record holder for 40 years as being both the deepest (72 metres) and most inaccessible lake in northern Germany. The surrounding region was recognised by UNESCO in January 2000 as one of 425 biosphere reserves worldwide. It is intended to promote sustainable tourism and an ecological awareness. Equally, it should demonstrate that preserving the environment can be a chance for development and that landscapes like these must be preserved. Almost 9 % of the region is made up of waterways and only 2.3 % is populated. This area is home to 12,300 people as well as 249 bird species.

In this sparsely-populated landscape great numbers of the kingfisher, swan, fire-bellied toad and dwarf dommel can still be found. Additionally, the bald coot raises its chicks here and wild boars, which are excellent swimmers, feel at home in this region. The bog bean, a botanical rarity and a relative of the gentian, can be widely found in this reserve. However, cotton grass has become rare due to fertilisation and drainage.

From Zarrentin to Lauenburg   41 km

Keep right behind the Pahlhuus, cross the railway tracks and turn right onto **Gadebuscher Straße**. At the end of this road turn left onto **Mühlenberg**, which you follow until you reach **Lüttow**. Continue along the main road until you reach Valluhn, where you turn left onto **Dorfstraße**.

Valluhn

Cross the A 24 - the petrol station on the eastern side used to be the GDR border clearance. **12** At the roundabout, turn right onto **Am Heisterbusch**. At the end of that road, after passing the Gudower Nase, turn right onto the **Neu Galliner Ring**. The street name refers to the settlement of Neu-Gallin, which fell victim to "Aktion Ungeziefer" in 1952. Shortly after crossing the Boize brook and part of the Neu-Galliner-Ring, a branched path leading to the right takes you to the north to the border.

Before the border strip – which you can easily identify thanks to the fact that the trees here are much lower - turn left onto the forest path and after a right turn you will come to an asphalted forest road, into which you turn left. This road was built for the Federal Border Guard and runs parallel to the former German-German border for the next 2.5 kilometres.

View to the Schaalsee

The next asphalt road continues as a signposted cycle path first to the left and then in the fields to the right until you reach **Langenlehsten**.

Arable flora

Most of the fields you cycle through here are "areas of natural conservation". Traditional agricultural methods on these sandy, marginal soils are financed by the state and through EU funds.

13 In Langenlehsten turn left towards Fortkrug and Leisterförde.

In **Fortkrug** continue straight towards the **"border installation"**. The complex was built in 2010 by the regional "Countryside trust" (contact: ☎ 038842-22432). It can be visited at any time. Different aspects of the "GDR border security" can be seen here with many original exhibits along a short part of the route.

Follow the main route towards the right and cycle on the rarely-frequented **K 28** via Bröthen towards Büchen. After 2 kilometres you will see a directional cross and a memorial stone on the left, from which a forest path leads to a memorial for Michael Gartenschläger.

Michael Gartenschläger

On the night of May 1, 1976, Michael Gartenschläger was shot at Grenzknick Bröthen by the special police force for the Ministry for National Security whilst attempting to dismantle a self-firing gun known as the SM 70. A display case and a commemorative cross with the inscription "He shook the conscience of the free world" pay homage to this brave act.

A few years earlier, in 1961, Michael Gartenschläger had been sentenced to life imprisonment in the GDR at the age of seventeen for resisting the government. In 1971, the Federal Republic of Germany bailed him out of prison. Shortly before his death, "Der Spiegel" reported that he had been successful on 30 March in dismantling an SM70. This made it possible for the West to look at the weapon in more detail and understand its impact.

These "death machines" typically released a salvo based upon even the smallest of movements along the border fence, resulting in a barrage of sharp splitters. Contrary to Michael Gartenschläger's expectations, the publication of these facts in the news did not cause a great amount of outrage in West Germany.

On 23 April, he then dismantled a second SM70. However, this did not reach Berlin until several years later, where it was presented to the public, with the help of the chairman of the "Working Group", Rainer Hildebrandt, in the museum "Checkpoint Charlie".

In the attempt to dismantle a third automatic firing weapon, with the aim of installing it in front of the permanent representation of the GDR in Bonn, Gartenschläger was shot by special police forces of the Ministry for National Security. On May 10, 1976, his body was buried under orders from the Stasi as an "unknown body found at sea" in the Waldfriedhof in Schwerin.

The three shooters were praised, rewarded and were even defended as recently as the year 2000, by the last interior minister of the GDR, Peter-Michael Diestel (CDU), and acquitted, along with the other Stasi officers.

After you have travelled through Bröthen, you will reach Büchen-Dorf, where you will find a preacher's cottage.

AUSFLUG If you want to visit the Schwanheide border station, turn left shortly before the church onto Schwanheider Weg, pass under the tracks and cross Riedebeck, the former German-German border stream. The forest path with sandy patches meets the Zweedorfer Straße, where you turn left and reach the border station with its threatening border clearance building that is itself under threat - from being torn down.

Büchen-Dorf (Büchen)
prefix: 04155

✳ **Priesterkate Büchen-Dorf (Preacher's cottage Büchen-Dorf)**, Gudower Str. 1, ✆ 6114, ⏲ Tu, Th, Fr 14-17:00, 1st and 3rd Su of the month 14-17:00. The old pastorate, called Priesterkate, was built in 1649 and is the oldest building in the Duchy of Lauenburg. In the historically preserved building,

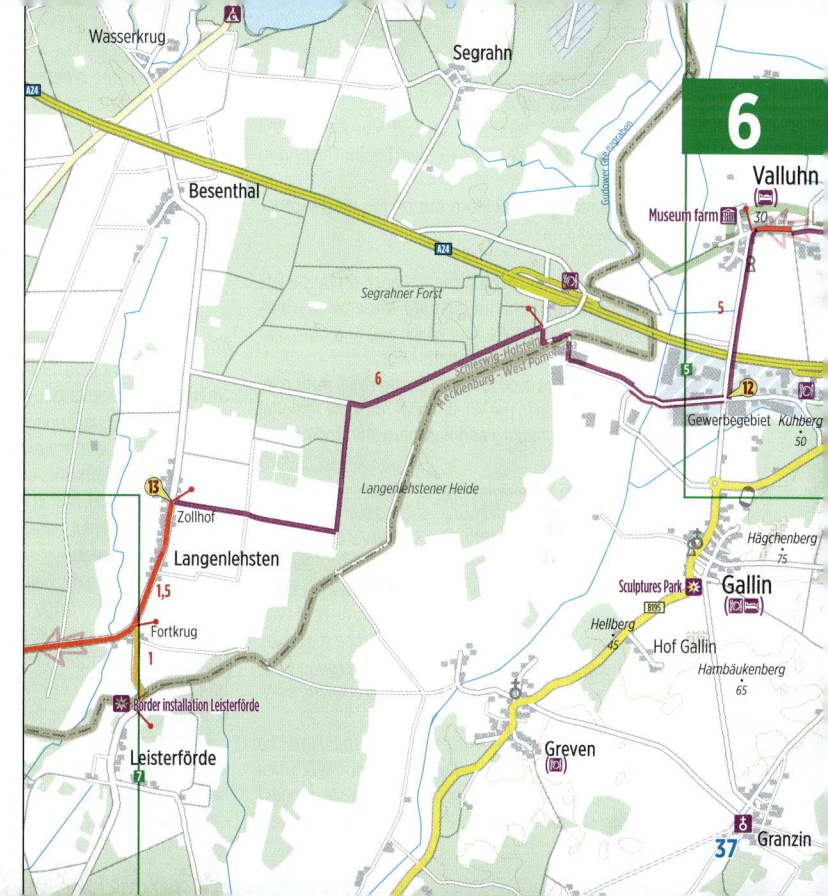

you will find a permanent exhibition concerning the German-German border. @ fgt362

From Büchen-Dorf, turn onto the L 205 over the Elbe-Lübeck Channel. **14** Take the road down behind the bridge to get to the channel.

VARIANTE You can already cycle before the bridge on the other side of the channel.

INS ZENTRUM If you want to cycle to the station, branch off to the left behind the bridge, continue left onto Wiesenweg, which leads into Bahnhofstraße, into which you turn right and you will then reach the train station.

TIPP All interzonal trains used to stop at Büchen train station, as it was the first stop in the West. Today, only the regional trains towards Luneburg and Hamburg still stop here.

Büchen

Büchen, which is surrounded by numerous lakes, was first mentioned in 1231 in the Ratzeburg Tithe register as „Boken" („Buche" or „Zu den Buchen"). The St. Mary's Church was built around 1200, and quickly became a meaningful place of pilgrimage known for a stunning picture of the Virgin Mary. This picture, however, was lost during the Thirty-Year War.

The town was in the border area twice: First on the Limes Saxoniae during the period of Karl the Great around 800, and the second time on the inner German border between 1945 and 1990.

The area became important through the construction of the Delvenau-Stecknitz Channel between 1391 and 1398: Since the salt city of Lauenburg transported the waste product to Luneburg via the waterway, it was called the "wet salt

street". It was the oldest channel in northern Europe and the first watershed of its kind. The channel was expanded to the Elbe-Lübeck channel in 1900.

Büchen also played an important role as a railway connection and transfer location since the Hamburg-Berlin line crossed the Lübeck-Büchen line here and was the only connection from Hamburg to Lübeck. In the 19th century, no other connection could be made since Holstein, which was in the middle, was occupied by Denmark.

At the end of the Second World War, the area became the target of bombing raids, with an ammunition factory located here specifically being targeted. The border situation during Germany's division caused problems for the community, but it profited from its location in the outermost belt of Hamburg. Today, local's hopes are pinned on tourism.

To continue from Büchen, cycle along the banks of the **Elbe-Lübeck Canal**. At first the path along the dike is a paved field path, but then it becomes asphalted as you approach the lock in **Witzeeze**.

After the watergate, continue on the dirt road until you reach Dalldorf. **15** Via the bridge you will reach the eastern shore of the channel where the trail is paved. Continue along the Stecknitz, the former border river with a forest adjacent on the eastern side. Afterwards you will find a wide field which remains from the former border strip.

After travelling around Lake Lanzer, the paved stretch comes to an end but begins again after the branch to Basedow. Continue straight ahead through the town of Lanze, cross the Stecknitz and you will reach the B 5 which you

will cross to the right. This road was of special importance to bicycle traffic through the GDR.

Bicycle transit through the GDR

The carriageway F 5 between Berlin and Hamburg was the only transit road through the GDR on which cycling was allowed. The Transit Agreement of 1972 it then stipulated that the new motorway from Berlin to Hamburg was the only road allowed for transit. Therefore, from the moment when the first part of this new motorway was in use (30th June 1981), cyclists were not allowed anymore. It was also not possible to cycle to East Berlin as bicycles were only allowed to be taken as "travel usage devices" – only in or on a car. In order to fight this discrimination against cyclists, the "Bicycle Initiative Berlin-Lauenburg" (FIBEL) was founded in 1979. Their goal was to raise public awareness of the problems cyclists were facing and on 12th August 1979 Dieter Hertwig organised the first bicycle tour from Berlin to Lauenburg. As the transit did not allow overnight stays and cycling was only allowed in daylight, the 69 participants started their journey early at 4.30 am at the border checkpoint of Staaken and reached Lauenburg 15 hours and 221 kilometres later at 7.30 p.m. It was hoped that these trips – in 1980 there were already 150 cyclists and in 1981 this grew to 260 – would persuade the authorities to allow bicycle travel through the GDR along the shortest route (136 km) from Berlin to Schnackenburg.

Unfortunately, their efforts were in vain!

16 After the bridge across the Elbe-Lübeck Channel, turn left onto **Hafenstraße**.

INS ZENTRUM In order to reach the town centre of Lauenburg, which is well worth a visit, continue straight where the main road bends to the left and continue cycling down Hafen Straße.

Lauenburg/Elbe

prefix: 04153

- **[i]** Tourist-Information, Elbstr. 59, ☎ 5909220, @ tlm376
- **⛴** Raddampfer Kaiser Wilhelm (Paddlesteamer Kaiser Wilhelm), ☎ 51086, ⏱ excursions on the weekends - from the end of May until the end of September, @ fqx548
- **🏛** Elbschifffahrtsmuseum (Maritime Museum on the Elbe river), Elbstr. 59, ☎ 5909219, ⏱ March-Oct., Mo-Fr 10-13:00 and 14-17:00, Sa/Su 10-17:00, Nov.-Feb., We, Fr-Su 10-13:00 and 14-16:30, @ kxb883
- **🏛** Mühlenmuseum (Mill Museum), Bergstr. 17, Lauenburger Mill, ☎ 5890, ⏱ daily 10:00-18:00. A former miller professionally operated the mill and tells stories of the life and work of his profession. @ ipg624
- **🚻** Maria-Magdalenen-Kirche (Saint Mary Magdalene), Kirchpl. 1
- **🚻** Schlossturm und Schloss (Castle tower and castle), Amtspl. 6 🚻 The castle tower is the oldest construction of the Ascanian fortification, built in 1182 and is open to visitors. Only one side wing remains of the once elaborate castle in which known personalities such as Wallenstein or King Wilhelm I and Bismarck spent some time. @ emg125
- **✳** Palmschleuse (palm watergate), Bei der Palmschleuse. The palm watergate is the oldest remaining chamber lock in northern Europe. @ jme886
- **🌿** Fürstengarten und Grotte (Fürstengarten and grotto). Created around 1590 by Duke Franz II, the garden was designed around 1656 as a baroque complex modeled on the Bohemian model. @ sdg237
- **🏊** Freibad (Outdoor pool), Am Kuhgrund, ☎ 4115, @ mem188

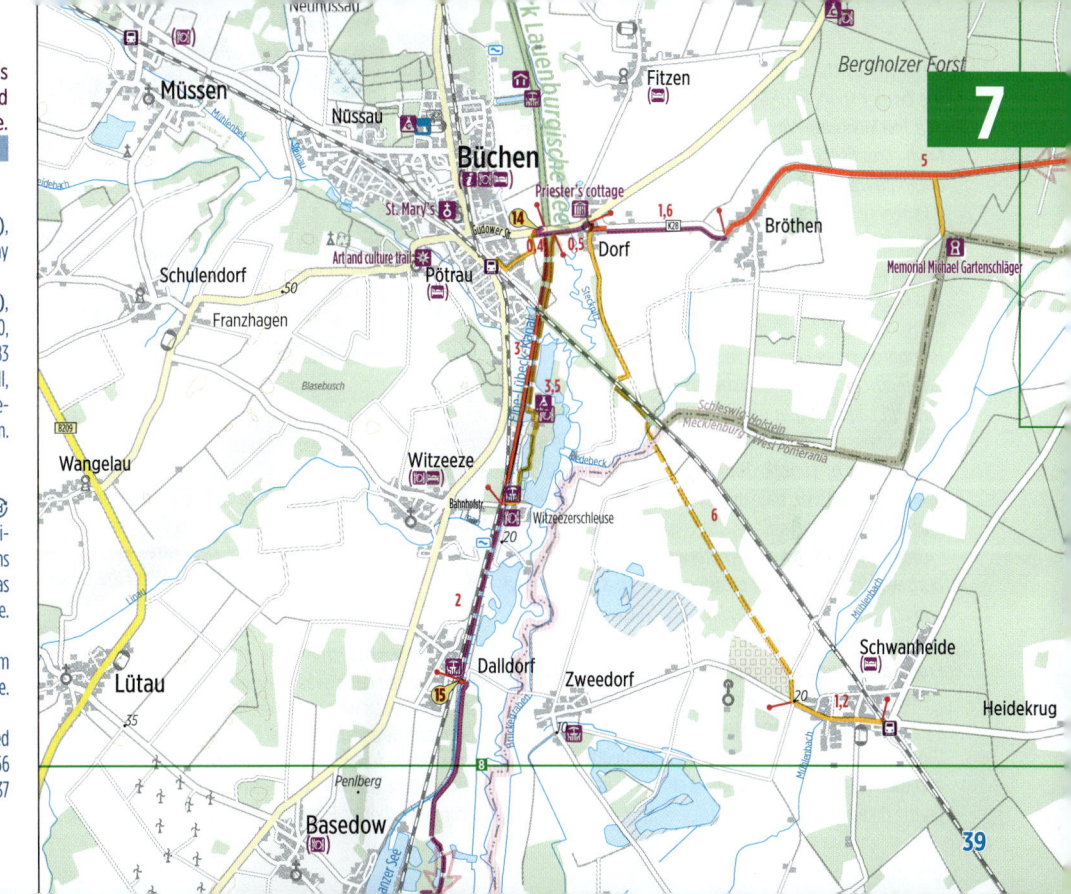

The city by the Elbe with a population of 12,000 lies in the border triangle of Schleswig-Holstein, Lower Saxony and Mecklenburg-Western Pomerania. The historical old town comprises about 600 timbered houses which mostly originate from the 17th and 18th century.

Lauenburg was built in 1182 as a fortress by Bernhard of Ascania, the successor of Henry the Lion, who was defeated by Friedrich Barbarossa one year earlier. In 1417, the city was the only to receive the privilege from Duke Erich V, to transport goods brought over the channel from Lübeck to Hamburg via the Elbe.

The so-called „Alte Salzstraße" (old salt street) leads through Lauenburg, a military and trade route on which the valuable Lüneburger salt was transported to the Baltic Sea harbour of Lübeck. Today one can travel this route over the Elbe by car, train or bicycle. Lauenburg lies on the northern Elbe cycle trail.

Until the completion of the motorway, Lauenburg/Boizenburg was the only border crossing point on a federal road and one of only three railway lines until the end of the GDR.

From Lauenburg to Neu Bleckede   22 km

After the left bend of Hafenstraße, cross the canal again. At the Lauenburg **railway station**, the route leads down to the right of the cycle path, crosses underneath the B 209 and then for the next 5 kilometres along the beautiful path on the dike along the Elbe.

Activists of FiBeL at Lauenburg checkpoint, 1980

The Elbe

The Elbe is a Central European river that begins its life in the giant mountains in the Czech Republic near the border with Poland. At 1,094 kilometres, it is the fourteenth longest river in Europe and one of the 200 longest rivers in the world. The Czech part is 367 kilometres long and the one flowing through Germany is 727 kilometres long. Before it flows into the North Sea at Cuxhaven, the Elbe crosses Decin, Usti, Dresden, Magdeburg and Hamburg. The most famous waters in its catchment area are the Vltava, the Saale and the Havel with the Spree. The river, which in the Czech part is called Labe, was regulated in the 1920s, 1930s and since the 1950s with a total of 24 barrages. In the 1920s, the German side decided against barrages and opted instead for the so-called "low water regulation" due to lack of money.

At Mělník the 430-kilometre-long Vltava and the 258 kilometre-shorter Elbe flow together. Normally, the name of the longer source river is adopted. But rivers such as the Aare and Rhine, Warthe and Oder, as well as the Havel and Spree are the exceptions that prove the rule. Otherwise Dresden and Hamburg would be on the Vltava.

At the end of the Second World War, the "handshake of Torgau" went around the world when Soviet and American soldiers met and offered out their hands on the remains of the Torgau Elbe Bridge on 26 April 1945. During the division of Germany, the Elbe between Schnackenburg and Lauenburg was also the inner-German border for 94 kilometres. Because the bank became a border area that no one was allowed to enter, the Elbe was - according to Axel Kahrs – "a phantom river" for those in the east and a "river without a counterpart" for those in the west.

But the Elbe has always been a border. Thus, the river separated Charles the Great's empire from the Slavs in the east and Konrad Adenauer also claimed in 1946: "Asia stands on the Elbe". But the separation is also visible in nature: east of the Elbe is the territory of the grey-black crows, while the black crows are more prevalent on the western side.

Without the decision in the 1920s, the inner-German border and the hermetically sealed GDR, there would be no natural area of beauty around the Elbe today with a free-flowing river 600 kilometres long. This should remain how it is and the chances are good for this happening, because in 2011 the German government - against the explicit protest from the Czech Republic - downgraded the Elbe to a "secondary waterway".

Uwe Rada's book "The Elbe" impressively describes "The flow of Europe's history".

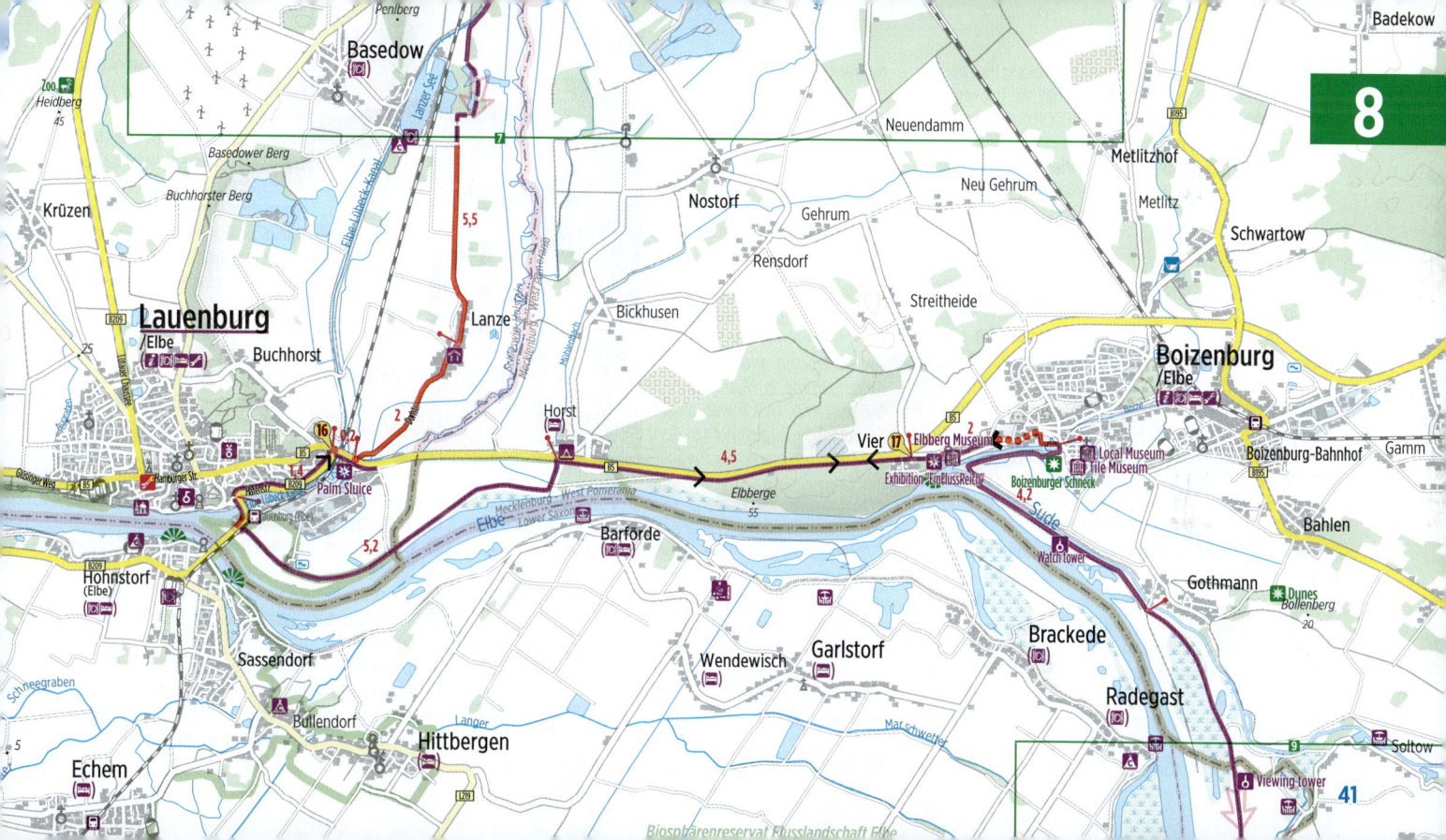

At the **B5** turn right onto the cycle path along the road. On the way to Boizenburg there are two small hills to overcome. A sign indicates that you are in the UNESCO protected nature park "Mecklenburgisches Elbetal".

17 Where the B 5 bends left in **Vier**, continue straight ahead until you see the Elbberg Museum at the end of the village.

Elbberg Museum

An auxiliary camp to the Neuengamme concentration camp used to exist on Reichsstraße 5 between 1944 and 1945. The prisoners, some 400 Hungarian Jewish women, were forced to work in the neighbouring armament factory. The only building which still exists today is a partially underground barrack in which food was stored for the camp kitchen. In this "kitchen basement" – used by the GDR border troops for paint storage – an exhibition can be found since 2002, which is dedicated to the "History of the town under Germany's dictators". The Boizenburg auxiliary camp can be viewed as a model in a scale of 1:100.

Another room is used for an exhibition about the German-German border by Boizenburg. This was the control location for the border crossing between Lauenburg and Boizenburg. Only the control tower is authentic, which was built in 1972/73 for the 5-kilometre-large restriction zone before the border which was only accessible by GDR citizens with special identification. This, however, was also the first control point for the transit passengers. Directly on the tower – it could hardly be worse – an advertisement for the restaurant of the same name, "Check Point Harry" can be found. An outdoor area also belongs to the museum. Although confined to a small area, various elements relating to the GDR border posts and vehicles belonging to the GDR border troops are exhibited here.

Neuengamme auxiliary concentration camp

Right after entering Boizenburg, you will find a memorial on the right "To commemorate the 400 Jewish women and girls of the Neuengamme auxiliary concentration camp, which was on the Elbberg from August 1944 to April 1945. This was erected by the Socialist Unity Party with the intention of "commemorating the prisoners of the Neuengamme concentration camp. The annual memorial event for the "Victims of Fascism" was discontinued in the mid 1970's due to the vicinity to the border. On contrast to the GDR inscription, the current plaque refers to the Jewish and female identity of the prisoners..

From the Elbberg Museum, continue straight ahead and up a steep hill until you reach the old and very charming centre of Boizenburg.

Boizenburg/Elbe
prefix: 038847

i **Stadtinformation (City information)**, Markt 14, ✆ 62667, @ tap456

Former inner-German border exhibition, Elbberg Museum in Boizenburg

🚢 **Fahrgastschifffahrt (Boat excursions)**

🏛 **Elbbergmuseum (Elberg Museum)**, Am Elberg ⟳ This location has two historical meanings: during the time of the National Socialism, it was the site of the former Neuengamme auxiliary concentration camp and later during the time of the GDR it was the initial transit control location of the former inner German border. The exhibitions concerning this topic can be found in the former kitchen basement of the auxiliary concentration camp. @ ogy541

🏛 **Fliesenmuseum (Tile museum)**, Reichenstr. 4, ✆ 53881, ✆ 56442 🚻 The first and only German tile museum, in a space of 500 m², displays thousands of artistic tiles from throughout history including amongst others Art Deco. @ oby143

🏛 **Heimatmuseum (Museum of local history)**, Markt 1, ✆ 62665 🚻, @ skw274

✳ **Ehem. Stadtmauer (Former City Wall)**

✳ **Weidenschneck**. The willow tapestry (18 m x 9 m x12 m) is connected to the old town by a 450-metre alley.

🌸 **Aussichtsturm Elwkieker (Viewing tower)**, Elberg 1

🏊 **Naturerlebnisbad (Nature Adventure pool)**, Boizestr. 5, ✆ 33245, @ syv746

In the „tile town" you can do a tour of the city showing you works from current artists on various house facades with tiles. There is a nice old town with beautiful timbered houses, restaurants and cafes. And a fantastic palace, adorned

with towers, oriels, domes and other decorative pieces. It is surrounded by a park designed by Peter Joseph Lenné.

Boizenburg was officially mentioned for the first time in 1158 and was granted city rights in 1267.

Over the centuries, trades, fishing and the trade with grain, wood and salt were developed. The City Hall and 150 houses were destroyed in a big fire in 1709.

After the Second World War, it was a German-German border town in the Soviet occupational zone. In the times of the Cold War, Boizenburg was characterized by the tile production and the ship construction on the Elbe shipyard, which was closed in 1997. The town on the Elbe with a population of 11,000 also offers the possibility to explore the nature park „Mecklenburgisches Elbetal" with a boat excursion.

In front of the old town, turn right onto the dike path and continue until you come to the well-signposted Elbe cycle path, into which you turn left. Shortly before Gothmann, pass a watchtower, cross the Sude over the old border troop bridge, cycle parallel to the Sude to Bleckede on the dyke and cross the border to the "Amt Neuhaus", which has belonged to Lower Saxony since 1993. Previously, the Elbe between Lauenburg and Schnackenburg was the border river between the two German states.

Amt Neuhaus

The community "Amt Neuhaus" to the right of the Elbe which now belongs to Lower Saxony, once again became part of Luneburg on June 30, 1993 through a contract between Mecklenburg-Western Pomerania and Lower Saxony. The area comprises approximately 240 km² and has a population of about 6,000.

After the fall of the Wall, eight independent municipalities existed in the current municipality (Sückau, Dellien, Neuhaus, Sumte, Kaarßen, Haar, Stapel and Tripkau). The first democratic elections of the community representatives in the GDR took place in May 1990. The eight municipal councils with a total of 92 council members at that time unanimously decided on the regrouping of the municipalities of Mecklenburg-Western Pomerania in Lower Saxony. These decisions were based on the background of the affiliation to Hannover until the end of World War II and the family, religious and economic ties from that period.

In "Amt Neuhaus" the route is very easy to travel on, with smooth paved slabs.

In Neu Bleckede, continue on the country road, keep right and after passing a watchtower you will reach Bleckede ferry.

Neu Bleckede (Bleckede)

🛥 **Fähre Bleckede-Neu Bleckede (Bleckede ferry)**, ✆ 2255, ✆ 0174/6896529, 🕑 ferry times: all year, Mo-Sa 5-23:00, May-Sept., Su/public holidays 9-21.30, Oct.-April, Su/public holidays 9-21:00, @ nrk836

🔵 **Grenzturm (Border tower)**

The train station and the train connection were taken out of operation in 1977.

From Neu Bleckede to Hitzacker	31 km
Bleckede	

prefix: 05852

Exhibition about the auxiliary concentration camp, Elbberg Museum

ℹ️ **Tourist-Information**, Schlossstr. 10, Bleckede castle, ✆ 951414 ⓣ, @ lgn588

🛥 **Fähre Bleckede-Neu Bleckede (Bleckede ferry)**, ✆ 2255, ✆ 0174/6896529, 🕑 ferry times: all year, Mo-Sa 5-23:00, May-Sept., Su/public holidays 9-21.30, Oct.-April, Su/public holidays 9-21:00, @ nrk836

🔵 **St. Jacobi**, Zollstr. 26-28, ✆ 1282

🔵🏛 **Bleckeder Schloss (Bleckede castle)**, Schlossstr. 10, ✆ 95140. Towards the end of the 13th century, Wilhelm von Luneburg had a moated castle built here. The tower and the moats are still preserved. The remaining buildings date from the 17th and 18th centuries.

✳️ **Heide-Express (Bleckeder small train)**, Bahnhofstr. 6b, ✆ 951414. Runs historic trains on the Bleckede-Luneburg line. Trips: May-July, Sept. 1st and 3rd Sun in the month, Aug. every Sun. @ riq111

🟢 **Biosphaerium Elbtalaue**, Schlossstr. 10, ✆ 951414 ⓣ Information about the Elbtalaue biosphere reserve can be found in the historical Bleckeder house and the tourist information centre. A variety of

Bleckede (1984/2006)

Elbe fish and beavers live close by and there is also a large natural history exhibition with a bird's voice piano, wind machine and much more. The live stork webcam offers a special bird's nest view from April to August. There is also an observation tower, a café, a shop and guided tours. @ ncd882

From the ferry, cycle on **Elbstraße** into the city. **18** Before you reach the big crossing, turn left onto Am Hafenstraße. A little later, the route turns right into Sanddeich. At the end of the road, go straight along the cycle path and then follow it to the left into Wendischthuner Straße. After the right turn in the road, turn left onto the Elbweg.

In Alt Garge continue on the main road and continue slightly to the left at the roundabout heading away from the railroad tracks on the cycle trail.

Alt Garge (Bleckede)
prefix: 05854
- ❇ **Gedenkstätte (Memorial).** The Memorial is dedicated to the prisoners of the Alt Garge auxiliary and labour camp, which existed for only half a year thanks to the end of the war. @ ebl883
- ❇ **Fahrraddraisine (Bicycle handcar),** Hauptstr. 1, ☎ 0176/84295779. Cycling in a different way: ride 13 kilometres on a former railway line through the Elbtalaue. Trips: April, May, Sept, Oct, Thu-Sun, 10.00, 13.00, and 16.00, June-Aug, daily 10.00, 13.00, and 16.00. Registration requested. @ rib678
- ✉ **Waldbad (Outdoor pool),** Am Waldbad 25, ☎ 334, @ osy374

At the end of town, continue along the train tracks. If you leave the street to the left, you will find a memorial on the left side of the Neuengamme auxiliary concentration camp.

19 Cross the railroad tracks and you will reach the Elbe. From here, continue on the pedestrianised street to Walmsburg and then on to Katemin.

At the beginning of Katemin, the community commemorates the fallen sons of World War I and II. The signs of the Elbe Cycle Trail continue in both directions to Hitzacker. At the Landhaus Katemin, turn left and continue on the cycle trail along the street which leads you to the ferry.

Neu Darchau
prefix: 05853
- ⛴ **Fähre Darchau-Neu Darchau (Darchau ferry),** ☎ 05853/1356, ☎ 0160/99162836, ⊙ Ferry connections: Mo-Sa 5.30-21:00, Su, Holiday 9-21:00, @ jkp436

From Neu Darchau, you can travel to Darchau with the Elbe ferry.

20 On the other side of the Elbe, in Darchau, immediately turn right onto the dike. Sometimes you've got a nice view, but mostly next to the dike the view over the Elbe is obstructed. In Darchau you will also find a watchtower. You will see numerous stones which pay homage to the dike's new construction which took place after the great flood.

Elbe flood 2002

In August 2002, severe rainfall in the Ore Mountains and in the Giant Mountains caused the highest water levels seen along the Elbe and the neighbouring rivers in over a century. Austria was also severely affected by the rainfall in the Alps. There was also extensive flooding in the Czech Republic and Poland.

The event was induced by an extreme and very rare weather condition which also led to the Oder flooding in 1997. Large masses of air were diverted in their west-east movement towards the south to the Mediterranean Sea. There, they absorbed moisture after being warmed. After crossing the Alps, they collided with cold air and cooled down which resulted in heavy precipitation in a relatively short time.

This unusual constellation is characterised as a 5b weather condition. Further areas were flooded by the Elbe, starting in the Czech Republic and Saxony (Bad Schandau, Pirna, Dresden, Meißen), over Saxony-Anhalt (Wittenberg) and Lower Saxony. The damage in Germany was estimated to be around 15 billion Euros.

In the year 2000, there was large flooding on the Elbe and Oder, which was the reason for raising and strengthening the dikes in the following years.

Continue through **Vockfey**, where a very informative information centre was put up in 2006.

Vockfey information centre

This memorial dedicated to the forced resettlement and the loss of many buildings consists of a "thinking pyramid" as well as a small house where the walls have written documents, photos, cards and further pieces of information displayed.

On the paved dike trail continue through **Pommau**, **Privelack** and **Bitter**. Along the route you will enjoy beautiful views of the Elbe and the Elbe Mountains on the other side. It is more pleasant than climbing them to the top by bike. **21** After 30 kilometres you will reach **Herrenhof**, where a stone commemorates the new construction of the dike in 2001.

Continue to Hitzacker by ferry, which is well worth a visit. In Hitzacker, you will find various places to stay overnight and restaurants.

Hitzacker
prefix: 05862

i **Kur- & Touristinformation Hitzacker (Tourist Information)**, Am Markt 7, ✆ 96970, @ qgo836

⛴ **Fähre Hitzacker-Bitter (Ferry Hitzacker)**, ✆ 96970, ✆ 0160/5960668, ⊙ Departure times: April 1-Oct. 15, Mo-Su 9-18:00 and upon arrangement. Ask about morning tours as Hitzacker is sensitive to low water. For passengers and bicycles. @ ura436

⛴ **Elbschifffahrtsbüro (Elbe shipping office)**, Am Markt 7, ✆ 969717, ✆ 0160/4402818. For round trips, @ yfr551

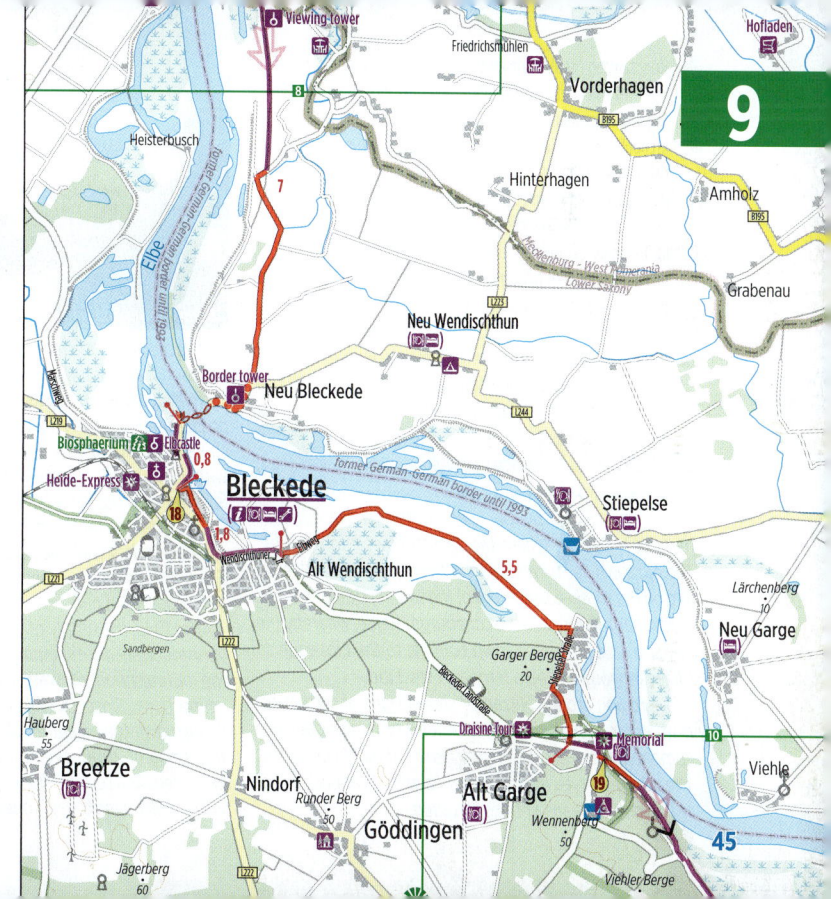

9

45

- ⛴ **Rundfahrten (Boat Excursions)**, ✆ 96970. On the former customs boat Hitzacker, Info: Tourist Information, @ qld456
- ⛴ **Sofafloß Herzogin Dorothea**, ✆ 8838, @ jcj837
- 🏛 **Archäologisches Zentrum Hitzacker (Hitzacker Archaeological Centre)**, Am Hitzacker See, ✆ 6794 ⏰, @ mjo623
- 🏛 **Das Museum im Alten Zollhaus (Hitzacker's old customs house)**, Zollstr. 2, ✆ 8838 🖼, @ dyf346
- ☧ **St. Johannis (St. John's)**, An der Kirche 7, ✆ 350
- ❀ **Historische Altstadt (Historical old town)**. The old town is located on the island, surrounded by the Jeetzel river.
- ❀ **Stadtführungen (city tours)**, ✆ 96970, @ ghs432
- ❀ **Weinberg (Vineyard)**. From about 1528 wine was grown on the Weinberg until a hail storm destroyed all the grapevines in 1713. Since 1983, this old tradition has continued in the most northern vineyard in Germany.
- 🏊 **HIDDO Freibad Hitzacker (Outdoor pool)**, Rieselweg 3, ✆ 05861/800980, @ ypy115

More than 5,000 people reside in the twelve different parts of Hitzacker, where the Jeetzel flows into the Elbe. The old town lies on an island in the middle of the Jeetzel and on the south-eastern foot of the so-called Elbe Heights. This already belongs to the Lüneburger Heide, whereby the lowland area of the old town belongs to the Elbtalaue. In Hitzacker you will find a ferry over the Elbe.

The region around Hitzacker shows signs of settlement from as far back as the Bronze Ages which have been documented in the Archaeological Centre at the Hitzackersee. The Jeetzel serves as a food source with its abundance of fish and as a means of transportation.

Border-tower and wall at Darchau

Hitzacker was officially mentioned for the first time in 1203 and was granted city rights in 1258. In 1260 a profiting customs fee was introduced for the Elbe, which secured the positive economic development of the city. This was mainly characterised by shipping, brewing beer and the grain trade with Hamburg. The economic upswing was, however, halted in its tracks by the Black Death epidemic and the Thirty-Year War as well as the Seven Year War. From the 1870's, the city had to deal with the results of the abolishment of the Elbe customs fee and Jeetzel's decreasing significance as a transportation hub.

After 1945, the supply of goods to Berlin via the Elbe was very important after shipping regained importance through the optimisation of waterways and improved channel connections. Since Hitzacker was not protected by dikes its historical town centre suffered a complete flooding in the spring of 2006. Even the record level from 2002 was exceeded. As a result, a flood protection facility was built in 2008, which even today is one of Europe's largest buildings.

Hitzacker, together with numerous surrounding villages as well as the small towns of Lüchow and Dannenberg, is part of the German Road of Timbered Houses.

Wendland Railway

The single track Wendland Railway leads from Luneburg through the Wendland to Dannenberg (Elbe). Until 1945, the stretch continued further over Dömitz to Wittenberge and was part of a route from Berlin to Bremerhaven, which was, however, never used for passengers. The stretch was opened in 1873. The railway bridge over the Elbe by Dömitz was destroyed in an air attack on April 20,1945. The remains can still be seen. The Wendland Railway operates as a regional train every three hours between Luneburg and Dannenberg. It would have been shut down a long time ago if it hadn't been used for the transportation of radioactive waste with Castor containers intended for nuclear waste storage in Gorleben. Since the stretch was frequently blocked by anti-nuclear activists, the passenger service on the Wendland Railway was discontinued during the time of Castor transports.

From Hitzacker to Dömitz/Kaltenhof   19 km

From Hitzacker, take the ferry to Herrenhof and turn right onto the dike where you can choose between the paved road along the dike, without a view of the Elbe, or the trail on top of the dike which is easy to travel on. The direction of the wind will also influence your decision.

Continue through **Laake**. In **Strachau** continue a few metres to the left away from the dike, then turn right through

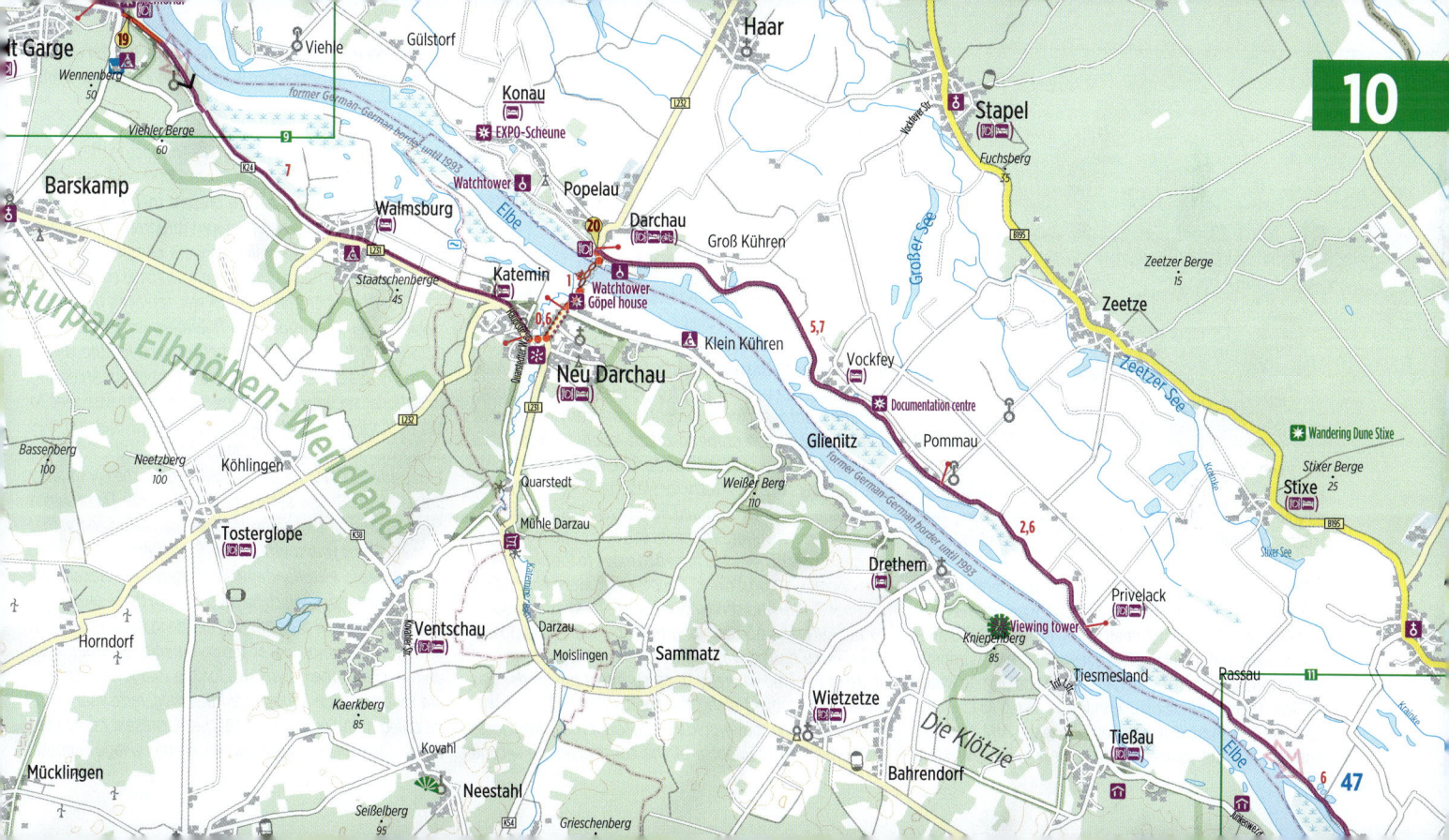

10

GDR-Border-police in the Elbe River in the 1950's

the town. You will again reach the dike. Remain by the Elbe and you will reach **Raffatz** where – as in Wilkenstorf as well – you will also be reminded of the new dike construction in 1999. Continue on a comfortable road until you reach **Bohnenburg**.

Before you reach Wehningen, the cycle trail bends around the arm of the Elbe "Alter Haken". Continue between Ort and Elbe and you will not need to travel on the B 195 after Wehningen, about 2 kilometres before Rüterberg. Continue on the firm sand road towards Rüteberg and Dömitz where you can then continue on a wonderful, paved road on the dike. After a short distance you will leave Amt Neuhaus and you will find yourself again in Mecklenburg-Western

Pomerania, where the first houses will start to appear from behind the trees.

Rüterberg (Dömitz)
prefix: 038758

🏛 **Heimatstube (Local Museum)**, Am Brink 3, ✆ 22314 🕐 In the „Elbklause" hotel restaurant you will find a Heimatstube which is the border museum belonging to the village of Rüterberg. Opening hours: by arrangement.

Republic of the village of Rüterberg

Rüterberg has existed on the eastern shore of the Elbe since 1340. A brick factory was built at the end of town in 1898 and a second in Broda seven years later. As of July 1, 1945, the border between the west and the Soviet occupational zone ran along the Elbe over a length of 95 kilometres. Rüterberg became a border town overnight. In the early morning of June 6, 1952, as part of the so-called "operation vermin", a convoy of trucks and cars rolled into Rüterberg/Broda. Police and members of the Ministry for National Security stormed and occupied numerous buildings. Several families had to pack their most important things in a hurry and leave their houses at once. They were forced to move to the hinterland.

In operation "cornflower", 26 premises were levelled on October 3, 1961 and some houses were used as cow barns by the LPG. The border along the Elbe shore was closed. In 1967, the border was further strengthened on the east shore of the Elbe whereby the securing of the border was increasingly moved along the shores of the Elbe. It was intended that nobody would be able to approach the shores of the Elbe. In the course of the construction, a second

border fence was built, turning the village into an exclave which could only be reached via a small road with numerous border control points.

"Your entry documents, please!". From now on this was the demand of the guards at the only entrance to the village. This entrance remained closed from 23:00 until dawn. The residents of Rüterberg had to present their identification papers in order to enter and foreign visitors required special authorization. The 150 residents were completely locked in and had little choice but to deal with these conditions.

In 1988 the inner border fence was replaced by a more stable model. The residents of Rüterberg were furious. On October 24, 1989, Hans Rasenberger, who led the village for many years, requested a resident meeting. According to national security regulations, the request was sent to the authorities in East Berlin. The resident meeting was authorised for Wednesday, November 8, 1989. From the 150 residents of Rüterberg, 90 gathered in the community house at 19:30. The atmosphere was tense. There was a feeling in the air that something was going to happen that evening. Many years before, Hans Rasenberger had studied the history of Switzerland and the villages there. He carefully chose a document, which he presented to those present. In this document, he suggested to decide in the original form of the Swiss democracy of the community, in order to be able to create their own laws for the village. "Those who are for the Village Republic of Rüterberg, raise your hand" he called to the residents. All of the 90 present raised their hand. They unanimously agreed on the village republic.

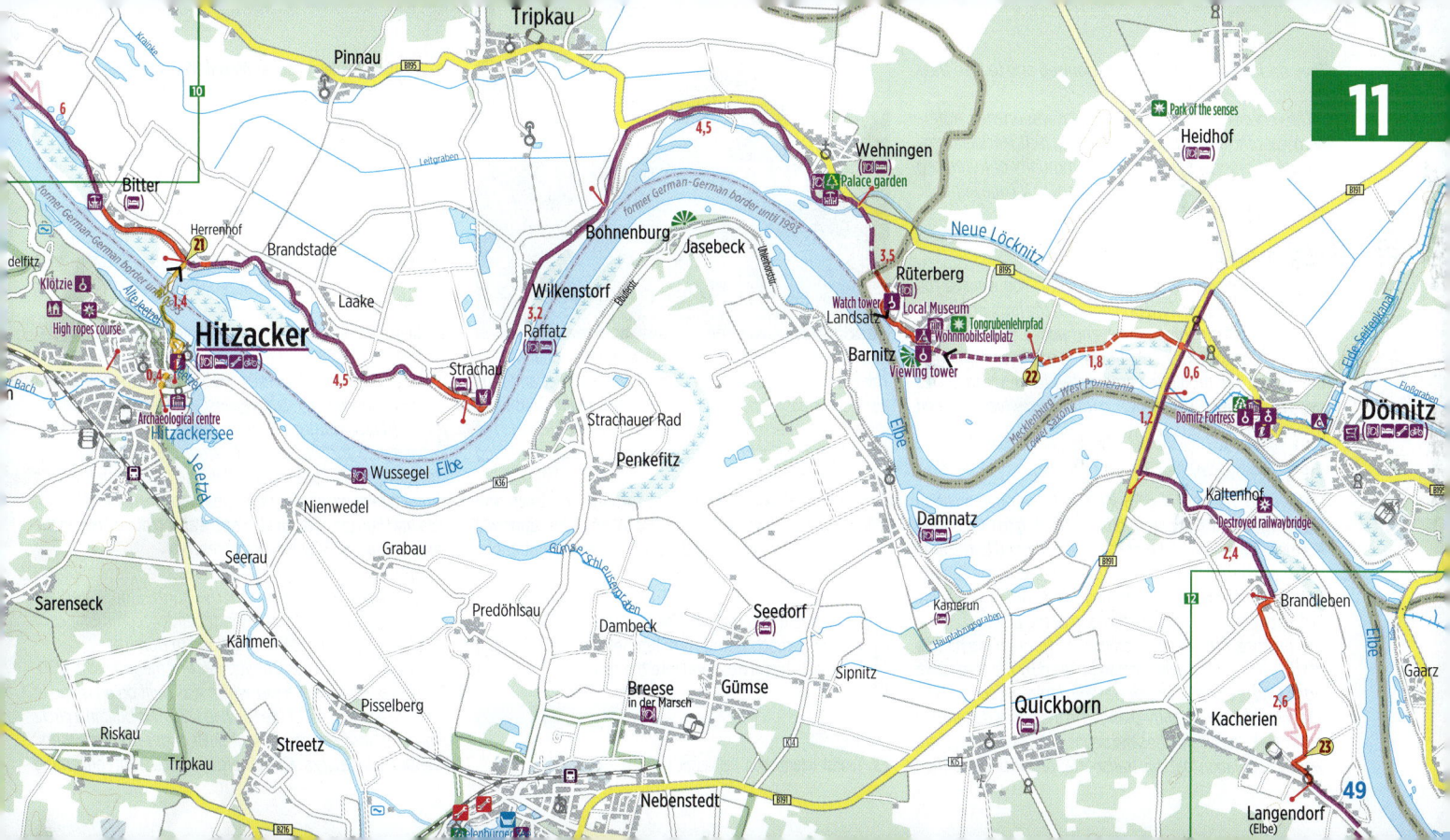

They decided to no longer be patronised and to take their fate into their own hands.

The very next evening, the Berlin Wall was opened. Rüterberg was officially recognised on July 14, 1991. Mecklenburg-Western Pomerania granted the community of Rüterberg the right to use the inscription "Rüterberg Village Republic 1967-1989" on their village sign.

Rüterberg Memorial

A memorial commemorates this story. You will see the barbed wire with a gate, a boulder with the inscription "For the victims of the inhumanity" and above that, a plaque with a kneeling soldier shooting. It is not known whether the barrier, the prohibited area or the fence stood at this site. There is also a watchtower in Rüterberg which has been turned into living quarters.

The Elbe border

The exact route of the 95-kilometre-long demarcation line on the Elbe caused problems. According to the London Protocol, the entire width of the Elbe belonged to the area of the western occupational zones and thus to the Federal Republic of Germany. The territory of the GDR accordingly began directly on the eastern shore of the Elbe.

In practice, the demarcation line ran through the middle of the river and the halves could be used by the respective sides. One problem however was the different course of the channel, which constantly changed in the bends depending on the water levels and the sand deposits. Furthermore, there was the regulation that ship transportation can be performed

Former entry-gate at the village Republic of Rüterberg

over the entire width of the channel in international waters. The Elbe was a federal waterway of the 1st order and thus also accessible to sport boats. Since these regulations were differently understood and interpreted by the FRG and the GDR, there were recurring problems and conflicts concerning the border of the Elbe.

From the "Elbklause" continue through the town and follow the trail towards Dömiz. **22** At the lake, signs will direct you to the left to the B195. Continue straight ahead on a fairly good concrete path to Dömitz which offers a wonderful view of the Dömitz Bridge. Once you reach the B191, take the first right onto the separate cycle trail.

INS ZENTRUM In order to reach Dömiz, turn left before the bridge and cycle past the fortress and into the town.

Dömitz
prefix: 038758

🛈 **Tourist-Information**, Rathauspl. 1, ☎ 22112, @ mpn636

⚓ **Fahrgastschifffahrt Andreas Heckert (Passenger ship)**, Hafenpl. 3, ☎ 0160/4402818, @ jsx732

🏛 **Museum Dömitz**, An der Festung 3, Fort Dömitz, ☎ 22401 ⬡ Various exhibitions are shown in the museum including the history of the fort and the city. There is also a memorial hall for the German author Frtiz Reuter. @ jjd517

⛪ **Evangelische Johanneskirche (Protestant St. John's church)**, Slüterpl. 8, ☎ 22189

⛪ **Festung Dömitz (Fort Dömitz)**, Auf der Festung, ☎ 22401. One of over 39 castles and manors of Mecklenburg-Western Pomerania. @ ykn832

🅿 **NABU-Besucherzentrum Elbtalaue (Visitor's center)**, Auf der Festung 2b, ☎ 26378

The small town of Dömitz with a population of about 3,300 in the county Ludwigslust, is the most southern town of Mecklenburg-Western Pomerania. It has the only Renaissance fortification in Northern Germany which is still standing. The pentagonal flat land castle from the 16th century is known as the "Pentagon along the Elbe". You can also find Europe`s biggest inland walking dune here, in the middle of a UNESCO biosphere reserve.

Dömitz is situated in the nature reserve "Mecklenburgisches Elbletal" and is the end of the Müritz-Elde Waterway. Since April 2004, the formerly independent communities of Heidhof, Polz and Rüterberg belong to Dömitz.

A priest, Heinrich von Dömitz, was first mentioned in 1230. There is also proof of a fort which was built on an island in the Elbe to the west of the town in 1235. It is built in a circle which is an indication that it is of Slavic origin. Dömitz was first mentioned as a city in 1259 whereby a document concerning

the city rights is only present from the year 1505. Over the centuries, the fort ruled over the fate of the city. This was even the case during the Thirty-Year War as well as during the Napoleonic Wars at the beginning of the 19th century.

Dömitz became an important traffic hub after 1870. During the construction of the railway stretch Wittenberge-Luneburg and Lübtheen-Ludwigslust, a railroad bridge was built over the Elbe, the ruins of which can still be seen today.

With the opening of the Müritz-Elde Waterway and the establishment of the Dömitz harbour as important shipping centres on the Elbe between Magdeburg and Hamburg, larger industrial settlements were formed in the city at the beginning of the 20th century. From 1934-36 a roadway bridge to Lower Saxony was also built.

Both of the big bridges were destroyed at the end of World War II. Dömitz suffered from the vicinity to the border during the division of Germany and the restrictions of the prohibited zone.

After the fall of the Wall, the roadway bridge was rebuilt in 1992. Little more than ruins remind us today of the railway connection.

The sand dune at Dömitz

At 42 metres high, the sand dune at Dömitz is one of the biggest in central Europe. It was formed around 12,000-15,000 years ago, when the Elbland was still a glacial veldt.

TIPP There are also two restaurants in Schweriner Straße in Dömitz: "Zur Festung" and further back the "Alte Zunft" with a terrace facing the Müritz-Elde-Waterway (✆ 35876).

From Dömitz/Kaltenhof to Gorleben   16 km

On the main route, cross the Elbe on the bridge and then turn left. Here you can cycle along the top of the dike or down below on the concrete path.

Cross under the ruins of the railroad bridge, the "symbol of the region", which was so impressively sung by Walter Moßmann in his "Lied vom Lebensvogel". The bridge was destroyed during the last days of the war by German soldiers and has not yet been rebuilt. It was, and still is, a symbol of the German division in the Elbe region.

Railway bridge at Dömitz

This 1,050-metre-long railway bridge was built from 1870 to 1873 and was the longest railway bridge in Germany for decades after its inauguration. On April 20, 1945 it was hit by American bombs and nearly completely destroyed. A segment fell into the Elbe and was not removed until 1948. Starting in the 1960's the north eastern head of the bridge was used by the GDR border troops. In 1978 the Deutsche Bundesbahn blew up the pillars on the western side and in 1987 the remains of the bridge on the eastern side were also destroyed. It is now a listed building. An old federal highway, which once connected the two regions with one another, was again completed in 1992 by the finished bridge.

Walter Mossmann (1941-2015)

When the people in West Germany protested against the "Atom Staat" (Robert Jungk) and attempted to stop the nuclear storage in Gorleben the West German song-writer

Dömitz (1984/2006)

Walter Mossmann wrote the "Lied vom Lebensvogel" in 1978. He wasn't afraid to express the unthinkable. The last verse of the "Lebensvogel" says:

There, where the Elbe comes out of the fence,
which is alive and shoots;
there, where the Elbe runs
along the fence through the green serenity;
for thirty-three years, far too long,
a broken bridge is a symbol of the region,
where right and left of the water
relatives live
for them the river is as wide as an ocean.
There I think of the Upper Rhine,
the border between Wyhl and Marckolsheim.
Why should such a coming together
be impossible here?
The men in the east and west
are playing an evil game with us,
look, the same hot trash is burning under our feet, and
still the neighbours remain strangers.
The country is quiet.
At the moment it is quiet...
sing bird, sing,
that Gorleben is alive, that there the gravedigger is
digging his own grave.

There, where the Elbe comes out of the fence,
which is alive and shoots;
there, where the Elbe runs
along the fence through the green serenity;

Bridgehead ruins at Dömitz

for thirty-three years, far too long,
a broken bridge is a symbol of the region,
where right and left of the water
relatives live
for them the river is as wide as an ocean.
There I think of the Upper Rhine,
the border between Wyhl and Marckolsheim.
Why should such a coming together
be impossible here?
The men in the east and west
are playing an evil game with us,
look, the same hot trash is burning under our feet, and
still the neighbours remain strangers.
The country is quiet.
At the moment it is quiet...
sing bird, sing,
that Gorleben is alive, that there the gravedigger is
digging his own grave.

Mossmann recited the last verse from the song "Noch" which his friend and East German singer Wolf Biermann had written after the crushing of the Prague Spring.

Biermann wrote:

Dann hing ich im DZug am Fenster, und
der Fahrtwind preßte mir Wind in' Mund.
Die Augen gesteinigt vom Kohlestaub,
Ohren von kreischenden Rädern taub,
hörte ich schwingen im Schienenschlag,
Lieder vom Frühling im roten Prag,
und die Gitarre im Kasten lag.
Das Land ist still.
Die Menschen noch immer wie tot.
Still. Das Land ist still. Noch.

I was hanging in the window of the train and
the wind was pressed into my mouth.
Eyes stoned by coal dust,
ears deaf from the screeching wheels,
I heard vibrations in the rails,
songs of spring in red Prague,
and the guitar was in the case.
The country is quiet.
The people are still like dead.
Quiet. The country is quiet. Still.

Eleven years later both dreams came true. The peaceful revolution in the GDR and in the Central Eastern European

Brandleben

Elbe

Gaarz

Viewing tower

2,6

23

erien

Langendorf
(Elbe)

11

4,2

Besandten

Brackwasser

Viewing tower

Unbesandten

Exhibition Green Belt

1256

Berg

Grippel

Pretzetze

Kietz

Laase

Slawenwall Kietz

Wootz

L256

Löcknitz

Polz

Breetz

Rhinowkanal

Lenzer Wische

Biosphärenreservat Flusslandschaft Elbe

Dannenberg
20

Mödlich

Eiseiche Mödlich

B195

Elbe

Seege

4

Eldenburg

Moasted castle

Seedorf

12

Lenzen
(Elbe)

Baekern

Stumpfer Turm
St. Katharina

Castle

Burgpark Lenzen

Qualmwassersteg Lenzen

Löcknitz

13

Watch tower

Haltepunkt Natur

0,5

Memorial stone

25

1,2

1,2

7

Höhbeck

Viewing tower

Schnackenschanze

24

1,5

Local Museum

Vietze

K28

4,2

Meetschow

Höhbeck

Pevestorf

Elbholz

Brünkendorf

Elbholz

Lange Berg
20

Laaser Graben

2,4

Gorleben

Gedelitz

L256

Laasche

Laasche

K28

Restorf

Finkenberg

Siedlung Binnenfeld

53

View of the Elbe river at Dömitz

countries ended the "Dictatorship of the Proletariat" (Biermann) which called itself socialism, and a great majority of the population stopped the construction of further nuclear power plants in Germany. The existing nuclear power plants in the GDR were shut down after 1989. In the Federal Republic of Germany, the red-green coalition (1998-2005) agreed to the phase-out of nuclear power in 2000, which the grand coalition of CDU and SPD did not dare to revoke.

The nuclear catastrophe in Fukushima happened just a few months after the ruling CDU/FDP government coalition had agreed in October 2010 to prolong the life of all 17 Nuclear power stations in Germany, prompting the agreement to shut the seven oldest nuclear power stations, and also the accident-prone reactor in Krümmel. After this, a law was tabled suggesting the gradual phasing out of eight more nuclear power stations and the last station to be switched off by 2022. This law was passed on the 30th June 2011 in the German parliament, and was supported not only by the ruling government CDU/CSU faction, but also by the opposition parties of SPD and Green. After the second chamber of parliament (Der Bundesrat) had also voted in favour of this law, the end of nuclear power plants in Germany was all but assured.

In **Brandleben**, leave the dike and pass the houses, keep left and continue on the road. **23** After the ponds, continue right at the T-junction and shortly after go left and enter the village of **Langendorf**. Turn left off the village road and the route will take you straight ahead to Grippel. Before you reach **Grippel** you will find an observation tower with a view of the former border and the watchtower on the opposite bank of the river Elbe. You can find some information boards about the "Niedersächsische Elbtalaue" biosphere reserve..

Biosphere reserve river landscape Elbe

Initiated by all five bordering states, the Middle Elbe was recognised by UNESCO in 1997 as a regional biosphere reserve "Flusslandschaft Elbe". It is one of 14 biosphere reserves in Germany and stretches over 400 kilometres along western Europe´s third largest river. The continuous protection and further development of the portions in Lower Saxony have been assured since 2002 by numerous regulations.

The Middle Elbe belongs to the few largely undeveloped rivers of Mid-Europe. The river with its wide bends and shores, plains and wetlands has changed little over the years. Extensive meadows, fields, wetlands and floodplain forests are home to numerous endangered plants and animals. Wood storks nest in nearly every location, cranes breed in remote wetlands and also the red kite feels at home here. The beaver, which nearly became extinct a few decades ago, regained this land as their natural habitat. Thousands of northern geese and swans use the Elbaue and bordering wetlands in the winter as a resting and feeding ground.

A stork family comprising five members needs 6.5 kg of food per day, which means for example 130 mice, 18 frogs, 658 earthworms and more than one thousand insects.

There is little traffic on the country road. In **Grippel** you can continue on a separate cycle trail on the right side of the street. In **Laase** cross the road and continue on the dam. There is a forest between the street and the cycle trail which gives travellers a beautiful view of the Elbe. Change to the other side of the street before you reach Gorleben.

Gorleben

Kirche mit Gedenkstein (Church with memorial stone), Gartower Straße. The memorial commemorating the years 1813-1913.

Gorleben (from "Goor" = Slavic for mountain and "leben" = heritage) was first officially mentioned in 1360 as part of the area ruled by Dannenberg. A fort stood at the site of the current community. The first impression you get is a place of idyllically situated farmsteads, deciduous groves in peaceful meadows and lush, green landscape.

The town became known as first an intermediate and then planned final storage for radioactive waste. Since the end of the 1970's, anti-nuclear activists have gathered here under the motto "Gorleben is everywhere". Such protests were encouraged (1976) by the GDR expatriate songwriter Wolf Biermann with his "Gorleben Song". The first verse:

Auf! Chauvies und Emanzen
kommt mit uns paar Bäume pflanzen!
Und dann einen trinken! Tanzen!
Das woll´n wir.
Du, komm! Wir pflanzen grade
eine grüne Barrikade

gegen diesen atomaren
Wahnsinn hier.
Einen „NACHSATZ FÜR DIE HERREN DA OBEN" fügt er
auch noch an
Glaubt nun ja nicht, dass wir zittern
kindlich vor Naturgewalten!
Glaubt ihr wirklich, dass wir zittern
so vor dem Atomkraft-Spalten?
Nein! Vor E u c h und Euresgleichen,
vor den Mächtigen und Reichen,
vor den Bossen, die nur messen
alles nach Profit-Interessen,
nein, vor euch müssen wir zittern!
Ihr! Ihr seid uns nicht geheuer!
Ihr! Euch können wir nicht traun!
Ihr könnt mit dem Sonnenfeuer
nichts als Scheiße baun.
Das Lied beendet er mit einem Refrain, der für jede der
fünf Strophen leicht abgeändert wird:
Gorleben soll leben!
Ja, ja, es soll leben
der Rest der Welt solls auch.
Ja, du pflanzt die Birke
und ich den Strauch.

Come on chauvinists and libbers
come plant a few trees with us
and then for a drink! Dancing!
That is what we want.
You, come! We are planting

a green barricade
against this nuclear
insanity here.
(AN „ADDITION FOR THE PEOPLE UP THERE" he adds)
Just don't think we are shaking
childishly from natures forces!
Do you really believe we are shaking
from the nuclear fission?
No! From you and your kind
from the powerful and rich
From the bosses, who only measure
everything according to profit interests
No, we have to shake from you!
You! You aren't normal!
You! We can't trust you!
You accomplish nothing but shit
with the power of the sun.
He ends the song with a refrain which is slightly altered
for each of the five verses:
Gorleben should live!
Yes, yes, it should live
as well as the rest of the world.
Yes, you plant the birch
and I the bush.
On 3 May 1980, the Free Republic of Wendland – the
former Interior Minister called this high treason – was
founded to prevent the planned final storage. The camp
created for that purpose was cleared by the police on June
4th of the same year.

When the annual autumn Castor transports reach Gorleben
from France, the anti-nuclear activists protest against the
use of nuclear energy and the storage of radioactive waste
in the "nuclear toilet" Gorleben by chaining themselves
to the railroad tracks at Dannenberg among other things.
In the "Wendland", even every-day normal people have
changed and you can find the yellow X everywhere, which
delivers the message that: "I am against nuclear power". A
police van can suddenly find itself surrounded by tractors
and in cases like these, the police officers are defenceless.
According to Nicolas Born, the mood in the countryside is
best described as a sort of quiet, seething rage.
Wolf Biermann wrote the Gorleben song "for Heinz B.",
which refers to Heinz Brandt, whose life does not just mirror
the past century but also the German history – the history
of both German dictatorships.

Heinz Brandt

It was supposed to be a short visit but it turned into a
long incarceration. Heinz Brandt had taken a plane from
Frankfurt am Main to West Berlin on 16 June 1961 – only a
few weeks before the construction of the Wall – in order to
participate in a trade union congress and to see a friend's
new flat. However, when he woke from a drug-induced sleep,
he unexpectedly found himself in Hohenschönhausen – a
Stasi-run prison.
The invitation had been a carefully planned trap, and his
abduction had been ordered by the Stasi boss Erich Mielke
himself. During his questioning he was offered to be let free
immediately, if he declared publicly, he had returned to the

GDR on his own free will and out of disappointment over West Germany. Heinz Brandt refused and was sentenced to 13 years' imprisonment in 1962, despite international protests. In 1964 he was freed again – a first success in a world-wide campaign led by the human rights organisation Amnesty International, which had been founded only three years before. Once back in West Germany, he wrote his book "Ein Traum, der nicht entführbar ist" ("A dream, which cannot be abducted").

Heinz Brandt, was born into a Jewish family on 16 August 1909 in Poznan. Throughout his life, he was non-conformist and never lost his idealism. Having joint the KPD (Communist Party of German) in 1930, he was arrested in 1934. His six years' imprisonment were followed by years in the concentration and death camps of Sachsenhausen and Auschwitz.

In Auschwitz he documented the elimination and managed to smuggle his notes out of the camp and into the hands of the Allied forces. At the end of the war, he was freed by the US Army from the Buchenwald concentration camp.

Like many of those persecuted by the Nazi regime, Heinz Brandt also believed that the enemies of his enemies were his friends. This was another reason why after the war he became an active member of the KPD/Socialist Unity Party (SED) and became secretary of the East Berlin district administration. At the same time, his criticism of SED-boss Ulbricht increased. Due to his support of the industrial action by workers belonging to the engineering company Bergmann-Borsig in 1953 during the "five days in June" (Stefan Heym), he was stripped of all his party posts in August 1953.

West German customs boat in front of the Elbe Bridge, June 1984

After the 20th party convention of the KPdSU (Communist Party of the Soviet Union) in 1956, where Khrushchev revealed the terror of Stalin to the delegates for the first time in a secret speech – "the most important speech in the history of Communism" (Wolfgang Leonhard) – Brandt travelled to Moscow in order to find out about the fate of his siblings, who had fled the Nazis in 1933 and emigrated to the Soviet Union. He discovered that his brother Richard had fallen victim to one of Stalin's anti-communism purges and his sister had been exiled to Siberia. From the reports he was able to gather in Moscow, he realised "that Stalinism had been a mass murder regime and not what I had previously assumed". Out of fear of being arrested, he fled the GDR in 1958, together with his wife and three children "because after ten years of Nazi imprisonment, I didn't feel like landing in Mielke's Stasi cellar."

However, the Stasi did not let the SED critic, who had fallen out of favour, out of their sight for long, and he and his children were permanently observed. This even continued in Frankfurt am Main, where he became trade union editor of the magazine "Metall". There his friend and IG Metall

colleague, the former NSDAP and later KPD member Hans Beyerlein, who lived above him, supervised him. This nice neighbour, a Stasi employee, arranged the kidnapping on the direct orders of Minister Erich Mielke.

Heinz Brandt just as before, continued his commitment to democracy and human rights in West Germany. He used his international contacts to organise the "Russell-Tribunal", named after the British Nobel prize winner, against the law known as "Radikalenerlass" which was initiated by the government in order to prevent people who were active in "anti-constitutional" organisations (e. g. the KPD) from working in the public sector. Not only the Russel-Tribunal in 1978 but also the European Court of Human Rights in Strasbourg found this law to be a violation of human rights.

Heinz Brandt always had an inquisitive eye on both German states. I will never forget the big demonstration in 1975 against the work ban in West Berlin, which had been imposed by the federal government, at which he declared his solidarity also with the victims of job bans in the East, in his speech on Wittenbergplatz. In place of the many others he mentioned Robert Havemann and Wolf Biermann as an example. The crowd's reaction was mixed: Half of the demonstrators booed, the other half applauded him. Despite his great efforts to set up a Russell-Tribunal in relation to the human rights violations taking place in the GDR, it never came to pass.

Later on, he criticised the trade unions' support of nuclear power and in 1977 founded the organisation "Aktionskreis Leben" ("Aktion Circle Life"), together with other members of the German trade union association DGB. This resulted

in internal proceedings within the trade union "IG Metall" to revoke his membership. However, as large parts of the trade union's members were on his side, the proceedings were stopped very quickly. Together with his friend Rudi Dutschke, Heinz Brandt was also involved in the founding of the Green Party.

In the autumn of 1980, he initiated the "Solidarity with Solidarność" movement, which collected funds for the oppositional Polish trade union Solidarność in many cities in West Germany. Unfortunately, he did not live to see the success of Solidarność, which was one of the main conditions for the fall of the Berlin Wall and the Iron Curtain in Europe. Heinz Brandt passed away in 1986 – he did not want a grave, as his parents and siblings, who had been killed by the Nazis and Stalin also do not have one. However, he is not forgotten in Berlin; a street has been named after him in the former border strip in Pankow, and in Weißensee a secondary school carries his name.

Wolf Biermann

The author and songwriter Wolf Biermann was born in 1936 as the son of a Jewish communist killed in Auschwitz in 1942. In 1953, Biermann moved from Hamburg to East Berlin, studied philosophy and mathematics at the Humboldt University, worked as a theatre director and had public performances from 1962-65 with ballads, poems and songs both in the GDR as well as in West Germany. After "The Wire Harp" was published in 1965, he was defamed at the 11th plenum of the SED central committee as a "watch dog of the reaction" who "aligns himself with his father's murderers". He was absolutely forbidden to publish or make appearances in the GDR. His books, songs and poems however appeared in the West and – as underground literature – also in eastern Europe. The song "Ermutigung" which was dedicated to the author Peter Huchel was his most well-known song in the GDR.

The first verse recites:

Du, lass dich nicht verhärten (You, don't become bitter)
In dieser harten Zeit (In these tough times)
Die allzu hart sind, brechen (which are all too hard, break)
Die allzu spitz sind, stechen (which are all too pointed, stab)
Und brechen ab sogleich (and take off)

Together with his friend, the communist and chemist Robert Havemann, Biermann became an integral figure in socialist opposition against the feudal socialism in the GDR. On November 16, 1976, he was not allowed to return after a concert he performed upon invitation by the IG Metall in Cologne for 7,000 people – although he had been assured that he would be able to return. Wolf Biermann was stripped of his GDR citizenship and expelled from the GDR. This resulted in a protest from authors, artists and citizens in the GDR.

The "Ballad of the Prussian Icarus" – the record cover showed the area of the Weidendamm Bridge in Berlin with the Prussian Eagle – was the last song written by Biermann in the GDR. The third verse recites:

Und wenn du weg willst, musst du gehn
Ich hab schon viele abhaun sehn
aus unserm halben Land
Ich halt mich fest hier, bis mich kalt
dieser verhasste Vogel krallt
und zerrt mich übern Rand

And if you want to go, you have to go
I have seen many leave
from our half country
I will hold on here, until the cold
hateful bird grabs me
and pulls me over the edge

Biermann dedicated his first song after the denaturalization, "Deutsches Miserere", to the philosopher Ernst Bloch (1885-1977). The first verse goes:

Und als ich von Deutschland
nach Deutschland
gekommen bin in das Exil
da hat sich für mich geändert
so wenig und ach so viel
Ich hab ihn am eigenen Leibe
gemacht den brutalen Test
freiwillig von Westen nach Osten
gezwungen von Ost nach West

And when I came from Germany
to Germany
in exile
there were so many changes
and so few
I took the brutal test
with my own body
voluntarily from West to East
forced from East to West

Dismantled Elbe railway bridge on the GDR-bank, June 1984

From Gorleben to Schnackenburg   22 km

Continue on a paved road which is not accessible to cars until you reach **Meetschow** where you will reach the Elbe after following the signs around a few corners. Continue on the street over the dike. To the left you will see the bridge over the Seege and reach Vietze.

Vietze (Höhbeck)

prefix: 05846

🏛 **Heimatmuseum Höhbeck (Museum of Local History Höhbeck)**, Hauptstr. 1, ✆ 9802828, ✆ 2201 ✉ The museum can only be visited with a guided tour. @ iub583

24 When the street makes a turn towards Gartow, continue straight ahead to Lenzen. Turn left at the next possibility towards Gartow and the "Schwedenschanze" and the radio towers.

At the end of this road, follow the signs half to the left towards Lenzen (5 kilometres). Continue straight ahead on the beautiful trail through the woods until you reach the radio towers. Turn left on the road to the Schwedenschanze where you will find a cafe and an observation tower.

„Schwedenschanze"

Brünendorf am Höhbeck was a Slavic fort 1,200 years ago which was commonly known as the Schwedenschanze. This characterization is somewhat misleading though since the fort had nothing to do with the Swedes. It is actually a Slavic fort from the early middle Ages. The wall runs to the southwest in a wide half circle arch. In the north and east it was protected by the Elbe and one of the side valleys. To the south, the wall is still maintained up to a height of 3,50 metres, in the west an approximately two-metre-deep trench protruded. Access to the fort was presumably in the north. Ceramic pieces were found during excavating which were determined to be of Slavic origin and from the 9th century due to the unique decoration.

Schwedenschanze was probably a Slavic bridgehead which secured the Elbe crossing by Lenzen. The excellent strategic position speaks for it. Until the construction of the dikes in the 13th century, the lowland of the Elbe was divided into individual islands by numerous arms. Crossing was only possible at a few locations. Whoever controlled the crossing of the river simultaneously secured the leadership in the area.

Since only a few findings were made, the construction was probably only used briefly.

Today the popular restaurant "Schwedenschanze" lies high on the Höhbeck. There the family Völkel welcomes their guests with homemade baked bread and sausages. Völkel's great grandparents came back to Höhbeck as settlers with several other families in the 1920's. Their story shows that the commune movement, which played a big role in the 1970's – also in connection with Gorleben – had its forerunners. Ecological agriculture and regional marketing were popular in the past as well.

Pass the tower and continue straight ahead into the forest following the signs toward Lenzen. The forest trail has a steep slope to the Elbe. At the bottom you will meet the street. Turn left towards the ferry to Pevestorf-Lenzen. This ferry connection is seen as a symbol of the areas surrounding the Elbe growing closer together, due to its more than 500-year-long history.

Watchtower Lenzen

Lenzen (Elbe)

prefix: 038792

ℹ **Tourist-Information**, Berliner Str. 7, ✆ 7302, @ tby486

⛴ **Fähre Lenzen – Pevestorf (Ferry Lenzen – Pevestorf)**, Fährhaus Lenzen, ✆ 7665. Ferry operation: April-Sept., Mo-Fr, 6-22:00, Sa, Su 8-22:00, Okt.-mid of April, Mo-Fr 6-19:30, Sa, Su 8-19:30, @ sut157

St. Katharina (Church of St. Catherine). The church was built in the 14th century and has a unique organ.

Burg Lenzen (Castle), Burgstr. 3, ☎ 1221 ⌨ Useful information about the surroundings, events and sights in the UNESCO Biosphere Reserve River Landscape Elbe can be found in the Burg Lenzen visitor centre. The permanent exhibition provides fascinating insights into the natural and cultural history of the river landscape on the „Green Belt". Special attractions include the virtual "flight on the grey heron" in the dome of the 24 metre-high medieval castle tower and the picturesque view of the more than thousand-year-old town of Lenzen. With its restaurant, castle hotel and romantic castle park, the historic castle complex of Slavic origin is a very worthwhile excursion destination. ⌨ uxg347

Stumpfer Turm, Berliner Str. 7. The medieval tower was part of the former city fortifications. It is the remainder of the Bergetor.

Filzschauwerkstatt (Felt demonstration workshop), Hamburger Str. 48/49, ☎ 504975 ⌨ In the largest felt demonstration workshop in Europe you will be informed about the development and history of hand felt. ⌨ jol872

Rathaus (Town hall), Kellerstr. 4. Restored town hall with an interesting clock that only has one hand, only showing the hours.

BUND-Besucherzentrum Burg Lenzen, Burgstr. 3, ☎ 1221, ⌨ tub746

Lenzer Wische. Landscape between Lenzen and Dömitz with Lower Saxony houses and Auenwald.

The town of Lenzen, with its half-timbered houses, is located between the Elbe and Lake Rudower. It is one of the oldest towns in Mark Brandenburg. Its first appearance in the history books was as far back as 929 BC when the famous battle between the Slavs and the Saxons took place here.

The historical town centre with its numerous half-timbered houses is well worth a visit.

After crossing the Elbe, right after the ferry landing, you will find a memorial stone. Engraved in the marble plaque is: „We are one nation. The Elbe separated the German nation from Cumlosen to Boizenburg for 40 years." Behind this memorial stone that is an oak tree and a memorial stone three times the size, which commemorates the 40 years of service of the dike captain Adolf Freiherr von Wangenheim-Wate. There you will also find an old watchtower, which has now been developed into a viewing tower. You can access the roof via the steel stairs and from there you can enjoy beautiful views of the surrounding landscape, which belongs to four different Bundesländer. In the border tower you will also find a little photo exhibition about the border history in this area and about the unique nature of the Lenzener Elbtalaue.

25 Turn right from the street onto the top of the dike, where you can cycle on a solid path. Immediately before Lenzen, you will see an area covering 420 ha that has been claimed back from the sea by moving the dike. In this stretch of land, the natural rhythm of low and high tides now allows for a new wilderness to develop. From the viewing point "Auenblick" you can see wild horses, storks and with a bit of luck, also sea eagles.

Continue on the paved path on top of the dike. **26** In Lütkenwisch you will come off the dike and join the road. A sharp curve to the right leads you to the ferry to Schnackenburg (1 kilometre). In order to continue on the German-German Border Trail, take the ferry from Lütkenwisch to Schnackenburg.

Lütkenwisch (Lanz)

🚢 **Fähre Schnackenburg-Lütkenwisch**, Schnackenburg, ✆ 03877/98814, 🕐 Fährzeiten: Mai-Sept., Mo-Fr 6-22 Uhr, Sa, So/Fei 8-22 Uhr. @ aer112

This village along the river Elber was located within the restricted zone and had 200 inhabitants before the Second World War, a school, smithy, wind mill, two restaurants and a shop selling colonial goods. When people were forced to leave their homes in order to make way for the GDR border facilities, these establishments as well as more than 40 of the village houses were destroyed. In 1990, only seven houses remained and they were also destined to go. However, this did not come to pass due to the disappearance of the GDR. An information plaque and a commemorative stone reminds passers-by of the village's history.

> **TIPP** If you would like to end the Iron Curtain Trail here, continue 21 kilometres along the Elbe to Wittenberge station.

Trip to Wittenberge   22 km

Continue along the road, either on top of the dike on a solid path or on the paved road to the east or west of the dam. At the sport boat harbour of Cumlosen, you will find a tower which is used as a residential building. Behind this you will get to the B 195 road but continue on top of the dike and cycle parallel to the road on the solid path.

Cumlosen
prefix: 038794

🏛 **Heimatstube Willi Westermann (Local museum)**, ✆ 30228. Life and works of nature-lover Willi Westermann

🎨 **Galerie Rolandswurt**, Dorfpl. 1, in the old sexton's office, ✆ 30228. Alternating exhibitions from regional artists.

Pass the church tower of Cumlosen, cross a control centre for flood control, continue through Müggendorf, pass under the bridge of the B 119 until you reach Wittenberge, where you can spend the night in the red brick building "Alte Ölmühle" at the banks of the river Elbe and take advantage of the superb food the "Kranhaus" offers. Continue along the shore of the river Elbe and pass the cafés. Head towards the town on Elbstraße, then continue straight on Bahnhofstraße until you reach the railroad tracks. Turn left towards Wittenberge train station. You can take direct trains from here to Hamburg and Berlin.

Wittenberge
prefix: 03877

ℹ️ **Tourist-Information**, Paul-Lincke-Pl. 1, in the Cultural and Festival House, ✆ 929181, ✆ 929182, @ wvh713

🚢 **Fahrgastschiff HERZ 2 (Passenger ship)**, Anlegestelle „Alte Ölmühle", landing Alte Ölmühle, ✆ 56799445, @ rkh257

🏛 **Stadtmuseum Alte Burg (City museum Alte Burg)**, Putlitzstr. 2, ✆ 405266, 🕐 Tue 14-16:00, Wed 10-12:00 and 14-16:00, Thu 10-12:00 and 14-18:00, Su 11-17:00. Restored timbered manor from the 17th century, former residence of the noble Gans zu Putlitz. The exhibition details the transformation of Wittenberge from farming village to important transportation and industrial hub, the history of the sewing machine with exhibits from 1850 to 1991 and the production thereof as well as the history of the city. @ ask356

🏛 **Museum Historischer Lokschuppen (Historic motive power depot)**, Am Bahnhof 6, ✆ 0152/09053353 🙂, @ tgh237

Memorial stone in Lütkenwisch

🚶 **Ev. Stadtkirche (Protestant Church)**, Kirchpl. The church was built 1870-72 in neo-Gothic style. Upon arrangement with the priest, the church tower can be climbed which gives you a great view over the city and the Elbe.

🚶 **Uhrenturm (Clock tower)**, Bad Wilsnacker Str. 48, ✆ 405266, 🕐 May-Sept, Tu-Su 10-16:00 and upon arrangement, guided tours: May-Sept., every first Saturday of the month at 14:00, tours starts at the clock tower. This landmark is located on the premises of the former Singer sewing machine works and is one of the largest clock towers on the European mainland. @ fky341

🚶 **Wasserturm**, Parkstr.

🎭 **Kultur- und Festspielhaus (Culture and Festival Hall)**, Paul-Lincke-Pl. 1, ✆ 929181, ✆ 929182. Modern, multi-functional location for theatre-, concert- und congress events; information and current program can be obtained from the tourist information centre. @ tnt873

✳ **Altstadt (Old Town)**. This was built in the form of a boat on sand. The tourist information offers informative city tours through the old town upon request.

✳ **Rathaus (City Hall)**, August-Bebel-Str. 10. Access to the tower from April-Oct, guided tours: ✆ 929181 od. 929182. The facade of this neo-

Borderland museum Schnackenburg

Baroque building (1912-14) is lined with sandstone. The interior comprises elaborately decorated representation rooms with luxurious glass paintings and valuable sculptures. The City Hall tower (51 metres) houses mechanical clockwork. Visitors can enjoy a beautiful view over Wittenberge from the observation platform at 37,5 metres.

✳ **Steintor**, Am Steintor. The Steintor was built about 1300 and is the oldest and most important construction in the Wittenberger old town. The former northern city gate also served as a jail. Today, there are parts of the collections of the City Museum on display. @ tub654

✳ **Industriedenkmal Alte Ölmühle (Industrial monument Alte Ölmühle)**, Bad-Wilsnacker-Str. 52, ✆ 56799410. In this former mill, there is a hotel with a show brewery as well as a festival stage, an indoor climbing tower with two parkour areas and a diving tower. There is also a charming café in the clock tower as well as a beach bar. @ ies282

✳ **Haus „Zu den vier Jahreszeiten" (House „Zu den vier Jahreszeiten")**, Johannes-Runge-Str. 16. This four-story Art Nouveau house was built at the turn of the century and has been lavishly restored.

✳ **Siedlung „Eigene Scholle" (Community „Eigene Scholle")**, in northern Wittenberge between Ahornweg and Lindenweg. The architect Walter Gropius (1883-1969) formed in 1914 a community upon the request of the subsidiary Eigene Scholle GmbH with the ideas he developed of constructions which can be rationally constructed.

✳ **Alter Fähranleger (Old ferry pier)**. At the old ferry pier you will find one of the most beautiful sandy beaches along the Brandenburg part of the river Elbe.

◻ **Friedensteich**. camping and overnight accommodation in log cabins, beach volleyball courts.

◻ **Prignitzer Badewelt**, An der Schwimmhalle 5b, ✆ 403515. sport and indoor adventure pool, @ ybi756

According to legend, there was once a castle in Witten-berge where the Stepenitz and Karthane meet, but it was burned down out of revenge by a lover who was cheated on.

Wittenberge harbour, the largest city of Prignitz, is one of the most important harbours on the Elbe. In the past especially petroleum, coal, herring and grain from Hamburg was shipped here. With the industrialization in the 19th century, Wittenberge enjoyed an economic upswing. The foundation was laid by the Berlin merchant, Salomon Herz, who constructed the first factory in Wittenberge - the oil mill.

Between 1832 and 1835 the Wittenberger Harbour was expanded. It still dominates the panorama of the city with its large storage. Between 1903 and 1990 the world-famous Singer, later Veritas sewing machines, were produced here.

Schnackenburg
prefix: 05840

ℹ **Tourist-Information Gartow**, Springstr. 14, Gartow, ✆ 05846/333, @ pqb433

⛴ **Fähre Schnackenburg-Lütkenwisch (Ferry Schnackenburg-Lütken-wisch)**, ✆ 03877/98814, ⏱ ferry operation: May-Aug., Mon-Fri 6-21:00, Sat, Sun/public holidays 8-21:00, Sept.-April, Mon-Fri 6-20:00, Sat, Sun/public holidays 8-20:00, @ aer112

🏛 **Grenzlandmuseum Schnackenburg (Borderland museum)**, Am Markt 4, ✆ 210, ✆ 294 ℻, @ swi455

✳ **Gedenk- und Begegnungsstätte Stresow**

Lower Saxony's smallest city with a mere 500 inhabitants is located at the border triangle of Lower Saxony, Saxony-Anhalt and Brandenburg. It received city rights around 650 years ago. This mini city is a picturesque mixture of timbered and red brick houses.

Borderland museum Schnackenburg

In May 1995 the museum was opened in the historical fisher house which provides information about the history of the German division. At the entrance is a copy of a border guard and the sign: "Stop, border!" It serves as a reminder of the 45 years of division and provides an extensive presentation of the former inner-German border. The permanent exhibition in the fisher house is not limited to simply documenting the GDR border facilities but rather attempts to also present the impact they had on the people. This border not only separated families and friends, it also influenced the economic development in all areas of the border region. Not only are uniforms and arms of the GDR border troops shown, but also the customs agents and border control agents used until 1990 in the West German border area. It can be easily demonstrated that the GDR border troops were mainly implemented against their own population.

From Schnackenburg/Wittenberge to Bad Harzburg/Ilsenburg 257 km

From Schnackenburg to Salzwedel   42 km

1 From the **borderland museum** continue straight ahead on the main road until you reach the end. At the end of the town, turn left onto the dike before the right curve and after the last timbered house. The trail is marked as **"Elbe-Radweg"** to Aulosen, Gummern and Stresow

Wooden information plaques provide information concerning the nature of the borderland.

TIPP

At the next bend, the signs for the Elbe cycle trail point to the left and the border education trail continues straight ahead. Turn left and after the bend in the direction of **Gartow** you will see the border facilities which serve as a reminder of the levelled village of Stresow. There you will see Clay masks, painted by the children of Osterberg's

GDR river-patrol boat at Schnackenburg

Grammar School, to remind us of the gruesome nature of the border.

Stresow

The village of Stresow was officially mentioned for the first time in 1310. After a great fire in 1922, rebuilding was started in the same year.

From 1952 to 1974, residents of the village were forced to move away and the houses were completely torn down. Today there is a memorial with commemorative stones at the site, border stones and plaques to explain the border facilities and the border closing elements. On April 16, 2005, a tree was planted by Marianne Birthler, Federal Commissioner for the Stasi records for the former GDR which commemorate the fate of the residents who were forced to leave Stresow.

Continue further on the cycle trail towards Gartow and Bömenzien. After a short distance you will come to a quiet, well-paved road which leads to Aulosen on the left and to Bömenzien on the right. **2** Turn right towards **Bömenzien**, continue through the town on the cobblestone road in the direction of Drösede and Gollensdorf. Ignore the streets going to the right towards Kapern/Gummern and Nienwald/Gartow where the former border crossing, "Königsbrücke", was located.

After passing the sign at the end of town, the street is paved again. In **Drösede** there is a road to a town with the odd name of "Deutsch" to the left, however continue straight ahead towards Arendsee, Gollensdorf and Ziemendorf. Between Drösede and Gollensdor, one can find the abandoned facilities of the former GDR border troops on the left side. In

Border stone at Stresow

these and the next town you will have to travel over some undesirable cobblestone roads.

The street between Gollensdorf and Ziemendorf is signposted as "Altmark-Radweg" and crosses the border to the municipal of Salzwedel. It continues for 6 kilometres through the forest and is very quiet.

Bernhard Simon

Halfway, a little off the road, a wooden cross pays tribute to 18-year-old Bernhard Simon, who stepped on a mine on 28.10.1963, that tore off his left leg. His brother, fleeing with him, was still able to drag him across the border, but shortly afterwards he succumbed to his injuries.

Ziemendorf

TIPP In Ziemendorf you can take a nice break at the restaurant "Zum Vierländer Eck" (four county corner) on the left side. A fitting name since this is where the counties Saxony Anhalt, Mecklenburg-Western Pomerania, Brandenburg and Lower Saxony come together.

Continue straight ahead on the Vier-Länder cycle path towards Arendsee. You will pass the old border barracks, on which land you will today find a small hotel, an exhibition about the green belt, and the 'Stairway of Human Rights'.

Vier-Länder Cycle path

On the "Vier-Länder cycle path", a circular tour between Elbe, Altmark and Wendland,

Old border barracks in Ziemendorf

there are also reminders of the past and of nature. The largest part of the trail follows the green belt for around 19 kilometres. Signposted border stations make the cyclist particularly aware of his surroundings.

On the right side a cycle trail runs parallel to the street. After 2 kilometres follow the road around to the right towards Zießau and Schrampe.

VARIANTE If you would like to cycle towards Arendsee, stay on the Vier-Länder Cycle path, and cycle on the southern side of the Ardensee, towards Schrampe. Between October and March, you can see flocks of wild geese here.

Arendsee (Altmark)

prefix: 039384

ℹ️ Tourist-Information, Töbelmannstr. 1, 📞 27164, @ Igx175

🏛 Heimatmuseum (Museum of local history), Am See 3, in former monastery. Alternating exhibitions in the monastery gallery. It presents the history of the town and explains the meaning of the Arendsee and nature reserve area

🏛 Klosterkirche und Klosterruine (Monastery church and ruins), Am See 3. The monastery was founded in 1184 as a Benedictine convent.

✉️ Strandbad Ardensee (Beach), Lindenstr., 📞 2251, @ Iwg381

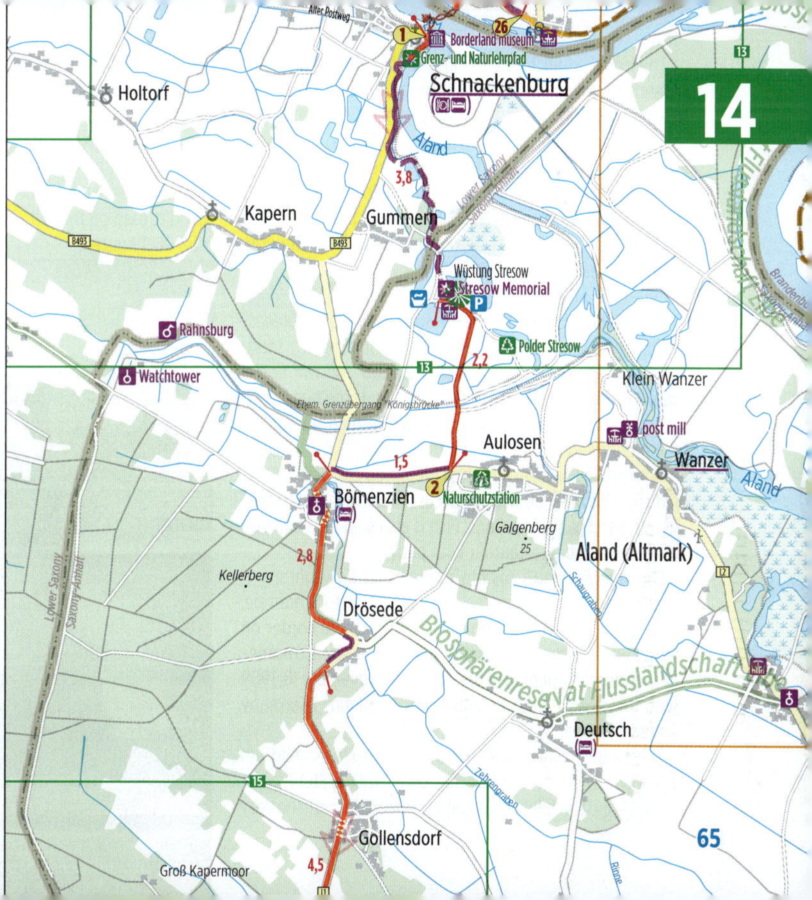

The Iron Curtain Trail continues on the Northern side of Arendsee, which was formed through the practice of salt leaching. The practically round lake is up to 50 meters deep and very rich in fish. One particular speciality is the unusual whitefish, which looks a little bit like a herring.

On the street towards Zießau, turn 300 metres left onto the paved dirt road with the railing leading directly to the lake. Continue on the car free, non-paved but cycle-friendly trail along the shore to Zießau.

Zießau (Arendsee (Altmark))

The historical fisher village is found in one of the oldest nature preserve areas of Germany on the northern shore of Arendsee. At the beginning of Zießau you will find a stone which commemorates the victims of the two World Wars, but the victims of the German-German border are not mentioned.

Remain on the lakeshore trail identified as "TK 9".

TIPP From this trail you will find access to the lake with swimming and picnic locations. Fish is also sold here and you will also find a restaurant with patio.

Once the dirt road turns into a paved road, turn right shortly afterwards onto the somewhat sandy trail to Schrampe.

TIPP When you pass the former German-German border on the way to Schmarsau, a round memorial stone commemorates the opening of the border on November 18, 1989 with the words "Deutschland einig Vaterland" (Germany united Fatherland).

The municipality of Lüchow-Dannenberg is reached - in Lüchow you can find the world's only "Rolling Stones museum" - and the following kilometres lead through the very beautiful countryside of Wendland. **3** On the little travelled country road, turn left onto the posted trail towards Gartow, cross the Lüchower Landgraben and then turn right. At the end of the trail, where it continues to Gartow and Schletau on the right, turn left onto the two-lane dirt road (convoy road). At the next right curve, a sign "Zum Mahnstein" points to a dirt road on the left, where you will reach a memorial after 200 metres.

Memorial to the victims of both world wars at Zießau

Memorial stone

There are a total of seven memorial stones in the border area and not a single one commemorates the death strip of the former German-German border. The largest stone of the "Landgraben Genossenschaft 1915 bis 1922" says:

„Hannover und Sachsen Hand in Hand (Hannover and Saxony hand in hand)

schufen aus Sumpf hier Bauernland (created farm land out of swamp).

Und was sie geschaffen in Zeiten schwer, (and what they achieved in difficult times)

nie geh es wieder zu Grunde! (should never be lost!)

Die Hände und die Herzen her, (The hands and the hearts)

zum Treueschwur im Wiesengrunde!" (to swear commitment in the Wiesengrunde!)

Here you will also find memorial stones from various banks: from the Welfenbank, the Prussian Bank and the Bank of Germany all with dates between 1922 and 1989. A further stone was erected in 1997: "This memorial stone is to commemorate the land reformation in the Lüchower Landgrabenplains." It also says:

"Through measures to improve the agricultural structure, the water management, the renewing of the village, the nature protection and the landscape maintenance from 1970-90, the foundation for the securing of agricultural existence and improvement of the life quality is provided in this area." Today, the consequences of these actions appear in a different light when considering environmental protection.

In a triangle on a round memorial stone it reads: "Old border until 1945" and "Old country border from 1549 to 1691" as well as "Princedom Luneburg, Electorate Brandenburg" and in Fürstenholze: "Province border from 1866 to 1945, border stone re-erected 1989".

The Haselnusshof on the Green Belt

The former farm between Arendsee and Salzwedel is maintained by Traudi, Jürgen and Christian Starck who have been committed to the "Green Belt" for several years. You can spend the night in the Sweden red wooden house "Lille Ville". The cycle workshop "Radkultur" offers the necessary cycle services.

Since the fall of the wall, the BUND bought 400 ha in the Altmark and secured it for the Green Belt. In the vast wetlands and swamps you will find orchids, cuckoos and other wild creatures. You can also listen to the tree frogs and the cranes which wander through the alder forests.

AUSFLUG If you would like to get information about the "Green Belt", turn left at the next crossing and continue for a good 6 kilometres via Mechau to the "Hasselnusshof" in Binde, Dorfstr. 14 (✆ 039036/96432).

The German-German border trail continues straight ahead at this and the following crossing towards Lübbow and Prezier. At the end of the road, turn left following the signs to Prezier and Lübbow and then again to the right.

A beautiful, idyllic landscape, totally quiet, singing birds; the fields are green in the spring. It is hard to imagine that this was once the death strip with watchtowers.

Memorial stone south of Schmarsau

4 Although the signs point to the right at the next crossing towards Lübbow and Prezier, continue straight ahead. There you will also find the levelled town of Jahrsau.

Jahrsau

Rundlingsdorf survived the Thirty Years' War because it was so isolated in the "Jahrsauer Sack", a small exclave. After "Operation Pest control" and "Operation Cornflower", Jahrsau was finally completely levelled and disappeared in 1970.

At the nature reserve the road continues to the right and later makes a left bend. Continue straight ahead until you hit **Volzendorf**. Turn right and then left onto the main road. After about 1.4 kilometres turn right towards Lübbow.

AUSSTIEG If you would like to continue the 9 kilometres to the train station in Salzwedel, stay on the circular road and continue straight ahead.

Ausflug nach Salzwedel

Cross the former border strip and continue via Klein Chüden and Ritze until you reach Salzwedel.

Memorial Ritzer Brücke

A total of 244 people were buried at this location comprising people who did not survive the railroad transport at the beginning of 1945 from the Neuengamme concentration camp to Salzwedel.

The prisoners died of starvation, neglect and illness. To commemorate them – as can be read from the inscription – this memorial was erected during GDR times under the title "The victims warn the living". The information on the memorial plaque concerning the nationalities and origin of the train from Neuengamme are questionable and not proven according to recent research.

After crossing the railroad bridge, continue straight ahead on a paved road until you reach Ritze.

Ritze

At the village square you will find a memorial stone with the following inscription: "Separation of Germany 1949-1990. Unification October 3, 1990".

When the cobblestones end after the railroad bridge, turn right onto Am Güterbahnhof and follow this road until you reach the train station.

Hansestadt Salzwedel
prefix: 03901

ℹ️ Tourist-Information, Neuperverstr. 29, ✆ 422438, @ yut367

🏛 Jenny-Marx-Geburtshaus (Jenny-Marx-birth house), Jenny-Marx-Str. 20, ✆ 423380 🚹 A small exhibition reminds of Jenny Marx (1814-1881), the wife of the famous philosopher Karl Marx.

🏛 Johann-Friedrich-Danneil-Museum (Kreis-Heimatmuseum), An der Marienkirche 3, ✆ 423380 🚹 The museum is named in honour of the prehistorian Danneil (1783-1868). He lived in Salzwedel and was the founder of the so-called Three Age System, the division of the early history in the Stone, Bronze and Iron Age. His collections are presented in the museum, numerous exhibits from the various historical periods of the region. Especially famous are the „Weinbergaltar" from the former Franciscan cloister church by Lucas Cranach and the Salzwedel Madonna, a Romanic wooden figure from the 13th century. @ asg468

⛪ Mönchskirche, An der Mönchskirche, ✆ 2501166, 🕐 April-Oct, Tu-Su 13:30-16:30; Nov-Dec, Sa, Su 13:30-16:30. The former church was built in the 13th century as Franciscan monastery. After the reformation, the cloister was used as a school, gymnasium and as City Hall in the 19th century. Since 1985 the former church is used as a concert hall. The valuable choir stalls are worth visiting. The Cranach altar can be admired in the Danneil Museum. @ igo146

⛪ St.-Marien-Kirche, An der Marienkirche, 🕐 Tu-Su 14:00-15:30, Jan.-Feb., Fr-Su 14:00-15:30 . Brick gothic from the 12th century and thus the oldest building in the city. The 86-metre-high octagonal tower and the 8 metre-wide and 6 metre- high Schnitzaltar from around 1500 is worth visiting. @ ddk372

⛪ Burg mit Burggarten (Castle with garden). Castle ruins from the 9th century which was first officially mentioned as „Saltwidele" in

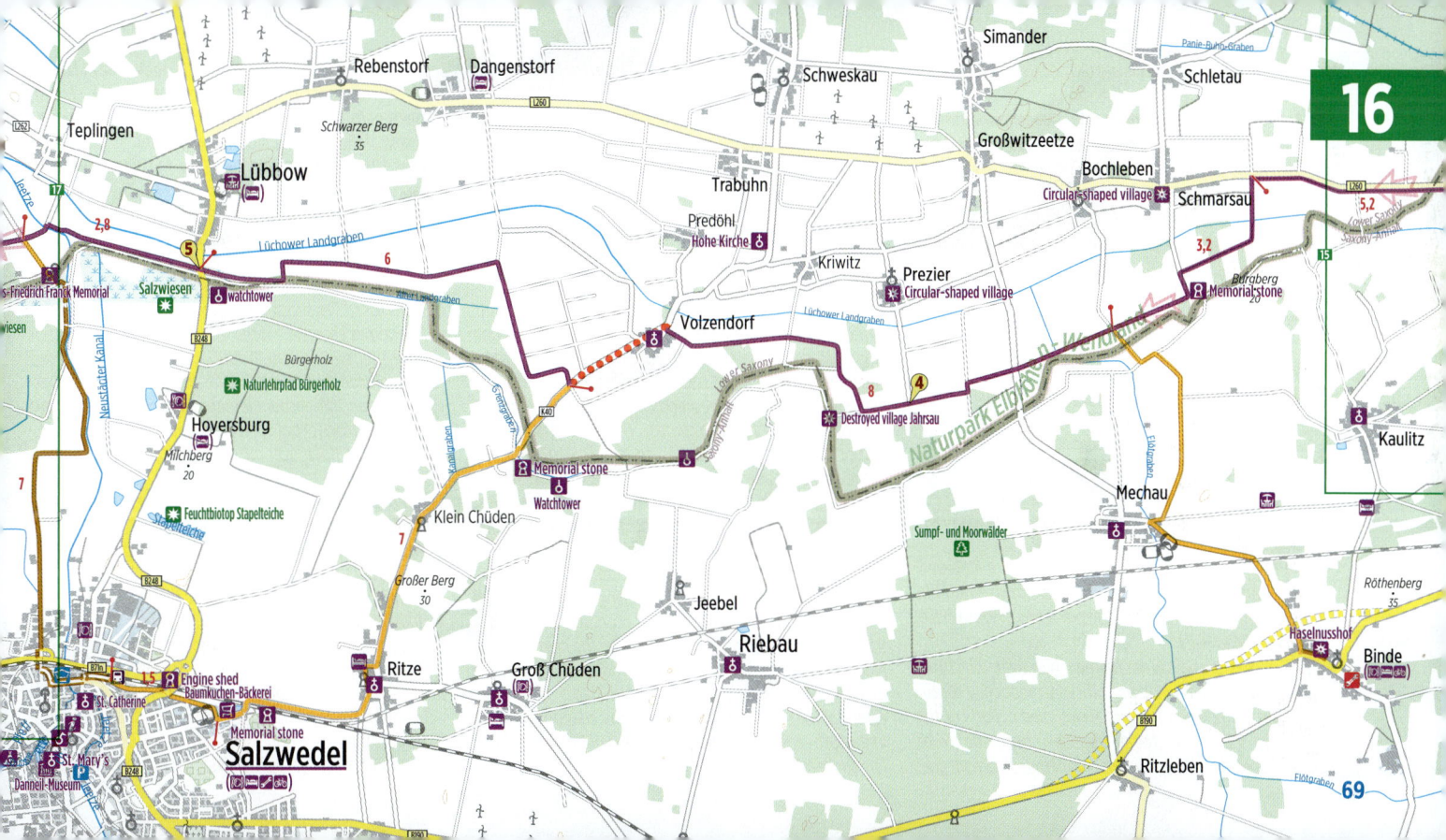

Teplingen

Rebenstorf

Dangenstorf

Simander

Schweskau

Schletau

Lübbow

Schwarzer Berg 35

Trabuhn

Großwitzeetze

Bochleben

Circular-shaped village

Schmarsau

16

2,8

5

6

s-Friedrich Franck Memorial

Salzwiesen

watchtower

Lüchower Landgraben

Zehra Landgraben

Predöhl
Höhe Kirche

Kriwitz

Prezier
Circular-shaped village

Lüchower Landgraben

3,2

Büraberg
Memorialstone

5,2

Lower Saxony
Saxony-Anhalt

15

wiesen

Bürgerholz

Naturlehrpfad Bürgerholz

Volzendorf

Lower Saxony

Naturpark Elbhöfen-Wendland

Hoyersburg

Milchberg 20

K40

Memorial stone

8

4

Destroyed village Jahrsau

Kaulitz

7

Feuchtbiotop Stapelteiche

Stapelteiche

Klein Chüden

Memorial stone
Watchtower

Predy-Amilel

Sumpf- und Moorwälder

Mechau

Röthenberg 35

7

Großer Berg 30

Jeebel

Riebau

Haselnusshof

Binde

Ritze

Engine shed
Baumkuchen-Bäckerei

Groß Chüden

69

1,5

St. Catherine

St. Mary's

Danneil-Museum

Memorial stone

Salzwedel

Ritzleben

Elötgraben

1112. The remains of the castle wall can still be seen, the moat, the chapel and the castle tower still remain.

- ❇ **Erste Salzwedeler Baumkuchenfabrik – älteste Baumkuchenbäckerei (First Salzwedel pyramid cake factory – oldest pyramid cake bakery)**, St.-Georg-Str. 87, ☎ 32306, ⊙ Viewing Mo-Fr 9:00-12:00, Sat upon arrangement, @ fal716
- ❇ **Neustädter Rathaus (Neustädter City Hall)**, Neuperverstr. 29. The octagonal Renaissance tower (1585) of the former City Hall can be seen for miles.
- ❇ **Stadtmauer (City wall)**. The wall was built in the 14th century at a height of 5 metres and a length of nearly 3 kilometres. Only two gates, the Neupervertor and the Steintor, remain from the original 10 gates.
- ❇ **Naturlehrpfad Bürgerholz (Natural path)**, Hoyersburger Landstr. Directly opposite the restaurant Bürgenholz in Hoyersburg, there is a boardwalk which takes you through an incredibly damp forest, in which cranes and black stalks nest.
- ✉ **Freibad Salzwedel**, Dämmchenweg 41, ☎ 3023923
- ✉ **Waldbad Liesten**, Liestener Dorfstr. 30, ☎ 039032/216, @ ckf188
- ✉ **Schwimmhalle**, Karl-Marx-Str. 14, ☎ 3023811

The town of Salzwedel has a population of a little over 25,000 and has an enclosed medieval old town ensemble. A well-known daughter of the town is Jenny of Westphalia, the wife of Karl Marx.

The city has its origin in a settlement by a castle which was built in the 9th century. It was officially mentioned for the first time in 1112 when Heinrich V occupied it. Parts of this castle can still be seen today, especially the castle tower, the so-called Bergfried. The founding of the settlement goes back to Albrecht the Bear (1100-1170) from the House of the Ascania who lived in the castle for some time.

Salzwedel was first mentioned as a city in a legal sense, as „civitas", in 1233. The development of the city is particularly interesting in regards to the century long division in an old and a new city; the latter was already founded to the northeast of the old town in 1247. Both were independent communities which functioned next to one another with their own administration; even two different churches existed: St. Marien (old town) and St. Katharinen (new town).

In 1263 the city became a member of the Hanseatic League. Strategically advantageously positioned at the intersection of important trading routes, the trade between Salzwedel and the cities of Hamburg, Lübeck, Luneburg and Magdeburg flourished and Salzwedel quickly developed into a grand Hanseatic city. By the 15th century, the general prosperity of the city in medieval times was reduced. Due to the defeat of the so-called beer tax revolt, which was focused against the introduction of a beer tax by the local rulers, the city lost significant rights such as jurisdiction, the right to free vote, the statute rights and the right to enter alliances.

In the Thirty Years War the city suffered financial and economic losses from various travelling armies. In order to protect themselves from difficult economic situations in the future, the unification of the old and the new city took place in 1713. From 1807 to 1813, Salzwedel belonged to the Kingdom Westphalia and acquired the status of a district capital of the Elbe department. Economic changes followed in the 19th century and the construction of the first railroad line to Stendal in 1870.

In February 1945, a bomb killed 300 people. The old town, however, was spared, including its Gothic brick church, remains of fortification facilities, two city gates, the former townhall of the old town, storage houses and 500 timbered houses. Due to the arrival of fugitives, the city grew within the inner German border area as of 1949. The increasing economic insignificance was somewhat reversed by natural gas drillings which were performed as of 1968.

On the wall of the former Stasi building you will find a memorial plaque from November 9, 1998 with the inscription from Perikles: "The secret to happiness is freedom. The secret of freedom is courage."

Since the reunification in 1990, the city has attempted to regain economic strength with the settling of mid-size companies and the encouragement of touristic infrastructure as well as with better transportation connections. The Baumkuchen, (a cylinder layer cake resembling a cross-section of a tree trunk) was invented here in 1807 and ordered by Emperor Wilhelm I in 1865 and is a must-eat treat here. Pop by café Kruse to see how it is made.

Salzwedel lies on the Romanesque Road and is a stage destination of the German Half-timbered Road. The townscape is characterised by half-timbered buildings from the early Middle Ages and North German Brick Gothic. The city gets its special flair largely from the mostly-preserved old city wall, the banks of the Jeetze and other waterways, densely lined warehouses and other old buildings.

To return to the main route, follow the left turn in the road and then turn right onto **Karl-Marx-Straße**. At the roundabout, turn right, cross under the railway line and the

main road and cycle straight in a northern direction. Passing the bridge over the Jeetzel, a little later you turn right over a canal and pass the Hans-Friedrich Franck monument (see below) back to the main route.

From Salzwedel to Wustrow   11 km

On the main route head towards **Lübbow** (13.6 kilometres). After about 2 kilometres, turn left despite the bike path signposting straight ahead into the direction of Dangenstorf, and then continue straight ahead. Ignore any possibilities of turning right. **5** Cross the B 248 and continue straight ahead along the stream. At the end of the road, turn left and cross the **Jeetzel bridge**.

If you would like to visit the memorial cross for Hans-Friedrich Franck, turn left at the next fork in the road. This will also take you to the re-naturalised Kusebruchswiesen with observation deck, with wonderful views over the underlying areas.

Hans-Friedrich Franck

The 27-year-old engineer from Meißen was able to climb over the metal mesh fence at Blütlingen on January 16, 1973 around 23:00. However, in doing so, he triggered a self-firing device (SM-70) which severely injured him with 80 pieces of steel shrapnel. Although he quickly received medical attention on the western side, he died the next day after long and complicated surgery. The irregularly formed, sharp and pointed metal splinters of the explosive body have a similar effect to a DUM-DUM bullet – according to the medical report from the western Wustrow by Hanno-

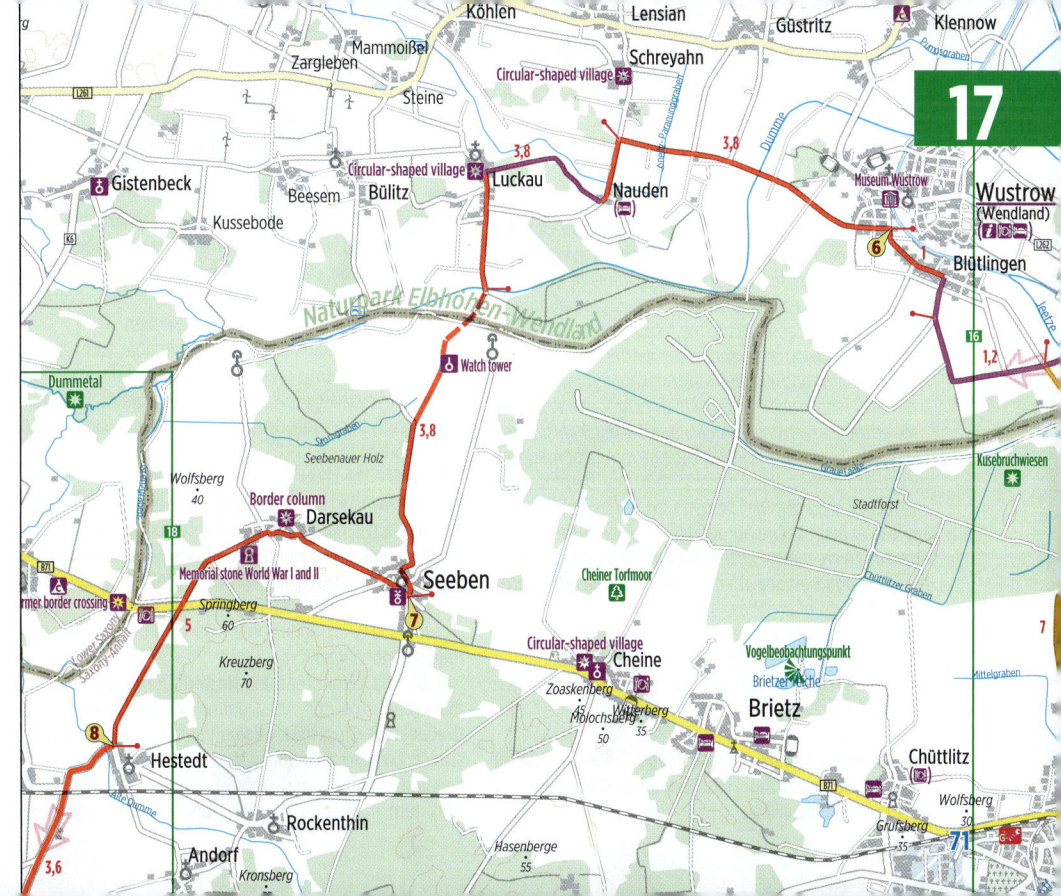

ver – which was the reason that Hans-Friedrich Franck's circulatory system irreversibly collapsed two and a half hours after completion of surgery.

Splittermine Modell 1970 directional antipersonnel mine

From 1971 onwards, the GDR installed 60,000 self-defence systems over a length of 200 kilometres on every fourth pole of the border fence, but had repeatedly denied their existence. They had been invented by SS-Sturmbannführer Erich Lutter in order to secure the fencing of concentration camps whilst saving on personnel costs. After Hans-Friedrich Franck's death - and Michael Gartenschläger's brave actions – the GDR were unable to deny their existence any longer.

When the German government under Helmut Kohl granted the GDR billions in loans in 1983, the government made it a condition that the splitter mines (SM-70) and the more than one million ground mines be removed. This did not make it any easier to cross the border, however, because security measures were moved further back into the hinterland and thus in doing so, escape attempts were no longer prevented under the eyes of the West German border officials.

Continue straight ahead on the cycle trail until it ends and then turn right. Continue straight ahead at the roundabout and turn left at the next possibility towards **Blütlingen** and Wustrow.

From Wustrow to Barnebeck/Schnega   23 km

6 In **Wustrow**, turn right into **Rudolphstraße** immediately after entering the village.

TIPP Continue straight ahead at this junction, pass the museum and reach the church. Once there, you will find various possibilities for refreshment and shopping.

Follow the sign-posted cycle trail to **Clenze**. The paved road is rather narrow and very quiet and leads you through some beautiful scenery towards Schreyahn and Nauden. After 2 kilometres, you will come to a fork in the road. Follow the sign-posted cycle trail towards Clenze to **Nauden** and continue past an elaborate timbered house. Behind the village, turn right and you will reach the town centre of **Luckau**, where you turn left towards Seeben.

After crossing the Dumme, the pavement turns into a dirt road. A short time later, continue a short distance on a paved convoy road, typical for the GDR, that has, however, been greatly improved. On the former convoy road, you will pass a watchtower.

7 Behind the church of **Seeben** turn right twice on the cobblestone road and come to a paved road towards **Darsekau** which is not signposted. There you will find border column number 416 where you turn left. At the end of the town, there is a memorial stone on the lefthand side which commemorates the fallen from the two World Wars. After crossing the B71 continue on the paved and little-travelled road straight ahead.

8 Shortly before reaching **Hestedt**, turn right onto the main road, cross the Alte Dumme and continue towards **Grabenstedt**. Cross the level single railed electrified railroad stretch, pass the abandoned station Bergen (Dumme) and continue straight ahead. About 1 kilometre after the town sign, turn right onto a cobblestone road towards **Groß**

Grabenstedt, which was destroyed during the expulsion. There you will see a number of abandoned and destroyed buildings.

Continue straight ahead on the road to **Henningen** where a border column still remains, just before the guesthouse. In Henningen you will also find a memorial stone which commemorates the World Wars with an unusual inscription: "Our fallen soldiers in gratitude". Turn right towards **Dahrendorf** and continue on the pavement in **Barnebeck** due to the cobblestone road.

AUSSTIEG After Barnebeck, turn right towards Schnega train station – from there the trains travel to Salzwedel and Uelzen – and to Schnega, where you can spend the night and find something to eat. Cross the Harper Mühlenbach, which through border times until today, was kept natural. Here you can see the remainder of a water mill.

Alternative ways to Schnega

Turn left after the town exit sign in Schnega towards the borderland museum in Schinmark and continue to Göhr. After 1.5 kilometres you will reach the borderland museum.

Göhr (Schnega)

🏛 **Grenzlandmuseum „Swinmark"** (Borderland museum „Swinmark"), Göhr 13, ✆ 05842/600, ✆ 05842/245 ☺ The museum is located in the city part of Göhr, about 5 kilometres from the former German-German border. Various original relicts from the times of the German division are displayed and the open-air area shows reconstructed border elements. @ jdk584

For the return journey, continue through Schnega and follow the signs towards Harpe and Schnega train station,

which is somewhat outside the town. After passing the town exit sign, a paved cycle trail runs along the left of the street which will lead you to the Schnega train station after one kilometre. Continue to the right towards **Warpke**, cross under the tracks and turn left after the tracks onto **Zum Bahnhof** towards **Bonese** (8 kilometres) and Harpe (3 kilometres). The quiet paved road curves its way through the deciduous forests to **Harpe**. After this little town, cross the former German-German border and reach **Dahrendorf**.

At the border, you will find a stone on the side of the road with a metal plaque and the following inscription: "1945 – This is where Germany was divided for 45 years – Never again – 1990." A few metres further on the right side of the road a wooden podest has been erected to watch wild animals. In the distance a watchtower still stands in an open field and soon you will see the abandoned facilities used by the border troops on the lefthand side.

From Barnebeck/Schnega to Brome   33 km

9 If you would like to continue of the German-German border trail, keep to the left after Barneneck – ignore the signposting pointing straight ahead - and continue over **Kortenbeck** to **Dahrendorf**. On this road the villages can be seen from the distance with their churches built from boulders.

Continue through Dahrendorf where a memorial stone commemorates the fallen of the two World Wars at the beginning of town by the church and a little later one under a tree which commemorates the division and reunification. Pass the church with the separate wooden tower and a nice

little house and continue further towards **Lagendorf**.

10 Behind the Grabower Graben, turn left onto **Lagendorfer Weg** to Winkelstedt, where you turn left onto the **L 7** and then right onto **Am Rundling**. After crossing the railway and later the Dumme you will reach **Eickhorst**, where you cross the K 1390 on the right. **11** Shortly before you reach the main road (Dährer Straße), turn right and cycle into Diesdorf on the mountain road, where you can go shopping and – as in the neighbouring Addendorf – can spend the night. The open-air museum (Freilichtmuseum) is highly recommended, where century-old timber houses have been relocated to and village life is very visible. There you will find a restaurant, the "Museumskrug" (☎ 03902/939857) which specialises in pancakes, old-fashioned dishes and home-made cakes.

Flecken Diesdorf
prefix: 03902

🛈 **Gemeinde Flecken Diesdorf**, Himmelreichstr. 1, ☎ 276, @ yxl131

🏛 **Freilichtmuseum Diesdorf (open air museum)**, Molmker Str. 23, ☎ 450 ⊜ The museum was founded in 1911 by doctor Dr. George Schulze and is a museum of folklore. You can view various farms with outbuildings, gardens and fields such

as Low German aisled houses, a granary, a blacksmith or a bakery. @ qbn126

⛪ **Klosterkirche (Cloister church)**, Kloster 1-2, ⏱ Arrange tours with the Evangelic priest's office ☎ 327 or 939640. Historically important Romanic brick church from 1182. @ ocv826

🛁 **Erlebnisbad (Hot baths)**, Molmker Str.

AUSSTIEG If you want to cycle to Wittingen station, 11 kilometres away, from where you can catch direct trains to Braunschweig and Uelzen, turn right onto Wittinger Straße. In Waddekath, which was separated from Rade in Lower Saxony by a wall due to its location, well-preserved remains of the wall with an observation bunker, a border column and a tank barrier are still visible. Information boards along the old patrol road provide information on border security and the opening of the border. To get to the remnants of the border, turn onto the asphalted road to Rade shortly before the border with Lower Saxony and follow the sign "Grenzmauer" (border wall).

The main route leads you across the state road, then immediately left onto **Lämmerstraße**. At the next junction turn half right onto **Molmker Straße**. Behind **Molmke**, but before **Drebenstedt**, continue straight on the Altmark-Radweg. Once you have conquered two small ascents,

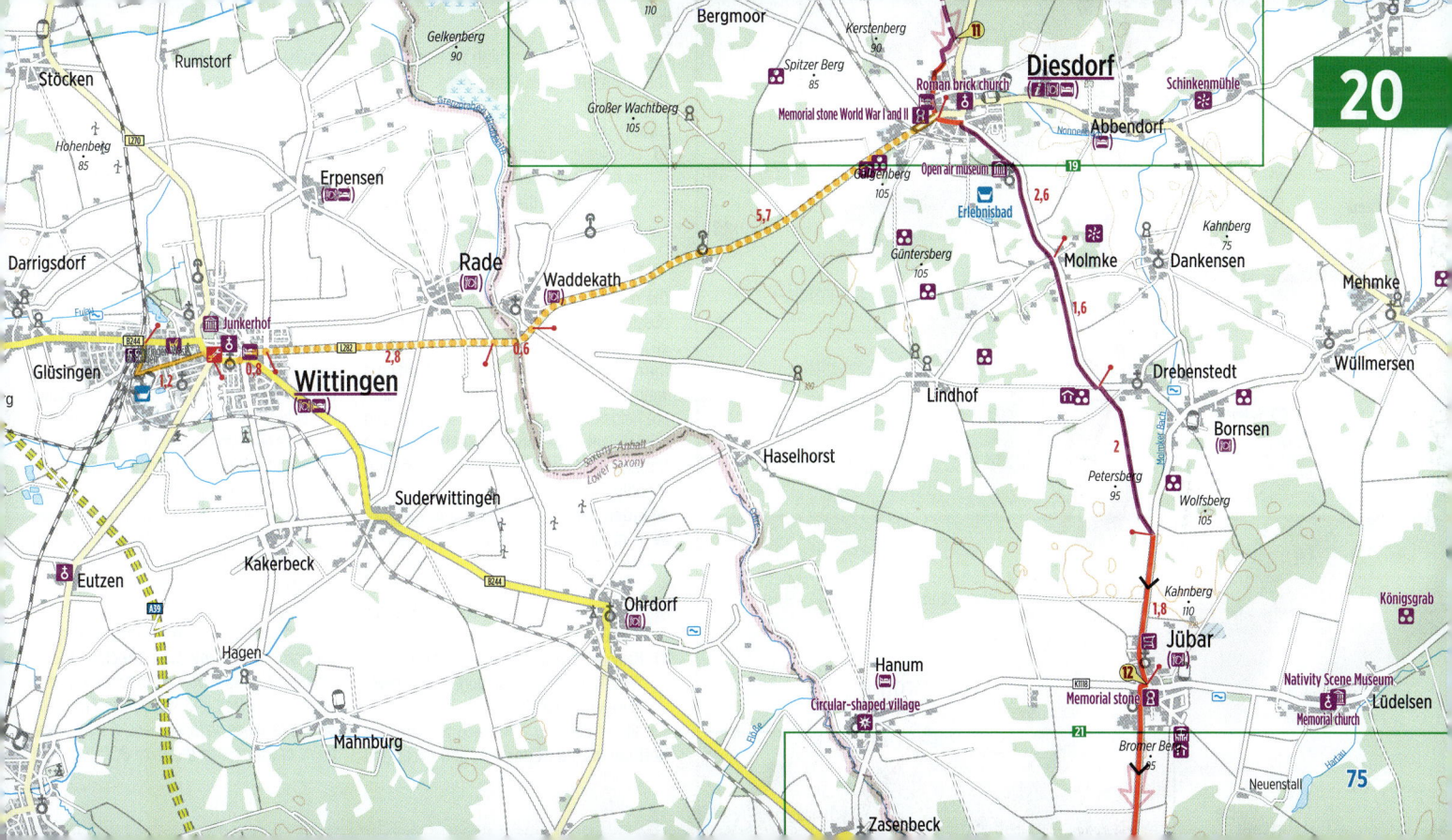

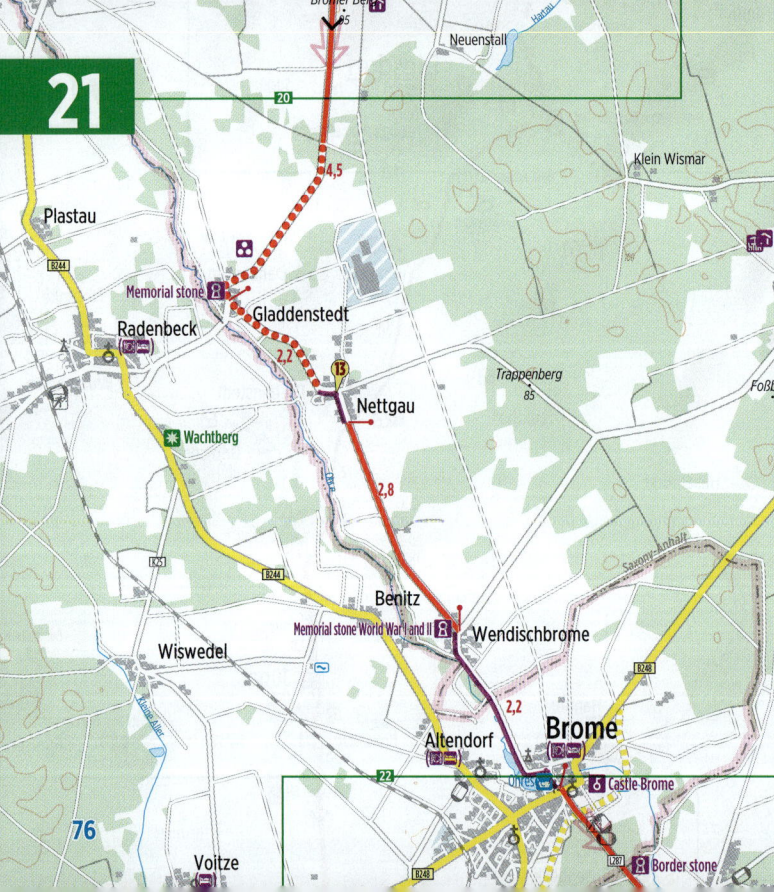

namely the 105-metre-high Wolfsberg and the 96-metre-high Petersberg, you will reach Jübar.

Jübar

🚏 **Gedenkstein auf dem Dorfplatz (Memorial stone on the village square)**. It was unveiled in the year 2000 during the 760-year celebration with the inscription: „October 3, 1990 Day of German Unification".

12 In the centre of Jübar, turn right at the restaurant "Zur Kastanie". At the next possibility turn left towards Gladenstedt (5 kilometres). After the sign exiting the town the route continues on a quiet road which is well-paved and leads to a slight hill. There are fields to the left and right and the road is lined with trees on both sides. Continue through Gladenstedt on a well-paved and friendly village road.

Gladenstedt

🚏 **Memorial stone,** in front of the fire department building (FFW Gladenstedt) – adjacent is the village community centre. The stone commemorates the opening of the border on February 2, 1990.

🚏 **Memorial** dedicated to the fallen of the Second World War and a memorial stone for the renewal of the street in 2002.

A little later you will reach the town of **Nettgau** with a pedestrian and cycle trail

parallel to the cobblestone road. **13** Do not continue on main road to Brome (12 kilometres) but rather turn right onto **Wendischbromer Straße** to **Wendischbrome** (2 kilometres). This lonely road is very seldomly travelled by cars – in spring you can hear the cuckoo calling – and continue from Nettgau via Wendischbrome, which was once in the GDR, over the former border to Brome. On a cycle trail, which runs parallel to the cobblestone road, cycle the last few metres to Brome.

Brome

prefix: 05833

🏛♿ **Burg mit Heimatmuseum (Castle with museum of local history)**, Junkerende, ✆ 1820 🌐 The castle originates from the 11th/12th century and was officially mentioned for the first time in 1203. Over the centuries, it was often destroyed and rebuilt. The remaining north wing and the stair tower are from the 16th century. In the main building you will find the museum of local history. Topic: The old trade in Flecken Brome. @ lex528

Brome, which was once in the western portion of Germany, was affected by the German-German border over a distance of 35 kilometres and surrounded by GDR border facilities on three sides. A significant point of interest in the over 800-year-old

city is the castle and museum of local history which took over the task of documenting this special situation after the fall of the Wall.

TIPP On the left side behind the entrance you will find the highly-recommend cafe "Rehfeldtsch Mühle" which is unfortunately closed between 12:30 and 14:30.

From Brome to Wolfsburg/Oebisfelde   30 km

In the centre of Brome, turn right and then after a stretch turn left towards Steimke.

TIPP When you once again cross over the former border, you will find a sign: "Altmark-Kreis Salzwedel" and an old border stone with the initials of the Kingdom Hannover (KH) in the direction of Saxony-Anhalt. On the other side of this stone you will find the initials of the Kingdom Prussia (KP). Signs also indicate the "Landkreis Gifhorn" and the "Kreis Salzwedel". It is not explained what "5.553" means. On the back side of the border stone you will also find "Kreis Isenhagen". There is no indication of the former border.

You will reach **Steimke** after about 2 kilometres traveling on a quiet road. **14** There you turn right shortly after the town sign towards Böckwitz. Continue on a smooth, quiet paved road which runs parallel to the former border. In spring, blooming rapeseed fields are found along the former death strip. You will see four windmills in the background. Turn right towards Böckwitz.

Böckwitz (Klötze)

🏛 **Landwirtschaftliches Museum (Museum of Agriculture)**, Im Rundling 2, ✆ 039008/80045 ↻ ☾ Relics from the German-German border are displayed. @ cuf434

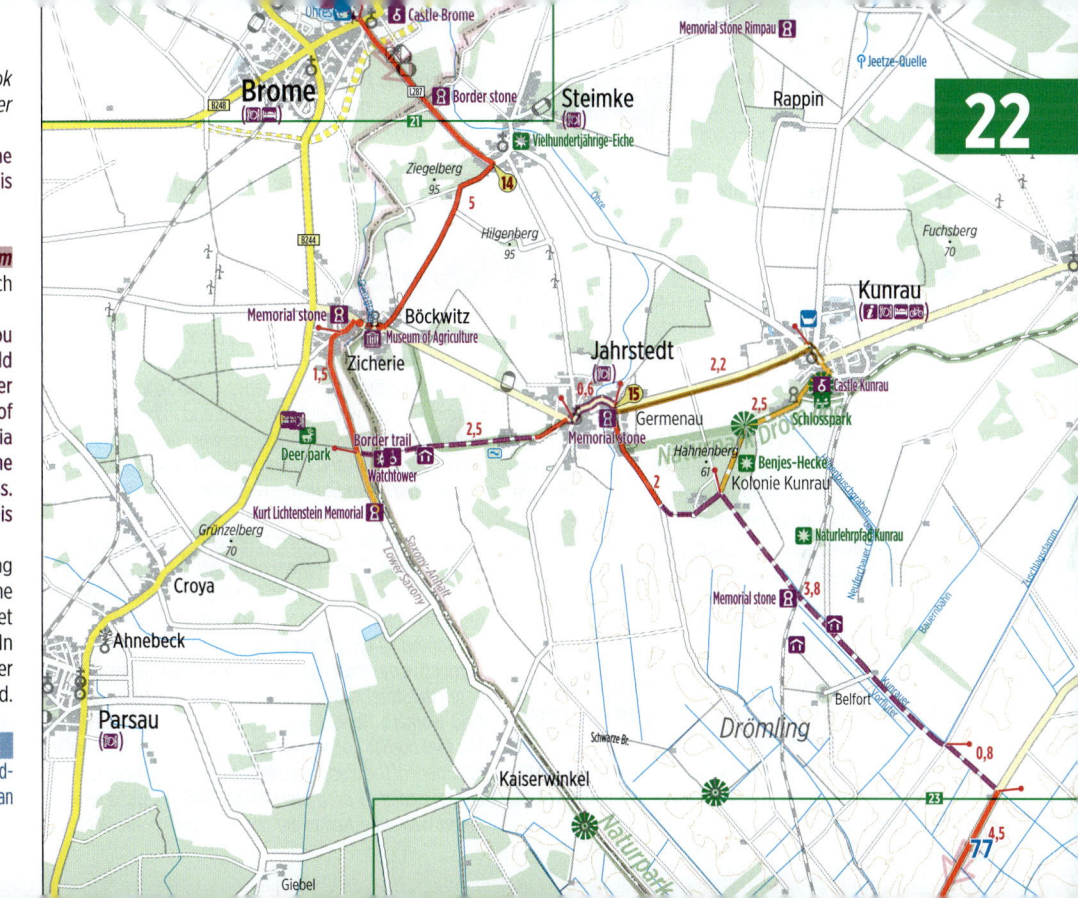

Upon entering Zicherie you will find a memorial stone.

Zicherie

🕱 **Memorial stone** with the inscription "Germany cannot be divided. Zicherie, 17 June 1958".

✱ **Educational border trail Zicherie-Böckwitz,** which documents the development of the border facilities.

Zicherie-Böckwitz

These neighbouring villages were connected by relatives over many generations. Zicherie belonged to the Kingdom of Hannover and Böckwitz to the Kingdom Prussia, but even the war of 1866 between Hannover and Prussia did not tear the residents apart.

That changed in 1945 when Böckwitz became part of the eastern zone and Zicherie part of the western zone. The towns Böckwitz in the Altmark and Zicherie in Lower Saxony were separated in 1952 by a wooden fence. Later these two towns were separated by barbed wire and fences and since 1979 the concrete wall kept Böckwith and Zicherie apart. Today you can still see original parts of this border facility on the 3.4-kilometre-long educational border trail. Heinrich Thies described the history of the double village called "Klein Berlin" very precisely in "Weit ist der Weg nach Zicherie".

In Zicherie turn left. The road is signposted with "**Kaiserwinkel**" and "**Grenzlehrpfad**". Follow the sign Kaiserwinkel and after about 2 kilometres, at the parking sign, turn left onto a dirt road into the forest which is marked as "Grenzlernpfad".

Before you turn into the educational border trail, you should continue a further 450 m – unfortunately there is no sign – to the memorial for the journalist from Dortmund, Kurt Lichtenstein, who was fatally shot here shortly after the construction of the wall. A weathered plaque on a cross reads: "A German shot by Germans. Kurt Lichtenstein †October 12, 1961".

Kurt Lichtenstein

The 59-year-old journalist was the son of a Jewish shoemaker from Berlin and had joined the KPD in the 1920's. In 1933 he disappeared into the underground, fought on the side of the International Brigades in the Spanish Civil War against Franco, was detained, fled and joined the French Resistance Movement. After the war, he supported the rebuilding of KDP and unions in the Ruhr and belonged to the Landtag of North Rhine-Westphalia from 1947-1950 as a KPD member.

The companion of Herbert Wehner became editor in chief of the "Freiheit" and other communistic newspapers. Due to his critical positions to the GDR he was banned from the KPD and later joined the SPD. For the "Westphalian News" he wanted to report about life within the inner-German border two months after the construction of the wall. When he left the street in Zicherie, to speak with the (east) German field workers, he was noticed, fired upon and fatally hit. The two border police were awarded for their "exemplary fulfilment of the pledge of allegiance and the order to fight" and immediately promoted. In the "Army news" a glowing report was published under the title "Well done, Peter".

From the memorial for Kurt Lichtenstein, cycle back and turn right onto the signposted educational border trail.

Educational border trail

The educational border trail documents the development of the border facilities: first the wooden fence between Böckwith and Zicherie as of May 1952, then the double barbed wire fence as of August 1961, the meshed metal fence as of 1968 and the wall as of 1979. Also, the SM70 mines can be viewed. Installations started in July 1979 and they were dismantled as of October 1984.

You can also see the anti-vehicle ditches which secured the border here as of 1968 and the convoy roads with control strips. An original observation tower also remains.

The linden tree planted by the former foreign minister Hans Dietrich Genscher on August 26, 1998 is part of the educational border trail.

Continue past the watchtower and straight ahead. Unfortunately, there are no signs indicating the town of Jahrstedt.

You will pass a signal fence which was erected here as border security after 1968 and is maintained in its original form. The base for the border troops was behind the meshed metal fence which is now used for other purposes. Some of the adjacent houses have been empty for a long time.

At the end of the trail, which is not signposted, you will reach the **Crojaer Weg** which leads onto the main road of **Jahrstedt** where you turn right. You will come to a red brick house which now houses the child care centre.

You can see a difference between the eastern and western development of this educational border trail. In the western

Zicherie the signposting is perfect, in the eastern Jahrstehdt there is no indication of the educational border trail. The trail is only signposted with "Kaiserwinkel" and "Schutzhütte".

Jahrstedt

🚶 **Memorial stone:** "10 years German unity. Jahrstedt"

On the red brick house "Gemeinde Jahrstedt" you will find a plaque which shows the educational border trail.

Continue towards Kunrau. When you cross the Ohre, there is a separate cycle trail which leads you past a memorial stone.

Across from the memorial stone the patrol road is indicated. **15** Shortly before you reach the cemetery which is on the left, turn onto **Germenauer Straße**, a cobblestone road, which you can easily avoid by traveling on the pavement.

AUSFLUG An alternative route leads straight on to Kunrau, where the castle is worth a visit.

Kunrau

In Kunrau you will find a castle built in the middle of the 19th century, which today houses an exhibition on the history of Drömling. The integrated castle tower offers a good view over the Drömling Nature Park with its old trees.

To continue along the main route, turn left at the first possibility in the unpaved, cycle-friendly trail.

Take the next turn to the right, which is prohibited for motorised vehicles of any kind, and continue straight ahead. The trail to Buchhorst (8.5 kilometres) and Belfort (3.1 kilometres) is signposted. Continue on the cycle trail signposted as **"Naturpark Drömling"**. Information plaques describe the flora and fauna. After a short while you will reach the railroad embankment.

TIPP There is a memorial stone at the railroad embankment: "Here the first moordamm was created by Theodor Herrmann Rimpau on 1 December 1862".

After crossing the tracks, you will come to the fork in the road to Kunrau. There you will find a covered information board concerning the educational nature trail Drömling. Continue straight ahead and follow the signs to **"Radrundkurs Altmark"**.

Drömling

Drömling is a lowland moor approximately 340km² in size and is located on the scarcely populated border between Lower Saxony and Saxony Anhalt. The larger section belongs to Saxony Anhalt and is around 260 km². There you will also find a nature park.

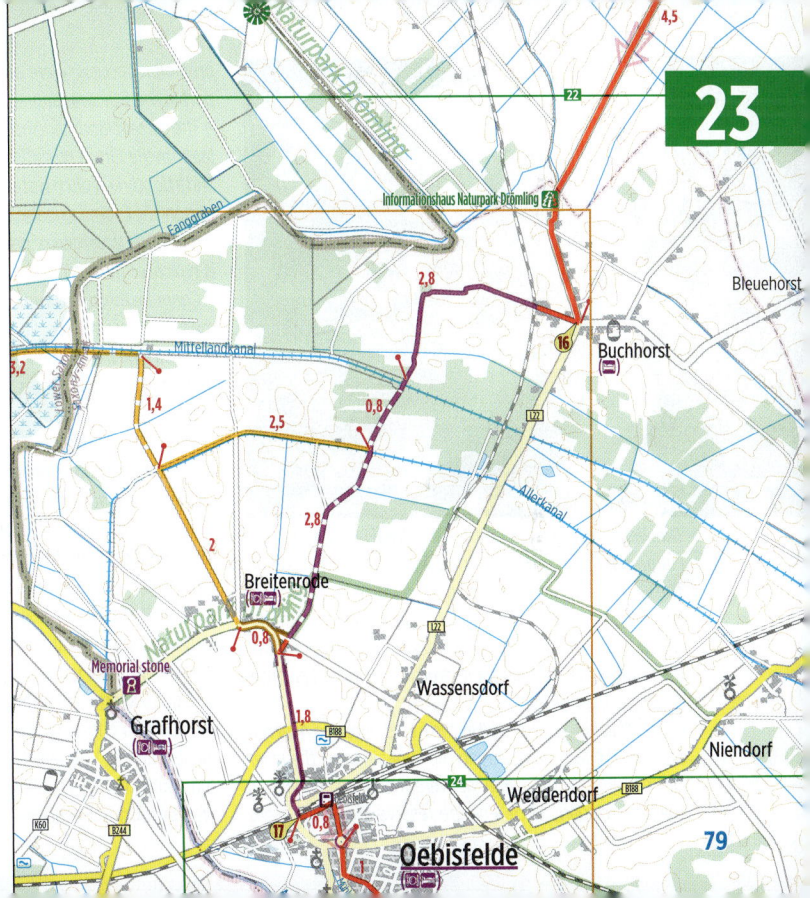

Cycle-path through the Drömling

The wetlands were turned from a natural landscape into a cultural landscape in the 18th century by Friedrich the Great. The valley is now a shelter for endangered animal and plant species. The next towns are Wolfsburg and Oebisfelde, which also make up the western and southern border of the nature park. To the east it stretches as far as Calvörde, to the north to Klötze.

The Midland Canal as well as the rivers Ohre and Aller run through the Drömling. During the separation by the inner German border, the wetlands were mostly maintained in the western part, since a nature reserve area (with areas prohibiting access) were arranged. Until 1990, the eastern part in the GDR was subject to intensive agricultural use.

The current landscape has its origin in drainage measures taken in the 18th century. There are vast green areas, forests and a tightly knit ditch system which is 1,725 km long. For this reason, the Drömling is also often called the land of thousand ditches. The long rows of poplars along the drainage ditches is typical of the region.

Continue through the impressive landscape along double rows of concrete slabs. Pass the wetlands, ponds, swamps and rows of trees. The entire area of Drömling is full of hundreds of small water ditches and narrow field and meadow trails. Here live, among others, peewits, snipes, cranes, bitterns, whooper swans, white storks, curlews and dabchicks. The nature park in Drömling is one of the largest midland wetlands of Germany.

Continue straight ahead on the right and left parallel to the drainage ditches towards Buchhorst. When a cycle trail goes to the left towards Röwitz, continue straight ahead on the pleasant, slab trail, cross another water ditch and continue with the water ditch on the right side, which was previously on the left.

About 5 kilometres after the railroad embankment, you will come to a road which leads to Röwitz and Kusey on the left and to Wassensdorf and Buchhorst on the right. Turn right there and follow the paved road through the **Wassensdorf** to **Buchhorst**.

TIPP Before you travel over the Ohre, there is an information centre on the right which provides information concerning the functioning of the drainage of the wetlands and the expansion of the flora and fauna in this area.

Cross over the Ohre. **16** In **Buchhorst** you will see a red brick house on the left side. Turn right there onto a cobblestone road. First follow the road for a distance on the sidewalk and then cross the railroad tracks. Afterwards the road is paved and takes you over the Middleland Canal after a bend (Weser-Elbe-Canal). Upon entering and exiting the bridge you will find old cobblestones, afterwards continue straight ahead on a dirt road until you reach the **Allerkanal**.
AUSFLUG Here you have the chance to travel to Wolfsburg.

Excursion to Wolfsburg

Turn right shortly before you reach the Allerkanal and continue along the northern shore. At the third crossing, turn right and continue until you reach the Middleland Canal. Turn left onto the southern side and turn right onto the B 244. Turn left before you reach the bridge and continue on the southern side of the Middleland Canal until you reach **Vorsfelde**. Cross the channel on the B 188 and continue on the northern side until you reach the next bridge at the Allersee. Once crossed, continue on the southern side of the canal as well as the railroad tracks until you reach **Dieselstraße** and turn right. Continue straight ahead over the Berliner Ring until you reach the **train station** which has direct trains to Berlin and Hannover.

Trip to Wolfsburg

Wolfsburg

prefix: 05361

- ℹ️ **Tourist-Information Wolfsburg**, Willy-Brandt-Pl. 3, directly by the main station, ☎ 05362/899930, @ ujm472
- 🏛️ **Automuseum Volkswagen (Volkswagen Car museum)**, Dieselstr. 35, ☎ 52071 ♿ Find out more about the history of the automobile with nearly 1,140 exhibits. @ hnc375
- 🏛️ **Kunstmuseum (Art museum)**, Hollerpl. 1, ☎ 26690 ♿ Exhibition and collection of modern works as well as classics and works by young artists. @ yro774
- 🏛️ **Städtische Galerie (City gallery)**, Schlossstr. 8, ☎ 281010 ♿, @ fwp427
- 🏛️ **Stadtmuseum Schloss Wolfsburg (City museum)**, Schloßstr. 8, ☎ 281040 ♿ Learn more about the history of the castle and of the city and its surroundings. @ vsm813
- 🏰 **Schloss Wolfsburg (Castle)**, Schlossstr. 8. The castle was built in the 14th century and later renovated. The current style, Weser Renaissance, is from the 16th century. In the castle you will find the city gallery, the art society and the city museum.
- ❄️ **Alvar-Aalto-Kulturhaus**, Porschestr. 51. An architectural masterpiece by the Finnish architect Prof. Dr. Alvar Aalto. It was opened in 1962. @ hxk826
- ❄️ **Autostadt**, Stadtbrücke, ☎ /0800288678238 🎡 This city of 25 ha with parks lakes shows and offers everything concerning cars and mobility. @ qkm354
- ❄️ **Phaeno – Experimentierlandschaft (Phaeno-Experiment landscape)**, Willy-Brandt-Pl. 1, ☎ 890100 ♿ A 9,000 m² environment concerning natural science and technology created by the architect Zaha Hadid. Inside you'll find an open landscape with craters, terraces, plateaus and caves. Numerous experiment stations and laboratories encourage you to experiment and help you understand natural phenomena. @ ifx632
- ❄️ **Planetarium**, Uhlandweg 2, ☎ 89025510. Extensive and varied program. @ kks456
- 🧢 **BadeLand**, Am Allerpark, ☎ 89000. Swimming and spa, @ exm555

Wolfsburg was officially mentioned for the first time in 1302 as the seat of the noble of Bartensleben and Neuhaus castle was officially first mentioned in 1372.

The founding of the Volkswagen production site on the northern side of the Middleland Canal in 1938 was a pivotal moment for the city where the 'beetle' would later be built. The „city of the KdF car by Fallersleben" (KdF = Kraft durch Freude, power through pleasure) was formed for the workers during the Third Reich through a combination of several municipalities.

During World War II the newly constructed car factory also served as an armament factory. The halls that produced the VW beetle – also, it must be said, by forced labourers – also manufactured jeeps, replacement parts for tanks and other munitions such as the V1 weapon.

The occupying British powers ordered the city to be renamed „Wolfsburg" in 1945. The VW factory was first under the management of the English Major Hirst, who prevented the transportation of the production machines to another location by ensuring factory orders for the British government. It was only thanks to this that the Volkswagen factory could remain after the end of the war and stimulate economic growth in Wolfsburg.

In 1995 the one millionth beetle was produced, an event that was celebrated with a special, one-off jewelled beetle.

Wolfsburg experienced an economic boom due to an influx of mainly Italian immigrant workers. In 1958 the City Hall was inaugurated.

During the communal reform of 1972, Wolfsburg's population exceeded 100,000 and was granted the status of a major city with a population of nearly 120,000. The city area had increased from 35 to 204km². In 1988 Wolfsburg became a university city (University Braunschweig-Wolfenbüttle).

Over the last few decades, modern urban visions have been realised in Wolfsburg. Three masterpieces by the Finnish architect Alvar Aalto now breathe fresh life to the city: The Alvar Aalto Kulturhaus, the community centre Church of the Holy ghost and the Stephanus Church. It is also home to a famous theatre which was built by the architect of the Philharmonic in Berlin, Hans Scharoun (1893-1972) and opened in 1973. The spectacular „Phaeno", a walk-in sculpture designed by Zaha Hadid and opened in 2005, is also worth a visit. It represents a unique mixture of natural science and technology.

From the train station in Wolfsburg, turn left onto **Heinrich-Nordhoff-Straße**, named after the first VW general director and then cross the Berliner Ring. At the intersection of Dieselstraße/Lerchenweg, turn to the north. Continue towards the east until you reach the next intersection, turn left, cross the railroad tracks and the Middleland Canal and then turn right. Continue on the norther side of the canal until you reach the next bridge in **Vorsfelde**. Cross the bridge over the B 188 on the southern side, turn left and continue along the water until you reach the B 244 and turn right. Turn left at the next possibility, remain on the shore of the canal

and turn right at the fourth intersection. Continue straight ahead over the Allerkanal to **Breitenrode**. Turn left onto the main road, continue through Breitenrode and keep to the right as you head towards Oebisfelde.

If you want to continue on the main route to Oebisfelde, cross the Allerkanal to **Breitenrode**.

In Breitenrode cross the country road, and shortly afterwards turn left onto the main road. **17** At the next crossing in the town, turn left after crossing the railway tracks to get to Oebisfelde **train station**.

Oebisfelde-Weferlingen
prefix: 039002

i **Stadt Oebisfelde-Weferlingen (Town of Oebisfelde-Weferlingen)**, Lange Str. 12, ✆ 8310, @ ytr258

▲ **Burg Oebisfelde (Oebisfelde Castle)**, Lange Str. 19, ✆ 86994, ◷ Sun/public holidays 14.00-17:00 and upon arrangement, Bergfried, Sun 14.30-17.30 and upon arrangement. Romanic castle with 27-metre-high tower was officially mentioned for the first time in 1267. This "swamp castle" is one of the oldest remaining constructions of its kind in Europe. Today, you can visit the castle museum and museum of local history,

and even the town archives, upon special arrangement.

▥ **Wassermühle Kasube (Kasube water mill)**, ✆ 05355/464, ◷ viewing upon arrangement. The mill is from the 14th century and is the only maintained mill of the region from the original six water- and five windmills.

The city in Börderkreis in Saxony Anhalt has a population of nearly 7,500. Drömling nature park is nearby. The origins of the city date back to the 10th century. It was constructed as a fortified city and provided protection from the Slavs who settled in the Altmark at that time. Between 1014 and 1073, Oebisfelde – „flat water island" – was officially mentioned for the first time, and later a fort was mentioned. During the Schmalkaldic War 1546-1547, a time when Karl V fought against the Schmalkaldic League, which consisted of individual princes and supported Protestantism – the city was devastated numerous times.

Border memorial

At the former border strip on the Aller, directly at the Büstedter Bridge (B 188), you will find the "border memorial" created by Manfred Böttcher with various elements symbolising separation and reunification. One way, one wall, one hole in the wall, a

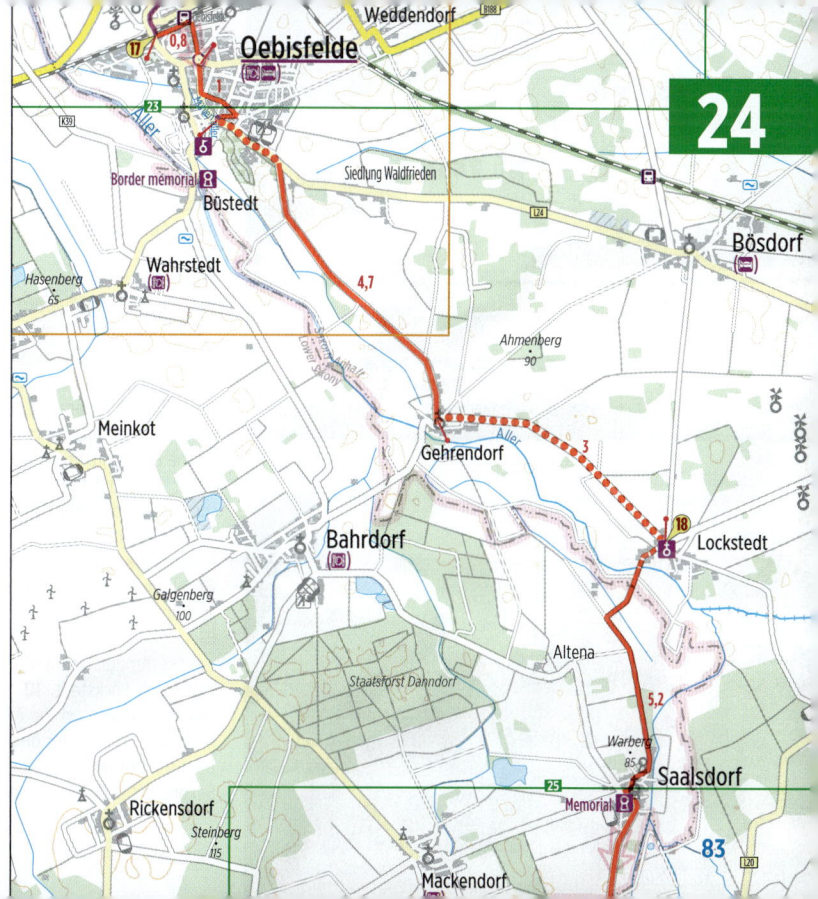

24

Oebisfelde (1984/2006)

step and a woman symbolize hope, whilst an owl symbolises nature. The former moor area "Drömling" was cultivated after the opening of the border and declared a nature reserve area. An information plaque provides information about the former border and the technical data of the facilities.

From Oebisfelde to Helmstedt/Marienborn   36 km

Continue straight ahead from the train station in Oebisfelde, cross the B188, continue straight ahead and turn right at the end over the **Mühlaller** stream. You will see the church tower, turn left and continue a short distance on the B188 until you reach the centre. Turn left at the church to the **Marktplatz** and from there towards Gehrendorf and Lockstedt. Shortly after leaving the town, turn right towards the signposted Gehrendorf and Lockstedt.

TIPP Continue parallel to the Aller and the border strip for some time, both of which can hardly be recognised.

Cross through **Gehrendorf** and follow the main road until you reach Lockstedt. **18** In **Lockstedt** turn right at the church. Continue on the Aller cycle trail to Saalsdorf, first on cobblestones, later on pavement. Cross over the Aller, then the border and you will then find yourself in Lower Saxony in the district of Helmstedt.

Border post in Saalsdorf

Saalsdorf

In Saalsdorf you will pass a huge oak tree and an old GDR border column, complete with hammer and sickle, reminding us of the separation: "125-year oak, 1871-1996. Those who remember can design the future."

Continue over the border straight ahead towards Weferlingen. On the **Elbe-Aller Trail** continue straight ahead on a dirt road which becomes paved again after 2.5 km.

Weferlingen

In 2000, Weferlingen celebrated the 850th anniversary of its first official mention. A memorial stone from October 7, 1951 commemorates "the village of peace". A further memorial stone commemorates the battle of Leipzig "1813-1913, With God for Emperor and Country", which was moved due to the roundabout.

TIPP There are numerous places to take a break – for example in the cafe "Le Village".

On the former border strip, you will find a cross and a memorial stone which commemorates the opening of the border on November 18, 1989: "Germany was separated at this site for 40 years, due to a dictatorial system. The communities Weferlingen and Grasleben. October 1990."

19 In Weferlingen, after the junction at An der Zuckerfabrik, turn left onto the cycle path leading to Tal der Aller. At

the pumping station pass under the railway and at the next crossroads continue straight on to Walbeck.

20 Turn left in Walbeck and then right onto Hauptstraße. Above the Aller on the left you will see the ruins of the **collegiate church**.

Walbeck

Ruins of the collegiate church St. Marien

The very old Ottonic town of Walbeck was first mentioned in the year 930. Today you will find the ruins of the collegiate church of St. Marien. The construction was already completed prior to 964 and significant parts of the construction can still be seen. The facilities were revealed in 1932. The funerary monument is one of few in good condition from the Ottonic period.

Keep to the right, pass through Walbeck and continue straight ahead. Upon leaving town a road branches off to the left, continue straight ahead on the comfortable gravel road. After travelling along a beautiful stretch of hills and fields, cross the Aller and you will reach the main road. Turn right towards Schwanefeld. The street winds down towards Schwanefeld and Beendorf.

In **Schwanefeld** you will most likely see a stork nest on the church tower. Continue past the soldier memorial from the first

World War, cross the Aller and und lave the town behind you. Directly at the entrance of Beendorf, turn right onto Mittelweg. Papenweg on the left takes you into the village.

Beendorf

After the sheave, turn right and cycle uphill through the village. Turn left at the memorial stone and follow the path along the former border.

AUSFLUG From Beendorf you can travel to the border town of Helmstedt via Bad Helmstedt. There are good connections in all directions from the train station. For the return journey from Helmstedt, turn right in Bad Helmstadt and re-join the main route again on the B 1.

Day trip to Helmstedt   11 km

Continue along Kreisstraße, through Bad Helmstadt and then along a hilly path. Soon after the motorway bridge, join **Beendorfer Straße** where you will find a cycle path on the lefthand side. At the intersection, turn left onto **Am Ludgerihof** and then continue straight on towards **Poststraße**. Turn right onto **Südertor**, and proceed in the direction of the city centre. Continue left until you hit the **train station**.

Helmstedt

prefix: 05351

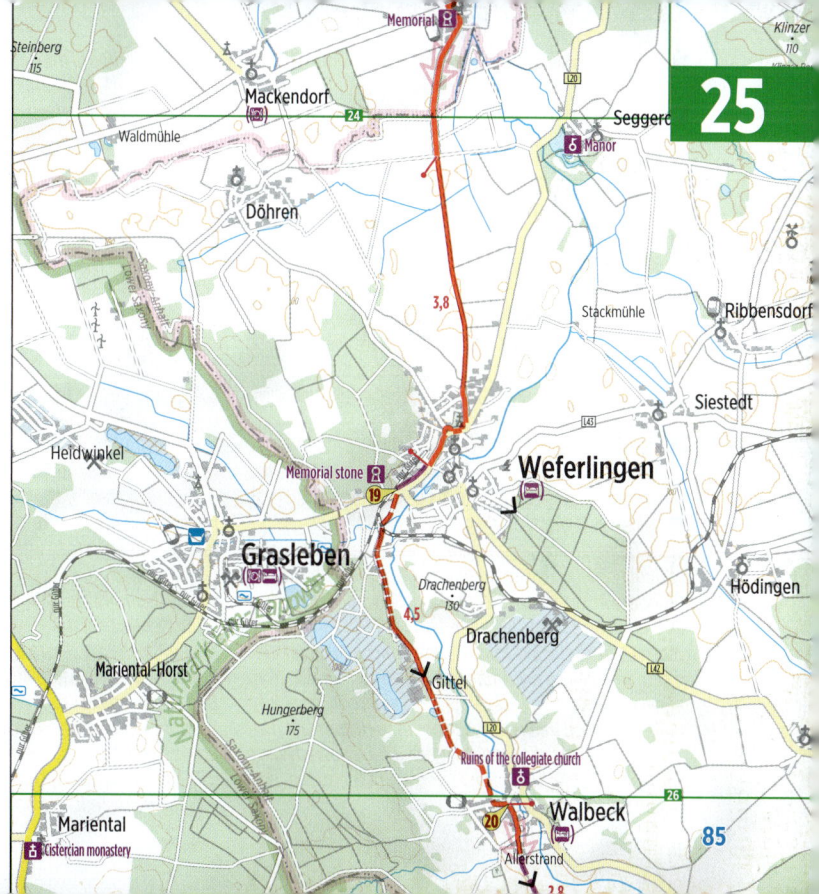

- ℹ️ **Touristinfo im Bürgerbüro**, Markt 1, in the citizens' office, 📞 171717, 📧 rey627
- 🏛️ **Kreis- und Universitätsmuseum (Local and university museum)**, Collegienpl. 1, 📞 1211132 🚻 The museum tells the history of the Helmstedt area from the Stone Age to the present with numerous exhibits such as early history excavations, metal works, old furniture or works from local artists of the present. 📧 mrw543
- 🏛️ **Zonengrenz-Museum (Border zone museum)**, Südertor 6, 📞 1211133 🚻 The history of the former inner German border is presented here in 5 periods. 📧 wly838
- 🔲 **Kloster St. Ludgerus (Cloister St. Ludgerus)**, Am Ludgerihof 1, 📞 58740, 🕐 Tours upon arrangement. It was founded by St. Ludger in the 8th century. The oldest building is the St. Peter chapel. The cloister was destroyed in 1553 and rebuilt at the beginning of the 18th century in Baroque style.
- ✳️ **Juleum**, Collegienpl. 1, former university, built 1592-97, 📞 120461, 🕐 tours upon arrangement. Famous professors such as Conring, Caselius or Calixt taught here until the university was closed in 1810.
- 🛁 **Julius Bad**, Stobenstr. 34, 📞 5385250, 📧 rhw515

The former university and hanseatic city has a population of about 25,500. It has a number of historical buildings, especially from the times of the Renaissance and more than 400 timbered houses from the 17th and 18th century. The central part of the old town is the market square (Marktplatz), where once the Amber road (Bernsteinstraße) from Königsberg to Aachen and the old Salt- and Troop road (Salz- und Heerstraße) from Luneburg to Halberstadt met. There you can also find the most beautiful timbered house with the imposing Haumann tower, which is also the most famous sight of the town.

During the time of the German separation, one of the most important border crossings (Helmstedt-Marienborn) was on the transit stretch between Hannover and Berlin.

Helmstedt, which is situated – like Rome – on seven hills, was officially mentioned for the first time in the year 952 as „Helmonstede". The founding of the settlement goes back to the Saint Ludger, bishop of Munster, whose missionary work led to the Benedictine monastery of St. Ludger. First settlements of the region go back much further: Because of the fertile loam soil, farmers settled here in the early Stone Age in the 6th century B. C. The so-called Lübbensteine in the area also originate from this period which are chambered tombs.

After the destruction of the town in 1199 by archbishop Ludolph of Magdeburg and the re-erection with the construction of a city wall in the year 1230 – just one city gate with tower and some remains of the city wall can still be seen – Halmstedt was granted city rights in 1247 and was the smallest member of the Hanseatic League from 1426 to 1518. The university was important, which was founded by Duke Julius as „Academia Julia" in 1576 and was a great influence on city life until the year 1810.

Today one can still view the buildings of the „Juleum Novum" in the city. There was a department for philosophy, theology, medicine and law. Between 1806 and 1813, Jérôme Bonaparte, brother of Napoleon, was ruler of the Kingdom Westphalia, to which Helmstedt also belonged. He had the university closed in the year 1810.

The brown coal mining, which dominates the landscape around Helmstedt, became one of the most important economic factors of the region in the 19th century. In 1874 the region's first open mine was brought into operation.

As of 1945, the city was in the border region between the two German states and for many West-Berliners it represented a small gateway to the big, wide world. The motorway to Berlin passed by Helmstedt, one of the three transit stretches from West Germany into the divided city. The border crossing of Helmstedt-Marienborn was a sorry sight.

When the inner German border was opened on November 9, 1989, the city experienced a flood of visitors like never before. In Helmstedt, which now calls itself "city of unity", an association now exists with the organisation „Without borders – roads to the neighbours", which aims to preserve the memory of this unique border during the 45 years of division.

According to two former West German border policemen, right up until 1961, East German border police would come into the bar at Klabautermann near Helmstedt - which was right at the border - hang their Kalashnikovs on the coat stand, drink a beer and leave again. At this time in history, they would even patrol together, talk, discuss football games and exchange cigarettes. They knew each other well and formed friendships. After the construction of the wall everything became more difficult. If you threw a pack of cigarettes over the wall to the colleague "over there", it would be intentionally stepped on and destroyed.

The route continues in the border strip, directly along the border.

21 Before crossing the B 1 there is a watchtower on the other side – turn right, continue somewhat parallel to the

highway, and then turn left and cross the B 1 and the A 2. At this point there is no reference to the imposing cast-iron memorial "La Voute des Mains", which rises 9 m into the sky. It can be reached by continuing on the B1 in the direction of Helmstedt.

La Voute des Mains

The memorial by the French sculpture Joseph Castell shows two hands over the broken remains of a wall made from thick granite blocks. In memory of "the victory of the people and humanity over an inhumane political system; but also as a reminder to all Germans to cherish their regained unity and to complete it through mutual respect."

Behind the motorway, when you see the original meshed metal fence, turn left.

Continue straight ahead to the signposted memorial site. At the entrance you will see: "The wall (1994) by Achim Borgsdorf, steel and original pieces of the wall. A gift from the residents of Helmstedt as an expression of their solidarity."

Marienborn memorial site

The allied checkpoint in Helmstedt/Marienborn was erected as early as July 1945. Members of the British, American, French and Soviet occupation troops all served here. Soviet soldiers, supported by the newly former border police of the Soviet occupation zone (SBZ) guarded the demarcation line between the Soviet and the western occupation zones. Here, one could observe the end of the blockade on 12 May

26

1949 when at midnight the first American cars began their journey to Berlin.

After the founding of the two German states in 1949, the Soviet military administration authorised the expansion of the site at Marienborn. Processing buildings were constructed as quickly as possible. In the beginning of the 1950's, the Soviet Union handed over the responsibility for the Marienborn checkpoint to the SED.

The use of firearms was then introduced to prevent fugitives from leaving the GDR. After erecting the permanent border facilities along the German-German border in May 1952, the guards at the crossing points also became stricter. After the construction of the Berlin Wall in 1961 and the complete enclosure of the German-German border, the border crossing point at Marienborn became the most important crossing point in the region - not only between the two German states but also between the two opposing political and ideological systems. At the end of the 1960's, the checkpoint facilities stretched over a length of one kilometre. New barracks were built to the south and north along the motorway.

On September 20, 1971, the Transit Agreement between the GDR and the Federal Republic of Germany was signed and on May 26, 1972 the Traffic Agreement followed as did the Basic Treaty on December 21, 1972. On June 7, 1971 the council of ministers of the GDR decided on the new construction of the border crossing point. They wanted it to lie one and a half kilometres from the German-German border and cover an area of 35 ha. From 1972 to 1974 the largest European checkpoint between East and West was built here for 70 million GDR Mark. It provided employment for over 1,000 people until 1989.

The members of the passport control units of the Ministry for National Security, the border troops and customs all worked there. In addition, there were civil employees in the exchange offices, German Red Cross, cafeteria workers and people employed to perform special checks for plant protection and veterinary medicine.

After opening the border in the fall of 1989, the border crossing point at Marienborn, which processed nearly 35 million travellers alone in the period from 1985 to 1989, stopped the border controls on July 1, 1990. Large sections were then completely destroyed or simply dismantled. In February 1992, the parliament of Saxony-Anhalt decided to erect a memorial site. On August 13, 1996 the "Marienborn memorial site" was opened. In the following period, an archive and information centre with permanent and special exhibitions concerning the former inner German border was created with a seminar area and a library.

Many original buildings, such as the covered terminal with the border houses, remain well maintained. The entire area of the facilities comprises approx. 7.5 ha. Today it is a place where "Germans tell Germans their biographies" according to the former president Roman Herzog who has visited the site.

TIPP Behind the memorial you will find a road leading to Morsleben on the left. This is where the GDR stored their nuclear waste.

Morsleben nuclear storage site

Morsleben, only 7 km from the former border crossing at Marienborn/Helmstedt, became infamous for being the GDR's main nuclear waste storage facility.

In 1897, both a potash and rock salt mine were brought into operation here. At the same location, the national socialists later forced labourers from the concentration camp at Beendorf to produce rockets.

As of 1972, the reopening of the salt mine at Bartensleben was approved despite numerous reservations regarding contamination from nuclear waste. The authorization for continuous operation was at first granted on a limited basis in 1981 and then on an unlimited basis in 1986.

Entrance to the Marienborn Memorial

After the German reunification, the Federation became owner of the mine and the responsibility for its future fell on the shoulders of the Federal Office for Radiation Protection. The unlimited authorization was changed to a limited use until June 30, 2000. Until then a total of (before and after the end of the GDR) 37,000 m³ of nuclear waste had been deposited in the salt mine.

On May 9, 1997, its closure was finally approved after a series of tough debates, mainly due to efforts by the red-green party of Saxony Anhalt. The German federal authority for radiation protection finally submitted an application for its closure in 2005.

Turn right into the town of Marienborn. After crossing the railroad tracks, immediately turn left, stay on the paved road and continue parallel to the tracks. Further straight ahead you will come directly to the train station.

AUSSTIEG Trains depart hourly to Magdeburg or Braunschweig from the station in Marieborn.

Marienborn
prefix: 039406

- 🏛 **Gedenkstätte Deutsche Teilung (Marienborn memorial site)**, An der Bundesautobahn 2, ✆ 92090 ℞, @ ofm178
- ⛪ **Klosterkirche (Minister)**, Altes Gut. The church was erected in the 12th century.
- 🔯 **Marienkapelle (Chapel of St. Mary)**, Hauptstr. This stone chapel with well dates back to 1836.
- ⛪ **Ehem. Kloster und Rittergut (Former Cloister and Manor)**, Altes Gut. The complex was built in the 15th century.

- 🔯 **Hügelgräber (Grave mounds)**. Around Marienborn you will also find grave mounds from the period of approx. 2,000-700 B. C. or megalithic tombs from the early Stone Age.
- ▭ **Räuberhöhle (Robber's den)**. East of Marienborn there is the robber's den. It said that the robber chief Rose (born 1816) was hiding there.
- ❋ **Orangerie (Orangey)**, Altes Gut. The building is located in front of the brewery and was constructed in 1810 in the shape of a Dorian temple.

Marienborn is a small community in Saxony Anhalt with a population of slightly more than 500 in the northwest of the Börderkreis, directly adjacent to Lower Saxony. It belongs to one of the historically oldest places of pilgrimage in Germany.

Legend has it that in the year 1000, the Virgin Mary appeared to a young shepherd at the site of the present Marienborn. Furthermore, at the same location, a statue of the Virgin Mary is said to have fallen from the sky and a spring with healing properties appeared in the 12th century. These events made Marienbord into a popular pilgrimage destination.

A very old minister from the year 1200 still exists as well as the respective cloister from the 15th century, the priest's house, and an orangery. Only ruins remain from the cloister and manor, the grounds of which were used as an agricultural co-op during the GDR period.

From Helmstedt/Marienborn to Hötensleben/Schöningen   16 km

From the **train station** in Marienborn, continue on the main road to the centre of town. Upon leaving the town, at the bus stop, a pedestrian and cycle trail goes to the right towards Sommersdorf which later turns into a concrete trail

Truck-clearance area at the Marienborn Memorial

which is good to travel on. The road served the agriculture and the border control.

In Sommereschenburg continue straight ahead on the street through the town.

Sommereschenburg (Sommersdorf)

- 🏰 **Schloss (Castle)**. The original castle was built in the 10th century as a border fortification and protection from the Slavs. It had an interesting history with numerous owners. In the 19th century the castle was built in neo-Gothic style under the Gneisenaus.

22 Turn right on the main road in town towards Sommersdorf. The beginning is downhill, later uphill. The cobblestone road turns into pavement a little while later.

Hötensleben (1984/2006)

Sommersdorf

From Sommersdorf continue towards Hohnsleben, cross the border, then follow the **B 245a** on a separate cycle trail to **Reinsdorf**. Turn left towards Offleben where you will find a memorial stone at the border, "Germany cannot be divided".

Continue through **Offleben** to the main road, turn left towards **Barneberg**, cross the border again and then immediately turn right towards Hötensleben.

Hötensleben

- ℹ️ **Gemeindeverwaltung (Municipal office)**, Zimmermannpl. 2, ☏ 039409/9160, @ vdv352
- ❈ **Flächendenkmal Hötensleben (Area memorial)**, ⏱ free access. Maintained border facilities along approx. 1 km can be viewed.

23 Before entering town a smooth convoy road goes off to the right, slightly uphill and straight ahead to the memorial at Hötensleben. Follow this trail and you will find yourself on a former access road to the German-German border. At the top of the hill you can enjoy a view of the entire border facility of the memorial at Hötensleben.

Carefully cycle down the convoy road to the road at the bottom.

The border memorial at Hötensleben

At its narrowest point, Hötensleben was only 35 metres from the border strip, but it was too big to force people to relocate. At the edge, approximately one kilometre of the original border facilities has been maintained. Shortly after the fall of the Berlin Wall, the "Round Table" in the community decided to preserve a piece of the border and the long-time mayor Dieter Buchwald (1990-2015) then implemented this decision. Due to the vicinity to the border, the "pioneer-technical development of towns" (GDR jargon) was used at a high level with walls which was uncommon for the rest of the inner German border. This memorial is one of the best preserved and looked after examples of the inner German border facilities.

The originally one-kilometre-long section is divided by the restored street to Schöningen. In the northern area, over a length of 350 metres and an area of 6.5 hectares, you can find the concealed wall, the border signal fence, the free view and illuminated firing field, the convoy road with car barriers, the control point strips, the border wall and the imposing hill tower. The "Hötensleber Kippe" is still visible in its original form and location.

In the southern area, the wall line is marked by trees, inspired by the motto: "Trees overcome walls". By personally planting poplars and oaks, the president Roman Herzog, important politicians, individual citizens, schools, parties, associations, communities and many others showed their commitment to German unity. The facilities can be visited around the clock. Information plaques provide information concerning the elements of the border facilities, tours can be booked (Border memorial association Hötensleben, ☏ 039405/50660 or at the Gemeinde Hötensleben, ☏ 039405/9610).

From Hötensleben continue on the cycle trail next to the street over the border towards Schöningen and past the coal mine.

Schöningen

Brown coal mine at Schöningen

The planning for the brown coal open-mine began after the first oil crisis in 1974. The nearly 470 ha large mine is divided into northern and southern fields by the country road 640. The northern field was added in 1979. Until 1996, 86 million m³ of earth and 15 million tons of brown coal were transported, which was used to produce electricity in the power plant at Buschhaus. The northern field has been filled with earth from the southern field since 1996. It is estimated that the last of the economically profitable coal supplies in the Helmstedt Revier will be exhausted around 2017/2018.

From Hötensleben/Schöningen to Hornburg   39 km

In order to continue on the main route, turn left into **Ohrsleber Weg** after the sewage plant. Continue on the asphalted road and cross a small stream a little while later. Then turn right into the first gravel road where you will see a tunnel under the railroad tracks at the end. Instead of turning right and crossing under the railroad tracks, turn left and shortly afterwards right again.

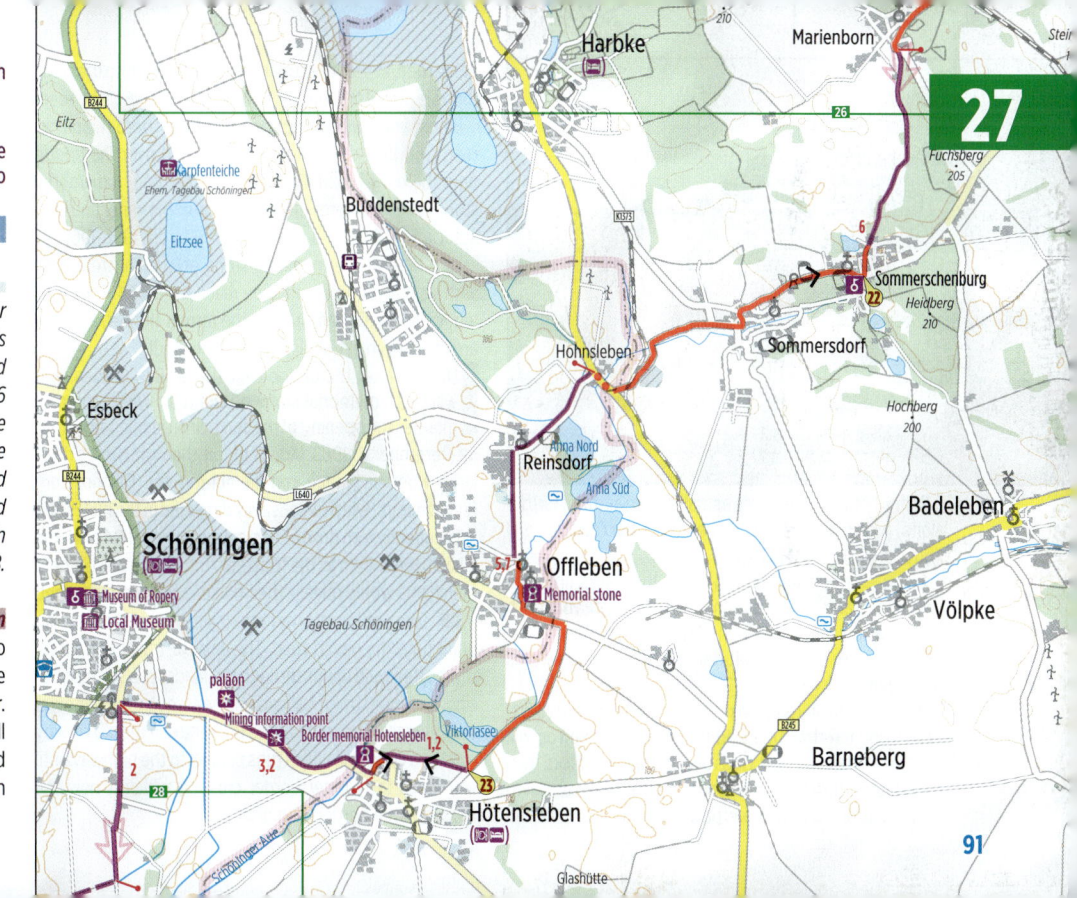

91

Hötensleben Border Monument

On the left side you will see a small stream and a bit further along, a large wind farm. At the end of the road you will find a large compost facility.

Again, turn left before you reach the tracks onto the paved road and continue along the tracks until you reach the road towards Ohrsleben. **24** Turn right under the railroad tracks and then left onto the main road towards **Söllingen**.

Where the main road makes a right bend towards Jerxheim, continue straight ahead through Söllingen. You will reach a cobblestone road, cross over the railroad tracks, then immediately turn right and continue somewhat parallel to the railroad on the paved road past the windmills. At the end

of the road, at the little stream, turn half right onto the comfortable gravel and turn right again at the end of the road.

Before you continue up the hill, turn left onto the paved road, and then turn left again at the end over the bridge onto the gravel road. At the end of the road, a memorial stone commemorates the melioration of the water and land association "Großes Bruch" performed from 1956-1965.

Turn right at the memorial stone onto a concrete road with several potholes until you reach the **B 244**. Then turn left, cross the Goßen Graben, the former border, and you are once again in the district of Halberstadt.

> **TIPP** Directly after the bridge over the Großen Graben, you will see a memorial stone on the right which commemorates the opening of the Jerxheim-Dedelegen border on December 8, 1989. Adjacent, on the righthand side, a large wooden plaque commemorates the Gasthof zum Kiebitzdamm, which was heavily damaged in the 1950's and subsequently torn down. For many years from 1714 onwards it had been known as the "Gasthof zum Zoll", a place where merchants would release their horses and spend the night.

25 Turn right at the next possibility behind the crossing point onto the paved road. The easy-to-travel but poorly signposted road winds through the landscape. At the crossing, continue straight ahead until you see the watchtower at Mattierzoll. Turn right at the B 79 and use the old convoy road as a cycle trail which runs parallel to the highway until you reach the former border crossing which is now the Hessendamm border memorial.

Mattierzoll border memorial

The memorial in the Winnigstedt district of Mattierzoll lies directly on the B 79. Prior to the opening of the border it was used as offices for the former federal Ministry for inner German Affairs. After the fall of the Wall, a section of the border facilities was reconstructed in a compacted form. Next to the border fences and two GDR border columns, the observation tower can be seen in its original condition. It is the last remaining, regularly-maintained border tower in Halberstadt. It commemorates the divided Germany and was placed under protection on the first anniversary of the opening of the wall. The stone directly on the border, "November 12, 1989", serves as a reminder to this piece of history. The facilities can be visited around the clock (except for the observation tower).

26 Turn left at the town sign of Mattierzoll into the gravel road that is good to travel and turns into a paved road after a short distance but is patched up at a few spots with gravel. The Neue Graben is on the right side. Continue on the beautiful road through vast corn fields and meadows.
27 When you reach the turn to Seinstedt, which is not signposted, turn left into the gravel road, pass the bridge over the Schiffgraben and continue on the paved road over the **Zieselbach**, where you will find a **refuge**, continue over the next intersection until you reach the signposted road towards Hornburg and turn right. After the town sign of Hornburg, the street is called the **Anna-Landmann Straße**.

January 7, 1997 was the 400th anniversary of the death of Anna Landmann, a woman who was accused of witchcraft, found guilty and was the last person to be burned alive in Hornburg in 1597.

Hornburg

prefix: 05334

- ℹ️ **Stadtmarketing Hornburg (City marketing/tourist office)**, Pfarrhofstr. 5, ☎ 94910, @ wxe323
- 🏛️ **Heimatmuseum (Museum of local history)**, Montelabbatepl. 1, ☎ 2234 ♿ The museum displays information about the history of the town and castle as well as items concerning the history of the German-German border. In front of the building visitors can also

Half-timbered houses in Hornburg

see a GDR border column, which once stood near Hornburg. It has the following inscription: „On 18 November 1989, the time of the division ended with the opening of the border between Hornburg and Hoppenstedt. To commemorate this special day, the museum for local history in Osterwieck presented this GDR border column to the museum of local history in Hornburg. Since 11 February 1990 a partnership connects these two museums." @ tic477

- ⛪ **Marienkirche (St.-Mary Church)**, Pfarrhofstr. 3, ☎ 1328, 🕐 April-Oct., Tu-Sun 14-17.00. The church contains important carvings dating back to the epochs of late renaissance and baroque. @ tto827
- ⛪ **St. Clemens-Kirche (Church of St. Clemens)**, Anemonenweg 5, ☎ 347. A small bust in front of the church commemorates Pope Clemens II, who was born in Hornburg and crowned King Heinrich III to Emperor of the Holy Roman Empire of the German Nation on December 25, 1046. To commemorate the 1,000th birthday of Clemens II the plastic created by the sculptor Sabine Hoppe was erected in the year 2005.
- ✴️ **Altstadt (Old town)**, Wasserstr. The old town dating back to the late Middle Ages is worth visiting with nicely restored half-timbered houses, nearly all of which have an inscription from the Bible on the beams.

From Hornburg to Bad Harzburg/Ilsenburg   27 km

Continue via **Pfarrhofstraße** into the old town and past the town hall. Turn right immediately behind the church into **Wasserstraße**. After 150 m turn left and then continue straight ahead and through a city gate. This will take you to the road **B 82**. Cross the river Ilse on this main road and then turn left into **Rimbecker Straße** towards Rimbeck. Continue

Hornburg museum of local history

on the quiet contry road along the Ilse where you can see the Harz with the Brocken on the horizon.

28 In **Rimbeck** turn right into **Dorfstraße** and then follow the **Wülperoder Weg** towards **Wülperode**.

In **Bühne**, on a fork in the road towards Stötterlingen there is a memorial stone dedicated to the fallen of the Second World War: "There are no words to thank them for their sacrifice, and we can never express enough gratitude to those who perished. For us".

At the end of the Wülperoder Weg turn left onto the **K 1338**, then make a sharp right turn and you will reach Wülperode. Follow the village road through the village. Then turn left onto the **L 90** and you will pass the border monument, where 50 metres of the original border fence

complete with vehicle barrier can still be seen. Behind the border monument at the border to Lower Saxony, turn left onto the unpaved field path along the pond. Here, close to the bank, Hans-Georg Kruse, a bulldozer driver by profession, fled the DDR.

Hans-Georg Kruse

The construction worker was commissioned to level an earth wall with a bulldozer and was supervised in this task by two border guards. At one point, he was left unobserved for a moment and he seized his opportunity. Seeing a BGS officer on the other side, he ran across the border as fast as he could. A GDR soldier pulled out his gun but Peter Puhle of the BGS, in turn, pointed his gun at the soldier, thus ensuring Kruse's escape and saving his life. The two men were reunited 30 years after the escape and regularly visit each other.

At the end of the pond, turn right along the pond onto an unpaved dirt road that leads straight on into **Weidenstraße**. In **Wiedelah**, turn left off the Weidenstraße into **In den Pappeln**, cross the Eckergraben, go up the small hill and take the next right towards Abbenrode.

> If you want to visit two art monuments, turn left towards the border. The second one can be found by turning right just before the border and then left.

29 On the main road, cross the busy road at the "Weißes Ross" guesthouse and then cross the railroad tracks.

> Upon leaving the county of Goslar and crossing the border to Saxony Anhalt, the former German-German border is not hard to recognise. In a field next to the road there is

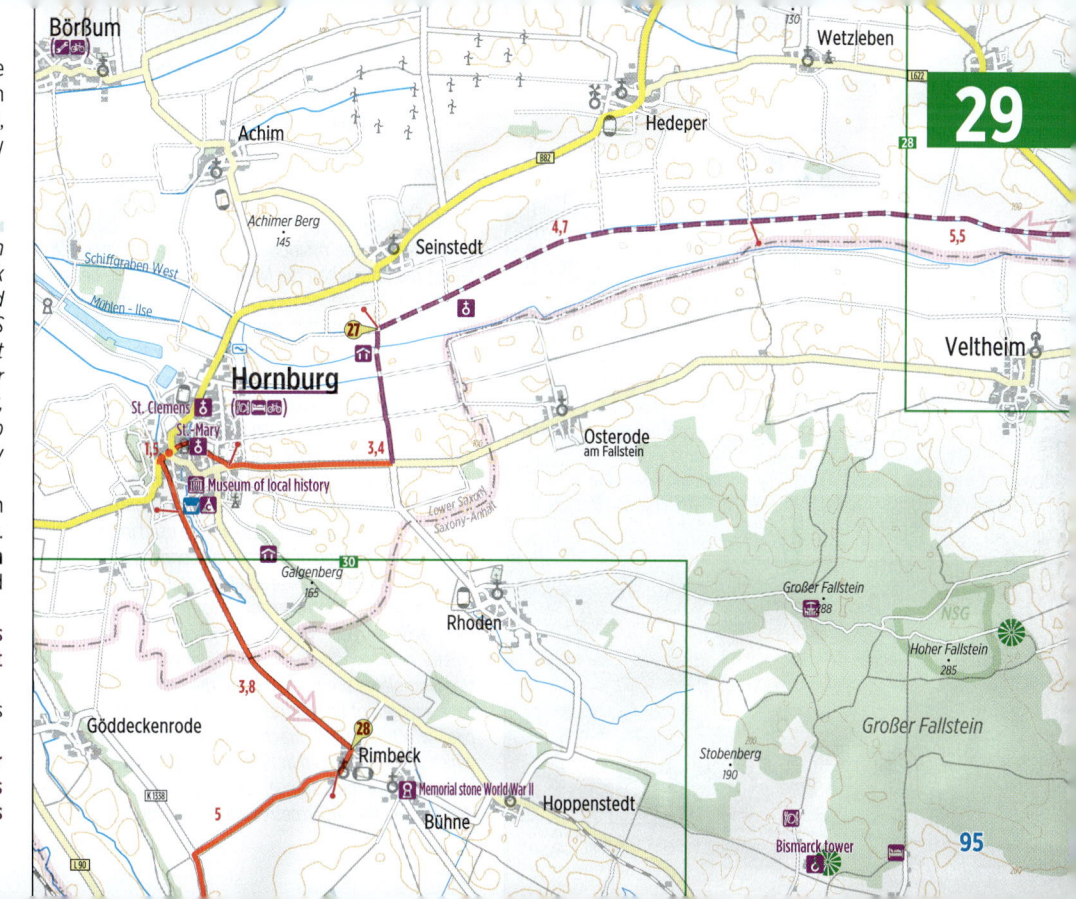

Stapelburg (1984/2006)

a rusty metal section which belongs to the "Environment Dissolution Iron Curtain memorial". For the uninformed observer it would be useful if an information plaque explained the significance of this part, which stretches over a distance of 3 km.

"Iron Curtain" memorial

The idea for the memorial was born in the mid 1990's during the time when the Nordharz railroad line between Abbenrode and Vienenburg was completed and the border facilities were completely removed. The former border area once again returned to farmland and only the patrol road was left to remind us of the past.

The architect and city planner Klaus Christian Wenzel created the memorial. It consists of ten unconditioned square steel plates which are three metres wide and four centimetres thick with a height of six to ten metres that were erected over a distance of three kilometres along the former border. A total of 80 tons of steel were used in connection with the introduction of the railroad connection.

At one point, six of these steel plates, half of which have in the meantime fallen over and lie forgotten on the ground, form a dense collection, which is characterised by the creator as a "configured scrap pile of world history". The standing plates are 6.60 m high; the ones on the ground have a length of ten metres. The distance from the "scrap pile" which is found directly next to the railroad tracks, which were completed in 1996, to the other steel plates is always double the distance – 200 metres to the next, then 400 metres, then 800 metres and finally 1,600 metres. The endless row is supposed to symbolise the expansion in the world and the timely and spatially unlimited division line between the formerly tow German states.

Afterwards cross the motorway-like B 6 and you will get to Abbenrode.

Abbenrode (Nordharz)
prefix: 039452

🏛 **Heimatmuseum (Museum of local history)**, Im Winkel 5, ✆ 9270, @ juw577

The power of water has been harnessed since the 12th century. A network of artificial ditches started from the Ecker. Several mills have survived to this day. The "Otto Mill" near the museum has been renovated and is now in good working order.

The mill village was first mentioned in 1129 and was the seat of a monastery that was largely destroyed in the Peasants' War of 1525 and has since completely disappeared. You can visit a memorial in Abbenrode commemorating the athlete Friedrich Ludwig Jahn. Victims of the tyranny from both wars are also commemorated.

The Heimatmuseum also informs visitors about the history of the German-German border region and in particular the first time a border within Germany was opened on 11 November 1989.

You will soon come across an old, red, British phone box, looking slightly lost on the right side of the road.

In the centre of town, follow the signs to Stapelburg which can be reached via a paved road.

Stapelburg (Nordharz)

🏰 **Burgruine Stapelburg (Castle ruins)**

In Stapelburg continue towards Bad Harzburg. **30** After the guesthouse "Rast an der Grenze" turn right and cross over the Ecker. Once you reach **Eckertal**, turn left at the "Eckerkrug" onto the paved road. "Welcome to Werningerode County" and "Goslar County" are written on the signs. When you reach the signs that say no through traffic, you have run into the Euro Route 1 through the Harz National Park.

AUSSTIEG If you would like to continue to Bad Harzburg, turn right here and continue to the train station. Trains depart from there to Hannover and Braunschweig. The route is signposted as "Europa-Radweg R1".

If you would like to continue on the main road to Ilsenburg, turn left here into the dirt road where the "Jungborn", once the first and largest natural sanatorium in Germany, is remembered, and continue over a bridge to the other side of the Ecker. Cross the convoy road with the perforated concrete slabs and continue on the Harz border trail towards Ilsenburg. The cycle route takes you down **Kastanienallee** into the city. At the roundabout, go straight ahead and pass the **trout pond** to the market place.

Ilsenburg (Harz)
prefix: 039452

🛈 **Tourismus GmbH mit R1-Service- und Infostelle**, Marktpl. 1, ✆ 19433, @ fvi441

🏛 **Hütten- und Technikmuseum (Museum of huts and technology)**, Marienhöfer Str. 9 b, ✆ 2222 ⊜ The museum of the city and regional history. Interesting functional models can be discovered and a small exhibition of the Brocken border facilities. @ hqq287

⛪ **Kloster Ilsenburg (Monastery)**, Schlossstr. 26, ✆ 80155, ✆ 0176/95607610 (Führungen/tours) ⏰, @ bnu745

🏰 **Schloss Ilsenburg (Castle)**, Schlossstr. 26, ✆ 970

🏡 **Nationalparkhaus „Ilsetal" (National park house "Ilsetal")**, Ilsetal 5, ✆ 89494 ⊜ The national park house is found near the hiking parking lot in lower Ilsetal. Alternating photo exhibitions and short movies concerning the fire salamander and Ilsetal. @ dms324

❀ **Erlebniswald Ilsetal (Ilsetal Adventure forest)**, Ilsetal 16b, ✆ 290015 ⊜ Climbing park, @ oct234

✉ **Ludwigsbad**, Schickendamm 6, ✆ 0151/56814458

Ilsenburg is surrounded on three sides by tree-covered mountains and is approx. 550 metres high. The Brocken, the highest elevation of the Harz, can be reached from here via Heinrich-Heine-Weg.

The empiric hunting castle Elysynaburg was built around the year 920, above the Ilse near the present town, where Otto III.

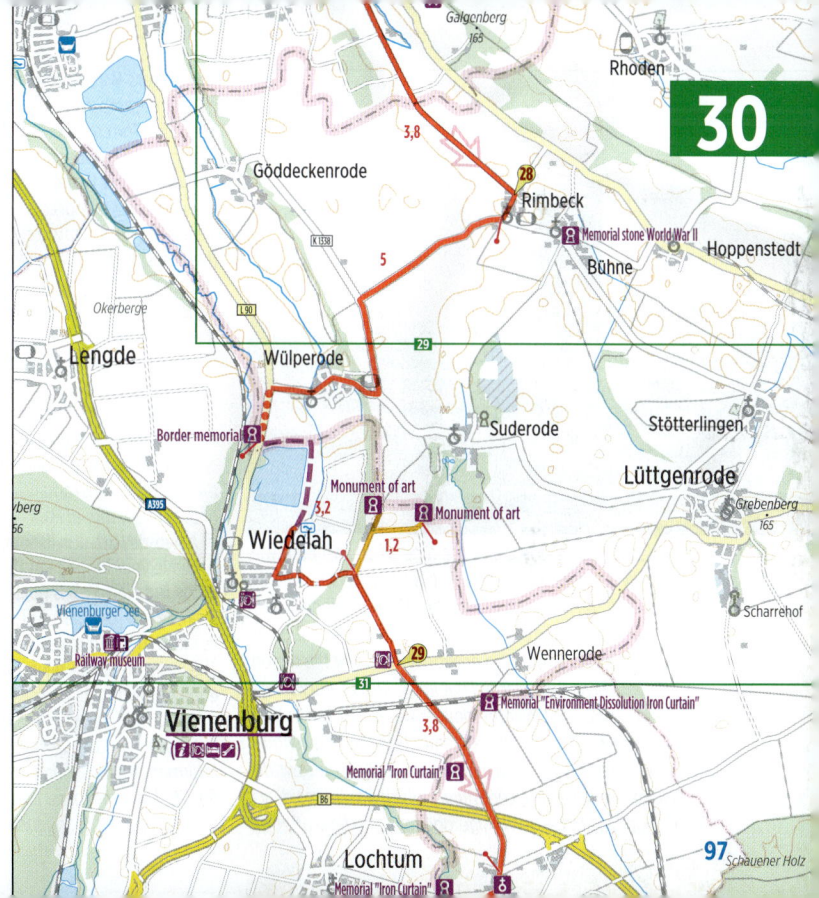

Memorial „Iron Curtain"

Thirty Years War. In the meantime (1609) the Bedetictine cloister became property of the county and became castle Ilsenburg. The community was also known beyond the Harz region for the production of stove plates and art castings.

During World War II, the military hospital was located in Ilsenburg and was occupied on April 11, 1945 by American troops. The Red Army occupied the city on July 3rd. During the times of the GDR, the community was considered an industrial and recreational centre and was granted city rights in 1959. On December 3, 1989, the „Harzfreunde" from Ilsenburg initiated the opening of the Brocken access and thus the inner German border at that location.

A walk through the city is also a stroll through its over 1,000-year-old history. The monasteries of Ilsenburg and Drübeck are well-worth a visit and are only 3.2 kilometres apart. Hike or cycle along the Harz monastery hiking trail through numerous romantic forests and discover the wonder of the Harz National Park.

A two-day break in Ilsenburg is definitely recommended. Leave your luggage at the hotel and climb to the top of the Brocken. This is possible by foot and also by bicycle. As a day tour, one can easily hike through the Ilsetal past the Ilse falls to the Brocken. The trail is really well signposted. The Heinrich-Heine hiking trail it is about 11 km from the edge of town to its peak.

Heinrich Heine, who was born in 1797 in Düsseldorf, was in the Harz in 1824, as mentioned in the Ilsetal by various information boards. First, follow the Ilse through thick, dark forests. Later the forest becomes lighter and at the end you will find yourself hiking through some pretty barren terrain.

The final few metres to the peak can be traversed by way of a concrete trail. Naturally, you can also reach the peak by bicycle, if you are willing to get off and push your bike along a few sections. If you do so, you will be rewarded with a wonderful downhill ride through the Ilse valley.

Due to the unpredictable weather conditions and the frequent fog, the poet Heinrich Heine wrote the following entry into the Brocken hotel's guestbook in 1824:
"Große Steine, (Big stones,)
müde Beine, (tired legs,)
saure Weine, (sour wine),
Aussicht keine. (no view.)
Heinrich Heine"

Harz National Park

The Harz National Park – a joint nature preservation area between the counties of Saxony-Anhalt and Lower Saxony – the largest forested national park with more than 25,000 hectares. It is also one of the most sparsely populated forest regions in Germany. It was created in 2006 and comprises nearly ten percent of the entire area of the Harz around the Brocken, from Herzberg in the south to Bad Harzburg and Ilsenburg in the north. In 2005, it was included in the European Charter for sustainable tourism in the reserve areas. It is internationally recognised by the IUCN (International Union for Conservation of Nature) and part of the European reserve system "Natura 2000".

Up to 95 per cent of the area is covered by forests, especially pine and beech forests. Fallen trees are not cleared away but are left to naturally degrade. On top of them, the

resided in 995. This was also the time when Ilsenburg was officially mentioned for the first time. Otto's successor, Heinrich II, gave the castle to the Bistum Halberstadt in 1003, which created a Benedictine cloister here that developed into the cultural and economic centre of the region. A reconstruction was carried out in the 12th century after a fire. In the Peasant War the cloister was destroyed in 1525. Ilsenburg was founded by settlements in the 12th century.

After the construction of two furnaces in 1545, the town developed into a wealthy community which was the residence of Count zu Stolberg-Wernigerode for some time after the

primeval forests of tomorrow are allowed to grow. Apart from the vast forest areas, moors have an outstanding position due to their special features. Granite cliffs and mountains streams are also found here. Due to its location in the former German-German border area, there are also many undisturbed plants and animals.

An immense number of waterways is also typical of the park – this is hardly surprising when one considers the 1,600 ml of precipitation per year. This allows many different varieties of moss to thrive, for example, the maidenhair moss with its long-stemmed capsules or the spade moss, which lives both partially and completely underwater.

The lynx fell extinct here a long time before the Cold War. Since 1999, a few biologists however, have been attempting to establish this predator here again. And they have been successful: after 200 years the lynx is now back in the Harz.

From Bad Harzburg/Ilsenburg to Fladungen/Fulda

331 km

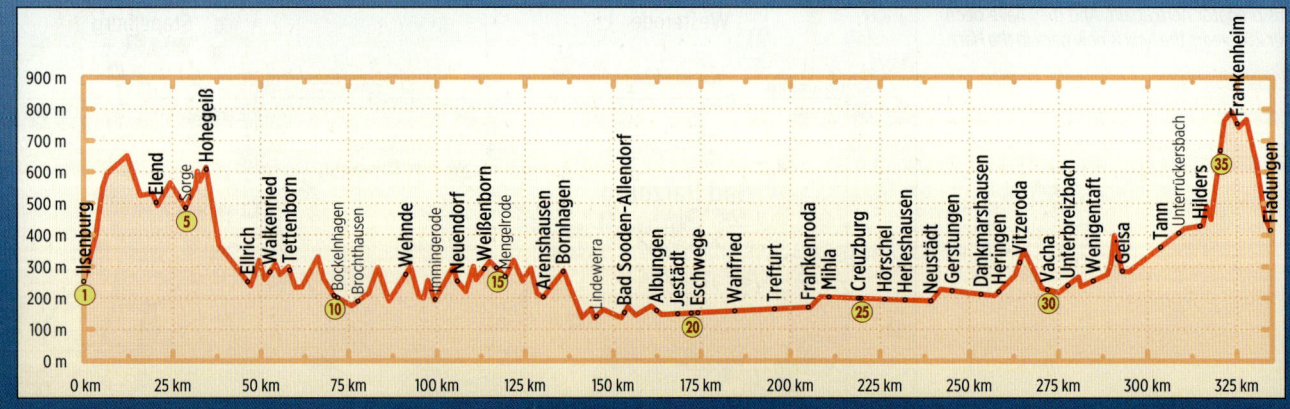

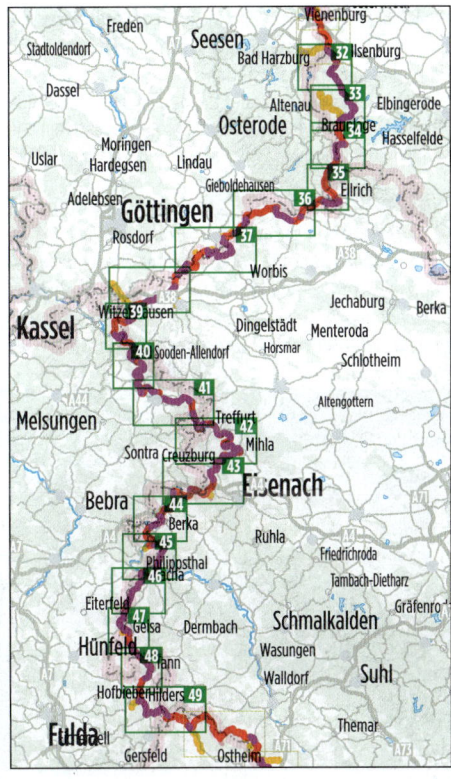

From the train station in Ilsenburg, turn left and a little bit later it branches off into Tannengang. Follow Kroatenstraße to Marktplatz, where you will hit the main route.

From Bad Harzburg/Ilsenburg to Sorge   29 km

1 The main route leads from the **market square** half left into **Rudolf-Breitscheid-Straße**, which shortly afterwards becomes **Mühlenstraße**. Follow the signs for hikers and cyclists towards the Ilsetal, the Ilse falls and the Brocken and follow the easy to travel cobblestone road which turns into a wide gravel road after crossing the Ilse at the "Ilsestein" **Waldhotel**.

At the next crossing, in around 2 kilometres, you'll see a bus stop. Make a sharp left turn up the steep hill away from the Ilse.

The gravel road signposted to the Waldgasthaus "Plessenburg" and to the train station of Drei Annen Hohne is quite steep and tiring, but the route is very good to travel on for mountain conditions. It is 2 kilometres from the crossing to the guesthouse. There are dense leaf trees on both sides which provide pleasant shade in the summer. Later the beech trees are replaced by fir and spruce trees. 100 metres before reaching the guesthouse you will come to a large crossing.

Apart from signs, you will also find the "Plessenberg" bus stop where bus 288 occasionally stops. This bus goes from Drei Annen Hohne via Ilsenburg to Werningerode.

On the right side you will find the "Plessenburg" **Waldgasthaus** (forest guest house) (✆ 03943/607535). Continue straight ahead up the hill until it begins to go down the hill to the **train station of Drei Annen Hohne** which is 9.5 kilometres from the guesthouse. Follow the respective signs. The gravel road is still good to travel on, the trees are

In Ilsenburg

Bus-stop in the middle of the forest on the way to Drei Annen Hohne

somewhat smaller and the landscape is not quite as dark as in the Ilsetal. Now and then the forest completely opens up. **2** ⚠ Attention: After cycling for 3 kilometres, you have to turn right at **"Bielstein" bus stop** towards Drei Annen Hohne. Then, continue straight towards Wernigerode.

The remainder of the stretch is rather flat, slight inclinations are rewarded with a small downhill ride. At the crossing to Hohnepfahl – you can also find a bus stop here - turn right towards Drei Annen Hohne and continue on the gravel road straight ahead to the train station.

Cross the street which leads from Wernigerode to Schierke and you will come to a car park where stands are set up in the warm seasons. A little later you will see Harz train station narrow gauge railway.

> **TIPP** You can buy drinks, fresh waffles, ice cream and the famous pea soup from the stands in the fields. In fact, the soup is so famous it is even exported to the USA in cans. You can sit right next to the railroad tracks on rustic wooden

benches and admire the trains in the narrow-gauge railway. Apart from the tracks, a historical lorry from the mines and caverns Bodefeld/Harz is displayed.

Follow the road towards **Schierke**. **3** After the Drei Annen Hohne train station, and shortly before reaching the railroad crossing, turn left onto a road which leads over the railroad tracks and continue straight ahead towards Elend, Mandelholz and Königshütte.

> **TIPP** The road to Elend is easy to travel on and does not have any large hills. Sometimes the road is rather compact with fine gravel and sometimes you will travel on forest trails. In any case, you will make good progress. The road through the beautiful fir and spruce forests is called "Alte Hagenstraße" or "Harzer Hexenstieg".

Shortly before you reach Elend, the road crosses the railroad tracks on the Harz narrow gauge railway again. Once you have reached the first houses in **Elend**, continue into the small town until you reach the charming **train station**.

> **TIPP** You can take the Harz narrow gauge railway from Elend to Nordhausen, from where you can take direct trains to Halle (Saale), Kassel, Erfurt and Göttingen.

Continue through town to the B 27 where you will find Germany's smallest wooden church. Follow the highway towards **Braunlage**, cross the Kalte Bode and cross under the Brockenbahn. **4** Shortly after leaving the town, turn left onto the quiet country road towards Sorge and Tanne.

The little-travelled road is in very good condition. Cross the Harz narrow gauge railway a few times and conquer a few hills. The last part before the B 242 at the edge of the town of Sorge goes downhill for quite a while. Turn left onto the B 242 and then right into the town of **Sorge**. Cross the bridge over the **Warme Bode** and continue straight ahead until you reach the **train station**.

> **TIPP** In the towns of Sorge and the 480 to 540-metre-high resort of Tanne you will find numerous places to eat and spend the night.

Harz narrow gauge railway

The Harz narrow gauge railway consists of a 140-kilometre-long network with over 50 stops with a gauge of 1,000 millimetres. This includes the Brockenbahn, the Harzquerbahn and the Selketalbahn. The network was created at the end of the 19th century with the connection of originally separate train lines.

Narrow-gauge train in the Harz

Due to the division of Germany after the end of World War II, the (western) Südharz railway was separated from the (eastern) network. The private railroad companies in the East were expropriated and as of April 1, 1949 operated by the Deutschen Reichsbahn. Since the Brocken was in the restriction zone near the border, the public transportation with passenger trains on the Brockenbahn was stopped in 1961. Later, only people with special authorization were allowed to travel to Schierke. The last train travelled to the West in 1963.

After the German reunification the Deutsche Reichsbahn reconstructed the Brockenbahn. Since the reopening on September 15, 1991, the stretch to the Brocken, the highest peak of the Harz, has become one of the most well-known stretches of the Harz narrow gauge railway.

On February 1, 1993, the counties Wernigerode, Quedlinburg and Nordhausen, the communities that lie on the stretch, the city of Quedlinburg, the community Tanne, as well as the resort Braunlage, took over the vehicles, lines and personnel from the Deutschen Reichsbahn. The "Harz narrow gauge railway GmbH" now finances the longest continuous narrow gauge railway network in Germany.

The trains travel daily and in addition to the diesel locomotives, you can also find steam locomotives. The Harzquerbahn also has diesel and electric trains. In Nordhausen, the trains have also linked up with the tram network.

The railway runs a few times per day and carries nearly 800,000 passengers per year from Wernigerode (234 m) over Drei Annen Hohne to the final stop at Brocken (1125)

Elend railway station

and back. Since 2006, there has been a regular train service to Quedlinburg as well.

TIPP It is best to begin the tour to the Brocken in Elend. If you spend the night in Sorge, you will travel the aforementioned distance back to Elend. You should plan to spend an entire day in Brocken. For one thing, there are several hundred metres of elevation to overcome!

From Elend to Brocken   29 km

From Elend, follow the paved road with a 12% gradient to Schierke, the most exhausting part to the peak of the Brocken.

After Schierke, the paved road up the Brocken is not accessible for cars and thus only maintenance vehicles and horse drawn carriages can usually be seen. The paved road is not in the best condition but is also not very steep. You can cycle almost the entire way to the top without getting off to push.

At first you will travel through thick pine forests, later it lightens up and at the end you will find yourself travelling through barren terrain. Signs provide information concerning the actual elevation. At 1,000 m you are almost at the top. There are only 141 metres of difference in altitude left before you reach the highest point.

You will see many walkers on the final stretch and you might have to dismount.

TIPP The oldest, still-maintained weather shelter in Germany is found on the peak of the Brocken. A sign explains: "Goethe found refuge here on December 10, 1777." On top of the Brocken you can have something to eat and if the weather is clear you have a fantastic view.

The down-hill ride from the Brocken to Schierke and further to Elend is an experience not to be missed: You can simply roll downhill for several kilometres.

ACHTUNG Be careful and pay attention to the road conditions, hikers, maintenance vehicles and the horse drawn carriages.

The Brocken

At 1,141 metres, the Brocken is the highest mountain in northern Germany. Its average temperature is 3.5 degrees Celsius, the strongest wind speed measured was 263 kilo-metres per hour. With 330 days of fog (1958), it is also the foggiest place in Germany.

The first proven ascent was in 1572. The Brocken was made famous by Goethe, who climbed it twice. The railroad line of the narrow-gauge railway was opened in 1899, the Brocken train station lies at an elevation of 1,125 metres. From 1945 to April 1947 the mountain was occupied by US troops. It was then passed on to the Soviets as part of a territorial exchange.

During the GDR, the Brocken was directly in the border area and until 1961 was accessed with easy to obtain authorization. By August 1961, it became a military restriction zone and a wall was built around the top – like in Berlin.

A view of a barred railway bridge on the line to Tanne, 1985

Various military objects were erected at the peak, as well as high performance listening posts operated by the Soviet secret service and the Ministry for National Security in the GDR.

On December 3, 1989, demonstrating hikers forced the opening of the wall. The military facilities were gradually removed after the reunification. On the former border strip, a watchtower, border fences, a water dam, dog training area, as well as an earth bunker, still remain. The last Russian soldier left the Brocken on March 30, 1994.

Since then, the surroundings have been re-naturalised, to let nature be nature once again. Where the wall once stood is now a nice walkway. Thousands visit the Brocken every year, mostly with the Brocken train and the horse drawn carriages but many also come by foot or bike. In the Brockenhaus you can view an exhibition concerning the opening of the Brocken and the original espionage facilities. There is also information concerning the cutlure, geology, climate protection and nature conservation.

From Sorge to Walkenried   24 km

5 Just before the train station in Sorge, you will find the "Raststüb" guesthouse (☎ 039457/3273), where you turn right onto **Ebersbachstraße**. The 2-kilometre-long road to the border museum, with an inclination of 200 metres, is signposted. You can easily cycle on the road because the slabs are in good condition.

First you will reach a piece of the border fence and pass the entrance gate. Continue on the slab trail through a forest until you reach the former observation tower of the

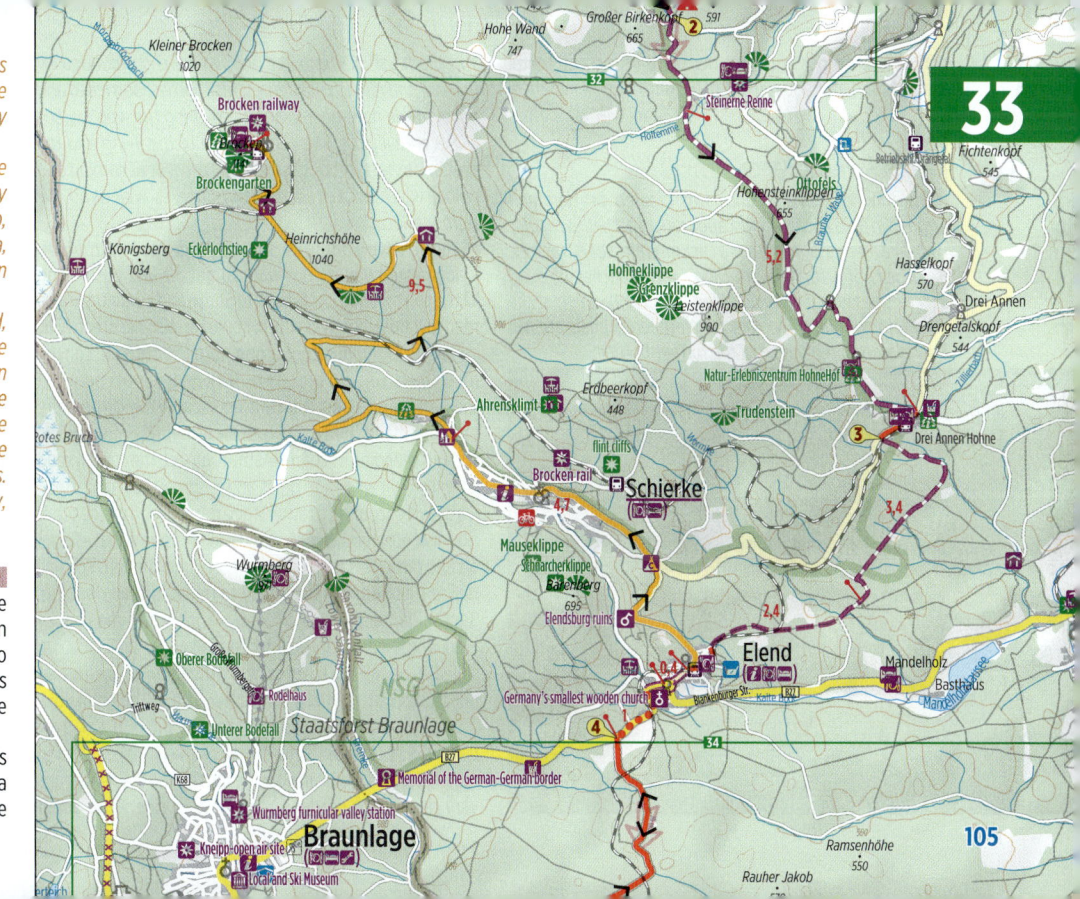

33

GDR border troops and a further piece of meshed metal fence. Afterwards you will reach the Ring of Remembrance.

Border museum
Ring of Remembrance

The Ring of Remembrance was created by Hermann Prigann in 1993 and is a landscape work of art with a circular wall, five metres high and has a circumference of 70 metres. It consists of artfully layered logs and branches of dead spruce trees which were obtained from the thinning of the surrounding forest. The nine concrete fence posts are the only elements remaining of the former border.

Shelter-hut on the Brocken

In the brush of the outer ring, which is surrounded by the wall and ditch, blackberries, raspberries, dog roses and honeysuckle have been planted, covering the wood which will eventually rot. The combination of the living and the dead material symbolises the cyclic process of coming and going, which applies to the landscape as well as to the historical location.

VARIANTE The following route is not recommended with heavy luggage. If you do not want to get off and push along the convoy road, cycle back to Sorge and continue on the road towards Hohegeiß which, however, also has steep hills.

From the **Ring der Erinnerung**, turn left onto the convoy road where you can cycle fairly well on the grass between the perforated slabs. It would be great if the community of Sorge made the convoy road a little better for cyclists without changing its charm. At the moment, the convoy road is overgrown with high grass and is somewhat neglected.

You will encounter a rather steep descent and on the other side another steep ascent, so most likely you will have to get off and push. This happens one more time later on. You will realise that nature is beginning to regain the border strip. Small pine trees have started growing next to the convoy road which were planted after the fall of the Wall. You can still see the tall old trees on the other side of the former border strip. In a few years the difference will be negligible.

Once you have reached the top you will find a narrow trail next to the perforated slabs which makes cycling rather pleasant. You can hear the cars on the B 4 which runs very close to the border on the western side. After about

A view of the Wurmberg over the border barrier installations near Schierke, 1988

2 kilometres, most of which you'll have to push, turn right onto a sign-posted trail towards the highway and Hohegeiß.

Turn left onto the paved cycle trail next to the **B 4** behind the guardrails. After 700 metres you will reach a large turning area. On the right side you will find a memorial stone dedicated to Helmut Kleinert.

Helmut Kleinert

Helmut Kleinert was 24 years old when he was shot on August 1, 1963 by members of the border troops. Together with his pregnant wife Marlit he was attempting to flee. "Due to good tactical behaviour" – according to the Stasi – it was

possible to arrest the woman without further use of firearms. Since Helmut Kleinert allegedly continued to flee, he was targeted. Although his leg was injured, he still attempted to get over the barrier. He was then fatally injured from a hail of more than 60 bullets.

Immediately after the death of Helmut Kleinert, adolescents who were spending their vacation in Hohegeiß erected a simple wooden cross with a wreath of barbed wire and the inscription "To the unknown". When the identity of the victim became known, the plaque carried his name and information about his life. In December of 1963 it was expanded and became a memorial site. Several years later the German Trade Union Federation had a plaque erected in the direct vicinity of the memorial with the inscription: "Live bullets are dangerous. Border police, do not murder people."

Flowers and wreaths are often placed at the memorial. Since there was a watchtower on the eastern side, visitors were bombarded with eastern propaganda via loudspeakers, especially on the weekends, which greatly upset the

Border-tower and fence near the Ring of Remembrance at Sorge

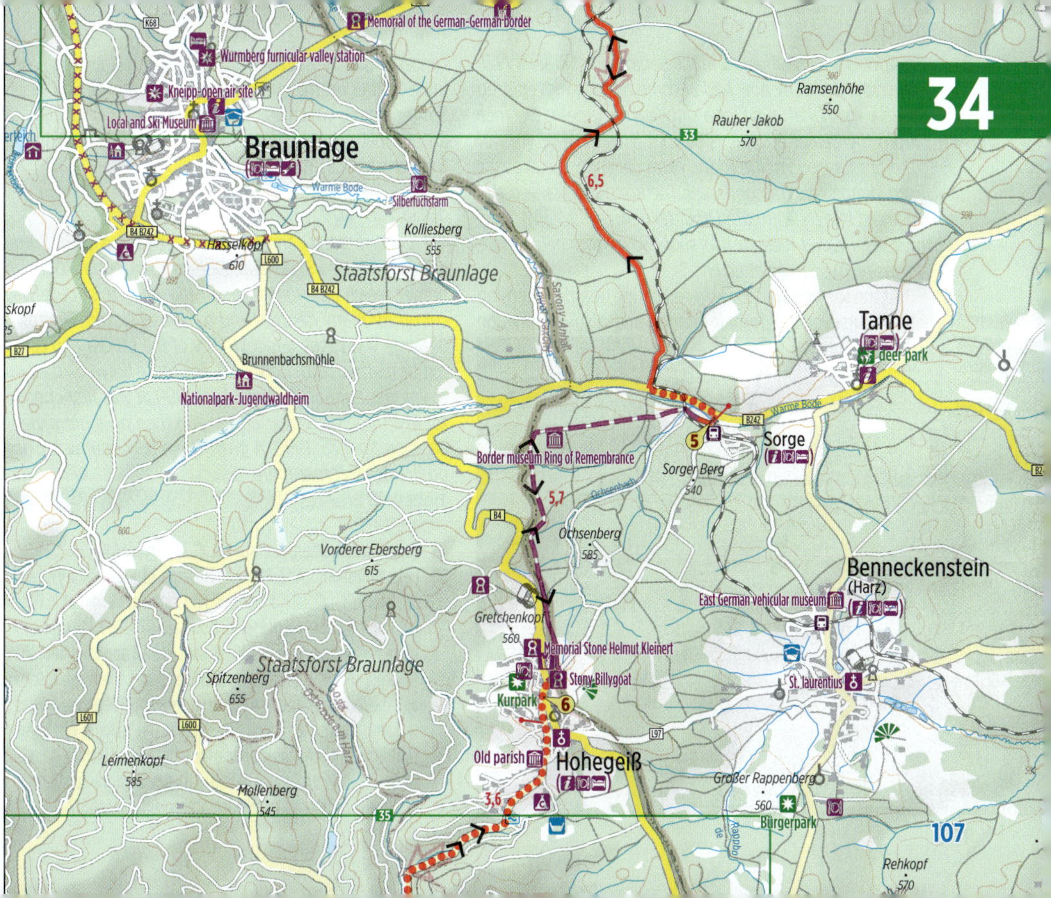

residents and vacationers. In the beginning of August 1971, the cross which by now had become rotten, was replaced with a memorial stone, at a significantly greater distance from the demarcation line, so that it was out of view of the border troops. Due to the extra distance, the acoustic propaganda was discontinued. The inscription carved and painted into the untreated boulder now reads: "On August 1, 1963, Helmut Kleinert was shot 150 m from here before crossing the demarcation line."

At the site you will find an information board concerning the course of the former border and also information concerning local points of interest and restaurants. Continue further on the cycle trail on the **B 4** until you reach **Sorger Straße** which leads to the left. There you will find an information board which describes the situation during Germany's division.

Sorger Straße

It is the shortest connection between the eastern Sorge and the western Hohegeiß. Due to the German-German border which ran right through the Harz, this route was cut off for many decades and remained closed. The town of Sorge was in the direct vicinity of the border and could not be reached from Hohegeiß. The route between the two towns was not opened until April 1990. It was first opened for just three days over Easter and then on a permanent basis on April 28, 1990. A grey, stone billy goat was place on the street corner there.

Hohegeiß (Braunlage)
prefix: 05583

- 🛈 **Tourist-Information**, Kirchstr. 15a, ☎ 241, @ eia445
- 🏛 **Heimatmuseum „Alte Pfarre" (Museum of local history)**, Lange Str. 54, ☎ 389, ☎ 241 ☺ This building is one of the oldest in Hohegeiß and probably originated from around 1600. At that time, there was a chapel here that was built in 1444 and used until 1704. Adjacent to the Priest's house and the chapel, there was a school and the cemetery. The Alte Pfarre was sold in 1830 and served as a residential house for a long time. In 1994 the building was bought by the museum and turned into a museum of local history. Adjacent to the Alten Pfarre you will find a memorial stone for Hermann Grote who composed the Niedersachsenlied. @ snb672

- ⛪ **Barocke Holzkirche (Baroque wooden church)**, Kirchstr.
- 🏊 **Waldschwimmbad**, Bärenbachweg

6 Continue straight ahead from the corner **Sorger Straße/B 4** and turn right into Lange Straße after about 100 metres. Continue straight ahead until you reach the main road where the road to Walkenried and Zorge is signposted. Continue following the signs and soon you will pass the **"Alte Pfarre"** on the right side. Continue along a rather long stretch from Hohegeiß down a steep hill on the paved road until you reach **Zorge**. Continue through **Unterzorge** towards Ellrich.

Ellrich
prefix: 036332

- 🏛 **Heimatmuseum (Museum of local history)**, Hospitalstr. 40, ☎ 260 ☺ tours: upon arrangement, @ lwr244
- ✳ **Stadtmauer mit Ravensturm und Wernaer Tor (City Wall)**. Remains of the city wall with Ravensturm and Wernaer Tor
- 🏊 **Waldbad**, Am Waldbad, ☎ /20431

Remain on **Zorger Straße** in Ellrich, pass a small church and continue towards the museum of local history. At a crossing, follow the sign "Gedenkort ehemaliges KZ – Außenlager Ellrich" (memorial site former concentration camp – Ellrich external camp) and turn right.

The train station is on the right side. The stretch Ellrich-Walkenried, which was interrupted during the division, was the first to be reopened towards the end of 1989. From here trains travel directly to Göttingen, Erfurt and Nordhausen.

7 Turn right after crossing the railroad tracks and follow the signs to the right onto the cobblestoned Pontelstraße to the memorial site with an information board in English,

Former GDR border-troop compound behind Sorge

French and German. A memorial stone from the Belgian city of Leuven also commemorates this dark chapter of history as well as numerous other information boards.

Ellrich-Juliushütte
Concentration Camp

Ellrich-Juliushütte was a subcamp of the Buchenwald concentration camp. More than 40 concentration camps existed in the Südharz and Ellrich-Juliushütte was the second largest with more than 8,000 prisoners. It stretched from the railroad tracks in the north to the Gypsum Mountains in the south. Massive buildings belonging to a former gypsum factory were used to detain the prisoners. Later, when even the capacity became insufficient, the prisoners had to build further barracks made of wood. One of the first buildings to be constructed was the kitchen, the basement of which still exists today. The meagre portions of food handed out to the prisoners was not nearly enough for the extremely hard work in the various construction projects. Indeed, malnutrition was one of the main reasons for the high death rate (50 percent) in the Ellrich-Juliushütte camp.

On the other side of the border you can still see the old gypsum rubble of the former Juliushütte, which was a gypsum factory in the 1920's and later a sawdust factory. During World War II, underground production sites for airplane parts and "V weapons", named by propaganda minister Joseph Goebbel, were built here, as in numerous other locations of the Südharzer Karstlandschaft. The V 1 was an unmanned airplane loaded with explosives and thus were the world's first cruise missile. The largest object of this kind was the nearly 40-kilometre-long tunnel system of the Kohnstein by Niedersachswerfen in which about 35,000 prisoners built the V 1 and V 2. 7,000 prisoners were detained in the Juliushütte, who brought the Niedersachswerfen every day by train, later also by foot. The camp was surrounded by barbed wire and watchtowers. The detainment was catastrophic. Just before their emancipation by the Americans in the spring of 1945, the camp was evacuated by the SS. Many prisoners died.

In the summer of 1945, the course of the demarcation line between the Russian and the British occupation zones was defined. Old border stones served as markers. An illegal route between the two occupation zones ran over the abandoned facilities of the concentration camp. The district of Juliushütte, which was the residence of the

35

The very last house on West German territory at Walkenried, 1988

camp guards in the years 1944/45, turned into a smuggler town for people and goods. With the erection of a permanent border fence in 1952, the GDR put a stop to the illegal border traffic and the active relationship between Ellrich and Juliushütte. The border fence and the ten-metre-wide control strip ran directly over the facilities of the former concentration camp. Over the next few years the rest of the concentration camp was levelled on the GDR side during the securing of the border and turned into the death strip. Passenger transportation was also disrupted and only freight trains were able to travel. During the GDR time, nothing remained of the former concentration camp.

On the western side, fugitives resided in Juliushütte after the war. The district became desolate after a fire in 1955 and was levelled under orders from the government in 1964. The remains of the concentration camp were removed, the rubble cleared away and the ground planted with spruce and larch trees and turned into a park. A border overview site was installed on a hillside above the crematorium. Due to the unique flora, the area is now a nature reserve.

Continue past the memorial stone on the forest trail which is signposted as the **Kaiserweg** and into the forest. After a bend in the trail, you will see a boulder on the western side with an inscription commemorating the concentration camp. Information bards explain the history along the way.

Turn left at the next big crossing towards **Juliushütte** and Walkenried. The route is in relatively good condition but has some challenging gradients. The last part is so steep that you will probably have to get off and push. Once you exit the forest, continue straight ahead on the dirt road which unfortunately is not signposted. From there the road goes downhill.

When you reach the fork in the road, turn right onto the paved road, cross the railroad crossing which is also closed and is only opened for cars upon request. After the railroad tracks keep to the left. At the next crossing turn left, cross the Wieda and continue over the bridge to the road between Wiedigshof and Walkenried. Turn right at the entrance of Walkenried and continue to the centre of town.

Walkenried

prefix: 05525

ZisterzienserMuseum Kloster Walkenried (Cistercian museum cloister Walkenried), Steinweg 4a, ☎ 9599064 ◉ Time travel through the fully restored cloister building from the 13th century which shows the Middle Age and cloister history with interactive exhibitions. Every summer concerts are held in the monastery. @ onl461

Jagdschloss (Hunting lodge). The castle was built by Duke August Wilhelm in the 18th century with rubble from the cloister. It is now private property and is used as a hotel.

Walkenried is known for its vast waters. The community has around 2,500 people and was surrounded by the inner German border in the east and south during the time of the division. Gypsum is also mined here today.

The pond region which surrounds Walkenried goes back to the time of the monks who constructed the Cistercian cloister in the year 1127 (part of the UNESCO World Heritage since 2010). These monks turned the swampy area into a pond region abundant with fish. According to legend, they created 365 different ponds in order to be able to fish from a different one every day. Today, evidence of only 50 can still be found, which have all become part of a bird sanctuary and nature reserve.

From Walkenried to Duderstadt · 33 km

8 In Walkenried pass the cloister church on the right, continue through the cloister gate and turn left towards Neuhof. Cross the railroad tracks at the end of Walkenried. On the right you will find Walkenried train station. From here, trains go directly to Göttingen and Nordhausen. Continue on a smooth road with guardrails on the sides toward Neuhof.

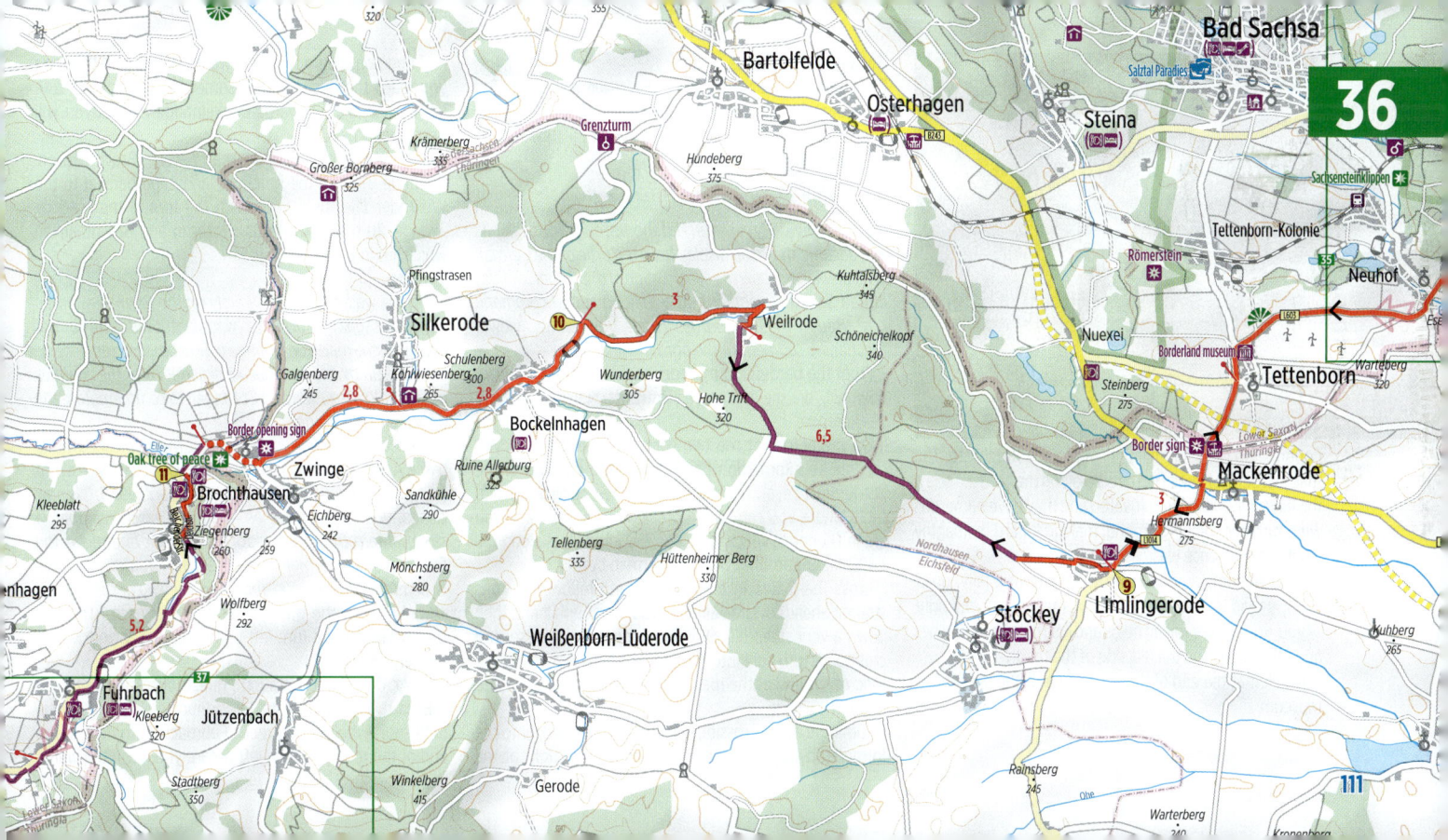

Tettenborn borderland museum

Continue up the slight hill until you reach **Kutzhütte**. The road just before Neuhof led directly along the border. Today, the fields have all been cultivated and they have numerous wind turbines spinning around, making it hard to imagine what this area once was.

From **Neuhof**, continue over the somewhat hilly, quiet country road to Tettenborn for 3 kilometres. Left and right of you, you will see rolling fields and lush meadows. Birches and other trees line the left side of the road.

Turn left at the end of the town towards the borderland museum.

Tettenborn (Bad Sachsa)

🏛 **Grenzlandmuseum Bad Sachsa (Borderland museum by Bad Sachsa)**, Am Kurpark 6, in the village hall, ✆ 0177/5319231 ☺ For groups over 10 people, other opening hours are possible upon arrangement. @ vom661

Borderland museum "Tettenborn"

In the community centre in Tettenborn, numerous exhibits and documents are on display from the time of the German division. Models show the construction of the border facilities in Bad Sachsa. In addition to a fully equipped command post used by the GDR border troops, you can also view a functioning segment of the border signal fence.

From the borderland museum continue straight ahead, downhill, on the main road towards Nordhausen and Mackenrode.

On the border of the two German federal states, you can see an information board about the opening of the border. Just beyond this you will find a wooden bench and table where you can take a break. For the first time you are in Thuringia, which stretches 750 kilometres along the 1,400-kilometre-long German-German border.

Cross the B 243 in **Mackenrode** and follow the signs straight ahead towards Limlingerode, first uphill and then down a very steep hill. **9** In **Limlingerode** at the second crossroads turn right into Mittelreihe. Keep right at the next fork. At the end of the road turn left, then right again and out of the village.

Turn right at the crossing, which is sign-posted, onto the former convoy road towards Weilrode. Turn right at the end and continue downhill towards **Weilrode**. **10** When you reach the bus stop at a somewhat larger road, turn left and continue towards **Bockelnhagen** which you will pass through.

Turn right at the end of the road towards Brochthausen. Continue through the beautiful landscape parallel to the Weilroder Eller until you reach the fork in the road by Zwinge. Turn right towards Herzberg and Brochthausen which lies in Lower Saxony.

Zwinge

Zwinge was in the GDR directly on the German-German border. An "oak tree of peace" was planted along the former border on the road from Zwinge to Brochthausen on December 15, 1999 by the regional administrators of the counties of Eichsfeld, Osterode and Göttingen to commemorate the opening of the border.

At the end of Zwinge you will still see the old meshed metal fence. A brick factory was on the other side of the fence which was in the border area and in operation until 1989. It is now closed. You can also see an original "Peitschenlampe", a street lantern, from the times of the GDR. The bridge over the Eller was on the former German-German border, and there is an information plaque about the opening of the border.

Continue on the quiet, smooth country road towards **Brochthausen** and turn left upon entering town towards the centre.

11 At the "Zur Endstation" **guesthouse** turn left onto **Deichstraße** - the bike trail is signposted - and continue until shortly before you reach Fuhrbach. Turn right at the end of the road and then left before you reach the water.

Continue on the paved road and turn right when you reach the end. Continue along a very nice, car-free, paved road on the edge of the forest along a small stream. Turn right at the end onto the country road. At the moment the cycle trail to Fuhrbach stops two kilometres short. Hopefully it will be completed soon.

The cycle trail to Duderstadt is signposted in Fuhrbach. Continue through **Fuhrbach** until you reach the end of town and the pedestrian and cyclist trail on the left side of the road. It is another 5 kilometres uphill to Duderstadt until "Rothe Warte".

Re-constructed command-centre at the Tettenborn border museum

„Rothe Warte"

"Rothe Warte" is a forester's house and was first mentioned in 1401. In the middle of the 18th century it had a bar license, and in 1854 it became a modern restaurant. After World War II, the British and the Russians had an agreement to straighten the demarcation line. The major part of the forest district including "Rothe Warte" and the district of "Lindenberg" were placed in the Russian occupation zone, causing Duderstadt to lose more than half of the 624-hectare forest as the city allowed wood felling in these districts. Entire caravans entered the forests on September 1, 1945. Everyone took what they were able to transport.

The black woodpecker

Once again, the black woodpecker is at home in this area. Despite its size and loud calls, it is hardly ever seen. It breeds in large areas of old forests and one pair claims at least 250-400 hectare of forest area as their own. The black woodpecker prefers to live from ants and bugs that live in wood. For the construction of their nests they prefer old birches or dead portions of stumps in which a nest is picked. Afterwards the nests are often used by wood pigeons, jackdaws, bats and other small mammals. The wood pigeon in particular depends on the black woodpecker for their nests.

AUSFLUG Turn right behind the "Rote Warte" restaurant towards the Natural Experience Centre at Gut Herbigshagen.

Cycle path towards Duderstadt

Gut Herbigshagen

This manor is home to a famous nature reserve. According to the founder's ideas - the wildlife filmmaker and scientist Heinz Sielmann (1917-2006) - "people of all ages, especially children and adolescents, should find interest in nature through personal experience and should find pleasure in dedicating themselves to the protection and maintenance thereof. Children are the nature activists of tomorrow."

The reserve has many visitors from kindergartens, school classes, associations and is well worth the visit.

From the restaurant, continue downhill on the cycle trail parallel to the road.

INS ZENTRUM If you would like to travel to Duderstadt, continue straight ahead and you will reach the pedestrian zone in the city centre.

Duderstadt
prefix: 05529

- **ℹ️ Tourist-Information**, Marktstr. 66, ☎ 05527/841200, @ ffn718
- **🏛 Heimatmuseum (Museum of local history)**, Bei der Oberkirche 3, ☎ 05527/2539 ⊖ The museum displays exhibits based on the history of the city and the culture of the region. It also shows the excavations of the medieval city wall. @ fnq273
- **⛪ St. Cyriakus**
- **⛪ St. Servatius**, Marktstr. 6
- **⛪ Sulbergswarte**
- **⛪ Westerturm (Tower)**, Auf der Spiegelbrücke 19. Landmark of the town. @ lni235
- **❇️ Historisches Rathaus (Historical City Hall)**, Marktstr. 66. The historical City Hall is one of the oldest and most beautiful in Germany and includes building styles from the 14th to the 18th century. There are various exhibitions on the following topics: Life in the Middle Ages, the plague, trade and economy and the legal system in the Middle Ages. There is a Glockenspiel in the west tower. @ pld283
- **✉️ Freibad (Outdoor pool)**, August-Werner-Allee, ☎ 911175, @ avy473
- **🔵 Hallenbad (Indoor pool)**, Auf der Klappe, ☎ 911174, @ rqi484

Duderstadt has a population of about 23,000 and lies in the county of Göttingen in Lower Saxony near the border to Thuringia. The medieval townscape is characterised by 600 half-timbered houses from different stylistic eras. The Westerturm is the last medieval town gate from Duderstadt's fortifications and is the city's most striking landmark. Due to a structural fault in the roof truss, the tower has a twisted tip. The Catholic Probsteikirche St. Cyriakus with two towers is the city's main church. It was built between 1250 and 1490 in three large stages. It was finally completed in 1854 with the erecting of the second tower on the west wing. The

historical City Hall is also worth visiting. There is a fountain of reunification on the market square.

The origin of the name can be traced back to a funny story: The city was built by three brothers who could not agree on the name. According to legend, the first one said to the second one: "You (Du) give the (der) city (Stadt) a name!" which he then repeated. The third one laughed and then they agreed on the simple name of "Duderstadt".

Church in Duderstadt

Duderstadt was officially mentioned for the first time in 929 and took possession of the monastery of Quedlinburg in 974. In 1237, the city became part of the fiefdom of Landgrave Heinrich Raspe of Thuringia and then it took possession of the Guelfs for about 100 years. Duderstadt was granted city rights around 1250.

In the late Middle Ages, the town developed into a prosperous and important city which lay on the north-south axis of the hanseatic cities in northern Europe ("Nürnberger Straße") to Italy and on an east-west connection from eastern Europe via Leipzig to Cologne and Belgium.

In the middle of the 14th century, the Guelfs gave the city to the archbischop in Mainz which ruled over the city for 450 years. Duderstadt continued to prosper and had a population of about 4,000 around the year 1400 and was thus just as big as Hamburg at that time.

During the 15th century, Duderstadt also suffered from the downfall of the Hanseatic League and the shift in trade routes. The economic situation worsened. Despite this, churches continued to be completed and a further fortification ring was also constructed. The current appearance of the city originated from this time.

The city completely lost its significance during the Thirty Years War (1618-1648) and the Seven Years War (1756-1763) and the residents were haunted by a series of epidemics. In addition, the shifting of the borders of the adjacent states became increasingly disadvantageous for the city: In the 19th century, the border between Hannover and Prussia ran right past Duderstadt, which pushed the city into the outskirts. It was only much later that the city became connected to the

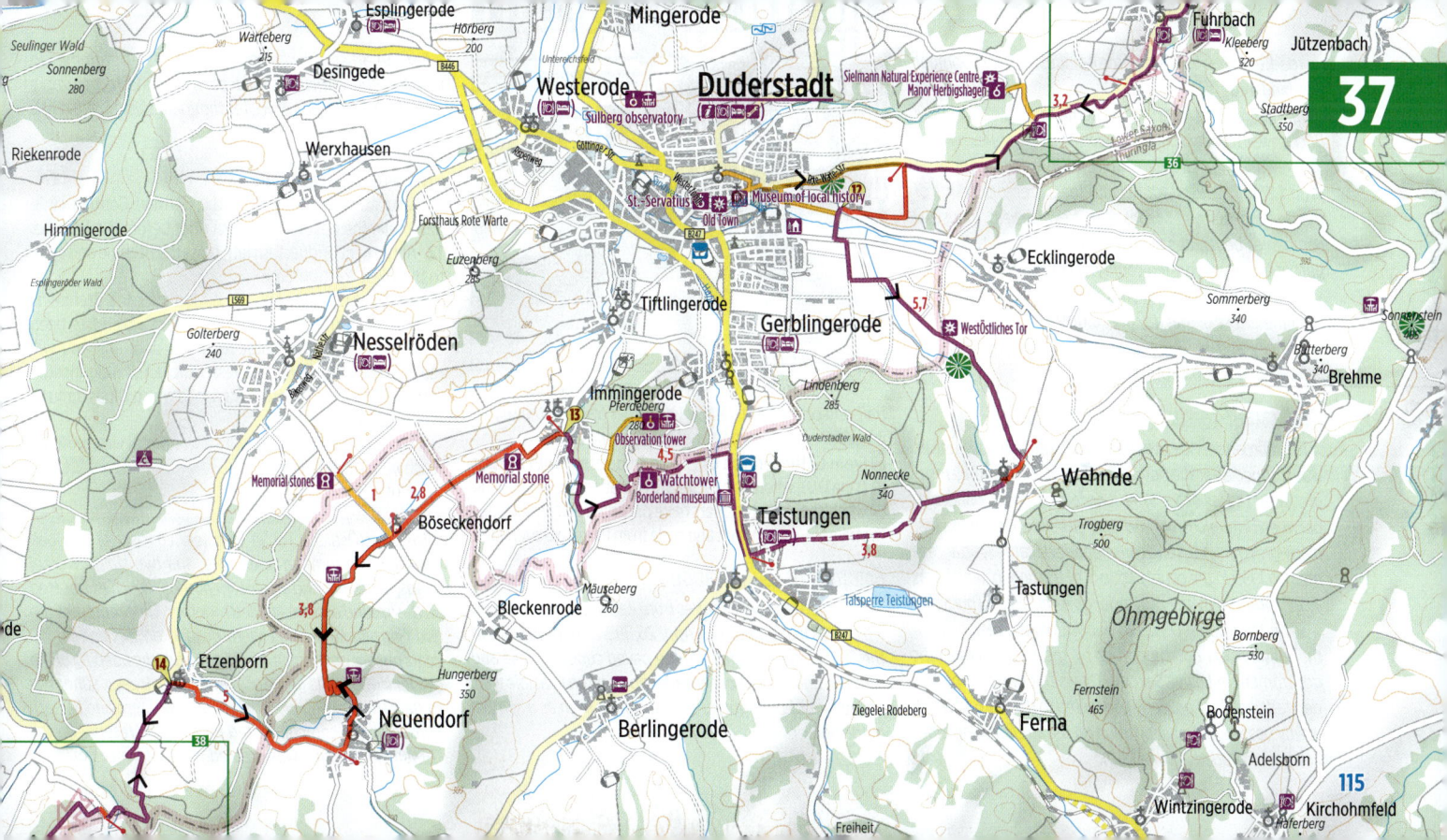

railroad, and thus for a long time its industrial development was hindered.

During the Third Reich, it was home to a subcamp of the Buchenwald concentration camp from 1944 to 1945 in which 755 Jewish Hungarians were subjected to forced labour. After World War II, Duderstadt fell into the extreme outskirts of the German-German border area. Nevertheless, industrial companies began to settle there. In 1973, the city became part of the newly formed county of Göttingen.

The border was opened on November 10, 1989 at 00:35. Over the course of that day over 6,000 GDR citizens arrived in the city and by the end of the year that number had increased to around 700,000.

Duderstadt-Teistungen

The railroad service between Duderstadt and Teistungen was stopped after the border formation and was only resumed after the fall of the Wall. It once provided a connection between Untereichsfeld and Obereichsfeld. One of the first black-green alliances on a communal level came to an agreement in 1999 in the county council of Göttingen, which was also supported by the provincial government in Thurngia.

Since the local SPD was in opposition, the re-joining of the railway was not supported by the social-democratic government in Lower Saxony. This is the reason why Duderstadt is still not properly connected to the railroad which is why passenger transportation on the stretch Leinefelde-Teistungen ended in June 2001.

Fountain of reunification in Duderstadt

Parts of the old railroad have since been turned into a bike trail, and connecting the line with other tracks in the region is no longer on the agenda of most politicians.

TIPP From Göttingen you can reach Duderstadt with the bus (Line 170), whereas bicycles are limited to two per bus and wheelchairs and strollers have priority. You can also take the train to Heiligenstadt and cycle from there to Duderstadt.

Fountain of reunification

The group of bronze figures from Karl-Henning Seemann which was inaugurated on April 26, 1994 stands in front of the St. Servatius church. On the paved cupola a male and a female figure meet but are kept apart by an invisible wall. At the foot of the figures, a moat can be seen as a symbol of the border.

For the artist, the sculpture represents an "attempt to visualise the difficulties that have become recognizable after the reunification as well as the unique historical event".

Von Duderstadt nach Heiligenstadt/Mengelrode   34 km

If you want to continue on the German-German cycle path, take the next left and turn right before the Brehme. **12** At the next bridge, turn left, cross the Brehme and cycle to the West-Eastern Gate.

After the first small hill, the bridge over the Brehme is on the left, turn right, cross the stream which has been developed up to the water retention pool and you will reach a crossing where the WestÖstliche Tor is signposted to the left. Follow the sign-posted road which winds through the landscape.

After a continuous incline with a wonderful view, you will reach your destination.

West-Eastern Tor

The WestÖstliche Tor in Eichsfeld consists of two oak trunks, which form an open gate, and two stainless steel bands, a western and an eastern portion, which are located on the ground and are welded together. They represent the two German states that were divided on this line for 40 years but are once again connected after the opening of the border in 1989. The grove of young beech trees is supposed to stand for thriving growth between Western and Eastern Europe and is complemented by a nature reserve on the "Green Belt" which was created on the former border. It

was opened on June 19, 2002 by Michael Gorbachev and the Federal Environment Minister Jürgen Trittin.

The concrete slabs on the eastern convoy road can still be seen. A paved cycle and pedestrian trail to **Wehnde** has been built parallel to this. Turn right at the end into the village. Turn left before the church and left again at the pump into **Teistunger Weg**. Unfortunately, at the time of writing, this is no sign In Wehnde for the borderland museum.

Where the road makes a right bend into the forest towards Gerblingerode, turn left onto the convoy road which is not in the best of shape. In Teistungen, turn right onto the cycle trail on the B 247, which is signposted. The borderland museum is shortly before the border on the left side.

Borderland museum Eichsfeld

🏛 **Borderland museum Eichsfeld**, Duderstädter Str. 5, ☎ 036071/97112, Opening hours: Tu–Su 10–17:00. The border crossing DuderstadtWorbis was between Teistungen and Duderstadt. The borderland museum was opened at the same location in 1995 and has several hundred square metres of exhibition area. The museum also comprises of the former customs administration building, the customs clearance building, the Mühlenturm and extensive outdoor facilities with the borderland trail. The detention cells in the basement are oppressive, illustrating the consistency with which the border was secured.

Big demonstration for German reunification

At this former German-German border crossing, a symbolic event took place on 21 January 1990, which was directed at the hesitating Modrow government. In order to demonstrate what would happen if the government did not allow free elections and support the German reunification, around 50,000 people armed with suitcases crossed the border into Gerblingerode in Lower Saxony and said that this time they would return but not the next time.

Memorial for the victims

On the 40th anniversary of the construction of the Wall, a memorial was erected in the direct vicinity of the borderland museum which commemorates the victims of the inner German border as well as the victims of communist tyranny. The zig-zag design of the memorial symbolises the division of the land by the former border. The eleven fugitives that died in this region between 1949 and 1989, and the four severely injured who reached the Federal Republic of Germany are mentioned by name.

From the borderland museum continue towards Duderstadt and turn left onto the convoy road, cross the stream and follow the sign-posted road to Immingerode. You will have to get off and push due to the steep hill and the perforated slabs (28 holes). Pass the dog-training facilities, the observation bunker, the car ditches and the observation tower.

Turn right if you would like to take a small tour to the woodland restaurant and the observation tower on the western side of the former border. Here you will find some information boards concerning the history and the flora and fauna.

Entrance-hall of the Eichsfeld borderland museum

From the western observation tower, continue past the woodland restaurant, turn left into the exercise trail and continue straight ahead to Immingerode.

If you would like to skip the visit to the woodland restaurant and observation tower, turn left at the forest. Continue on a nice downhill ride on a paved road and keep to the right. **13** In **Immingerode** keep to the left, turn onto **Bismarckstraße** and follow the signs to **Böseckendorf**. When the road turns into the fields, turn right. Turn left at the next corner and you will see the stones on the former German-German border which remind us of some local history that took place in 1961

Mass escape from Böseckendorf

Böseckendorf lies two kilometres southwest of Immingerode and was surrounded on three sides by the border strip. On October 2, 1961, the village made headlines when one fourth of the population successfully fled over the mined border. 16 families with 16 men, 14 women and 23 children had made the decision and prepared themselves after they had heard that the village was to be evacuated. In another escape, on the night of 22 February 1963, a further 13 people from Böseckendorf managed to successfully cross the border to Immingerode, because the frozen ground had made the landmines less dangerous. The priest belonging to the fugitive camp Friedland by Göttingen – Monsignore Scheperjans – helped the fugitives to form a community. With the support of the Federal government and Lower Saxony, the town of Neuböseckendorf was developed by Nörtenhardenberg. On September 8, 1965, the foundation stone for the small church was set.

At the beginning of Böseckendorf you will see a huge linden tree with the following text from NABU: "This summer linden tree was planted right after the Thirty-Year War, approximately 350 years ago. The tree is a living symbol of a new beginning after the murderous war, under which Eichsfeld especially suffered. The centre of the tree is very damaged, but a linden tree can survive many years despite such damage."

AUSFLUG Turn right in Böseckendorf towards Nesselröden, cross the convoy road and you will see a group of memorial stones on the left.

Border memorial

The sculpture was dedicated to commemorate the division on June 26, 1991 and interpreted as follows by the artist and sculptor Roger Bischoff, a German-American who resided for some time in Nesselröden: "The two leaning stones represent people who want to be together, as indeed the people of Nesselröden and Böseckendorf once were. The triangular stone between them, with a base that reaches deep into the earth, is buried, and symbolises how the prejudices of the people in the world should also be buried. The stone is there to remind us that many people lost their lives in front of the border fence, behind it and in the death strip. The stones are supposed to be a reminder that such a division of the German people should never happen again."

Back in Böseckendorf, turn right towards Neuendorf and continue up a long hill. Cross the convoy road and continue downhill to **Neuendorf**. Continue through the village and past the church.

Keep to the right at the end of the village and continue downhill towards **Etzenborn**. You will recognise that you are on the border again by the convoy road with the perforated slabs. **14** At the end of Etzenborn, turn left before the little bridge into the paved cycle trail which is signposted to Weißenborn. After a hill, continue downhill on a beautiful road through a very thick forest.

Once you reach the street, turn right towards Weißenborn and then left again a few metres behind the bend onto a paved trail which is signposted as the cycle trail to Weißenborn. Here you have to overcome a small hill. Turn right at

the end of the paved road, continue through **Weißenborn** to the main road and turn left towards **Siemerode**. At the end of town, a bus turning point serves as a reminder of past times. After Siemerode, continue uphill. Directly after the sign "Landkreis Eichsfeld", a memorial stone commemorates the opening of the border Siemerode-Weißenborn on 20 January 1990.

Continue straight ahead in Siemerode and left on the main road towards Heiligenstadt. **15** Turn right shortly before the bridge over the Beber River onto the paved cycle trail downhill towards Mengelrode.

Mengelrode

AUSFLUG In the centre of Mengelrode, turn left towards Heiligenstadt country road. Cross under the A 38, pass the brick factory and turn right at the next crossing. Keep to the right at the railroad tracks and you will reach the train station of Heilbad Heiligenstadt where direct trains depart to Göttingen, Gotha and Erfurt.

Heilbad Heiligenstadt
prefix: 03606

ℹ **Tourist-Information**, Marktpl. 15, ℓ 677903, ℓ 677142, @ qin144

🏛 **Eichsfelder Heimatmuseum (Eichsfelder Museum of Local History)**, Kollegieng. 10, ℓ 677480 ⊜ The museum provides information concerning the history of Eichsfeld, the history of the city, shows works of art, plus furniture and paintings and there is also a Riemenschneider exhibition commemorating the most famous son of the city: Tilman Riemenschneider (1460-1531) was a famous sculptor of the late Gothic and Renaissance. @ olq734

🏛 **Literaturmuseum Theodor Storm (Literature Museum)**, Am Berge 2, ℓ 613794 ⊜, @ pcq576

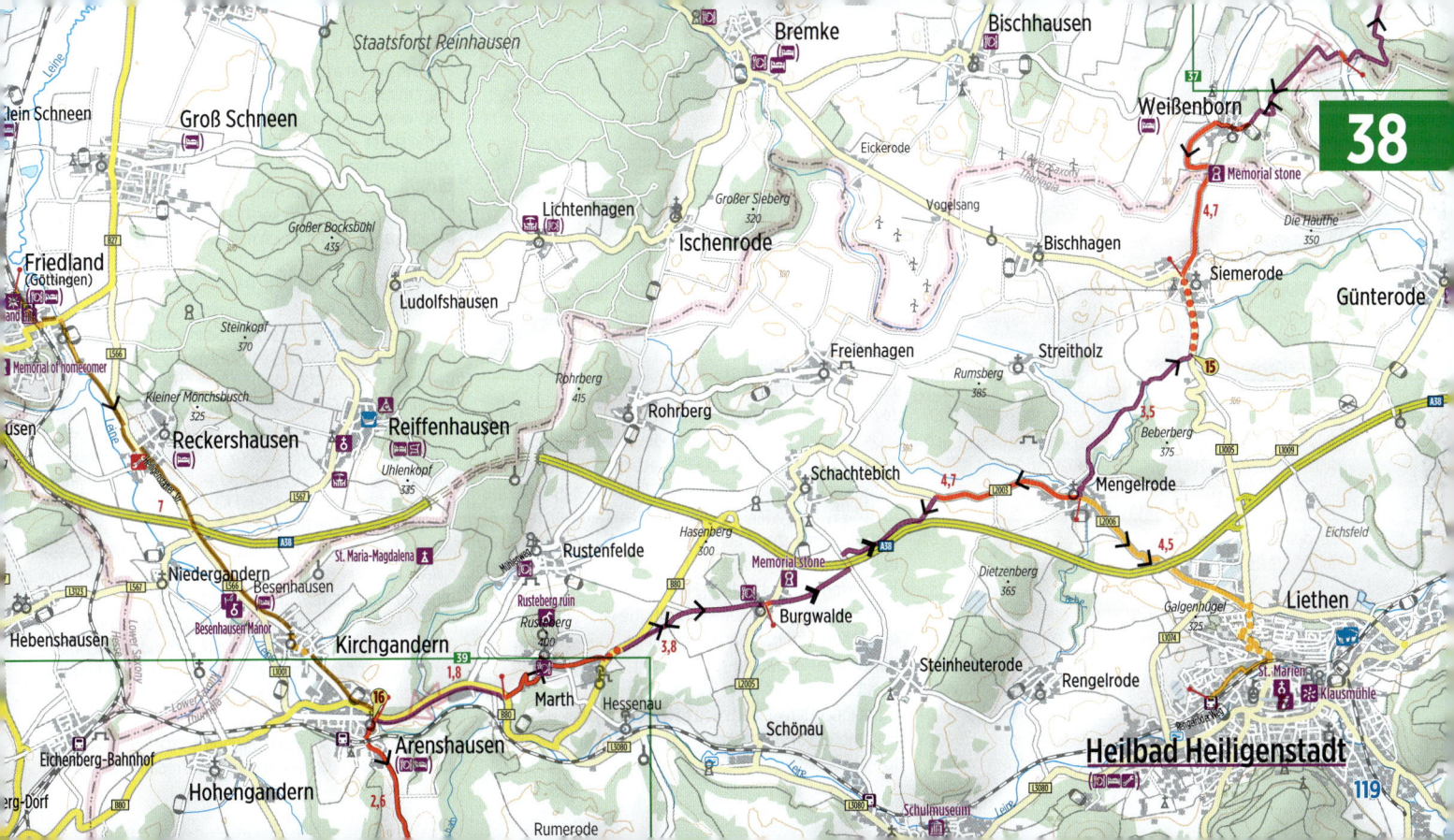

Staatsforst Reinhausen

38

Bremke

Bischhausen

Weißenborn

37

Memorial stone

4,7

Die Häuthe
350

Siemerode

Günterode

Eickerode

Vogelsang

Bischhagen

Kein Schneen

Groß Schneen

Friedland
(Göttingen)

Memorial of homecomer

Lichtenhagen

Großer Bocksbühl
435

Großer Sieberg
320

Ischenrode

Freienhagen

Rumsberg
385

Streitholz

Beberberg
375

3,5

15

Kleiner Mönchsbusch
325

Steinkopf
370

Reckershausen

Reiffenhausen

Uhlenkopf
335

Ludolfshausen

Rohrberg
415

Rohrberg

Rumsberg
385

Schachtebich

4,7

L2003

Mengelrode

L1006

4,5

Eichsfeld

L1005

L1009

A38

7

Niedergandern

Besenhausen

St. Maria-Magdalena

Besenhausen Manor

Rustenfelde

Hasenberg
300

Memorial stone

Burgwalde

Dietzenberg
365

Galgenhügel
325

Liethen

St. Marien

Klausmühle

Hebenshausen

Lower Saxony

Kirchgandern

39

1,8

Rusteberg ruin

Rusteberg
400

3,8

A38

Steinheuterode

Rengelrode

16

Marth

Hessenau

Schönau

Eichenberg-Bahnhof

Hohengandern

2,6

Arenshausen

Rumerode

Schulmuseum

Heilbad Heiligenstadt

119

Vital-Park, In der Leineaue 1, ☎ 66390. Here you will find the Eichsfeld thermal spa, the indoor pool and also a bowling alley. @ fkc344

The city was first mentioned in 973. The royal court with the Martin Church and the village "Heiligenstadt" were transferred to the archbischopric Mainz around 1000. Apart from Erfurt, the town became an important base of the Mainz churches and territorial politics in mid Germany. The granting of city rights and the city seal took place in 1227 by Archbishop Siefried II. Afterwards the city was fortified. It was very damaged by a fire in 1333 and haunted by the plague in 1350.

Tilman Riemenschneider was born here around 1460, Thomas Müntzer was in Heiligenstadt in 1525 which was voted capital of Eichsfeld in 1540. The counter-reformation began in 1575. The Jesuits came to Heiligenstadt which was devastated several times by passing troops during the Thirty-Year War (1618-1648). The first newspaper was published in 1722 and in 1739 the city was devastated by a second large fire. In 1773 the Jesuits left Heiligenstadt and in 1802 the city was transferred to Prussia.

Heiligenstadt was occupied by Napoleon from 1806-1813. In 1838 Jakob and Wilhelm Grimm prepared the final version of their "German Dictionary". From 1856-1864 Theodor Storm was active here as district judge and in 1856 enthused about Eichsfeld: "I never thought that I could be so inwardly touched by the enchanting beauty of a place on earth." The first Kneipp bath with spa facilities was built here in 1929 and in 1932 the Eichsfelder Museum of Local History was opened.

The city survived World War II without any significant damage. Eichsfeld was divided after 1945. In 1973, Heiligenstadt turned 1,000 years old and became the county seat of Eichsfeld in 1994 after the end of the GDR. The 1,100-year anniversary of the official first mention of Eichsfeld was in 1997.

From the centre in Heiligenstadt continue north into the direction of the road A 38, then turn left into Mengelrode, pass under the motorway and then in **Mengelrode**, turn left into the direction of Freienhagen.

VARIANTE You can also reach Arenshausen by taking the Leine-Heide bike path.

From Heiligenstadt/Mengelrode to Bad Sooden-Allendorf   32 km

On the main route in **Mengelrode**, continue through the town and after the exit, take the second road left, which is slightly uphill, towards Burgwalde. Continue parallel to the motorway for a while and pass a linden tree with a bench and memorial stone commemorating Napoleons defeat in the battle of the nations of Leipzig: "In memory of the 100-year memorial festival, March 10, 1913."

Follow the street until you reach the end and then turn left. Ignore the trail on the left. Once you have reached **Burgwalde**, follow the road straight ahead to Marth for about 2 kilometres.

The lonely street leads you to the top of a hill. Reach the new motorway access road and continue straight ahead to Marth.

Marth lies on a small hill. Continue straight ahead at the first crossing, and from there on continue downhill to the B 80 where you turn right towards Arenshausen. Parallel to the street – signposted EV 13 – a cycle trail runs on the southern side along the Leine.

AUSFLUG Once you have reached Arenshausen, continue over Kirchgandern and Reckershausen to the former fugitive camp of Friedland which now serves as a museum.

Friedland Refugee Transit Camp

Friedland became known as being home to the Refugee Transit Camp. The district of Klein Schneen was first officially mentioned in 1036. It was constructed by the British occupying powers in 1945 and initially received fugitives from the former East German areas and from Sudetenland. The location was predetermined since the three occupation zones met here (Lower Saxony: British, Hesse: American and Thuringia: Soviet). Friedland was also on the railroad stretch between Hannover and Kassel.

In the years after World War II, returning war prisoners arrived here, a period that lasted until 1955 with the so-called "return of the ten-thousand". Afterwards, the camp received fugitives from the GDR. A total of 3.6 million have people passed through the camp since its construction. In 1956 about 3,000 refugees came from Hungary and in the 1970s many of Pinochet's political opponents from Chile made their way here. Later "boat people" from Vietnam also passed through.

A station, built in 1890, through which well over four million refugees, displaced persons and repatriates reached

the camp, was renovated and a permanent exhibition added - supplemented by a theme trail - showing the eventful history of the camp.

Arenshausen

16 In Arenshausen turn left right after the Leine bridge towards **Gerbershausen**.

There is a memorial stone in front of St. Matthäus Church: "Unforgotten - the soldiers 1914-1918. Lord, grant them eternal peace." The names of the fallen soldiers follow. "Erected in gratitude by the community on November 12, 1922."

The fact that Arenshausen actually belonged to Hessen and was allocated to the Soviet occupational zone in the Wanfried

Agreement after 1945 as well as the reunification is hardly mentioned.

Cross under the train tracks and you will reach the train station.

AUSSTIEG From the Arenhausen train station, you can travel directly to Kassel-Wilhelmshöhe and Eichenberg.

Arenshausen–Eichenberg

The stretch Halle-Kassel was disrupted during the division. The section Arenshausen-Eichenberg was the first stretch to be brought into operation again on May 26, 1990.

Keep to the left after the railroad tracks and continue on the narrow, paved road uphill towards Gerbershausen. After leaving Oberstein, turn right onto the agricultural forest trail which is sign-posted as the Werra/Leine connection cycle trail.

Cross the street to Bad Sooden-Allendorf and continue straight ahead on the signposted "Deutschen Märchenstraße" to Bornhagen.

Bornhagen
prefix: 036081

i **Gemeinde Bornhagen**, Am Kulturzentrum 11, ☎ 61311, @ hgo821

⚥ **Burgruine Hanstein (Hanstein castle ruins)**, ☎ 67856 ⁷ᵈ According to records, the castle

View from Hesse to Hanstein Castle, 1985/86

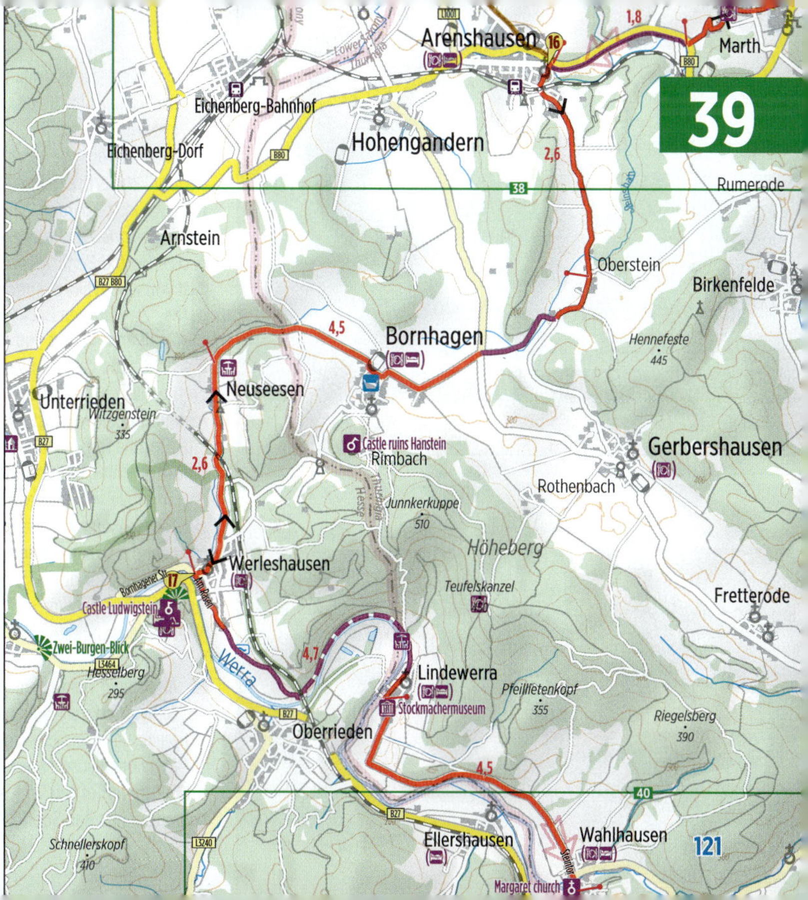

originated in the 9th century. It was officially mentioned in 1070 for the first time. The towers and the renovated great hall are well maintained. @ Ich337

In Bornhagen, the director of the "Centre for Political Beauty", the artist Philipp Ruch, rented a house and set up 24 steles in the garden, a nod to the Holocaust Memorial in Berlin designed by Peter Eisenman, because his neighbour had called the Berlin Memorial a "Memorial of Shame".

TIPP If you would like to spend the night here, you can stay in the "Zweiburgen Blick" Hotel Garni. It is recommended to call first so that you don't have to slog your way up the hill to the castle in vain. Since there is no restaurant on the hill, you can enjoy a meal in the Klausenhof, an old restaurant below Hanstein (✆ 036081/61422).

In Bornhagen, continue on **Friedensstraße**, turn right before reaching Klausenhof onto the **Bauernweg** and after a short while you will reach Neuseesen.

In **Neuseesen** continue into the village before turning turn left over the stream. At the end of town, you will be warned to watch out for ducks! Cross the train tracks through the tunnel and you will reach Werleshausen.

Werleshausen (Witzenhausen)
prefix: 05542

🏰 **Jugendburg Ludwigstein (Castle Ludwigstein)**, ✆ 501710. The 600-year-old castle was acquired in 1920 and made into a youth centre. On the mountain you will find a hotel. There is no charge for looking around the mountain. @ iqc282

17 Turn left at the Werra and continue on the northern shore towards Bad Sooden-Allendorf.

The salty Werra

The Werra originates in Thuringia at the seam between the Thuringian forest and the Thuringian Slate Mountains. It flows through Hesse to Lower Saxony where it combines with the Fulda to form the Weser. Since the middle of the 19th century, salty waste water has been directed into the Werra from the industrial mining of potassium salt in the region.

Since the potassium miners were allowed to pump their salt loads into the river unregulated, the Werra was extremely contaminated with sodium chloride (salt) during the GDR rule. Afterwards, due to some improvements over the past years, the current limit of 2,500 milligrams per litre is at least complied with. However, this figure originates from 1942 and was at that time defined as an "exception due to the war". The Werra is therefore still considered one of the most polluted rivers in Europe.

As the current limit was only valid until 2012, the European water rights guidelines should also have been implemented for the Werra.

Another problem is the diffuse chloride entries from discharged production waste waters, the cause of which has only been known since 1994. They cause the Werra to already exceed the limit when the water is low – even without introduction of the brine. That is why only sculpin live in the Werra, a smaller fish from the family of the Cottidae, which normally lives in the northern (salty) Pacific Ocean.

If the waste water was pumped into the Main, there would be problems with the EU since the Main flows into the Rhine. There, the International Commission for the Protection of

Hanstein castle (1984/2006)

the Rhine prohibits the introduction of brine since the limit in European rivers is 100 milligrams per litre. This figure is what water experts consider to be acceptable for the Werra so that the river is able to regenerate itself.

In 2016, the Weser Ministerial Conference agreed in its "Master Plan Salt Reduction" to reduce salt concentrations by half so that negative effects on flora and fauna can be avoided from 2027 onwards at the latest.

The potash mining not only endangers the water quality of the Werra, however. It is today mainly used as a fertiliser.

Cross the railroad tracks by Oberrieden and continue to **Lindewerra**. Turn left there, as signposted, and then right again. On the shore of the Werra you will reach **Wahlhausen**. Cross the Walse River and continue towards Bad Sooden-Allendorf.

AUSFLUG After Wahlhausen, turn left on the former convoy road with the 38 perforated slabs to the Thuringian-Hessian border museum in Schifflersgrund. This trail is only really suitable for pedestrians.

Shortly afterwards you will see an artistic object advertising "Art on the cycle trail". A few metres further, on the corner where the street also continues to the borderland museum, you will find a memorial stone under the big linden tree "Unity, freedom, fatherland". Shortly before you reach the borderland museum you will find a memorial "For the victims of the separation of Germany" and a wooden cross which commemorates Heinz Josef Große, who was shot in an attempt to flee in 1982.

Heinz Josef Große

While Heinz Josef Große was working on the convoy road, he noticed that the border soldiers often wandered off, leaving home alone in the border section. Since he believed he was not being observed, he drove over the car ditch with his digger to the border fence, lifted the bucket, climbed up and jumped over the fence from the bucket. His daring escape was then discovered and he was shot in the safety section by two border soldiers shortly before reaching the border to Sickenberg.

According to the report from the border police, "the attempt to cross the border in the direction GDR/FRG was prevented by the use of firearms and the person involved was recovered with fatal injuries". The District Court Mühlhausen (Thuringia) sentenced the two border soldiers who shot Heinz Josef Große to a youth and prison sentence of one year and three months on November 20, 1996.

Borderland museum Schifflersgrund

The Schifflergrund borderland museum has been open since 1991 in Bad Sooden-Allendorf. In the outer area you will find several hundred metres of border facilities, a 1,500-metre-long metal meshed fence and the original observation tower erected in 1982. There are two Soviet combat helicopters and several vehicles to be seen on the museum grounds. You can view an exhibition in numerous rooms which focus on the separation of the local region. There is also a model of the building in which the American and Soviet occupational officers negotiated the Wanfried

Wahlhausen (1984/2006)

Asbach (1984/2006)

Agreement in 1945 and one of few existing copies of the agreement. In front of the grounds of the museum you will find a brick memorial dedicated to German unity "separated – united".

After visiting the borderland museum, turn right onto the street and turn right again at the next possibility. Before entering the village, turn right again onto a bicycle trail. Continue straight ahead on the paved road until you reach the gate, then turn left and you will once again reach the linden tree.

18 Once you have reached the main route again, cross the street soon after the street art and take a right towards Werra. You will reach Allendorf along the river. Cross a side river of the Werra, continue under the bridge, a stretch on a dirt road, pass the weir plant and reach a market place with a fountain, the pool of which was in the Saline Soden until the year 1573.

Bad Sooden-Allendorf

prefix: 05652

- **Tourist-Information (Tourist information)**, Landgraf-Philipp-Pl. 1-2, ✆ 95870, @ isq726
- **Salzmuseum im Söder Tor (Salt museum in Söder Tor)**, Rosenstr. 1-3, ✆ 958716 ☺ The museum provides information about salt springs, salt procurement, transportation of salt and the history of the spa. @ ltb818
- **Grenzmuseum Schifflersgrund**, Pl. der Wiedervereinigung 1, Asbach-Sickenberg, ✆ 036087/98409 ⓝ Es sind Teile eines Grenzzauns und ein Beobachtungsturm erhalten, außerdem werden Hubschrauber und Fahrzeuge gezeigt. Die Ausstellung widmet sich hauptsächlich erfolgreichen und gescheiterten Fluchtversuchen. @ cov642

- **Luditzer Heimatmuseum (Luditzer Museum of local history)**, Brunnenpl. 2, ✆ 95870. Museum dedicated to the Bohemian city of Luditze, established in 1961. Various photographs are exhibited, an Egerland farmhouse room, traditional clothing, porcelain etc., information about the former home of many World War II fugitives. @ iur321
- **St. Crucis (Church of St. Crucis)**, Kirchpl. The Feldsteinkirche has been around since the beginning of the 13th century and the mighty tower was added in the 15th century.
- **Rathof.** The Rathof, built of stone, is considered the oldest building in the city next to the Church of St. Crucis. It lies directly on the city wall and was used as a town hall until about 1500.
- **WerratalTherme (Werratal spa)**, Am Gradierwerk 2a, ✆ 958780 ⓝ Bad Sooden-Allendorf is one of the best German salt water spas. @ ayg753

Bad Sooden-Allendorf lies in the Werra-Meißner district in Hesse and has a population of about 9,500. In the direct vicinity of the town you will find the Hohe Meißner and the border to Thuringia. The city also lies close to the geographic centre of Germany.

The town was first officially mentioned between 776 and 779 when Charlemange awarded the Fulda Abbey the tribute and toll of the Westera settlement and the salt springs, market, salt pans and salt workers.

For about 1,000 years, until the end of the 19th century, salt was mined from brine originating in the reservoirs below the city in so-called evaporation houses.

During the Thirty-Year War, the city completely burned down in an attack by the Count Isolani in the year 1637. Only the Rathof built of stone and the Church of St. Crucis

survived the fire without damage and are still the oldest buildings of the city.

With the decline in salt production due to the Prussians lifting the salt monopoly is 1866 - the infrastructure of the city slowly changed and became a resort area.

From Bad Sooden-Allendorf to Eschwege   22 km

TIPP To the east of the Werra lies the district of Allendorf and to the west of the river you will find Bad Sooden. On the shores of the Werra, on the bridge, over which the Bahnhofstraße runs, you will find many old historical alleys with numerous timbered houses and also a selection of accommodation and restaurants.

Continue straight ahead on the scenic **Hauptstraße** until you reach the Werra. Turn left before the bridge onto the Werratal cycle trail. Continue straight ahead on the sign-posted road, pass the public pool until you reach the end of Bad Sooden-Allendorf. Follow the signs and turn right onto the separate cycle trail which leads along the shores of the Werra until you reach **Albungen**.

TIPP The wooden posts with the bicycle symbols are nice to look at. In the background you will see the forest-covered hills and the Castel Rothestein.

On the smooth, flat Werratal cycle trail you will come to Albungen via Kleinvach. The cycle trail winds through the valley parallel to the Werra.

You are surrounded by rolling hills. Continue through **Kleinvach**. **19** In Albungen, cycle over the bridge on the western side of the Werra. Continue straight ahead, follow the sign-posted street to the left and cycle between Werra and the railroad tracks, later parallel to the tracks, on the paved road towards Eschwege. Cross under the B 249 and over the dams in **Niederhone** by continuing to the left over the bridge.

Continue straight ahead until you reach **Jestädter Straße** and turn left. Cross over the B 249, later over the Werra and continue straight ahead until you reach **Jestädt**. Continue through the village on the main road and at the end, turn right onto the cycle trail to Grebendorf. You will pass Lake Meinhard with its swimming area shortly before you continue over a small bridge to the other side of the stream. Turn left here and cross the former railway line. **20** At the end of **Grebendorf**, turn right.

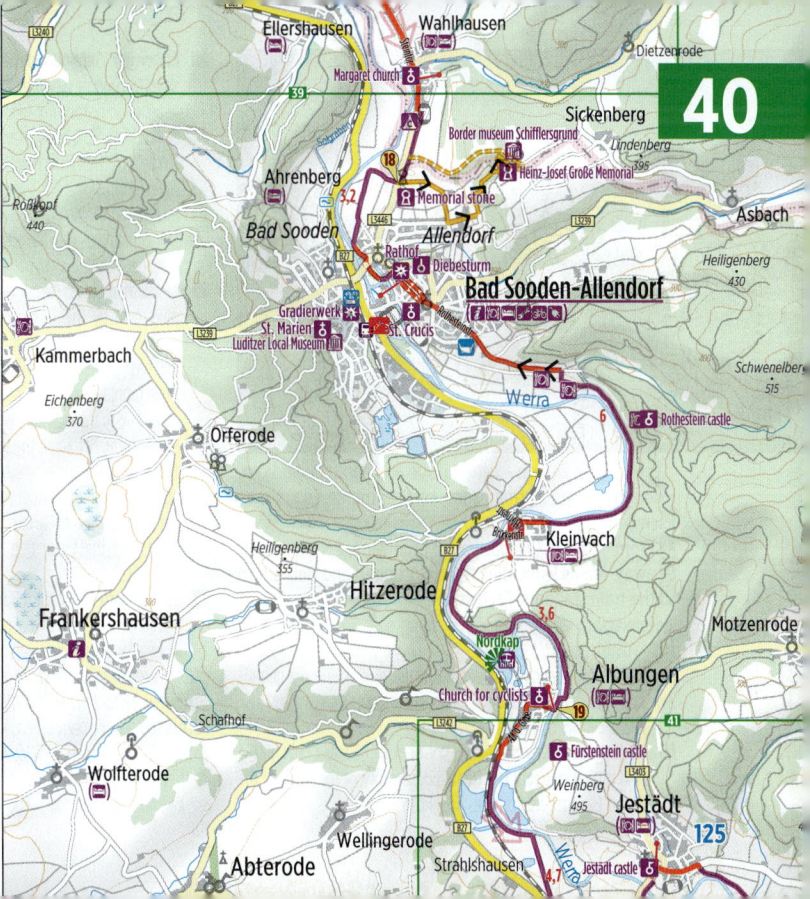

40

Eschwege on the River Werra

Cross the B 249 on a cycle bridge and continue straight, through the pedestrian zone to the market square in Eschwege.

From here a road leads you to Eschwege, 2.5 kilometres away. Trains leave directly to Göttingen and Bebra fom the train station in Eschwege.

Eschwege
prefix: 05651

🛈 **Tourist-Information Eschwege**, Hospitalpl. 16, ☎ 331985, @ qem413

⛴ **Ausflugsschiff „Werranixe" (Passenger shipping)**, Am Werratalsee, ☎ 338032, @ qgp783

🏛 **Stadtmuseum (City museum)**, Vor dem Berge 14a, ☎ 304281 ☺ Find out more about the tumultuous history of the town of the Werra-Meißner district here. @ hdd185

🏛 **Eschweger Zinnfigurenkabinett**, Hospitalstr. 7, ☎ 331985 ☺ The small version of world history can be seen here as well as 5,000 years of tin history. @ rqd364

⛪ **Marktkirche St. Dionys (Market church St. Dionys)**, Bei der Marktkirche 5 ♿ Hall church with three naves from the year 1466 with royal tomb.

⛪ **Neustädter Kirche St. Katharina**, Neustadt. The stylish late-Gothic hall church was completed in 1520. The stone pulpit from 1509 is considered unique.

⛪ **Landgrafenschloss (Landgrave Castle)**, Schlosspl. The castle, originally built by the Thuringian Landgrave Balthasar in 1386, was converted into a Renaissance castle in the 16th and 17th centuries and has served as the seat of district administration since 1821. Frau Holle fountain can be found in the courtyard, which was designed according to the fairy tale written by the Brothers Grimm.

⛪ **Nikolaiturm**, Nikolaipl. The tower from 1455 originally belonged to the Godehardi Church, which was demolished more than 400 years ago. An all-round corridor provides a wonderful view.

✿ **Botanischer Garten**, Gartenstr. 9, ☎ 9527055. Park with some exotic plants like the ginko tree or the primeval world sequoia tree. @ ywt122

✿ **Sophiengarten**, Vor dem Berge, ☎ 70331. The beautifully laid out Bürgergarten is an oasis of peace in the middle of the old town and open all year round.

Eschwege was first mentioned in a document from Emperor Otto II in 974 (973-983). However, "eskinivvach" refers to the existence of a much older Germanic settlement from about the year 500 A.D. The first beginnings of the settlement were around the Cyriacus mountain with the so-called "Karlsturm", the only remnants of the former women's organization which existed from about 1000 to 1527. The settlement stretched down to the river which was the best location to cross the Talaue.

The Allstädter of Market Church is the eastern border of the large market place and was dedicated to the holy Dionysis. Excavations in 1991/92 showed that the origin of the church goes back to the early Middle Ages. The oldest part and remainder of the former church is the church tower from the 13th century. The current church was added to in stages in the 15th and early 16th century. Extensively damaged in 1637, the reconstruction took nearly half a century. The windows in the chancel originate from the turn of the 19th to the 20th century.

Eschwege has two women to thank for the further development of the settlement to a market (around 1188) and city (before 1236). With the first official mentioning, Emperor Otto II granted the settlement to his wife Theophanu from Byzantium as a "retirement plan" and, after his death, his daughter Sophia founded the women's sanctuary on the mountain named after the Holy Cyriacus around the year 1000.

Eschwege's early economic success was based on cloth and leather products in the early modern ages and later became an important trade location in Lower Hesse.

In the Thirty Years War, during which Eschwege was almost continuously occupied, the city was pillaged during Easter of 1637 by the empiric Croatians and much of the city was burnt. Thriftiness, durability and diligence displayed by the residents at that time led to the town being almost entirely rebuilt within just one generation. More than 1,000 timbered

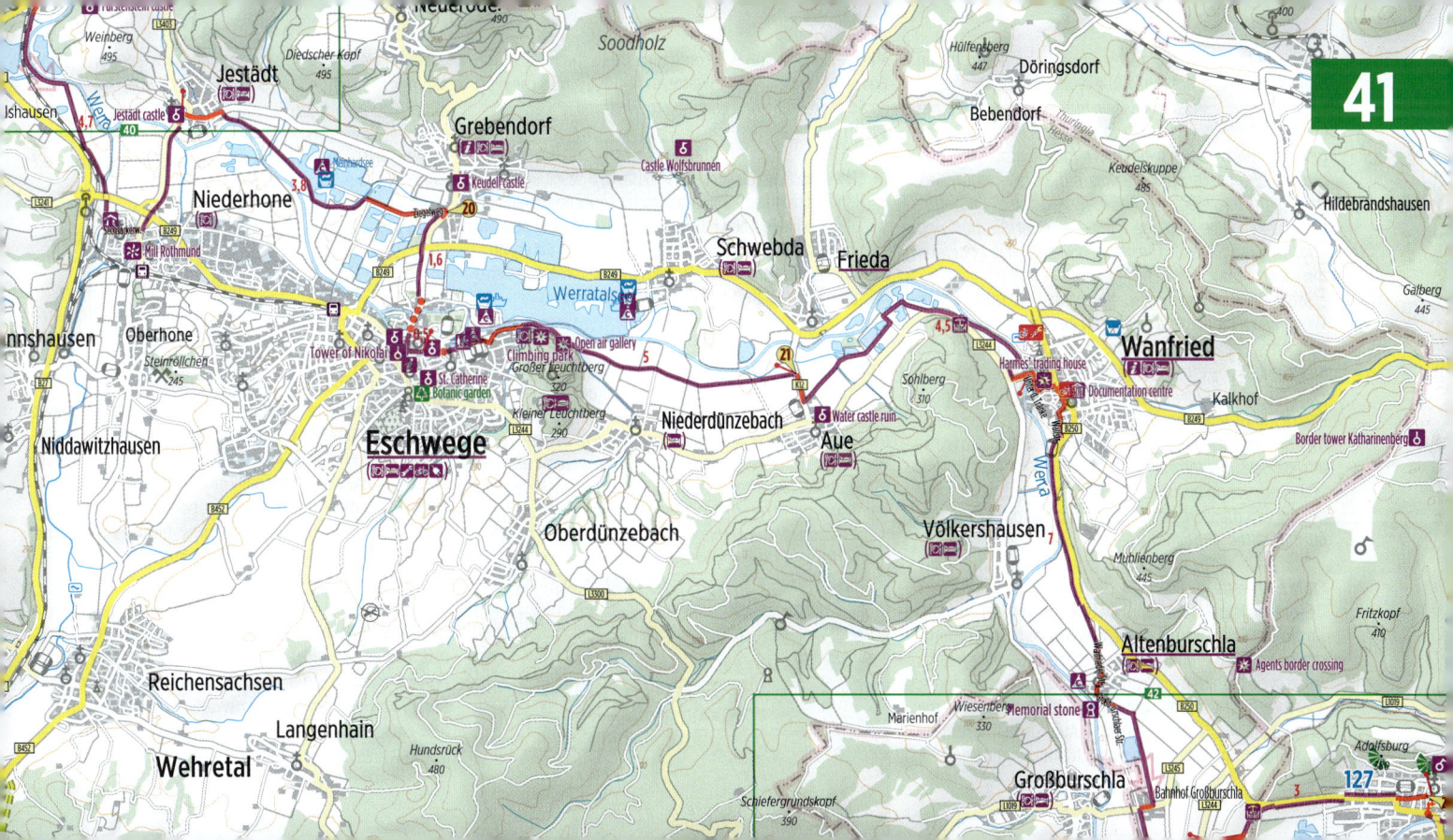

41

houses in the old town, nearly all of which are from the time after the fire, are the visible proof of their hard work.

Today, the city still specialises in the production of leather and thus Eschwege is proud to be called the "city of the tanneries". It was also well-known for the processing and refining of tobacco which thrived in the Werra landscape. Despite the decrease in small businesses, the city was able to expand far beyond the Middle Age fortification ring prior to World War I. The railroad (1875) also benefited the town greatly.

Around 1930, it had a population of about 12,000. Prior to World War II there was a significant increase in the population. After 1945, a large number of refugees and expellees had a revitalising effect on the city. After the reformation of 1973, the population increased to about 24,000. After the end of the GDR, Eschwege moved from the "zone area" to the "middle of Germany" and acquired new significance as a "regional sub-centre".

The interesting history of the city can be explored in the nearby city museum which is found on a former tobacco farm from the 18th century.

From Eschwege to Mihla — 35 km

From the **Marktplatz**, continue through a small park onto **Jardin-de-Saint-Maudé** street, which leads to **Leuchtbergstraße**. Follow this until you reach the forest, where it turns into a cycle path that first runs along the edge of the forest and then later through some fields. **21** Turn right at the roundabout. At the first possibility in **Aue**, turn left and follow the signs for the Werratal cycle path through the ponds. A little while later you will come directly to the bank of the Werra. In Bogen, head towards the bridge, cross the river on **Schlagdstraße** and continue to Wanfried.

Wanfried
prefix: 05655
- **Stadtverwaltung (Municipality)**, Marktstr. 18, ☎ 98940, @ arq542
- **Heimatmuseum und Dokumentationszentrum zur deutschen Nachkriegsgeschichte (Local Museum and archive detailing post-war German history)**, Marktstr. 2, ☎ 923547, ☎ 92134 ☺, @ brp476
- **Harmes'sches Handelshaus**, Schlagdstr. 6. The baroque timbered house has elaborate flat carvings and unique designs.

Wanfried Agreement

On September 17, 1045, the Wanfried Agreement was made in Kalkhof, in which the Americans agreed on an exchange of territory with the Soviets. The Hessian towns within the American zone were affected: Asbach, Weidenbach, Vatterode, Sickenberg and Henningerode were all allotted to the Soviet zone. The Thuringian villages of Neuseesen and Werleshausen in return became part of the American zone.

The reason for the exchange of territory was the fact that the north-south railroad line from the American exclave

Schlagd, historical harbour at Wanfried

Bremerhaven to the American zone in the south ran three kilometres through the zone occupied by the Soviets leading to numerous disruptions on the line. After a German engineer was shot by a Soviet soldier, the two ruling powers negotiated the Wanfried Agreement which was not changed until after 1989.

After the main road bends to the right, turn right into **Unter der Tränke**. A little later turn left into **Bornweg**, then later continue along **Steinweg**. Turn right onto the main road, then right again into **Klauskirchstraße**. The signs for the **Werratal cycle path** lead you left into **Wallstraße** and along the main road to the beautiful village of **Altenburschla** with its half-timbered houses. From there, cycle on to **Großburschla**.

> **TIPP** On the border of Großburschla you will find a stone at the "Rastplatz im Lerchenfeld", which was placed on the 10th anniversary of the border opening: "At this historical site, the Iron Curtain was finally lifted on November 13, 1989 at 15:46. For more than forty years, people were separated from each other by border security facilities along the 296-kilometre Thuringian-Hessian border."

Wendehausen border tower memorial

Preserved at its original location, this watchtower has operated as a small museum since 2008. Text and images provide information about life in the formerly restricted area. The view from the border tower over the Hainich is also wonderful. In clear weather, you can even see as far as the Wartburg.

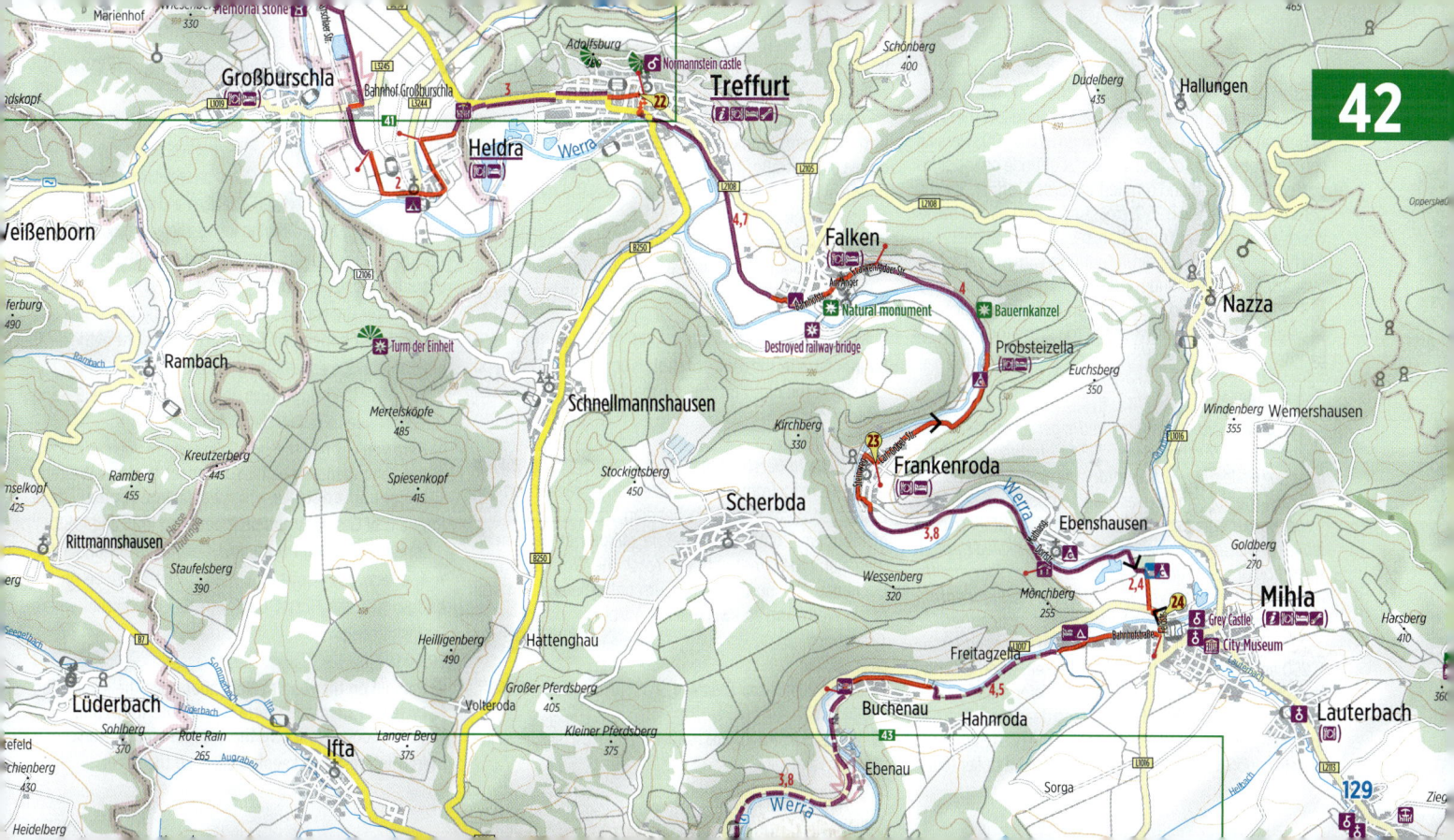

Continue on the western side of the border since this Hessian area once protruded into the GDR like a nose. Continue parallel to the railroad tracks and follow the signs to **Heldra**, where you will be welcomed by the 2003 Hessian competition winner of "Our Village". Continue on the signposted paved road and turn left towards **Treffurt**. Shortly before you reach the B 250, cross under the railroad tracks which are no longer in operation, pass the watch post. You will find yourself once again in Thuringia with a great view over **Adolfsburg**. Continue on the lightly-travelled highway.

TIPP The pedestrian and cycle trail can be ignored since the height differences between the roads are too great.

Frank Mater

The 20-year-old Frank Mater tried to get across the border just north of Treffurt on 22 March 1984. He triggered a splinter mine, fell while still on GDR territory and was found by border officials. The doctor who was called pronounce him dead.

His mother was told her son had had a "fatal accident while committing a crime". Frank Mater was killed through the automatic shooting device, even though four months beforehand the UN convention had prohibited the use of mines against civilians and this had come into force in the GDR.

22 In Treffurt turn right towards Werra, pass under the B 250 and continue on the road to **Falken**. Upon entering the town, shortly before you reach the Werra Bridge, you will see a nature memorial of stone and dead trees. The trail in Falken is sign-posted. You will enjoy the pretty timbered houses. Upon leaving the town you will come closer to the

Werra again, pass a cliff on the left side and reach **Probsteizella** where you will find a camping site and a restaurant.

Cross under the old railroad tracks again and continue further towards **Frankenroda**. **23** In the village, turn right onto **Lindenstraße**, then left onto **Steinweg** before the bridge over the Werra. A little later, cross the river on the cyclist's bridge.

At **Ebenshausen**, turn left down to the Werra bank, but stay on the southern bank. Pass the **outdoor swimming pool** and continue until you come to the main road where you turn left.

24 Cycle across the Werra and then turn right into **Bahnhofstraße**, the centre of **Mihla** is on your left. There you can spend the night directly by the Werra in the "Grauen Schlosshotel".

From Mihla to Gerstungen   34 km

On the road from Mihla to Creuzburg, remain on the eastern shore of the Werra heading west. After the end of the town, continue on the old railroad embankment, then along the street until you reach the Werra bridge in **Buchenau**. Behind the village turn onto the western side of the Werra and you will reach Creuzburg.

Creuzburg
prefix: 036926

🛈 **Tourist-Information Creuzburg**, at Creuzburg Castle, ✆ 98047, @ uvh677

⛪ **Nikolaikirche**, Marktpl. The church from 1215 has a semicircular Romanesque choir.

⛪ **Liboriuskapelle (Liborius chapel)**, An der Werrabrücke, ✆ 94711. The chapel was erected in 1499. @ qhi463

🏰 **Burg Creuzburg (Castle Creuzburg)**, Burgberg 1, ✆ 98047. Built between 1165 and 1170, the castle now offers visitors a museum with Elisabeth-Kemenate, concerts and presentations on the open-air stage, a Michael Praetorius exhibition and monthly alternating exhibitions in the great hall as well as a hotel. @ upo456

Shortly before the B 7 turn left and cross the Werra over the oldest stone arch bridge north of the Danube, which was rebuilt after the war. With its seven sandstone arches and the **Liborius Chapel** set in the structure, it is one of the most beautiful bridge ensembles in Central Europe.

25 After the bridge, turn right, cross under the B 7 and then continue to **Wilhelmsglücksbrunn**.

TIPP Here you will find the cafe Salina where you can enjoy a meal and spend the night. You can see the large Werratal bridge from a distance, which was financed by the Federal Republic of Germany and built between 1986 and 1988.

Continue through **Pferdsdorf-Spichra**, cross under the A 4, afterwards also the railroad tracks, continue on the bridge over the Hörsel until you reach Hörschel where Rennsteig begins.

Hörschel (Eisenach)

TIPP Remain on the road to Neuenhof since the signposted cycle trail along the Werra is unusable. If this trail is not paved soon, it will give the impression that Hörschel is merely interested in keeping bikes off the street.

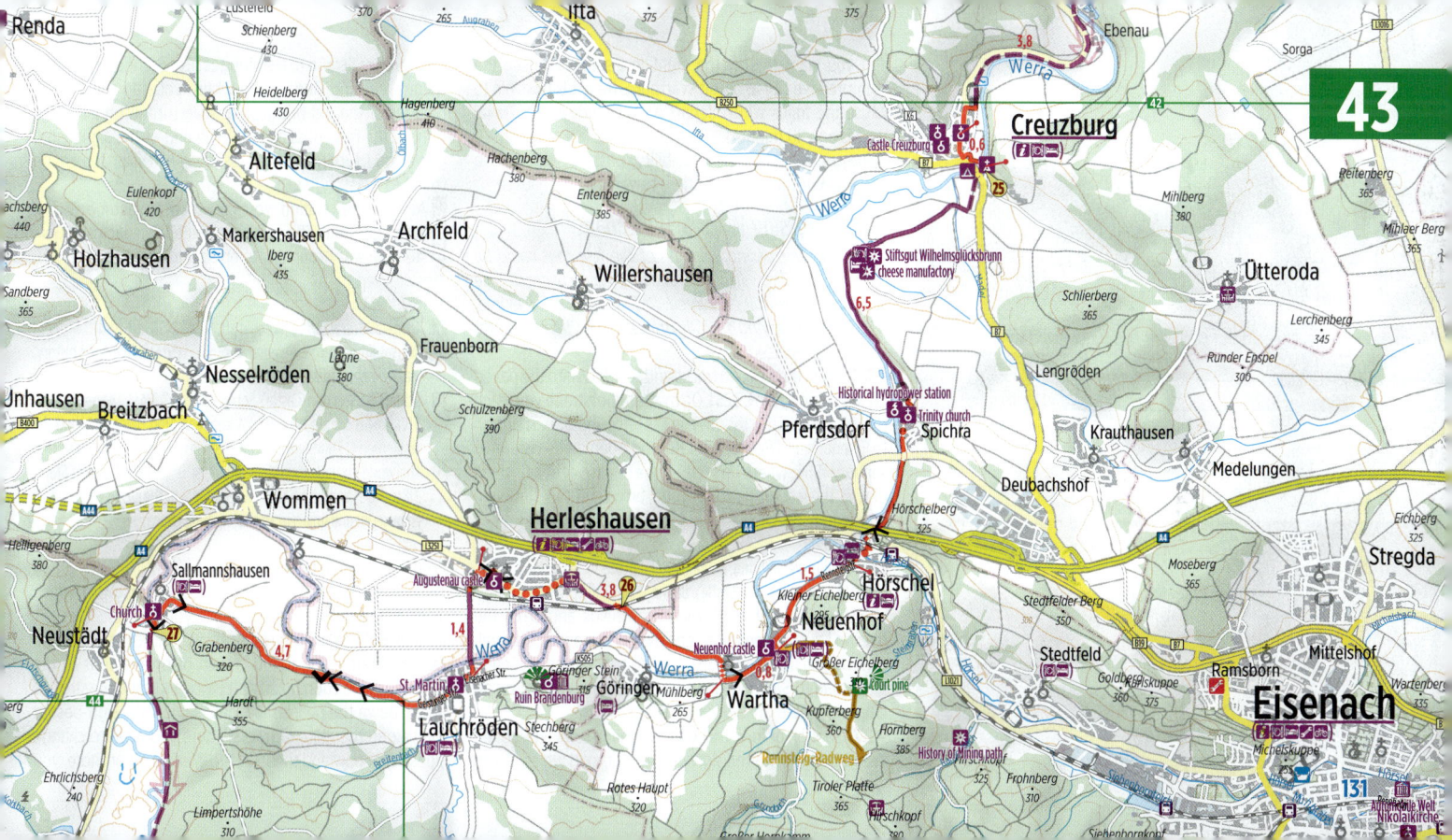

Lauchröden (1984/2006)

AUSFLUG If you want to stay the night in Eisenach, or see the impressive city and visit Wartburg, then it is possible to use the trains which depart on an hourly basis. Travel time is only 10 minutes.

Turn right at the next possibility, pass over the Werra towards **Wartha** and from there towards Herleshausen.

Border crossing Wartha/Herleshausen

This border crossing was one of the few that could be crossed by car. The watchtower and the former customs office in Thuringia are still preserved. In 1981 Günter Guillaume, who had been spying on Willy Brandt in the Chancellery for years, was replaced here.

26 Cross the railroad tracks and turn left onto the paved cycle trail along the **L 3251**. On the **Bahnhofstraße** you reach Herleshausen. The station is on the left hand side. Trains go to Eisenach and Bebra. After Konrad Adenauer's visit on 16 January 1956, where he secured the release of all prisoners of war, the last group to be freed, arrived at this station.

Herleshausen
prefix: 05654

- **Gemeindeverwaltung**, Bahnhofstr. 15, ✆ 98950, @ tpv562
- **Schloss Augustenau (Castle)**, Bahnhofstr. 10, @ pfy853

Cycle straight ahead through the fields and cross the river. In **Lauchröden** the signposting is somewhat unusual.

Turn right, travel through the village on the cobblestoned main road to **Sallmannshausen**, where the Werra was no longer the German-German border.

27 Shortly before the end of town, turn left at the Werra bridge onto the sign-posted dirt road which is also the **Herdaer Straße** to Gerstungen. Cross under the bridge before reaching Gerstungen where you can still see the remains of the old bridge, and then turn left again. Turn right at the next possibility. At the end of the signposted gravel road, turn right and cross the Werra using the bridge to get to Gerstungen.

AUSSTIEG At the train station you can take advantage of the Werratal-Bahn. The section between Eisenach and Gerstungen was brought into operation again on May 1991.

Gerstungen
prefix: 036922

- **Gemeindeverwaltung**, Wilhelmstr. 53, ✆ 2450, @ tvs411
- **Werratalmuseum**, Sophienstr. 4, ✆ 31433 ⊕ Exhibitions on history, geology and life in Werratal. @ fda688
- **Schloss Gerstungen (Castle)**, Sophienstr. 4, ✆ 31433. The Gerstungen Treaty was signed here in 1074 between King Heinrich IV and the noblemen of Thuringia and Lower Saxony. A plaque informs us that the world-famous mountain geologist Dr. Friedrich Moritz Stapff (1836-1895) was also born in Gerstungen. In the castle you will find a museum and adjacent to this, a round church.

From Gerstungen to Vacha   27 km

Turn left just after the bridge into **Löbersgasse** which leads to the main road, into which you turn left. Turn left immediately again into **Nauenstraße** and cross under the railroad bridge. The round church of **Untersuhl** is to the right. After the **church**, turn left twice and continue straight ahead down the pedestrian zone. Follow the sign-posted road along the railroad tracks where you need to change sides every now and then. On the Werra's other shore, you

will see the potash factories of Alexanderhütte and the gigantic Monte Kali on the horizon, a rock salt pile which glows different colours according to the time of the day.

TIPP The Monte Kali is an artifical mountain which is however, often included on maps.

Berka/Werra
prefix: 036922

🛈 **Verwaltungsgemeinschaft Berka (Municipality)**, Kirchstr. 9, ☏ 330, @ yvs457

28 In Berka continue to the left past the Werra bridge, continue straight ahead and parallel to the railroad tracks towards Dankmarshausen.

Dankmarshausen

In Dankmarshausen, stay on the western bank of the Werra, follow the **Bahnhofstraße** to **Widdershausen**, where you cross the Werra to the left from **An der Brücke**. Turn right at **Dippacher Straße**. **29** Behind Leimbach and shortly before Heringen turn left onto **Fülleroder Weg**. If you want to visit Heringen or the potash mining museum, continue straight ahead.

Heringen (Werra)
prefix: 06624

🛈 **Tourist-Information**, Dickesstr. 1, ☏ 919413, ☏ 5127, @ qrf845

🏛 **Werra-Kali-Bergbau-Museum (Werra potash mining museum)**, Dickesstr. 1, ☏ 919413 ☺ The museum shows the history and the present potash mining operations in Werratal. Take a tour of the Monte Kali, the impressive rock salt pile in Wintershall. @ xoo151

✉ **Fritz-Kunze-Bad**, Badstr. 5, ☏ 435, @ jhw313

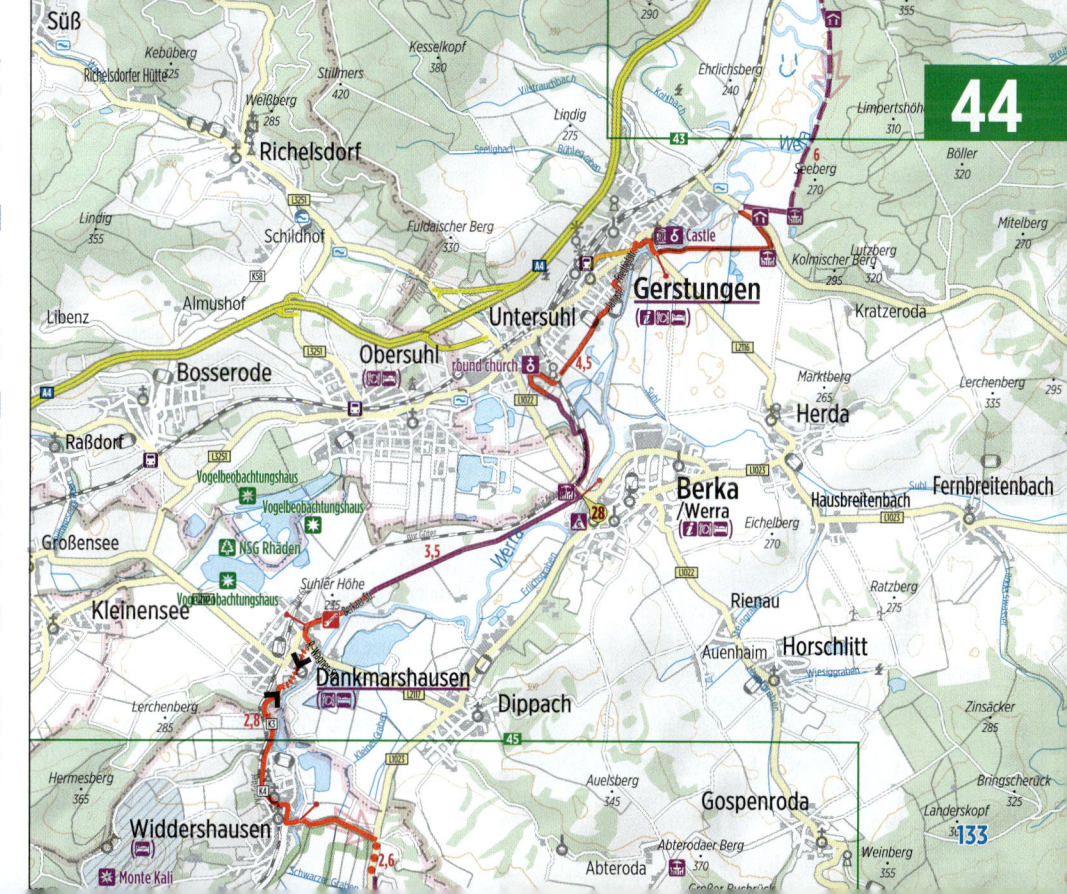

The Bridge of Unity at Vacha (1986/2006)

Potash and the results

Potash is mainly used today as a fertiliser with limited results. Since only a portion reaches the plants, the vast remainder of product is washed from the field by the rain and ends up in the ocean via streams and rivers. There the fertiliser feeds the algae. The flourishing plants consume oxygen and the result of this is the ocean animal start running out of air. Experts speak of "death zones" which have already spread in the Baltic Sea.

The main route leads over the **Fülleroder Weg**, crosses the border to Thuringia and remains on the **Gasteroda**. At the end of this road, turn right onto **Abterodaer Straße**, which in turn leads to **Vitzerode**. Follow the main road straight ahead.

Pass the villages of **Heiligenroda**, **Schwenge** and **Niederndorf**, whose history is explained on information boards along the way. In **Oberzella**, follow **Martinstraße**, turn left onto **Mittelstraße** and then straight ahead onto **Vachaer Straße**. Cross Sachsenheimer Straße and turn right onto the separate **Werratal cycle path** in the direction of Philippsthal.

Before the border to Hesse, turn left and cross the **bridge of Unity** to Vacha, on which Napoleon crossed the Werra after the Battle of Leipzig on March 27, 1813 during his urgent return journey to Paris.

Bridge of Unity

The "Bridge of Unity" built in 1342 between Vacha and Philippsthal was completely blocked off as of 1961. The bridge was in GDR territory and was integrated into the border security facilities. At the south end there was an observation tower used by the GDR border troops. After the opening of the border, the old bridge was extensively renovated and mad available to pedestrians and cyclists. It became a symbol of the German separation and the German unity. On the Northern end of the bridge you can see Hoßfeld printing house, which was once divided in two.

Hoßfeld House

Hoßfeld house residence and print shop was built around 1890 in Hesse directly on the border to Thuringia. The print shop belonged to the publisher of the Rhön newspaper which mainly appeared in the Thuringia area as a daily newspaper from 1893 to 1941. The company expanded its offices over the border in 1928 and thus moved the printers to the Thuringian territory.

When the German-German border became more and more closed off, the printers were moved to Hessian territory on New Year's Eve 1951/52 as a preventative measure. The connecting door between the properties was quickly bricked up. Afterwards GDR officials prohibited the owner of the print shop to enter the Thuringian part of the building and even repairs were not allowed.

Not until after the completion of the fundamental contract and a measurement of the border, and one twelfth of the house was transferred to Mrs. Hoßfeld effective as of January 1, 1976.

Vacha
prefix: 036962

🛈 **Stadt Vacha (Vacha administration association)**, Markt 4, ✆ 2610, @ atd214

- 🏛 **Heimatmuseum (Museum of local history)**, Untertor 8, ✆ 22839, ✆ 25757 ⊜, @ mar735
- 🏰 **Burg Wendelstein (Castle Wendelstein)**, Untertor 8 ⊜ The castle houses a museum of local history with exhibitions on the historical trades of Vacha as well as Thuringia's largest doll collection with approx. 2,000 dolls. @ bjm811
- ✳ **Brücke der Einheit/Werrabrücke (Bridge of Unity/Werra bridge)**. The bridge connects Vacha in Thuringia with Philippsthal in Hesse.
- ✳ **Haus Hoßfeld (House Hoßfeld)**. Formerly divided house belonging to the Hoßfeld printer
- ✳ **Histor. Marktplatz (Historical market place)**. With timbered houses
- ✳ **Rathaus (Town hall)**, Marktpl. The Town hall was built in 1613 from Caspar von Widemarkter.

Since the town, with a population of about 4,000, was in the restricted zone of the inner German border during the GDR times, many historical timbered buildings still exist. You can also still see a watchtower as well as a piece of the Wall. No alterations have been made to the optics of the city since the war's end. Therefore, the city is now an insider tip when it comes to historical buildings.

The city was first mentioned as Vacha in 817 in the so-called "Codex Eberhardi" of the Fulda Abbey. The name goes back to the old German "vah" which means "fish trap" or "dam". Vacha was first mentioned as a city in possession of the Fulda Abbey in 1186. It was one of the first towns in Thuringia to be granted city rights. Vacha changed ownership many times. As of 1406, portions belonged to the territory of the Landgraves of Hesse, and then completed transferred to them after 1648 with the end of the Thirty-Year War. In

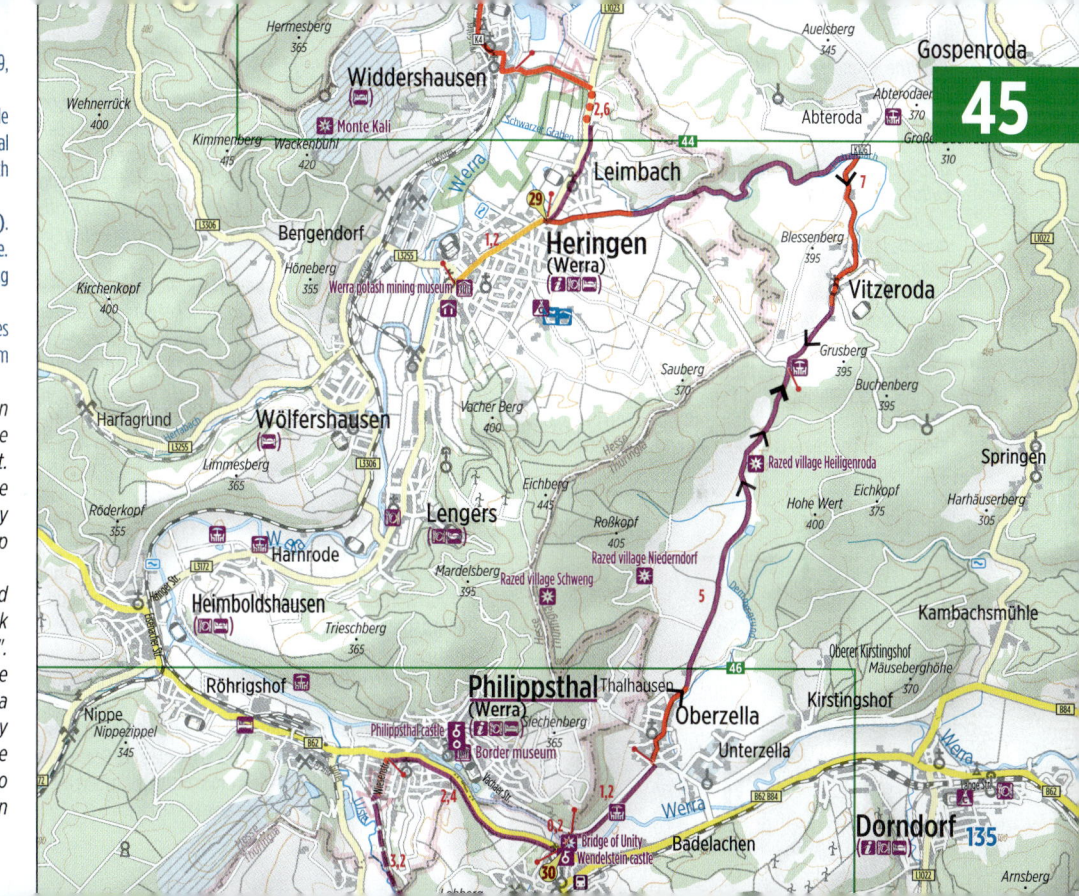

45

135

1816 the Grand Duchy of Saxony-Weimar-Eisenach took possession of the city.

Vacha also played an important economic role in the early modern ages since it was ideally placed on the old trade route between Frankfurt and Leipzig. It was also the cultural centre of the region.

It is worth visiting the market square with its historical houses, Vitusbrunnen well and the splendid timbered town hall as well as the Werra bridge and the Castle Wendelstein from the 12th century where you will also find one of the largest doll museums in Thurningia with 2,000 dolls.

30 At the south end of the historic bridge, turn right onto the cycle path along the **B 62** and after 2.5 kilometres you will reach Philippsthal. If you want to visit the Merkers Adventure Mine, turn left after the bridge and cycle to Bad Salzungen. The mine is located about 8 kilometres east of Vacha on the B 62.

The formerly divided Haus Hoßfeld

Merkers Adventure Mine

The Merker Adventure Mine is found east of Vacha on the B 62 between Dorndorf and Bad Salzungen. You can experience what it feels like to be a miner 800 metres below the surface. Apart from gaining an insight into the running of a modern mining company, it also provides information concerning the history, development and tradition of potash mining.

Experienced miners accompany the visitor to the hall-like bunker with the largest underground bucket wheel excavator in the world and to the crystal cave which was discovered in 1981, with salt crystals up to one metre in length as well as to the "Adventure museum".

The entire gold and currencies of the Reichsbak were stored in the gold room after the end of the war as well as art works of priceless value.

From Vacha to Point Alpha   19 km

Taking the bike path on the left side of the **B 62** you will get to Philippsthal. Once there, turn right at the traffic light and you will get to the palace as well as the border museum.

Philippsthal (Werra)
prefix: 06620

- **Gemeindeverwaltung (Citizen advice bureau)**, Schloss 1, ☎ 92100, @ omu728
- **Schloss Philippsthal (Philippsthal Castle)**, Schlossstr. The castle was built in 1685 by Prince Philip of Hesse on the ruins of a Benedictine monastery, of which the three-nave monastery church (built at the end of the 12th century) is still preserved today.

Border incident at Vacha in the 1950's

✉ **Sportbad**, Am Bad 3, ☎ 918638

The town was originally the noble residence of the knight lineage of „Cruceburg" and was first mentioned in 1191 in a writ of protection from Pope Cölestin III for the founded Cloister of the Benedictines. This cloister also took on the name of the knight lineage and was called „Kreuzberg", which was also the original name of the town Philippsthal.

The very wealthy cloister was destroyed in a peasant revolt in 1525, abandoned by the nuns in 1568 after the reformation and secularised in 1593. The three-nave cloister church which was built at the end of the 12th century remains and is still used by the Evangelic community today. In 1685, Prince Philipp from Hesse had a castle built at the site of the cloister ruins which he named „Philippsthal".

Just before the end of Philippsthal, turn left onto **Wiesenstraße**, where the way to Unterbreizbach in Ulsertal is signposted. After a brief right-left bend, continue along the tracks of a former railway until you reach the Ulster. You will see a white pyramid, the **Hattorf salt mountain**.

Cycle on the Rhön-Ulstertal bike trail, which is identical in this part to the Hesse Railway Bike Trail and then cross the river Ulster at **Unterbreizbach**. Continue towards **Pferdsdorf** and stay on the western side of the river on the paved track, which later turns into gravel. Before **Wenigentaft**, the paved bike path takes you over a bridge with blue railing. Cross the river Ulster on the bridge, turn right and cycle through the town along **St. Georg Straße**. **31** At the southern end of town turn right into **Gänseweg**, which leads to the **Kegelspiel bike trail** after 800 metres.

A short while later, turn left at a **cycle shelter** before a bend. Do not continue along the Kegelspiel cycle trail to the left but rather continue under the **railroad bridge** to a very pretty Talau along the stream. When you reach the street, turn left, cross the Grüsselbach, turn right, continue through the town of the same name until you reach the **R 2** and turn left.

A view of the barred Werra Bridge and border-tower at Vacha from Philippsthal, 1985/86.

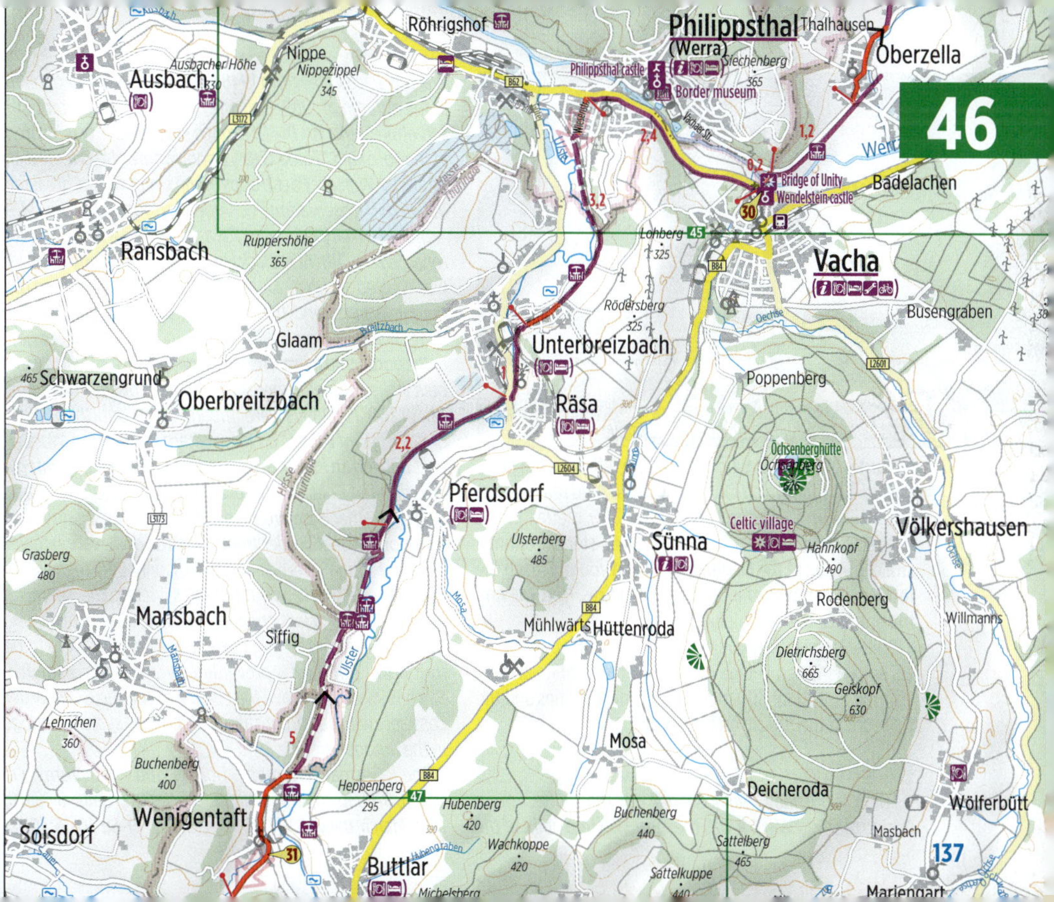

46

137

Freedom wind-play sculpture at Point Alpha

Shortly after the B 84 crossing, turn left onto the sign-posted dirt road which runs into a paved road after a short distance where you turn right. After 800 metres in the "Hessengraben", which is at times very steep, continue straight ahead at the **Lindendreieck** and you will reach the former US camp after a further 500 metres. You will find the entrance to Point Alpha at the end.

On the Hessian side you will find the military base of the US soldiers called "Point Alpha". On the Thuringian side you will find about 300 metres of border facilities and the museum in the "house on the border".

Point Alpha

For Peter Ustinov, "Point Alpha" was the "hottest point during the Cold War". It was the most Western point of the Warsaw Pact states from 1948 and until the border opened in the autumn of 1989, also one of the most important observation points for the US troops in Europe. It was located in the so-called "Fulda Gap", a spot where NATO feared an attack by Warsaw Pact troops in the event of war breaking out. In the "Observation Post Alpha" an outpost of the "14th Armored Cavalry Regiments" was stationed which was later renamed the "11th ACR Black Horse". In 1945 a wooden tower was erected at "Point Alpha" from which one could see the border facilities and the city of Geisa. In 1985 a concrete tower was built which still remains and is a permanent part of the border museum. The sheet metal barracks which were built in the beginning were later replaced by solid buildings. About 200 US soldiers were stationed here. Until the autumn of 1989, "Point Alpha" on the western point of the Warsaw Pact fulfilled an important role in NATO's defence strategy.

During the Cold War, direct eye contact could be made with the other side from this location. The observation tower of the GDR border troops and the observation tower of "Point Alpha" were separated by only 200 metres. On the seam between two different systems, the so-called "Klassenfeinde" (class enemies) were in close contact.

After the fall of the Iron Curtain, the facilities were to be torn down but it was prevented by a citizens' initiative. Since 1995 you can have the chance to see the GDR border complete with patrol path and running rope system for dogs in the outdoor area.

The German-German borderland museum (☎ 06651/919030, opening times: April-Oct., daily 9-18:00, Nov.-March daily. 10-17:00, Dec.-Feb., Tu-Su 10-16:30) is separated into three sections. On the Thuringian side you will find a newly constructed museum building and about 300 metres of border facilities, on the Hessian side are the grounds of the actual "Point Alpha". In front of the entrance to the newly constructed museum, which was on the Thuringian side until recently, a large symbolic "round table" and an original segment of the Berlin Wall complete the facilities. In total there are 30,000 m² on the Hessian side and 40,000 on the Thuringian side.

Rudi Arnstadt

Between the Hessian Setzelbach and the Thuringian Wiesenfeld, the 36-year-old Captain of the National People's Army, Rudi Arnstadt, lost his life on August 14, 1962 in cross-fire between soldiers of the Federal Border Guard and the National People's Army. Suddenly and without warning, is what was later said, a GDR officer fired a shot to the west. The Federal Border Guard officer, Hans Plüschke, who was on inspection with an officer, shot back and fatally hit Rudi Arnstadt above his right eye. According to the Western side, Plüschke, who was 23 at the time, acted in self-defence and saved his own life and the officer in front of him.

The GDR saw the situation differently and claimed that only a warning shot had been fired. Arnstadt was defending the GDR territory and was made a hero. Numerous public facilities and schools carried his name. Without being present, Plüschke was sentenced to 25 years imprisonment for murder.

Due to security reasons, Hans Plüschke left the Federal Border Guard in 1970 and founded a private taxi company.

He was considered endangered and was allowed to carry a handgun. "I was always afraid that they would kidnap my children, put me under pressure so that I surrender and hand myself in", explained the father of five in 1997 on the 35th anniversary of death, when he dared to appear on public television for the first time.

Seven months later, on March 15, 1998, he was found murdered at four in the morning on the B 84 between Neuwirtshaus and Rasdorf. The fatal shot hit the 59-year-old

above the right eye into the brain, the same death as Rudi Arnstadt.

For his great uncle, Lothar Plüschke, who secured the other side of the GDR border as a dedicated NVA soldier, it was clear: "Former members of the Stasi do not release their target persons. That did not change after 1989." The murder was not solved.

From Point Alpha to Fladungen/Fulda

42 km

If you would like to avoid the route to Geisa on the main road, turn left at the road block and continue on the level dirt road past the parking lot and somewhat uphill to **Rasdorfer Berg**. The route signposted with the red triangle crosses the convoy road with the perforated slabs. Continue straight ahead on the gravel road through the forest, which is easy to travel through and which later turns into a road through a field. Follow the signs and turn right, where you will then have a beautiful view of Geisa.

The tip of the triangle shows the way to Geisa.

This very steep meadow descent, which is not necessarily recommended in the opposite direction, meets the unmarked **Buttlarer Straße**, into which you turn right.

GDR border post at Point Alpha

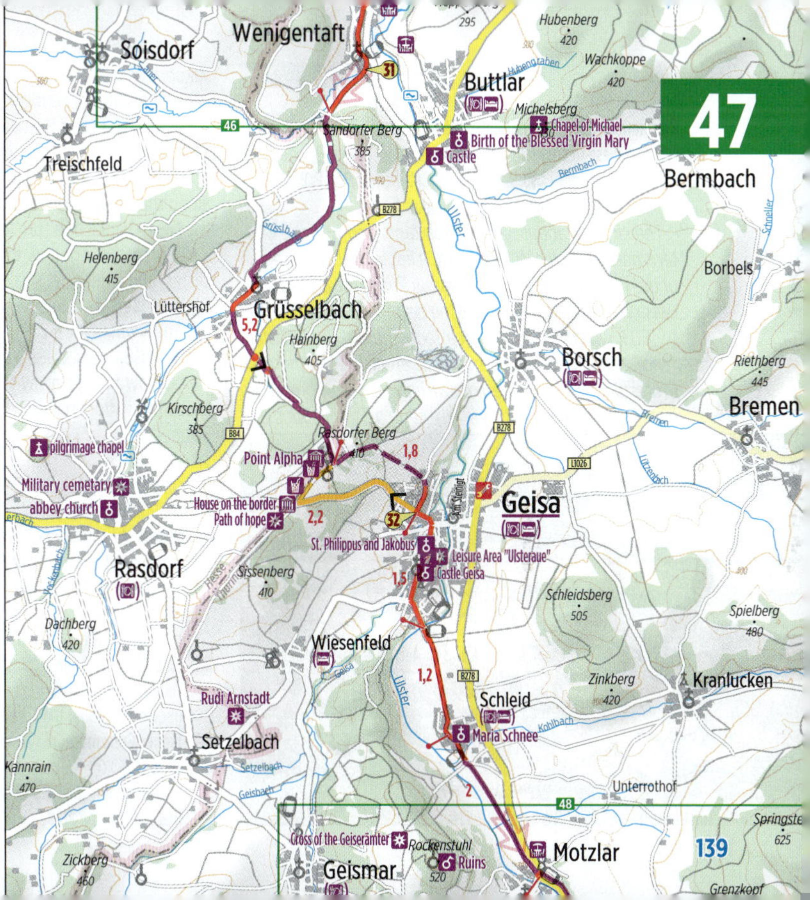

47

Geisa

prefix: 036967

- ℹ️ **Stadtverwaltung Geisa (Municipality)**, Marktpl. 27, ✆ 690, @ buj146
- 🏛 **Anneliese Deschauer Galerie**, Schlosspl. 1, ✆ 69115, 🕐 June–Sept., Tu, Thu, Fr 11:00-15:00, Su 11:00-16:00, Okt.-May, Tu, Thu, Fr 11:00-15:00. City museum and art gallery, @ mdu856

The city has about 5,000 inhabitants and was the westernmost city in the Warsaw Pact. It lies in the border region of the Thuringian-Hessian-Bavarian Rhön. The area around Geisa was in the possession of the bishops of Fulda from 817 to 1803, which is why the area today beside the Eichsfeld represents one of the two Catholic areas in the otherwise Protestant Thuringia. The old town has many well-preserved historical buildings with the city church St. Philippus and

View of Point Alpha city of Geisa

Jakobus as well as the castle district, which used to be the old administrative centre.

32 At the end of the road turn left onto the **Rasdorfer Straße**, cross the Geisabach, turn right at the **roadhouse** "Zum Goldenen Stern", immediately left again and continue along the stream. After crossing the Geisabach again, pass the Geisschänke and turn left over the wooden bridge.

Keep to the right at the next intersection, cross the Ulster and continue straight ahead on the signposted **Rhön-Ulstertal cycle trail** through **Schleid** and **Motzlar** to **Günthers** where the B 278 runs parallel after the intersection.

33 In Günthers, cross a country road, the Ulstertal cycle trail is now further away from the highway, and you will reach Tann after changing sides on the B 278.

Tann

prefix: 06682

- ℹ️ **Tourist-Information Tann**, Marktpl., ✆ 961111, @ byw218
- 🏛 **Freilichtmuseum „Rhöner Museumsdorf" (Open air museum Rhöner Museumsdorf)**, Schlossstr., ✆ 961127 🚪 The museum village consists of a double and triple winged building and a bakery. The residential houses of the courtyards are furnished with typical old furniture from the Rhön and there are also numerous every day utensils in the individual rooms and stalls. @ ypf524
- 🏛 **Naturmuseum Rhön**, Schlossstr., ✆ 8977 🚪 The nature museum can be found in the vicinity of the museum village and provides information about the flora and fauna in the Rhön. @ xps841
- 🏛 **Tanner Grenzmuseum (Tanner border museum)**, Am Kalkofen 6, ✆ 961111 🕐 🌐 The museum explores the history of the division of Germany with the help of newspaper reports, photos and other material. @ mmk818

Market place of Tann

- 🏰 **Schloss der Freiherren von und zu der Tann (Castle of the Barons von und zu der Tann)**, Schlossstr. The compound consists of the red castle from 1558, the blue castle from 1574 and the yellow castle from 1714. It is also worth visiting the castle fountain, a baroque construction with the heraldic animal – the jumping trout as waterspout – from the year 1686.
- ✳️ **Elf-Apostel-Haus**, Markpl. Oldest town house in the city.
- ✳️ **Sagenkeller**, Schlossstr. 3. Various myths are presented in the basement rooms of the former castle brewery in the form of artistic works made out of wood chips and sawdust. More information available at the tourist information centre.
- ✳️ **Stadttor (Town gate)**. The town gate was erected by Eberhard von der Tann during the fortification of the city (1557-1563).
- 🛁 **Geriethbad**, Am Geriethpark 3, ✆ 917452, @ ehu547

Tann lies in Ulstertal in the Hessian Rhön and was first mentioned as a town in 1179. The first castle complex was built between the 11th and 12th century and the town was fortified in the 16th century. In 1879, a fire destroyed large sections of the medieval construction. With the opening of the German-German border, which surrounded the town with a half circle for over 40 years, Tann is once again in the middle of Germany. The town has a population of about 5,000 and is mainly Evangelic.

Tann has several points of interest such as the renovated town gate from 1557, the city fountain, an old community centre and the castle compounds of the Barons von und zu der Tann.

Remain on the western highway in Tann. Keep to the right twice (the sign is missing!), cross the Ulster and continue on the western side of the river on the Ulstertal cycle trail signposted as the **R 3** towards Fulda and Neustädtges. You will reach **Aura** via **Wendershausen**, **Lahrbach**, **Unterrücksbach** and **Neuschwambach**.

From here you can continue to Fulda on the Milseburg cycle trail which is signposted as R 3. Turn right and continue on the former railroad for 31 kilometres and through a 1,100-metre-long tunnel to Fulda.

34 The main route makes a sharp left. Continue on the **R 8** towards **Hilders**.

Remain on the **Ulstertal cycle trail** until you reach **Findlos**, turn left and then turn left again.

At the end of the separate cycle trail, turn right onto **Ulster Straße** towards Batten. Turn left on the **B 278**, then right at the next intersection, past a fountain and follow the sign "Frankenheim 7.2 km" up the hill. Keep to the right at the cemetery. This paved road, signposted with the tip of q red triangle, continues up a very steep hill for the next 3 kilometres where all but the fittest cyclists will have to get off and push. Shortly before reaching the street it becomes a comfortable gravel road.

35 Turn right onto the **L 3176**, continue to the parking lot "Spinne", turn left onto the paved road which is signposted with the red triangle.

Remain on the road which leads to the "Berghotel Eisenacher Haus" from Findlos via Batten and is signposted as **hiking trail "W/O 3"** (WestEast 3) with a red triangle. Following the tip, you will reach the former German-German border after 1.5 km which is marked with an erected barrier. Shortly afterwards turn right onto the paved road.

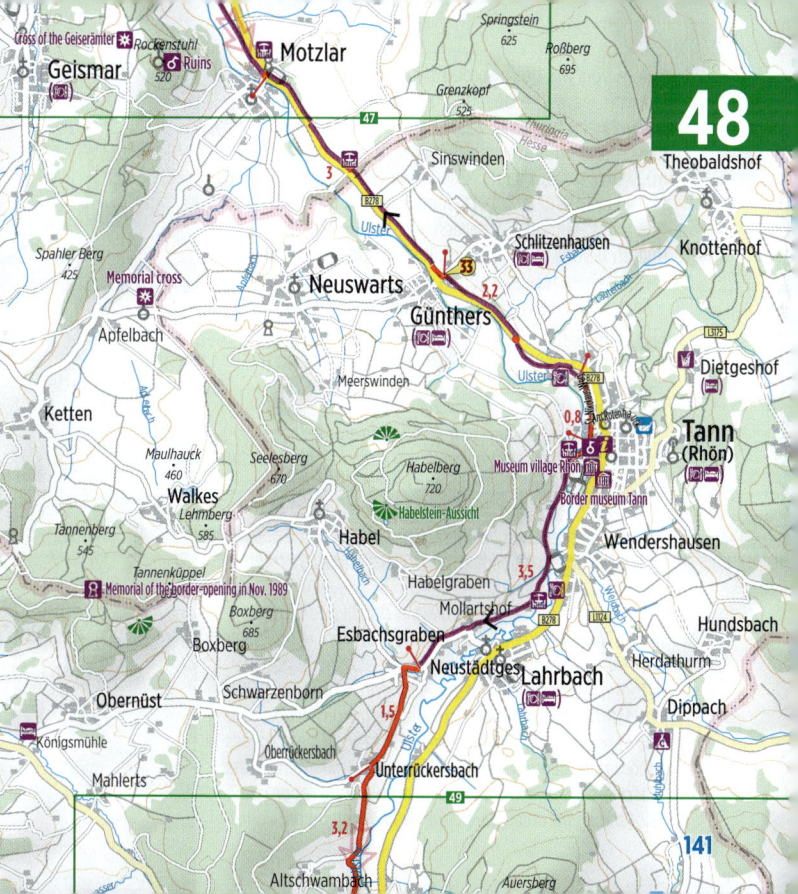

48

Here you will be rewarded for the steep climb with a fantastic view. The beautiful, almost level road towards Frankenheim turns into a quiet street. To the left you can reach a hill with a wonderful view, the Ellenbogen (814 m), with the restaurants "Eisenacher Haus" (☎ 036946 or 149914 or 149915) and 1,000 metres further the "Thüringer Rhönhaus" with a beer garden (☎ 036946/32060). Information boards at the parking lot provide information on the biosphere reserve in Rhön.

To the right you will reach **Frankenheim**, the highest town in Rhön at 750 metres, three sides of which were surrounded by the border when Germany was divided.

Rhön Biosphere reserve

The Rhön biosphere reserve is the main area in the mountain range of the same name which stretches beyond the borders to Bavaria, Thuringia and Hesse. It was recognised as a valuable cultural landscape by the UNESCO in 1991. Their aim is to protect the variety and quality of the habitat in light of the surrounding agricultural industry, tourism and other industry.

Sustainable development plays a decisive role and it is hoped that industry and agriculture can work in harmony with the nature reserve and the habitat, as much as possible.

The entire area of the reserve is currently approx. 185,000 ha. With the help of a "frame concept for the protection, care and development", designed from 1991 to 1995 by employees of communes, counties, official offices and organizations, the biosphere reserve was divided into main areas (approx. 2.5 % of the entire area), care zones and development zones.

The „Geschlossenes Band" sculpture by Waldo Dörsch

In the first zone, the direct use for agricultural or forestry purposes is strictly forbidden and in the care zones, the land is to be used in a gentle and natural manner. The last zone includes the populated areas of the Rhön, the villages and cities. Typical regional products and wildlife are encouraged, such as the "Rhönschaf" (sheep) and the mixed orchards which are often very natural.

The mountains in the three-county triangle of Bavaria, Hesse and Thuringia are called the "land of the open distances", as the Rhön with its open basalt summits, meadows and pastures gives the impression of incredible vastness. 1,000 years ago, the monks called the Rhön "Buchonia" – land of the beech trees. Even today, he beech tree is the most common tree in these forests.

The black stork also feels at home here. It is much rarer than its white relative and has completely different habits. Black storks do not greet each other by clattering but by whistling. They also cannot see their prey, which is why they have to fish blindly. However, they do this successfully. They ideally need untouched old forests and they are very sensitive to human interferences – including forestry.

"The closed circle"

When you cross the former border strip between Simmershausen und Oberweid, you will see "The closed circle" on the left. It was created by Waldo Dörsch from Oberweid after the fall of the Wall. His idea was to honour his son Thomas, who, at the age of 20, successfully fled from Oberweid over the Staufelsberg to Simmershausen during a snowstorm in 1986.

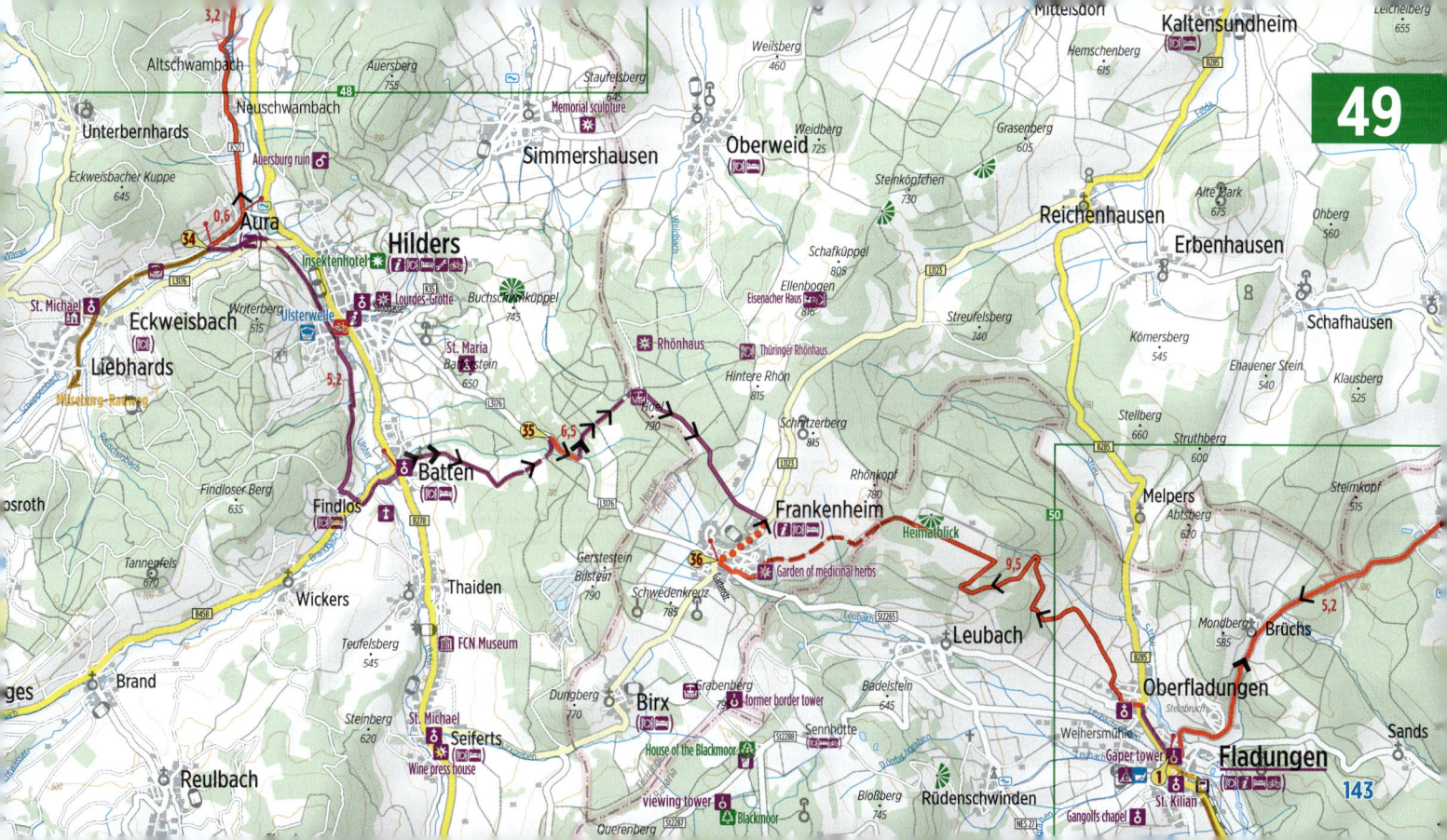

The plaque reads: "The closed circle, a symbol of being connected in unity in Rhön. December 3, 1989, the day and site of the first reunification of the neighbouring towns Simmershausen and Oberweid after 40 years of separation."

36 In **Frankenheim**, which was formerly surrounded by the border on three sides, turn left and slightly downhill towards the east to **Leubach**, turn left into **Leubacher Straße** and pass the restaurant "Schweinebucht".

Continue somewhat uphill after a bend, turn right at the next intersection onto the paved road signposted with the "Museumtour im Grünen Band Thüringen" which turns into a gravel road after a short distance ("border information trail").

Fladungen

Cross the convoy road with the perforated slabs and continue straight ahead on a narrow dirt road. After the bushes a better hiking trail goes off to the left towards the **"Heimatblick"**. Continue on the dirt road through the forest and you will reach a comfortable gravel road (**"Schwedenwall"**) where you turn right. You can enjoy some beautiful views from the top at an altitude of 800 metres, which is the highest point of the inner-German bike trail. You will reach a street at the end of this dirt road.

Ignore the road on the left leading to Heimatblick. At the next crossing, to the right you will reach the ObereSee, turn left and continue on the paved road down the hill. In **Oberfladungen** keep to the left, pass the city hall and you will come to the lightly travelled B 285 with a separate cycle trail, into which you turn right.

AUSSTIEG Since there is only one railroad in Fladungen which only operates from May to October on Sundays and holidays, you must continue on the cycle trail on the B 285 to Mellrichstadt, the next train station south of Wilmars, and 30 kilometres away. From there direct trains depart to Schweinfurt, Würzburg and Erfurt.

Fladungen
prefix: 09778

🛈 **Tourist-Information**, Marktpl. 1, 📞 919111, @ kow244

🏛 **Fränkisches Freilandmuseum Rhön (Franconian open-air museum Rhön)**, Bahnhofstr. 19, 📞 91230 🚲 Seven-hectare large museum grounds with farms and typical community buildings such as a church, village restaurant and community brewery. The flour and oil mill are particularly good highlights. @ nbo411

Open air museum, Fladungen

🏛 **Rhönmuseum**, Marktpl. 1 🚲 The museum shows early historical findings, historical maps and many significant objects relating to Rhöner folk art. It provides some insight into the farming culture in the Rhön area with typical furniture, pictures, costumes and carvings.

❄ **Rhön-Zügle**. Historical steam railroad of the Franconian open-air museum Fladungen. The „RhönZügle" operates on selected Sundays and holidays from May 1 to the beginning of October between Fladungen and Mellrichstadt through the beautiful Streutal.

❄ **Stadtmauer mit Wehrtürmen (City wall with defence towers)**. The wall was erected in the 14th century. The fortification has been restored including historical parapet.

🛏 **Freibad (Heated outdoor pool)**, Flurstr. 16, 📞 1621, @ bql373

From Fladungen/Fulda to the Czech Republik border   308 km

From Fladungen/Fulda to Herbstadt   52 km

1 From Fladungen, continue on **Brüchser Straße** to the north towards Brüchs and Weimarschmieden. After a short journey on a very beautiful country road, slightly uphill, you will reach **Brüchs** and downhill, Weimarschmieden.

Weimarschmieden

Here you will find the most northern Bavarian restaurant in an old, rustic timbered house.

TIPP

You will also find a memorial stone with a rare inscription connecting the two World Wars and the German separation. "In memory of the victims of both World Wars 1914-1918, 7 dead, 1939-1945, 10 dead. They thought they were protecting

Restaurant „Zur Weimarschmiede"

their homeland and were dedicated to the end. Erected in 1990 when the German separation finally ended."

From Weimarschmieden, follow the road a short distance towards Helmershausen, continue along the nice birch trees and then turn right towards Filke and Willmars. On the Bavarian side follow the former border on a quiet, very pretty street. First you will travel through some dense pine forests and later on you will pass through some meadows and fields. **2** After passing through Filke, turn left in Willmars towards Stedtlingen.

The stretch from Willmars to Stedtlingen is on a quiet street, past some lonely forests and fields and crosses the former border where you will be welcomed to the county of Schmalkalden-Meiningen. On the Bavarian side you will see three trees on the left and a bench you can use to take the weight off.

Gerd Palzer

A memorial stone approximately 400 metres before the border and a memorial plaque about 800 metres after the border commemorate the customs officer Gerd Palzer who was shot on July 29, 1952. The reason for the fatal shots is still unclear. It is, however, certain that he was shot on the western side, although the opposite was claimed by the GDR.

Shortly after the border you will see the convoy road, on the one side with perforated slabs, on the other side as a gravel road. The former border strip can still be recognised by a row of small trees.

After crossing the Sülze stream, turn right onto the sign-posted cycle path that winds through the valley and leads

Damaged former GDR watchtower at Henneberg

to Sorghoff. There, turn right, cross Hermannsfeld and to the right, perched upon a hill, you will see an observation tower used by the former border troops and also a cross at the same height.

500 metres after leaving town, turn right onto the convoy road and you will reach Friedenskreuz.

TIPP

Friedenskreuz on the Dachsberg

The so-called Weltfriedenskreuz originates from an initiative by Gotthilf Fischer. Since 1980, the leader of the Fischer

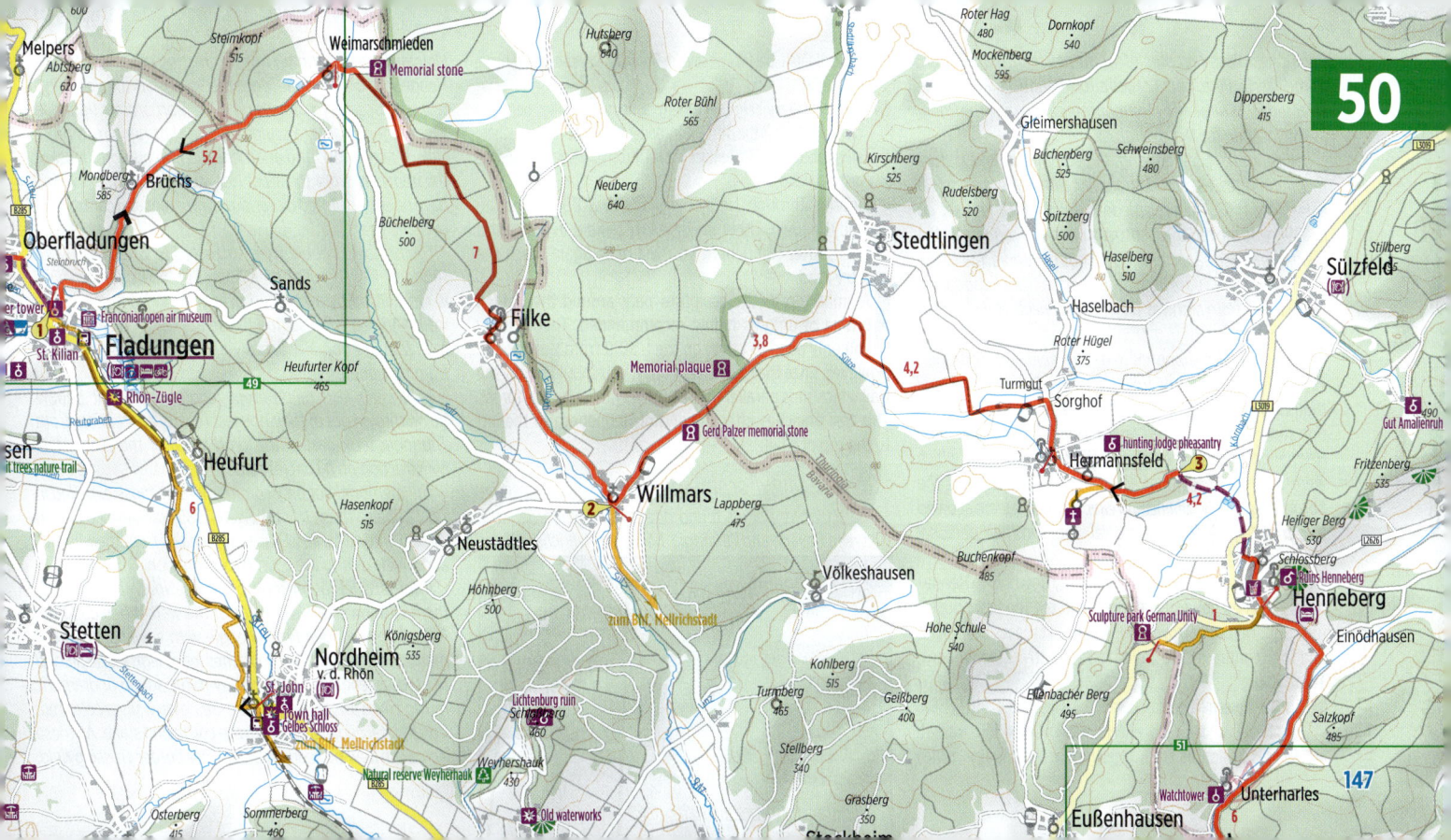

50

Melpers
Abtsberg
620
Steinkopf
515
Weimarschmieden
Memorial stone
Roter Hag
480
Dornkopf
540
Dippersberg
415

Gleimershausen
Schweinsberg
480

Mondberg
585
Brüchs
5,2
Büchelberg
500
Büchenberg
525
Spitzberg
500
Haseberg
510
Sülzfeld
Stillberg
Oberfladungen
Steinbruch
7
Neuberg
640
Roter Bühl
565
Kirschberg
525
Rudelsberg
520
Stedtlingen
Haselberg
510
Gut Amalienruh
590

tower
Sands
Franconian open air museum
Fladungen
St. Kilian
Rhön-Zügle
Filke
Memorial plaque
3,8
4,2
Haselbach
Roter Hügel
375
Turmgut
Sorghof
hunting lodge pheasantry
Fritzenberg
535
3
4,2
Heiliger Berg
530

trees nature trail
Heufurt
6
Heufurter Kopf
465
Gerd Palzer memorial stone
Willmars
2
Lappberg
475
Hermannsfeld
Schlossberg
Ruins Henneberg
Henneberg
Einödhausen

Hasenkopf
535
Neustädtles
Völkeshausen
Buchenkopf
485
Hohe Schule
540
Sculpture park German Unity
1

Stetten
Königsberg
535
Höhnberg
500
zum Bhf. Mellrichstadt
Kohlberg
515
Salzkopf
485

Nordheim
v. d. Rhön
St. John
Town hall
Gelbes Schloss
zum Bhf. Mellrichstadt
Lichtenburg ruin
Schlossberg
460
Turmberg
465
Geißberg
400
Ellenbacher Berg
495

Osterberg
Sommerberg
460
Natural reserve Weyhershauk
Weyhershauk
430
Old waterworks
Stellberg
340
Grasberg
350
Watchtower
6
Unterharles
147
Eußenhausen
49
zum Bhf. Mellrichstadt

Choirs has placed crosses of world peace in Washington, Rome, Jerusalem, the Bregenz forest and in Rhens. He selected St. Wolfgang by Hermannsfeld, a town in the Rhön, as the location for the sixth cross.

The church of St. Wolfgang, famous throughout history for pilgrimages, has stood on an island in the Hermannsfeld Lake since 1462. The Weltfriedenskreuz, which was set up in 1991, was moved to Dachsberg upon the request of the residents of Hermannsfeld. It is now directly adjacent to the former command base used by the border troops and can be seen clearly from highway 19, which connects Mellrichstadt with Meiningen.

The cross is also supposed to be a reminder of "operation vermin". In the weeks following May 26, 1952, several thousand people were forcibly relocated from the restriction zone. With the forced relocation of 18 families in 1952, Hermannsfeld belonged to the GDR communities, which were the most heavily affected by the "cleansing of the border area". Only "politically reliable" people were allowed to remain and received a special stamp in their personal identification.

From Hermannsfeld, continue slightly downhill to Henneberg. **3** When you exit the forest and see the first houses, turn right onto a narrow road. The road crosses the L 3019 and then continues as a paved road directly to Henneberg.

Henneberg

🏛 **Schiller-Museum**, Friedrich-Schiller-Str. 1, Bauerbach, ✆ 03693/43666
ⓔ Dieses schöne Fachwerkhaus war im Jahre 1782 Friedrich Schillers Zuflucht, als ihm 14 Tage Arrest wegen einer unerlaubten Reise drohten. Die Räume sind im Originalzustand zu besichtigen. @ ehn374

♂ **Burgruine Henneberg (Henneberg castle ruins)**, Schlossberg. The castle was built in the 11th century under the Count von Henneberg and peaked in the 13th century. In the 17th century it was abandoned and neglected.

Continue through Henneberg. The **L 3019** is directed around the town. There is a small restaurant in the centre of town. After Henneberg you will once again reach the country road.

> **TIPP** A small trip to the sculpture park around the golden bridge of unity is highly recommended. Theoretically you only need to travel on the L 3019 from Henneberg. However, since the road is very busy, you should follow the trail which runs parallel to the highway through the forest. This trail branches after the end of Henneberg to the left to the top of a hill.

"German Unity" sculpture park

The sculpture park is found directly on the border strip between Bavaria and Thuringia, between Mellrichstadt and

At the Henneberg Sculpture Park „Deutsche Einheit"

Meiningen, at the former border crossing of Eußenhausen-Henneberg on the B 19. There the "golden bridge of unity" was constructed, comprising of a Barbarossa figure, a silver federal eagle, a sculpture of a shot fugitive, a piece called "homeland" and another called "expulsion". Most of the items are from the artist Herbert Fell, but many works have been performed by various companies and contractors over the years.

The brutality people were subjected to when they were suddenly kicked out of their homes in "operation vermin", is symbolised by a knocked over chair in front of a house wall. And you will also find the sentence: "You can expel a man from his homeland, but you can't expel his homeland from his people."

Bent chair legs of different lengths represent people being thrown out of their houses. Twenty apprentices from Thuringia took part in the production of the black steel construction on a concrete slab.

The memorial not only commemorates those expelled in 1952 but also those from the year 1585 when Prince Bishop Julius Echter expelled Evangelic families from their homes and towns during the counter reformation.

A large celebration took place on November 9, 1999, the 10th anniversary of the fall of the wall. When darkness fell, a large wooden federal eagle with a wingspan of ten metres was set on fire. The flames leapt high in the air and the federal eagle burned brightly to the sound of dramatic music. Like a phoenix from the ashes, a new, silver coloured, iron federal eagle arose from the collapsing stake. All these items can now be seen on the former border crossing field.

Memorial plaque in Berkach

Friedensweg

Along the border strip from Eußenhausen to Birx in the Rhön, a 40-kilometre-long "Friedensweg" was constructed as a cycle and hiking trail, which is part of the German-German border trail.

On the same road return to the beginning of Henneberg. There turn right, travel through **Einödhausen** and you will find an observation tower used by the border troops in **Unterharles**, which is in the middle of some light-coloured timbered houses that are on the hillside. On the quiet country road, with slight hills, you will reach **Schwickershausen** where you keep to the left on the main road.

AUSSTIEG From Schwickershausen you can cycle to the train station in Rentwertshausen where trains depart to Erfurt and Würzburg.

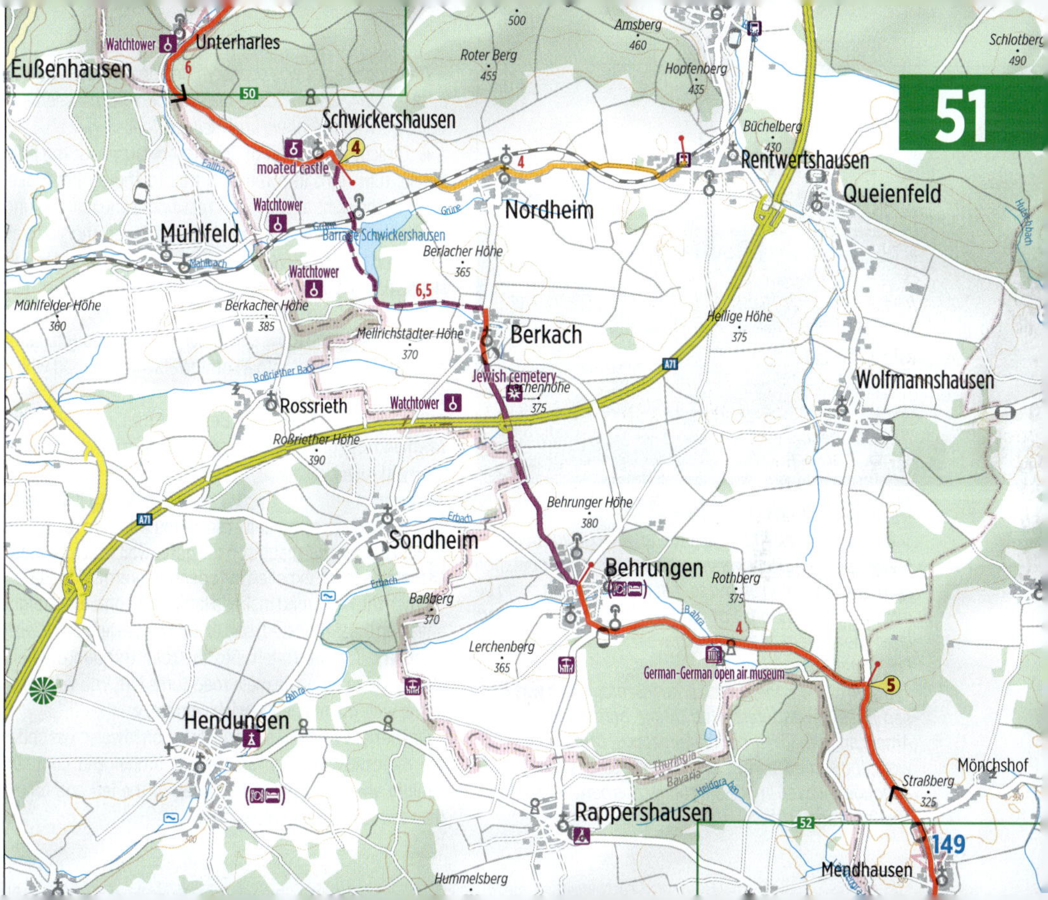

51

Eußenhausen
Unterharles
Watchtower
6
50
Schwickershausen
moated castle
4
Rentwertshausen
Queienfeld
Büchelberg
Mühlfeld
Watchtower
4
Nordheim
Baracke Schwickershausen
Berlacher Höhe
365
Wolfmannshausen
Heilige Höhe
375
Mühlfelder Höhe
380
Watchtower
Berkacher Höhe
385
6,5
Mellrichstädter Höhe
370
Berkach
A71
Jewish cemetery
Zehnhöhe
375
Rossrieth
Watchtower
Roßriether Höhe
390
Behrunger Höhe
380
A71
Sondheim
Behrungen
Rothberg
375
Baßberg
370
4
Lerchenberg
365
German-German open air museum
5
Hendungen
Straßberg
325
Mönchshof
52
149
Rappershausen
Hummelsberg
Mendhausen

Roter Berg
455
Amsberg
460
Hopfenberg
435
Schlotberg
490
500

The Behrungen German-German open air museum

Mellrichstadt-Rentwertshausen

After the reunification, the (second) railroad line between Mellrichstadt and Rentwershausen was taken into operation again in the autumn of 1991 so that Meiningen can again be directly reached from Schweinfurt. One and a half years later there were also trains travelling directly between Erfurt and Schweinfurt.

In July of 1945, the stretch Erfurt-Bebra, which was opened in 1847, was interrupted by the border between the American and Soviet occupation zones. During the repair work, the second railroad stretch was disassembled in 1946 although it was an important connection between southern Thuringa and Erfurt.

The second track was disassembled on the Bavarian side between 1947 and 1950. As of 1971, there hasn't been any trains between Mühlfeld and Mellrichstadt.

4 Directly at the end of Schwickershausen, at the little house, turn right into the slab trail to the artificial lake. Keep to the right at the lake, cross under the railroad and on the right you will see an old border tower. The slab trail is comfortable to travel on since there are no perforated slabs. When you approach the border tower, turn left and continue past the dam. Occasionally this trail leads directly over a meadow and is hard to get through. Later on, however, it turns into a comfortable gravel road which you can follow to Berkach.

Once you have reached Berkach, turn right into the town and straight towards a small, distinctive church with a curved tower.

Berkach

In the Berkach community centre you will find a restaurant with a memorial plaque on the outer wall which commemorates those expelled in "operation vermin" in 1952.

When the main road makes a left bend, continue straight ahead on the signposted road to Behrungen and the Jewish cemetery. If you turn left into the road through the field about 400 m after the main road turns left, you will come to the well-maintained **Jewish cemetery**.

On the right you will see an observation tower, cross under the motorway through an elegant tunnel and continue straight ahead to Behrungen. Keep to the left and follow the road towards Mendhausen.

Behrungen

Deutsch-Deutsches Freilandmuseum Behrungen (German-German open-air museum Behrungen), ☎ 09720/951212. At the edge of the Behrung forest you will find various border closing elements: an original piece of the border fence, a tank trap and an earthen observation bunker which was meant for defence purposes. There is also a watchtower with an information board. The open-air museum has made the most of the few resources it had and is well done. You can see the wide border strip, the original parts and can get an impression of the former border.

Shortly before you reach the sign at the end of Behrungen, you will find the former GDR border troops compound on the right. A little further on the right you will find the German-German open-air museum Behrungen.

The road is in Thuringian territory directly on the border. **5** After 3 kilometres you will come to a larger street where you turn left towards **Mendhausen** which you will reach after 2 kilometres downhill. Continue through the town, cross the former border and travel straight ahead towards Irmelshausen.

6 Turn left into the very busy main road without cycle trail shortly before you reach Irmelshausen towards the swimming area. Follow the signs and turn right at the second possibility and right again at the end. Immediately afterwards turn left over the stream onto a very nice road through the fields. Turn right at the end of the road with a view of **Wasserburg**.

Irmelshausen (Höchheim)

Wasserburg Irmelshausen. The water castle is one of the nicest in Bavaria, but can unfortunately only be viewed from outside. Built

in the 15th century as a timbered house, it lies in the middle of a former swamp area which was transformed into a small lake with an island in the middle by daming the Milz. The previous constructions are from the 11th century. The current owner of the castle, since 1376, is the von Bibra family, who were active in political matters at the end of the Middle Ages in Franconia and South Thuringia. Since they still live in the house, it is not currently accessible to the public. The view from the outside is impressive though and the castle has served as a movie location.

Turn left again at the next possibility, also over a stream, and continue straight ahead on the signposted road towards **Herbstadt**. The sloping pathway on the large mountain Gelichbueg, just before Herbstadt, allows you to take an alternative route. On the hill on the left is a watchtower, the mountain is called the **Große Gleichberg**. The paved road leads to a country road where you turn left and then reach Herbstadt.

A quiet country road leads to Bad Königshofen on the right after 6 kilometres. Cross the country road and continue to the centre of the city. At the end of the road, turn left and you will find the church.

Bad Königshofen im Grabfeld
prefix: 09761

Kurbetriebs GmbH, Am Kurzentrum 1, 📞 91200, @ soj672

Archäologisches Museum (Archaeological museum), Martin-Reinhard-Str. 9, 📞 3979011 ⊜ The museum tells the history of the city Bad Königshofen from the early history to the present. @ qqe431

Museum für Grenzgänger (Museum for border crossers), Martin-Reinhard-Str.9, access via the archaeological museum, 📞 3979011 ⊜, @ pwu342

Stadtpfarrkirche Mariä Himmelfahrt (Parish church of the assumption of Mary)

FrankenTherme, Am Kurzentrum 1, 📞 91200, @ oas234

The town, with a population of 7,000, is a resort area. It has a lake with supposedly healing waters, the first of its kind. In Ipthausen you will find a very nice pilgrimage church dedicated to Maria. There is also the largest compound with beos in Bavaria, the black bird with the strong voice.

In the town of Bad Königshofen, which was first officially mentioned in 714, you will also find the Frankentherme. The name originated from the story of a queen who lost a valuable ring in the „Grabfeld". According to legend, the queen ordered the entire area to be dug up in search of the ring, which then gave the area its name. She is said to

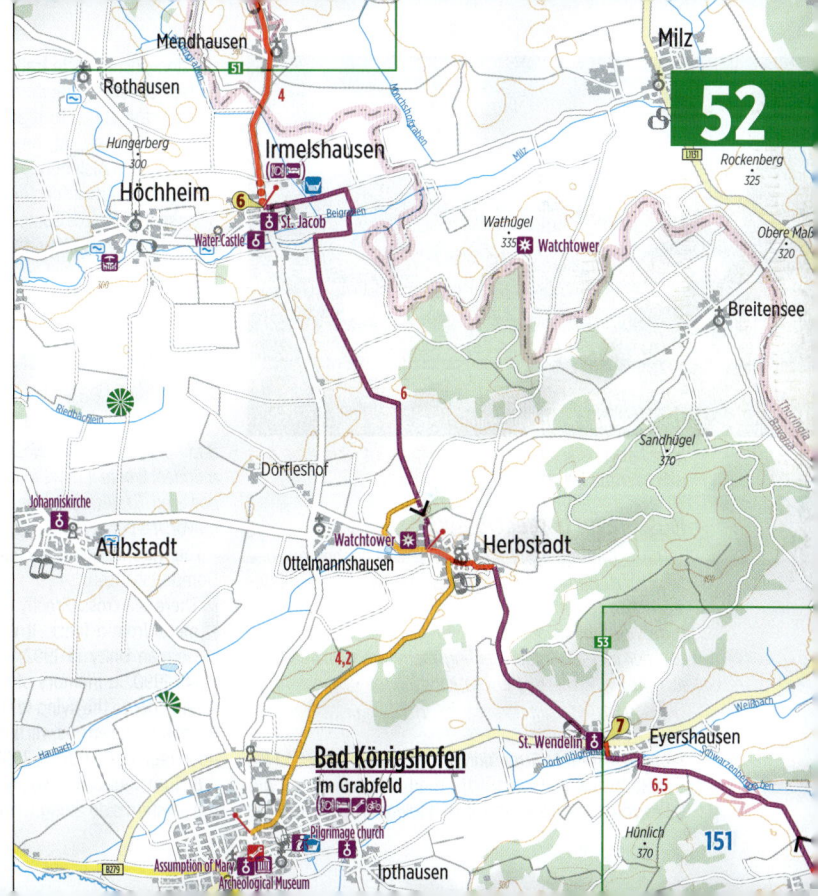

The "Bayernturm" at Zimmerau

have had a palace built exactly on the spot where the ring was eventually found.

Museum for border crossers

The "Museum for border crossers" was opened on June 17, 2007 in Bad Königshofen and is not limited to the demarcation and borders under the title "People in Grabfeld". It provides information about the personal stories of the "border crossers", representing many other "neighbours in Grabfeld". There is also a copy of the original inner-German border.

From Herbstadt to Streufdorf   57 km

In Herbstadt, at the fork in the road, where the road right takes you to Königshofen, turn left towards Eyershausen in the sign-posted **cycle trail "Rhön-Grabfeld"**. **7** In **Eyershausen** continue straight ahead over the main road until you reach a concrete road, which unfortunately has no sign, and turn left. At the end of the road, turn right and you will reach **Alsleben**.

Keep to the left and continue on the signposted Franconian Saale spring towards Gompertshausen on the **"Erlebnisstraße der Deutschen Einheit"** (The German Unity Experience Road). When the street bends around to the right, continue somewhat to the left on a concrete road to the **Franconian Saale spring**. Turn right at the next possibility and you will find a bench next to the spring.

Franconian Saale

The Franconian Saale winds over 135 kilometres through Bad Königshofen, Bad Neustadt and Bad Kissingen to Gemünden, where it flows into the Main. In the past, the Saale powered 16 mills in the area of Königshofen. According to the mayor, it is perfectly safe to drink the water from the spring.

You will once again reach the street and turn left towards Gompertshausen.

TIPP There is a cross directly on the border made out of the metal from a fence. It was erected on the day of the German Unity in 1992 with the following inscription: "1945-1990. In memory of those who died at the border. A reminder to the living for the future." In the direction of Gompertshausen you will find a tower which can be viewed upon request (℡ 09720/890).

8 Turn right before you reach the cross and continue on the western side along the border. Turn left after a right bend. The paved road winds through the landscape. At the end, turn left and follow the signposted road straight ahead. At the end of the gravel road you will find a barrier. Continue straight towards **Sternberg**. You will come to a small street where the **Bayernturm** and the cycle trail are signposted on the left. Follow this sign on the paved road towards Zimmerau.

Zimmerau (Sulzdorf an der Lederhecke)

Bayernturm. The 38-metre-high tower was built in 1966. It is square and has an observation platform from which one was once able to view the border facilities of the GDR.

AUSFLUG You can reach the Bavaria tower if you turn right onto the 3rd road to the sign-posted Berggasthof Bayernturm.

9 At the end of the road turn right and then left onto the country road and cycle towards Rieth, which is 4 kilometres away.

TIPP Cross the former border and travel through Thuringia again. Directly next to the street you will find a memorial stone on the former border with the inscription: "For the eternal reminder of the separation of our German Fatherland 1945-1990 Rieth/Zimmerau October 3, 1990." Next to a GDR border column and a memorial stone there are numerous segments of the border fence to be viewed. There is also a crucifix which was probably not there during GDR times.

Bush-crickets

Large numbers of bush-crickets can still be found in the fields of Thuringia and in the Black Forest. There are almost extinct in the rest of Germany because the fields

are mowed too early and are too heavily fertilised which is why there aren't enough herbs left for them to eat. The bush-cricket is the largest cricket in Germany with a length of up to 4.5 centimetres. It cannot fly or jump and plays dead when in danger.

Shortly before you reach **Rieth**, continue downhill and from there towards Hellingen. Cross a stream, continue through **Hellingen** and then further through **Volkmanns-hausen** towards **Poppenhausen**, which was once directly in the border area.

From there, continue towards Bamberg over the border to the county of Hildburghausen until you reach a country road and turn left.

On the right there is a sign to the border stone "Drei-ländereck". Continue on the paved road past the forest. When the forest begins, turn left over the field to the border stone, where the counties Coburg, Hildburghausen and Hassberge come together.

The country road to Lindenau is signposted. Continue through **Gleismuthhausen**. At the end of the village, follow the sign towards **Autenhausen**. **10** At the next intersection turn left towards Lindenau. Cross the convoy road and continue on the mostly-paved road towards **Lindenau**. Cross the little stream and you will reach the main road where you turn right. Pass the beautiful timbered houses and continue towards Ummerstadt which is 4 kilometres away.

On the uphill road you will pass the levelled village of Erlebach, a village which originated in the Middle Ages, which was located to the right of the street. A memorial plaque and numerous stones commemorate the fate of the

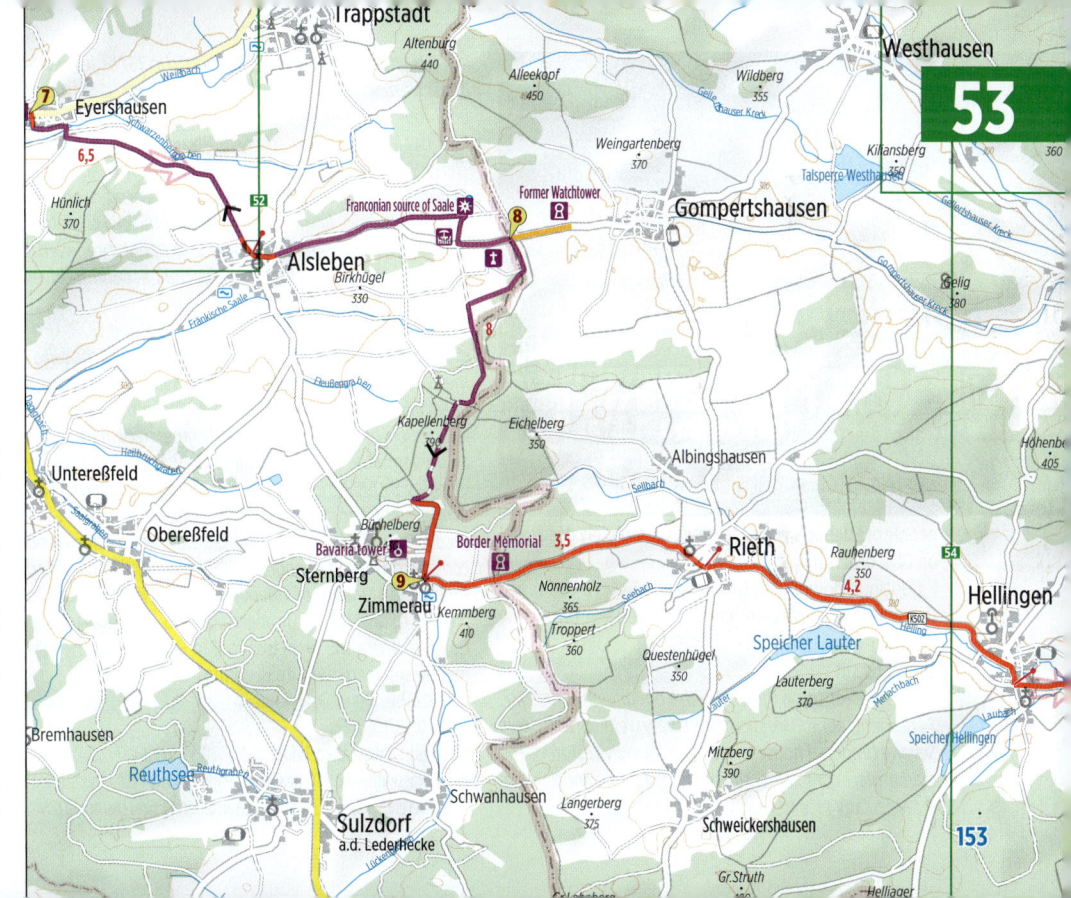

In Ummerstadt

people of Erlebach, whose town was completely destroyed on GDR orders.

Continue downhill to Ummerstadt. Before you reach the historical old town, cross the Rodach on a new bridge.

Ummerstadt

The smallest city in the GDR with a population of just 527, 34 residents per square kilometre, is very well kept and clean. Several timbered houses have been lovingly restored. The market place complete with city hall, restaurant and fountain is particularly nice to visit.

The town was first officially mentioned in 837 as „Undrungen novu mocru". The spelling of „Ummerstadt" is not found until four centuries later (1223). The town was fortified in 1319, but it was not granted city rights until 1394. During the Thirty-Year War, all public buildings were destroyed in 1632 as well as 52 houses. Eleven years later there were only 26 occupied houses. In the following years, the city therefore only had a population of 100. From the 18th century onwards, the pottery trade was the most important economic driver for the small town.

Due to the location in the border area of the GDR, Ummerstadt was subject to heavy emigration before the fall of the Wall. Already in 1952/53, citizens who were considered politically unreliable were forced to leave the town. The population of nearly 1,000 that Ummerstadt had at the beginning of the GDR in 1949 almost halved in the following decades. By 1982 Erlebach was completely evacuated. Thus, Ummerstadt became the smallest city in the GDR in the second half of the 1980's. After 1990 the emigration trend continued without change. In 1992 the population voted for the maintenance of independence in a public decision.

Keep to the left in Ummerstadt and continue to Bad Colberg where the cycle trail to Bad Rodach and the Billmethausen memorial site is signposted.

Bad Colberg (Bad Colberg-Heldburg)
prefix: 036871

- ℹ **Tourist-Information**, Hauptstr. 4, ✆ 20159, @ jci887
- ✉ **Terrassentherme (Terrass spa)**, Parkallee 1, ✆ 230. There are 11 different pools in this modern spa, in different sizes cascading down from one another. The leisure centre has numerous saunas and salt pools which offer a diverse range of wellness benefits. @ xth674

Heldburg (Bad Colberg-Heldburg)
prefix: 036871

- 🅿🏛 **Veste Heldburg und Burgenmuseum**, Burgstr. 1, ✆ 21210 ⊜ The castle was built in the 12th century on a cliff over 400-metres-high and expanded in the 14th and 16th century into an impressive Renaissance construction. @ vct744

Pass the spa and continue on a small road towards Gauerstadt. About 2 kilometres after Bad Colberg you will find the **Billmuthausen memorial site**, which became symbolic of the many levelled villages along the GDR border.

The razed village of Erlebach

Billmuthausen

The town was first officially mentioned in the year 1340 as "Billmethehusen". Today, not much is left of Billmuthausen after its complete demolition in the year 1978. Only the remains of the cemetery and the transformer tower still exist, the latter having been used by the GDR border troops. The beginning of the end of Billmuthausen was in the summer of 1945. Billmuthausen, which belonged to Thuringia since 1920, was occupied by US American troops on April 7, 1945. On July 1, 1945, the Americans retreated behind the Bavarian border and the Red Army approached. The demarcation line separated Billmuthausen from the neighbouring Franconian villages.

On May 26, 1952, regulations concerning the 500-metre-protection strip and the 5-kilometre-restriction zone came into effect where Billmuthausen was located. Now, entering the restriction zone and the protection zone was only possible with a permit. On the night of May 27 "operation vermin" began. The second wave hit the affected towns on June 4 starting at 0:45. Under police supervision, numerous families were forced to leave their houses with immediate effect and forced to relocate to the hinterland. In Thuringia, 3,423 people were affected, including numerous residents in Billmuthausen. On June 20, seven families with 34 people and their personal belongings crossed the demarcation line to Bavaria. At that time, the village was half desolate. In September 1961, the next emigration wave took place with "operation cornflower". In January 1965, the final destruction of Billmuthausen began with the demolition of the town

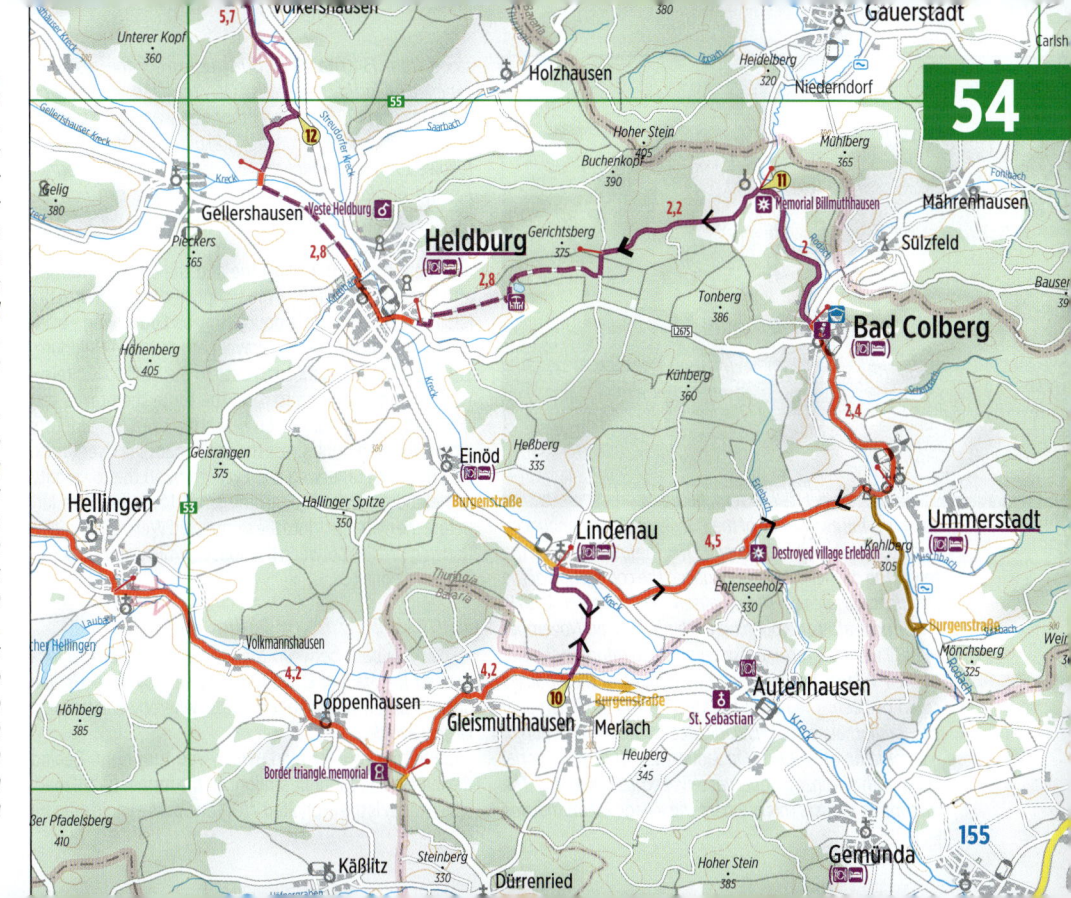

Former millstone and info-board at Billmuthausen

church. A full evacuation of the village was then announced by the officials. On September 1, 1978, the last family left the town. The district council announced the completion of the "border measures at Billmuthausen" on December 4, 1978.

Not until after the opening of the border on November 9, 1989 were the former residents able to return to the site of their village. Not even the foundations of their houses could be seen. The newly founded association "memorial site Billmuthausen e.V." is dedicated to the construction of a commemoration town. On January 22, 1992, a memorial stone with a bronze plaque was unveiled in a ceremony. The inscription reads: "This is where the village Billmuthausen

stood from 1340 to 1978. 1978 destroyed, the residents expelled." A further text reads: "Only the dead were allowed to remain." In 1996, the cemetery wall was reconstructed. In the summer of 1999 construction of the memorial chapel followed. At the entrance to the chapel a quote from former Federal President Richard von Weizsäcker can now be read: "Those who close their eyes to the past will be blind to the present."

11 Pass the former **millstone** and the **watchtower** and after the **memorial**, follow the signposted hiking trail to the left in the direction of Heldburg. Stay on **Lutherweg** – even when it bends right into a gravel path to Veste Heldburg. Then take the non-asphalted path to the right to Kuhteich, where there is an area to rest. The route then takes you downhill. Continue until you reach the road in Heldburg, where you turn right. Cross the main road, the river Kreck, turn right on Lutherweg and cycle through the town gate of Heldburg. Cycle through the small town and turn left before the river Kreck into the signposted Werra-Obermain-Radweg (WOM) between the houses, which later ceases to become asphalted.

Werra Obermain cyle path

The cycle path between the Werra in southern Thuringia and the Main in Bavaria through an idyllic landscape on well-paved or asphalted paths, whereby car traffic is largely avoided.

Come to a country road, where you turn right. Behind the river Kreck, continue straight on the former patrol road, which today is the asphalted WOM and pass a liquid manure

storage unit in Hunshaug. **12** Before the road, turn left and continue until you reach **Völkershausen** on the asphalted forest road. Stay on the WOM and reach **Seidingstadt**, where there is also a **railway museum**.

At the end of the village, the WOM turns right. Take the signposted "Grünes Band Thüringen" until you reach **Streufdorf**, where you can shop, stop for refreshments and spend the night.

Streufdorf

With a current population of 850, the town, which lies directly on the border between Thuringia and Bavaria, is now part of the Straufhain community. Streufdorf bore witness to the only active resistance which took place against the unjust regime of the GDR before 17 June 1953. In May 1952, the politically "unreliable elements" were removed from the GDR border area and relocated to areas further away from the border in what the SED called "Aktion Vergeziefer" (Operation Vermin).

At the time of the operation, Streudorf had a population of 1,400 inhabitants, most of them opponents of collectivization, factory owners, businessmen or "big farmers" with more than 20 hectares of land. The operation was jointly carried out by the Ministry of State Security (MfS) and the People's Police.

In Streufdorf, barricades were erected after the arrival of the People's Police and the possessions of the inhabitants, which had already been loaded on trucks, were quickly returned to the houses. On the market square, rubber truncheons were snatched from the police and used against

them. The "messengers" of the party were also beaten. More than 350 Streufdorfer, the Stasi noted, took part in the spontaneous resistance. It was only stopped when the People's Police sent another 500 men and the Soviet army threatened to deploy units.

After the uprising, 80 families left their village and were part of approximately 3,000 people who escaped the GDR by fleeing to West Germany. A total of about 12,000 people were resettled in "Aktion Vergeziefer" and "Aktion Festigung". The "Zweiländermuseum" also commemorates the victims of these events.

Rodachtal Zweiländermuseum

The museum has been exhibiting displays since 2009 on the last 100 years of life in this rural region and the history of the region in Franconia and Thuringia that was divided for 40 years. One particular exhibition is how life was in the restricted area from the construction of the border fortifications and "Operation Vermin" in 1952 to the opening of the border in 1989.

From Streufdorf to Neustadt near Coburg   50 km

In Streufdorf, follow the main road. **13** At the end of the village, turn left after the petrol station onto the well signposted (WOM) agricultural forest road that leads to **Stressenhausen**. WOM is shown at the InfoPoint, follow the sign straight ahead to Steinfeld. Once you are back on the WOM, pass an observation tower for the local scenery and turn right at the road. After about 200 metres turn left onto WOM. Here you will see an asphalted path, into

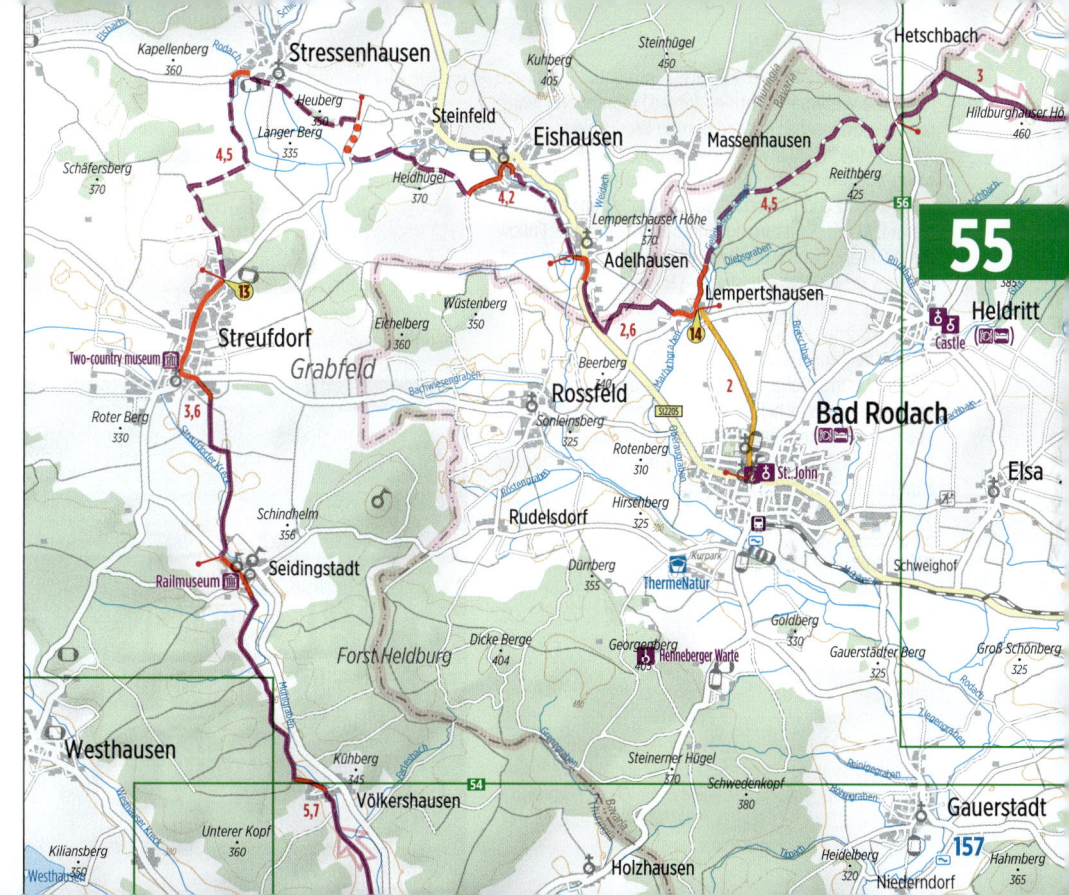

which you turn right up to the forest and continue until you reach the **Wehrmacht (armed forced) monument**, which commemorates the First and Second World Wars.

Follow the **"Mühlenwanderweg"** until you reach a road where you turn left and continue until you reach **Eishausen**. In front of the church, you will see the castle depicted in miniature. At this point turn right onto **Brunnenstraße**. Follow the WOM and behind the stream turn left onto a dirt road.

Follow the WOM to **Adelshausen** and cycle along the cycle path on the left side of the road. At the former German-German border a sign indicates the opening of the border. The border strip with the paved path is still visible. After 200 metres in Bavaria, turn left onto the asphalted dirt road and continue over a hill on an apple tree-lined avenue until you reach **Lempertshausen**. From there you can cycle to Bad Rodach, 2.5 kilometres away, where you can stop for a bite to eat and spend the night.

Bad Rodach

prefix: 09564

- ℹ️ **Gästeinformation (Visitor information)**, Schlosspl. 5, ✆ 1550, @ siq235
- 🛁 **ThermeNatur (Natural spa)**, Thermalbadstr. 18, ✆ 92320, @ fax481

The first official mentioning of the king's court "Radaha" dates back to the year 899, the beginning of the town however is said to date back as early as the second half of the 8th century.

Around 1300, a community was formed around the market place with its own system of law and order. In 1347, Rodach was granted its city arms, the Lion of Meißen, a black lion in a yellow field. In 1350, the church of Rodach was upgraded

to that of a parish church (St. Johannis) and the entire community was surrounded by a wall in 1386. The Castle of Straufhain was destroyed in the peasant war of 1525 and the ruins still remain today. With the expansion of the city wall in 1531, Rodach became a regional fortress.

During the Thirty Years War Rodach suffered from fire in 1632, leaving only a few original houses. Two years later the city was pillaged by the Emperors troops. Friedrich Rückert spent time in Rodach in 1814 where his poem "Idylle Rodach" was written. On July 1, 1892, the railroad line between Coburg and Rodach was opened. The "Free State of Coburg" which was formed after World War I, with a population of 75,000,

The Bad Rodach Town hall

which included Rodach, Neustadt and over 100 communities, became part of Bavaria in 1920.

On April 10, 1945, Rodach came under fire from American artillery.

Since drilling for a mineral spring was successful in 1972, Rodach was able to develop into a spa area. The warmest thermal spring in northern Bavaria bubbles at a depth of 652 metres and is 34° C. The 1,075th anniversary of the city was celebrated in 1974 and in 1976 the thermal spa was opened.

Following the completion of the regional reformation in 1978, Rodach now comprises 14 districts and has a population of about 6,500. In 1999 Rodach was recognised as a "spa" and has been called Bad Rodach ever since then. There are direct trains to Coburg and Lichtenfels from the train station.

Werra Railroad

The 130-kilometre-long Werra railroad from Eisenach to Coburg via Meiningen was inaugurated in 1858. Due to the demarcation line after World War II, the railroad operation was stopped between the stations of Eisfeld and Görsdorf as well as between Neustadt and Sonneberg.

In order to celebrate the connection between the Free State of Bavaria and the State of Coburg that has existed since 1920, the train station in Coburg was the first to receive electricity after the war. Today, regional trains travel between Coburg and Lichtenfels every day at two-hour intervals.

14 The main route takes you left in **Lempertshausen** towards **Massenhausen**. At the barn at the end of the village, keep right, cycle along an asphalted path that leads up into

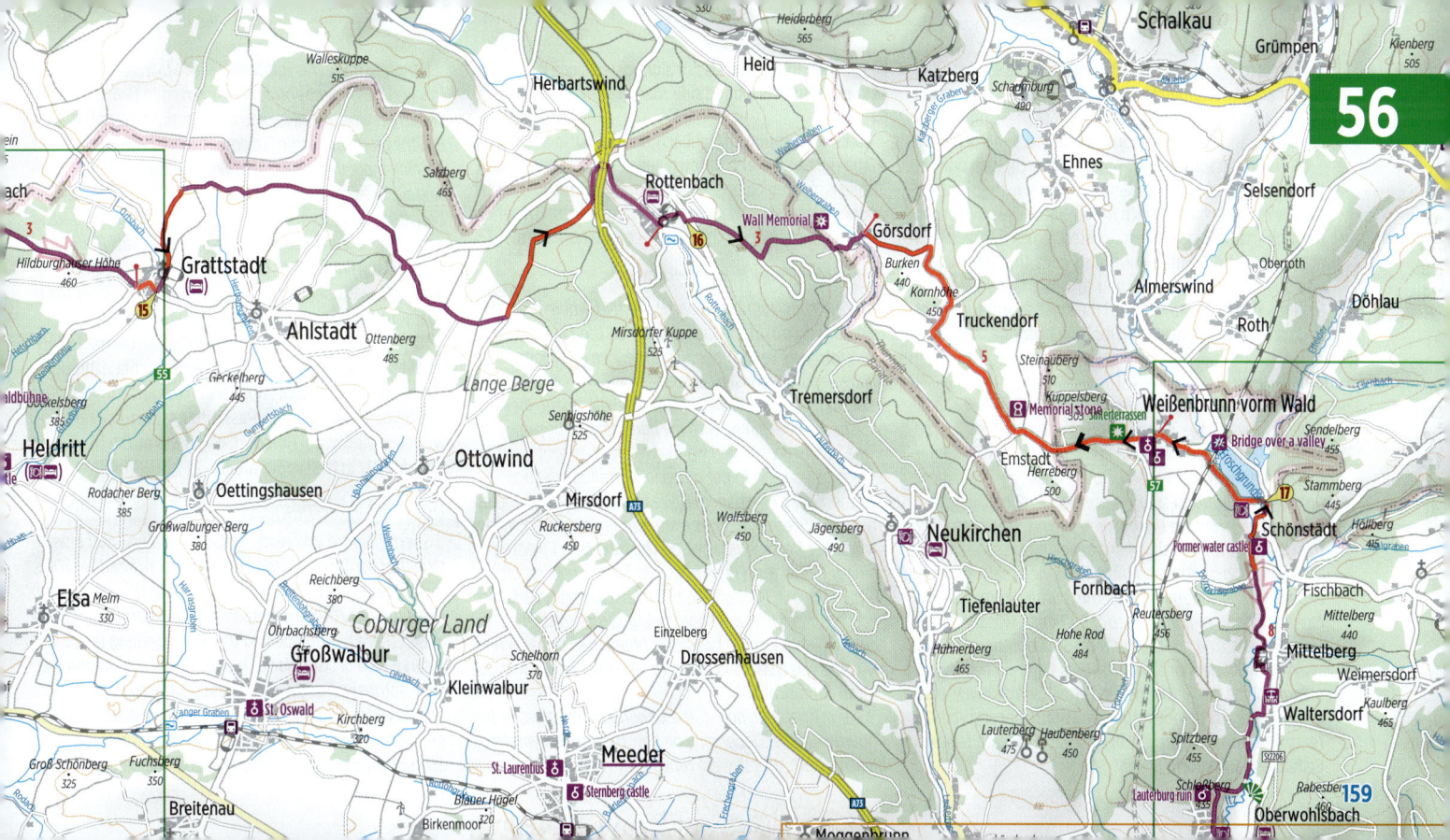

the forest to a gravel path, and follow the little stream. Stay left for about 3 kilometres on the main path, turn left at the crossroads with signs and a bench, cross the asphalt road on the left and follow the signs to Grattstadt in the forest.

15 In Grattstadt turn left, pass the church, turn right at the end of town towards Harras and follow the signs for the cycle trail until you reach Rottenbach. The paved road through the fields is well signposted. Cross the road and at the end of the path, which also goes through woods, you come to a road where you turn left. Continue uphill towards the motorway. Behind the small forest, turn right and continue underneath the motorway bridge.

Thuringian Waldbahnen

The A 71 motorway was planned in parallel and simultaneously with the railroad. While the last section on the motorway was inaugurated in 2008, it took 10 years longer for the railway to be finished. Due to allegedly insufficient finances, it only progressed in piecemeal. Progress was often just enough to secure the building permit. One reason for this was that the new railway line mainly crosses the Thuringian Forest on bridges and through tunnels making it very expensive and time-intensive. The journey from Berlin to Munich, with a maximum speed of 300 km/h, was shortened from 6 hours to 4 hours after a construction period of 20 years and a budget of 10 billion euros.

*Turn right at the fork in the road after the motorway, pass a rather interesting-looking transmission tower and you will reach **Rottenbach**. Turn left in the centre of town towards **Eisfeld** and **Görsdorf**.*

TIPP | The road to Görsdorf is not signposted since it is hardly known. But it is a good side road.

Continue through Rottenbach and take the small road to the right at the end of town which leads slightly uphill. Eisfeld is mentioned on the town exit sign as being the next village. After just a few metres you will reach the **B 4**, which these days is rarely used since the completion of the A 73.

Everyday life in the border area

The B 4 leads from Rottenbach to Eisfeld, where Wolfgang Thierse grew up. In the introduction to the first edition of this book on 17 September 2007, the Vice President of the Bundestag shared his experiences:

"During the inner German border's development, the town of Eisfeld, where I lived with my parents, also became part of the border area. If you wanted to enter, to visit relatives or friends, you had to get a special permit in advance.

In the 1960's I first lived in Weimar, where I completed my apprenticeship, later as a student in East Berlin. When my mother became ill, I got on the next bus. I wanted to be with her as quickly as possible. Since I had no official permit with me, I got off the bus a few stations in advance in order to get home without being discovered. My plan, however, went wrong. I was caught and had to pay a fine. My crime was that I had dared to visit my mother without official authorisation!

Near my parent's house, the Bahnhofstraße crossed the Coburger Straße. Depending on how the political wind was blowing, both streets were repeatedly renamed.

Bahnhofstraße was suddenly called Stalinallee, and when this was no longer opportune it reverted to Bahnhofstraße. The street which once lead to Coburg, the current B 4, even had the grandiose name "Street to Unity"! However, this was nothing more than an illusion! When a "GüSt" (border crossing site) was constructed in the late 1970's on the connection between Thuringia and Franconia, the optimistic-sounding name was cause for some consternation in East Berlin. The name was immediately changed to that of a communist leader. It was only in 1990 that it received the old name again. Today it is once again Coburger Straße."

16 Cross the highway and follow the narrow road which leads to the right up the hill. Afterwards, continue through a forest until an old tunnel appears on the left. This is where the railroad previously ran. Pass through the tunnel and you will reach the town of **Görsdorf**, which was on the Thuringian side directly in the border area.

Görsdorf Wall memorial

Shortly before you reach Görsdorf you will find a small stretch of border wall made from cement on the left. In 2003, this piece of wall was completely full of graffiti, however in the autumn of 2005, the memorial was painted a bright white again. There is a sign behind the wall regarding the nature reserve area of "Görsdorfer Heide" with the following text: "The border wall at Görsdorf was constructed in the 1980's and served to block the view towards the west. At the behest of the former mayor, Reinhold Meier, an approximately 30-metre-long piece of the wall was maintained after 1989."

Today the piece of wall is part of the "Görsdorfer Heide" nature reserve area as well as a cultural memorial and living space for small animals. In combination with the extensive fields of gorse, it is intended to be a habitat for small animals and butterflies. It is particularly suitable for the latter's hibernation. Located in a pipe, there is an entrance to a bat refuge and the cracks are perfect for insects, lizards and small animals.

Keep to the right in Görsdorf and continue towards **Katzberg**. One kilometre after leaving the town, turn right towards Emstadt. On the way you will travel through **Truckendorf**. Shortly before you reach **Emstadt**, which is somewhat secluded in the former border area, follow the road to the left towards Weißenbrunn.

The streets in this area are all pretty quiet, good to travel on and lead you through some beautiful scenery.

On the way to Weißenbrunn, you will cross the Thuringian-Bavarian border. A memorial stone was installed there on October 3, 1999: "10 years open border – in neighbourly solidarity Lauertal Schalkau Rödental."

Continue through Bavarian **Weißenbrunn** and you will come to the **Froschgrundsee** behind the town. Follow the road towards Fischbach, Rödental and Coburg.

In order to avoid unnecessary mounting and demounting, continue on the cycle trail to Neustadt/Coburg via Rödental.

17 After the dam, on the left is a parking lot with restaurant and cafe, turn right onto the cycle trail to Coburg. Once

A view from Bavaria of the barrier near Görsdorf, 1985

you have this steep stretch behind you, turn right again. Unfortunately, there are only signs in the opposite direction.

Continue directly along the river, after **Schönstädt** on the other side, cross a street and continue straight ahead. Cross a little bridge with a wonderful trail set apart from the street, pass sports areas and tennis courts, cross the river again over a bridge and continue on a good gravel road, which is later paved again, until you reach **Unterwohlsbach**.

18 For the main route, turn left in Unterwohlsbach towards Gnailes and Mönchröden. Continue through Rödental and cross the railway tracks.

Rosenau (Rödental)
prefix: 09563

🏛 **Museum für Modernes Glas (European museum for modern glass)**, Rosenau 10, ☎ 1606 📠, @ byj342

⛪ **Schloss Rosenau (Castle Rosenau)**, Rosenau 1, ☎ 3084-13, ⏰ April- Oct. 3, daily 9-18:00, Oct. 4-March, Tu-Su, So 10-16:00. Tours at the top of the hour. @ qbr834

Rödental
prefix: 09563

⛪ **St. Johannis (St. John's)**

🏨 **Rödenbad**, Bürgermeister-F.-Fischer-Str. 6, ☎ 1302, @ rvq526

The city was founded in 1971 from a merging of 16 independent communities. The oldest official mentioning of a settlement refers to the „Waltsassyn", the current community Waldsachsen, and is from the year 1317. There was once a castle in the centre of Waldsachsen but it was sadly destroyed by fire in 1822.

The picturesque Castle Rosenau in the Itz valley was the summer residence of the Dukes of Coburg. This is also where Prince Albert, later husband of the British Queen Victoria, was born. In the beautiful English landscape gardens, the classical teahouse now serves as a park restaurant. It is also worth visiting the late Gothic Church of St. Johannes. In 1863, Queen Victoria had it renovated at her own expense, in memory of her late husband.

In 2005, Rödental became known for the construction of the Itztal bridge, which belongs to the newly constructed section between Nuremberg and Erfurt. Due to lack of funds, however, it will probably remain unused for some time.

Turn right shortly before you reach the railroad tracks and you will once again be on the main route. Turn right here towards Neustadt.

AUSFLUG At this point in the main route, you can also travel to Coburg some 8 kilometres away.

A visit to Coburg

Continue straight ahead until you reach the country road to Kipfendorf where you turn right towards Einberg. In Waldsachsen, turn left before you reach the Krebsbach and continue along the river to the Mühlteich. Turn right before you reach the lake and in a left bend you will come to a country road where you turn right. Turn left shortly before you reach Rögen and follow the regional cycle trail through Seidmannsdorf to Coburg.

Coburg
prefix: 09561

ℹ️ **Tourist-Information**, Herrng. 4, ☎ 898000, @ nht614

🏛 **Coburger Puppenmuseum (Coburg doll museum)**, Rückertstr. 2-3, ☎ 891480 📠 900 dolls and numerous doll houses, doll carriages as well as toys from between 1800 and 1955 are exhibited here. @ efq768

🏛 **Naturkundemuseum (Museum of nature)**, Park 6, ☎ 80810 📠 The museum, founded in 1844, dates back to a collection of the dukes of Coburg. Since 1912 it has been housed in a separate building on the edge of the Coburg Court Garden. Exhibits include, among others: Earth history, evolution, man, minerals. @ pft176

⛪ **Heilig-Kreuz-Kirche (Holy Cross church)**, Hintere Kreuzg. 7

⛪ **Veste Coburg**, ☎ 87979 📠 The fortress originates from the 13th century and houses a significant art collection. You can see suits of armour, weapons, artistic works, the oldest carriage in the world,

the Lutherstube, pictures from Dürer, Cranach or Grünewald. @ mgr368

- 🏰 **Schloss Callenberg (Castle)**, Callenberg 1, ☎ 55150 🚋 The castle was first officially mentioned in 1122 and was the summer residence of the Dukes of Coburg. The compound is a significant architectonic work of neo Gothic in Bavaria and now houses the Duke's art collection (tours ☎ 55150) and the German Rifle Museum (tours ☎ 0611/4680739). @ isfz212

- 🏰 **Schloss Ehrenburg (Castle)**, Schlosspl. 1, ☎ 8088-32 🚻 The former Residenzschloss with arcades and garden at the foot of the hill with a neo Gothic facade from the 19th century houses the Coburg library. Tours at the start of every hour. @ xvq231

- 🏰 **Schloss Ketschendorf (Castle)**, Parkstr. 2, ☎ 15330. In the romantic castle of the singer Rosine Stoltz, you will now find the youth hostel of Coburg.

- 🏰 **Bürglaßschlösschen (Castle)**, Str. Oberer Bürglaß. Today the Coburg registry office is housed in the 18th century classicist building. Until the 1950s the house was called the Bulgarian Castle, because it was the residence of Tsar Ferdinand of Bulgaria for 30 years until 1948.

- ✳ **Coburger Erker (Coburg gazebo)**. The Coburg gazebo is a special architectonic feature from 1593, found at Castle Ehrenburg, at the city hall, at the registry office and a house in Markt 6; a total of 5 gazebos, which all have the same features unique to Coburg.

- ✳ **Reste der alten Stadtmauer (Remnants of the old city wall)**. The old city wall from the 15th century and the two city gates, the Judentor and the Spitaltor from the 13th century areall that remains of the fortification with 4 inner city gates. The only remaining outer gate is the Ketschtor from 1303.

- ✳ **Stadthaus (Townhouse)**, Markt 10, ☎ 891111. Elaborate construction of the late Renaissance from 1597-1601.

- 🏊 **Aquaria**, Rosenauer Str. 32, ☎ 7491640, @ cox483

This was first mentioned in 1056. In 1248 the "Veste" Coburg, the second largest active fortress in Germany, came into the possession of the Dukes von Henneberg. The city received the right of self administration and their own jurisdiction in 1331. In the year 1353, the Veste was transferred to the margrave von Meißen (House Wettin), whose descendants ruled until the end of World War I.

During the Diet of Augsburg (1530), Martin Luther lived in Coburg Veste for six months. When the dukes moved into Castle Ehrenburg, Coburg became its own state in 1547. In 1632 the Veste was occupied by Wallenstein without success. After a changing history and decades of probate disputes, the Grand

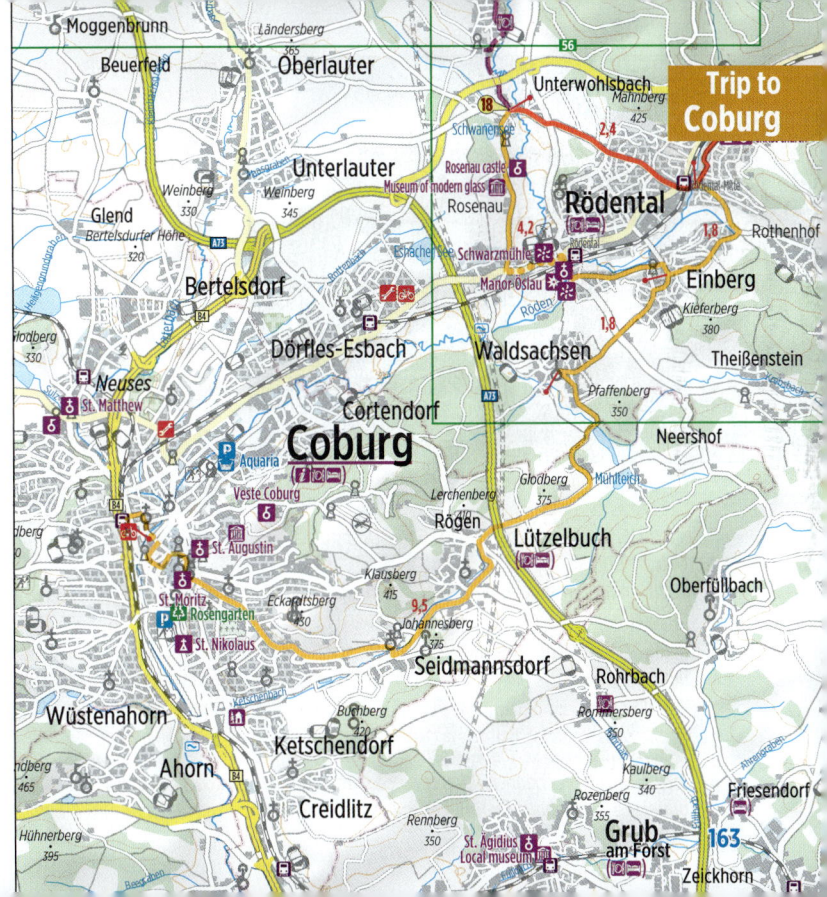

Coburg, Townhouse with Prince Albert Memorial

Duchy of Saxony-Coburg-Saalfeld was created in 1735 with Coburg as its residency.

In 1826, Duke Ernst I founded the Grand Duchy of Saxony-Coburg-Gotha.

The Coburg "marriage offensive" began which led to a relationship by marriage to nearly all European dynasties over the course of the 19th century. In 1840, Queen Victoria married her cousin, Prinz Albert from the Coburg house of Dukes.

In 1860, the first German sport festival took place in Coburg, and in 1862 the German Singers Alliance was founded. In 1866 Friedrich Rückert passed away here. His burial site is in Coburg-Neuses. On November 14, 1918, the

monarchy ended with the resignation of Duke Carl Eduard. In the first popular vote in Germany in 1919, over 88 percent of the voters were against the unification of the Free State of Coburg with Thuringia. Thus, Coburg became part of the Free State of Bavaria in the following year.

After 1922, Coburg turned into an important centre for National Socialism. Already in 1929, the NSDAP achieved the absolute majority for the first time in the town council election with 43 percent. On February 26, 1932, Coburg, was the first German city to grant Adolf Hitler Freedom of the City (revoked in 1946), and as such, as of 1939, it was allowed to carry the honorary title of the NS period "First National Socialistic City of Germany".

The city arms, which since 1430, had included Saint Maurice, the patron saint of the city, and was depicted as a "Mauretanian" with dark skin colour, was replaced in 1934 with a sword and swastika during National Socialism.

With the separation of Germany into four occupation zones, Coburg, surrounded on three sides by the Soviet occupation zone, became geographically and economically isolated as of 1945 due to its proximity to the border. With the integration of numerous expelled citizens and fugitives, the population grew to approx. 55,000 by 1950. After the end of the GDR, Coburg once again regained its function as the "interface" between Bavaria and Thuringia.

The city became a European City in 2005, in the same way as Würzburg, Frankfurt and Görlitz have done, due to its dedication to European thoughts and ideals. Coburg maintains very lively European city partnerships, is active in

the cultural exchange and has honoured citizens who stand for European values.

From Coburg continue on the same way back to Seidmannsdorf, Waldsachsen and Rödental until you reach Mönchröden and turn right shortly before reaching the railroad tracks.

From Coburg continue on the same way back to **Seidmannsdorf**, **Waldsachsen** and **Rödental** until you reach **Mönchröden** and turn right shortly before reaching the railroad tracks.

On the main route to Naustadt, continue along the Röden on the well-signposted cycle trail **"Main-Coburg-Tour"** until you reach the city centre of **Neustadt** by Coburg.

Turn left at **Bahnhofstraße** and immediately right again onto the cycle trail parallel to the main street.

AUSTIEG If you would like to travel to the train station, continue straight ahead until you reach the tracks and turn right to the train station in Neustadt by Coburg. From there you can travel directly to Lichtenfels, Nuremberg or Sonneberg and therefore also in the Thuringian Forest.

Connection Neustadt-Sonneberg

With the completion of the connection between Neustadt and Sonneberg on September 28, 1991, the decade long interruption of the route Sonneberg-Coburg-Lichtenfels was ended and a popular train connection was provided between the new and the old Federal States.

Neustadt bei Coburg

prefix: 09568

Stadtverwaltung (City adnministration), Georg-Langbein-Str. 1, ☏ 81133, @ qjv782

Informationsstelle über die Teilung Deutschlands (Information concerning the division of Germany), Austr. 99, ☏ 81126 ☺ The main focus is on the historical development of the division of Germany as well as life in areas formerly close to the GDR border.

Museum der Deutschen Spielzeugindustrie (German toy industry museum), Hindenburgpl. 1, ☏ 5600 ☺ The museum provides information about the mechanical and manual production of toys and about the doll making profession. A collection of over 800 traditional dolls from over 100 countries are on display. A special children's museum includes a "Father Christmas workshop" and the presentation of various fairly tales are a highlight for small visitors. @ csu366

Prinzregententurm. The Prinzregententurm (1905) on the Muppberg is a 28-metre-high observation tower and landmark of the city.

Märchenbad, Am Moos, ☏ 85239, @ ddd381

Hallenbad (Indoor pool), Wildenheider Str. 11, ☏ 89199-0, @ yui828

The city originated with the construction of a toll castle in the Rödenfurt in the second third of the 12th century. Due to the advantageous location on Judenstraße, a long trading street which connected northern and southern Germany, it soon developed into a market as a document from the year 1248 shows. Neustadt was granted city rights in the year 1316. Frederick the strict, landgrave of Meißen, gave the city the double tailed, red armoured black lion as the city arms.

To protect the citizens, the city council soon had a city wall erected with five fortified gate houses. They were, however, not able to protect them from dangers from within. In the years 1636 and 1839, large fires occurred and nearly burned the entire town down. From 1918 to 1920, Neustadt belonged to the Free State of Coburg until both were allotted to the Free State of Bavaria by a popular vote in 1920.

The residents of the city practiced carving utensils for a long time. In the 17th and 18th century, the weaving and nailery trade became common. At the beginning of the 18th century, the residents turned their attention towards the fabrication of dolls. In the following period, doll production in Neustadt was significant. Glass blowers from the Thuringian Forest complemented this line of business with the production of Christmas ornaments in Neustadt after World War II.

With the division of Germany after World War II, Neustadt became a border town. In the course of the territorial reformation, the guarantee of regional autonomy in the agreement with Bavaria from 1920 was lost and it was integrated into the county of Coburg as a "large district town" in 1972. Since May 1, 1978, no less than 21 districts belong to the city.

On November 12, 1989, the border to the neighbouring city Sonneberg in Thuringia fell and Neustadt was once again in the middle of Germany.

From Neustadt near Coburg to Stockheim   30 km

In Neustadt by Coburg, turn right from **Bahnhofstraße** and continue on the cycle trail until the end where you turn right. Keep to the left towards Sonneberg and continue on the cycle trail on the southern side until you reach the **"burnt bridge"**.

"Burnt bridge"

Die „Gebrannte Brücke" war am 1. Juli 1990 der Ort der Unterzeichnung des Vertrages über die Abschaffung der Personenkontrollen an der innerdeutschen Grenze durch die beiden Innenminister Peter Michael Diestel (DDR) und Wolfgang Schäuble (BRD). Bereits am 12. November 1989 wurde hier um 4.48 Uhr die Landesgrenze zwischen Bayern und Thüringen geöffnet und die Sperranlagen durch die Feuerwehr beseitigt.

Nach 1945 wurde die „Gebrannte Brücke" aufgrund ihrer Lage zwischen den Städten Sonneberg und Neustadt bei Coburg zum stehenden Begriff für die Auswirkungen der Deutschen Teilung. Ihr Symbolwert steigerte sich, als es während eines Fußballspiels zwischen einer Sonneberger und einer Neustadter Fußballmannschaft am 31. Juli 1949 zu einer Massenflucht über die Grenze kam. Letztmalig erfolgte eine Öffnung des Grenzübergangs 1951.

Sonneberg

Die Stadt Sonneberg erstreckt sich auf etwa 45 Quadratkilometer über die Linder Ebene bis an die Landesgrenze Thüringens. Von den Bergen rund um Sonneberg eröffnet sich ein weiter Blick in das oberfränkische Land.

Auf dem Gebiet der heutigen Stadt waren während des 11. und 12. Jahrhunderts mehrere Siedlungen entstanden, die Angehörigen des niederen Adels Möglichkeiten zur Etablierung eigener kleinerer Herrschaften boten. Ende des 12. Jahrhunderts errichteten sie eine Burganlage, nach der sie sich auch nannten.

Unterhalb der Burg entstand eine kleine städtische Siedlung, die bereits 1317 als „Rotin unter (der Burg) Sonneberg" genannt wurde. 1349 wurde sie mit den gleichen Rechten der Nachbarstadt Neustadt ausgestattet.

Wirtschaftliche Grundlage war im späten Mittelalter der Abbau von Schiefer und Grauwacke und deren Verarbeitung zu Wetzsteinen. An dessen Stelle trat im 17. und 18. Jahrhundert der Handel mit Holzwaren, später auch mit Spielwaren, der seit dem 18. Jahrhundert den Schwerpunkt bildete. Dadurch wurde Sonneberg zu einem Zentrum des Weltspielzeughandels.

Obwohl nach dem Ersten Weltkrieg dessen Bedeutung zurückging, blieb Sonneberg Mittelpunkt eines durch vielfältige Industriezweige (Spielzeug, Porzellan, Glas, Maschinenbau) geprägten Wirtschaftsraumes, mit regem Austausch zwischen Nord/Süd und Ost/West.

Die Teilung Deutschlands beendete diesen Handelsverkehr. Die Stadt lag nun im Fünf-Kilometer-Sperrgebiet am Rande der DDR, was die wirtschaftliche Entwicklung stark einschränkte. 1952 und 1961 wurden Oppositionelle zwangsausgesiedelt, die letzten Privatbetriebe der Spielzeugindustrie 1972 verstaatlicht und zu volkseigenen Betrieben zusammengefasst.

In Sonneberg traten am 23. Januar 1990 der Bürgermeister und alle Ratsmitglieder aus der SED aus und folgten damit dem Magdeburger Oberbürger-

Sonneberg (1984/2006)

meister Werner Nothe, der das eine Woche vorher getan hatte und damit ein Beispiel gegeben hatte, dem immer mehr Städte und Gemeinden folgten. Danach wurde Sonneberg mit Neustadt bei Coburg kulturell und wirtschaftlich immer enger wieder miteinander verbunden.

19 Turn right from the "burnt bridge" towards **Ebersdorf**. This is where the first portion of the 10,000-kilometre-long European Iron Curtain Trail was opened on June 2, 2009 by the mayors of Neustadt by Coburg and Sonneberg. The cycle trail between the "burnt bridge" and the levelled village of Liebau was built in a very bicycle friendly way and is signposted with the EuroVeloRoute EU logo.

Turn left at the next road onto the cycle trail signposted as the **"Iron Curtain Trail"** which meets the street again in Ebersdorf. Turn left and continue until you reach **Heubisch**, cross the main road and continue straight ahead on the sign-posted cycle trail along the Steinach until you reach **Mupperg**. **20** Turn left, cross the Steinach and turn right onto the main road. Continue to Bavarian **Fürth am Berg**.

After the former hotel "Grenzgasthof", continue straight ahead past the sign-posted cycle trail and pass the memorial stone which commemorates the levelled village of Liebau on the other side of the border.

Two stones and a map inform visitors of the levelled village of Liebau: "This is where the village of Liebau once stood, first mentioned in 1317, its

residents fled in 1952, the village demolished in 1975 upon order of the SED regime. Mupperg 1992."

Continue straight ahead, cross the border again and you will reach the street which later turns left towards **Schwärzdorf**. Turn right there, pass the fire department building that looks like a church, pass **Schnitzerswüstung** and you will reach **Neundorf**. **21** Turn left towards Bächlein, cross the Föritz, and you will reach **Bächlein** on a slightly uphill street. There you will find the Waldhotel and beer garden directly on the street.

Ignore the cycle trail to Kaltenbrunn and continue towards Haig. Pass the **Krötendorfwustung** and the **Schaumbergwustung** and you will come to a country road which leads to **Haig** roughly 2 kilometres away.

Sylvester Murau

The former border crossing near Kronach was the site of a gruesome German-German family drama. The former Stasi major Sylvester Murau (1907-1956) had left the GDR in October 1954 and found a new home in the town of Heubach in Hessen. Operation "bounder" was supervised by Albert Schubert. Murau´s own daughter Brigitte, helped the Stasi in luring her father into a trap so that he could be taken back fo the GDR by two criminals on 24 July 1955. After a 300-kilometre-long drive, they took her father, who had been subdued by alcohol, in their car to the GDR border near Kronach and from there to the Stasi headquarters in Berlin Lichtenberg.

Sylvester Murau had the dubious honour of being the first opponent of the Socialist Unity Party to be kidnapped by the Stasi in West Germany. He was sentenced to death by the district court in Cottbus by judge Lucie von Ehrenwall, whom the people aptly called "Bloody Lucie". The public was not allowed at his trial. Murau allegedly "waived" his right to a judge as he believed, rightly, that his death sentence had already been fixed and quite literally signed off five weeks before the start of his trial due to Ulbricht´s signature in the head office on 13 January 1956. On 16 May 1956, Sylvester Murau was beheaded by a Nazi-guillotine in the courtyard of a Dresden prison at the hands of the hangman Walter Böttcher, who by this point, had already executed over 60 prisoners.

His daughter went on to have a career in the Ministry for State Security (Stasi) and later married the Stasi general major, who had led her father`s kidnapping. Albert and Brigitte Schubert lived in Berlin Hellersdorf for 50 years afterwards, where Jürgen Schneider was able to interview them for his book "The Stasi lives".

On the cycle trail signposted as "Oberfranken Radweg 2", "Obermain-Frankenwald Tour" or "Main-Coburg Tour", you will reach **Rottelsdorf** after two kilometres. **22** Once there, turn left towards Haßlach.

If you want to cycle to Kronach, go straight on to Knellendorf and from there continue along the railway line to the city of Kronach which you'll reach after about 5 kilometres. From the train station in Kronach there are direct trains to Saalfeld (Saale) and Lichtenfels.

Kronach

prefix: 09261

A view from Bavaria of the barrier before Sonneberg, 1985/86

ℹ️ **Tourismus- und Veranstaltungsbetrieb der Lucas-Cranach-Stadt Kronach (Tourism- and events in Lucas-Cranach town of Kronach)**, Marktpl. 5, ☎ 97236, @ bvg731

🏛️ **Fränkische Galerie (Franconian gallery)**, ☎ 60410 ♿ In the Franconian gallery you can see significant works from Lucas Cranach and Tilman Riemenschneider. In the summer months the popular Rosenberg Festival takes place every year with various theatre performances. @ aca433

🏰 **Festung Rosenberg (Castle Rosenberg)**, ☎ 60410. The castle was first officially mentioned in 1249. In the 14th century, it was promoted to an Episcopal regional castle and was expanded in the 15th and 16th century. This well-preserved, stone, monster of a fort was

Kronach

The district town with a population of 16,000 is the centre of the Franconian Forest and belongs to the most beautiful medieval cities of Upper Franconia.

The Lucas-Cranach town celebrated its 1,000th anniversary in 2003. Lucas Cranach the Elder (1472-1553) is one of the main masters of the southern German Renaissance painting and the most famous son of the town.

Kronach was officially mentioned for the first time as "Urbs Crana" in 1003 and the fortress Rosenberg in 1249. As the most northern fortress of the bischopric, the city had an excellent defence function with the fortress on the Rosenberg. It is considered to be one of the largest and best maintained fortresses in Germany.

The Jewish synagogue only remained during the Pogrom because the former head of the Jewish congregation sold the synagogue to the city of Kronach at the right time. Since 2002, the victims of the auxiliary concentration camp are commemorated in Kronach before the doors of the city.

The inner German border separated the area over a distance of 102 kilometres from the neighbours in Thuringia. The local railroad Pressig-Tettau was closed because it was no longer allowed to travel the 6.8-kilometre-long stretch in GDR territory.

The opening of the border began in Kronach on November 11, 1989, when thousands of GDR citizens crossed over the border between Probstzella and Ludwigstadt. At Falkenstein, which marks the middle of the 600 kilometre-train distance between Munich and Berlin, the first road crossing from Thuringia to Bavaria was opened one day later.

never taken or destroyed. During the Thirty-Year War, the fortification with 14-metre-thick walls resisted massive attacks by the Swedes – not least thanks to the women pelting the fleeing enemy with paving stones and throwing boiling water on them. During the First World War, the castle served as a prison camp and its most famous inmate was Charles de Gaulle. The last major renovation works to be carried out were completed in the 17th and 18th century. @ fil817

✿ **Obere Stadt (Upper town)**. Historical old town worth visiting with completely maintained city wall, elaborately restored houses, medieval towers, idyllic squares and romantic alleys.

⚓ **Crana Mare**, Gottfried-Neukam-Str. 25, ✆ 2377. Adventure pool, @ spk312

On the main route, travel towards Haßlach along the stream of the same name, cross under the railroad tracks, cross the main road, stay on access roads and continue on the Rennsteig-Main-Lions cycle trail along the Haßlach between the houses and the stream.

AUSFLUG From Haßlach you can also visit the Friedenskapelle in Burggrub.

Peace Chapel in Burggrub

On the former inner German border to Thuringia, you will find the "Border and Peace Chapel" which was constructed in 1992 out of gratitude for the peaceful reunification. There you can find information concerning the period of separation and the opening of the border and enjoy the view over the former Bavarian-Thurinigian border area.

Since there was no counter-reformation, Burggrub is one of the few villages in southern Kronach which is mostly Evangelic-Lutheran. The town between the Evangelic Saxony (now Thuringia) and the Catholic Bamberg was destroyed many times during the Thirty Years War.

If you continue straight you will reach Stockheim where you can stay the night.

Stockheim (Oberfranken)

From Stockheim to Lauenstein/Ludwigsstadt   **31 km**

Where the road goes off to the right over the bridge towards Wolfersdorf, continue over the river, through **Wolfersdorf** and turn left onto the **R 3**. After the Grössan brook, turn left and then right again to **Neukenroth** into

Rosenau. Behind Schwedenstraße, turn sharp left onto **Dorfäcker** street and at the next possibility turn right onto the small narrow trail next to the green fence. Cross the Haßlach on a beautiful pedestrian bridge and then take the B 85 on the right. On **Am Schwarzenbach** street, cross the tracks, behind which you immediately turn right and cycle past a lake.

Continue along the railroad tracks until you come to the fork in the road and follow the signs of the Rennsteid cycle trail to the left.

TIPP Pressig lies to the right. The interzone trains also stopped at the train station Pressig-Rothenkirchen on their journey between West Berlin and Munich.

In order to climb the Frankenwaldrampe between Pressig and Ludwigstadt, the trains had to be strengthened with a helper engine. Since they had to stop here anyway, the passengers were allowed to enter and exit. After the end of the GDR, stronger locomotives came into use and there wasn't any need for the stop anymore. Today, regional trains travel from Pressig-Rothenkirchen to Saalfeld (Saale) and Lichtenfels.

23 Turn left at the next crossing, not up the hill to the right, pass a small lake on the left and continue on the "western" side of the border. Cross the border strip, continue along the former convoy road and turn right at the road towards Heinersdorf, which was escaped being levelled even though it was very close to the border.

Heinersdorf (Judenbach)

🏛 **Gedenkstätte Heinersdorf-Welitsch (Memorial site)**, Welitscher Str. 17. The outer area can be visited around the clock. In the wooden

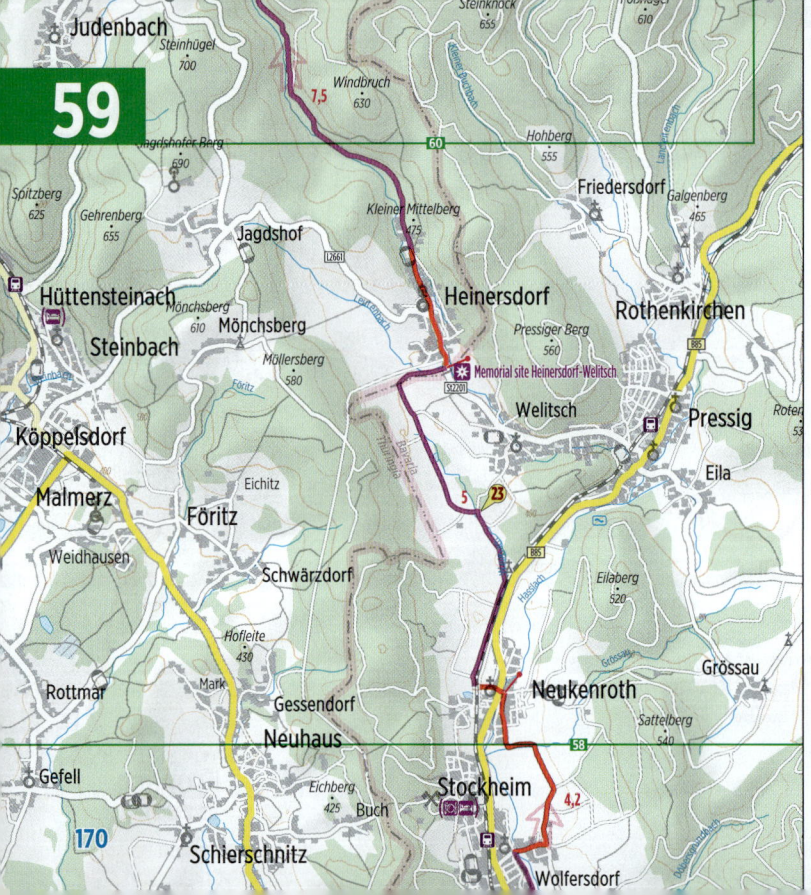

barracks of the small former border crossing Heinersdorf-Welitsch there are exhibits from the time between closing the border and the fall of the wall. The exhibition is only open upon request ☏ 03675/744516 or 09261/20480. @ kkd554

Heinersdorf-Welitsch memorial site

At the beginning of town, the association of the same name opened a memorial site consisting of three partial areas. For example, 30 metres of the once 750-metre-long and 3.30-metre-high concrete wall have been maintained. This wall completely separated the two towns from each other. Furthermore, there are one-metre-deep car trap ditches, six-metre-wide control strips, a convoy road, a watchtower and behind that, a further three-metre-high border fence which was adjacent to the five-kilometre-wide restriction zone. Furthermore, there is a barrier in the Tettau river which was created to prevent escape via the small river.

Continue through Heinersdorf and then on the paved forest road along the Tettau in the former border strip. Cross the border from Sonneberg county to Kronach county, continue following the Rennsteig cycle trail which leads through Tettau valley. **24** Turn right at the road towards Schauberg.

Schauberg (Tettau)

At the end of town, you will find a memorial with the inscription: „For all the victims of violence – love one another as I loved you". It commemorates six border police who died when a truck fell from a cliff on August 26, 1962. The cross is opposite the accident site. The text is unusual since it commemorates the dead on both sides of the border.

Continue on the **"Rennsteig-Main-Lions Cycle Trail"** towards **Tettau**. In order to get to the nature park information centre Spechtsbrunn (here you can find information concerning the three nature parks, Thuringian Forest, Thuringian Slate Mountains/Upper Saale and Frankenwald as well as about the "Green Belt") continue straight behind the border in Thuringia and then to the left.

The main route turns right behind the border onto an unpaved forest path along the border and you will then reach the Rennsteig monument as well as the old army and trade route with the Rennsteig. You will come to a rest area with an information board commemorating the reopening of the Rennsteig on 28 April 1990.

At this location, the so-called slate field, you can get some information concerning the "Green Belt".

TIPP

The Rennsteig

The Rennsteig was first mentioned as "Rynnestig" in 1330 and, with 100,000 visitors per year, is the most popular hiking trail in Germany. It is 170 kilometres long, originated in Eisenach on the banks of the Werra and runs southwest to Blankenstein an der Saale. The largest part runs through the Thuringian Forest and only 12 kilometres are in Bavaria. Rennsteig and Rennwege, two out of over 220 trails in the German speaking area, were used by an ancient network of messengers, who traversed them by foot or on horseback because they were the shortest distances between the important towns.

The prehistorical age of these trails has also been confirmed by archaeological findings. The courier trails usually led through forests on ridges, far away from settlements, to avoid attacks. The bordering Frankenwald not only forms the water divide between the Elbe and Rhein but also the language border between the Thuringian and the Franconian dialect.

25 After the rest area, continue straight towards **Lichtenhain**. Cross the street, continue on the paved road, turn left to the restaurant called "Grüner Baum", turn right after the church and continue straight ahead until you reach Lauenstein. Turn right at the first crossroad, the next leads to the convoy road towards Lauenstein. The short compact section soon turns into perforated slabs.

After two kilometres, the road goes down a very steep hill. Afterwards turn left from the convoy road onto the forest trail and continue further downhill until you reach a gravel area. Keep to the right and you will soon reach a street.

TIPP On the corner to the left is the "cook grave", also called "women's grave". According to legend, at this location in the 16th century, under the rule of the "Knights of Thüna", a cook from Castle Lauenstein was tied to a stake and buried alive because she was convicted of infanticide according to the Mirror of the Saxons.

Follow the street to the right and you will reach Thüringer Warte.

Thüringer Warte

At the summit of the 678-metre-high Ratzenberg in Bavaria you will find the "Thüringer Warte" observation tower. The nearly 27-metre-high tower stands about 200 metres from the former German-German border.

60

A view from Bavaria over the border-wall at Heinersdorf, 1985

The construction of the tower began on April 3, 1963 and was opened on June 17, 1963. About 6,000 to 7,000 visitors came to the opening ceremony. Five years after the opening, there were 180,000 visitors, and by the end of 1992, 905,943 individual visitors had been counted.

The observation tower was renovated in March 1994. Although the tower no longer has the importance it once had, for example when you were able to view the border facilities, the view over Thuringia is still impressive. An exhibit inside the observation tower sheds some light on the history of the inner German border.

Pass Thüringer Warte and continue downhill to Lauenstein Castle, at the foot of which you can enjoy a meal.

Lauenstein (Ludwigsstadt)
prefix: 09263

🔊 🏛 **Burg Lauenstein (Lauenstein Castle)**, Burgstr. 3, 📞 400 ➡ Medieval castle in the Thuringian-Franconian Slate Mountains. The oldest construction materials date back to the 12th century. The castle was first officially mentioned in 1222. In the years 1551 to 1554, the main part of the castle, known as the Thünabau, was built. In 1622, the castle was bought by Margrave von Brandenburg-Kulmback-Bayreuth. In 1791 it fell to the Prussians, in 1803 to Bavaria. In 1896 Dr. Erhard Messmer purchased the neglected castle and had it renovated and newly decorated. Since 1962, the castle has been under the ownership of the Free State of Bavaria. The main castle now houses a museum with over 20 rooms. @ sjk514

From the Lauenstein Castle continue downhill until you reach the **B 85**.

AUSSTIEG If you would like to travel to Ludwigstadt, where trains depart to Saalfeld, Kronach and Lichtenfels, you must turn right. Roland Jahn has some uncomfortable memories of this former border station.

Roland Jahn

On 8 June 1983 the civil rights campaigner arrived at the border station in Ludwigstadt at around 3.17 am. A group of six to eight people had taken him to the GDR border station in Probstzella in chains and had put him into a separate compartment at the end of a regular train. They locked the door behind him and the train conductor was ordered to only open the compartment once they had crossed the border. There he told the federal German customs agents: "I am still a GDR citizen!"

Roland Jahn (*1953) was one of the famous GDR civil rights campaigners and co-founder of the Jena Peace Union. After his public protest against the expatriation of Wolf Biermann 1976 the student was expelled from university and worked as a transport worker. He did not want to leave the GDR but instead, wanted to change it. He uncovered many injustices and used his imagination to make them known to the public, often with the help of the Western media. For example, in 1977 he took an empty white banner to the official Labour Day demonstration on 1 May or flaunted the symbol of the GDR peace movement "Swords into Ploughs" at one of the peace demonstrations of the Free German Youth (FDJ) in Jena. The Soviet Union gifted this sculpture and it has been decorating the entrance of the UNO headquarters in New York since 1959. They took up the biblical motif of the prophet Micah: "In the last days the nations will come to Zion and they will forge their swords into ploughs".

After a protest at the military parade on 1 May 1982 he was arrested and interviewed by the police. Because he had mounted on his bike the Polish national flag with "Solidarność" written on it, he was arrested again on 1 September 1982 and this time sentenced to 18 months' imprisonment as a result of "publicly vilifying the state order". After this, the Stasi tried hard to convince him to leave the country.

After six months of solitary confinement and psychological torture, he was released due to protests from the Federal Republic of Germany. He was expatriated against his will and deported to the West, where he worked as a journalist

for the RIAS (Radio In the American Sector), the newspaper "tageszeitung" and the ARD TV magazine "Kontraste".

In West Germany he was one of the most vocal GDR opponents, along with Wolf Biermann and Jürgen Fuchs. He was a contact person for rallies and organised printing presses, video cameras, books and computers and had them smuggled into the GDR with the help of a courier network. This way, for example, he was able to contribute to the film "Bitter things from Bitterfeld" ("Bitteres aus Bitterfeld".)

In 1985 he used the landing of a plane on the East-Berlin airport Schönefeld, in order to pay a short and illegal visit to his friends in Jena and East Berlin, despite his entry prohibition. For the Ministry for State Security, that watched his every move right until the end – also in the West, he was a great enemy and they accused him of cooperating with Western secret services. This resulted in his honorary membership of the East-Berlin Environment-Library, which had been given to him in 1987, being renounced again in 1988.

His biggest "success" was the video camera, which opposition members Siegbert Scheffke and Aram Radomski used to film the mass demonstrations in Leipzig on 9 October. Roland Jahn had not only organised the camera but also managed to get national TV stations to air the first pictures the next day. This demonstration with 70,000 participants – all were afraid of the "Chinese solution" as supported by Egon Krenz, with which the opposition movement on Tiananmen Square in Beijing had been struck down – is today seen as a deciding factor for the success of the peaceful revolution in the GDR.

After the end of the GDR he helped in the unravelling of all the facts of the SED-Dictatorship and began researching the

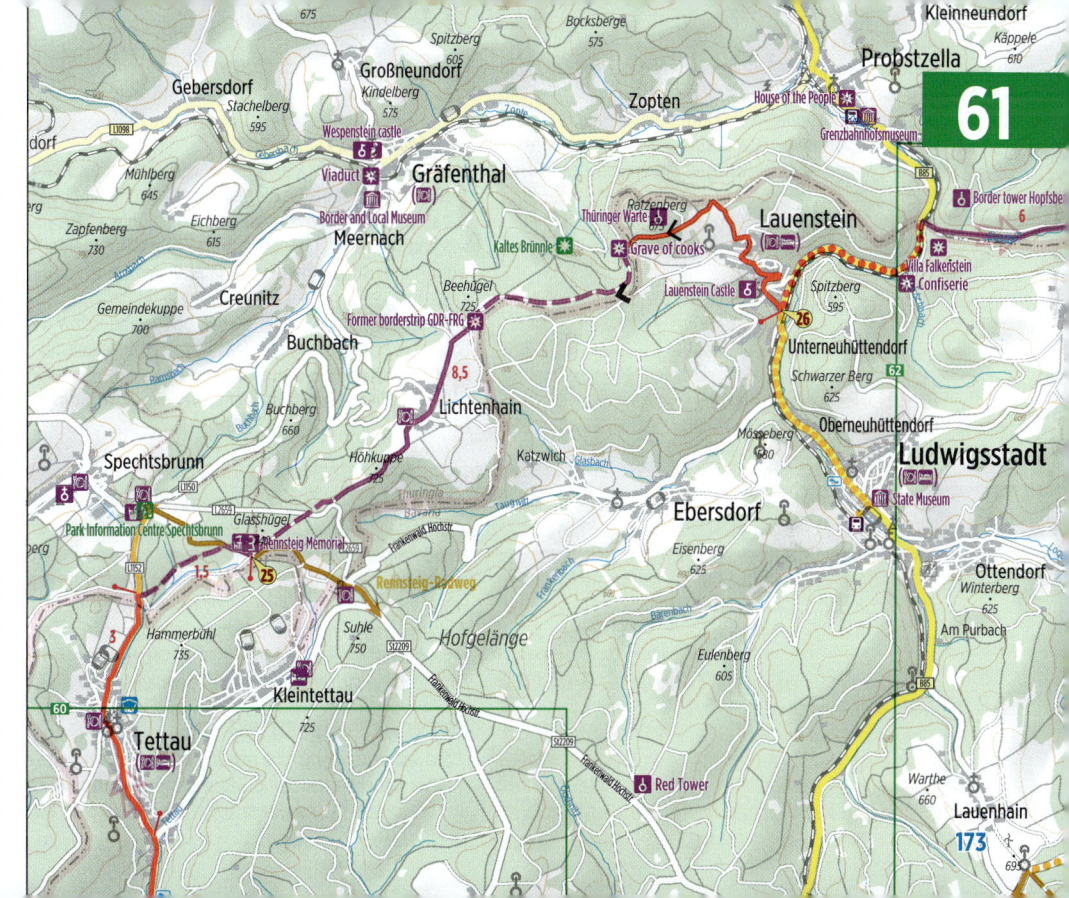

61

German-German past and present. In March 2011 Roland Jahn took over from Joachim Gauck and Marianne Birthler and became commissioner for the documents of the former GDR national secret service (*Bundesbeauftragte für die Unterlagen des Staatssicherheitsdienstes der ehemaligen DDR"*).

Ludwigsstadt

prefix: 09263

- ℹ **Tourist-Information (Tourist information)**, Lauensteiner Str. 44, ✆ 974541, @ sit482
- 🏛 **Schiefermuseum (Slate museum)**, Lauensteiner Str. 44, ✆ 974541
  - 🌐 The production of slate boards was very important in Ludwigsstadt. The museum tells the history of slate mining and the slate industry. @ ryc762
- 🔲 **Marienkapelle**, Lauensteiner Str./Ecke Thünahofer Str.
- ✳ **Altes Rathaus (Old city hall)**, Marktpl. 1. Simple timbered construction from 1746-49.
- 📧 **Freibad (Outdoor pool)**, kronacher Str. 35, ✆ 1623, ✆ 9490
- 🔵 **Hallenbad (Indoor pool)**, Kronacher Str. 34, ✆ 9920245, ✆ 9490

The origin of the city is said to originate some time before 1269, since a reeve already had his seat in the city at that time. The idyllic city with the districts Edersdorf, Lauenstein, Lauenhain and Steinbach an der Haide and as of 2008, has a population of nearly 3,600 and lies at the meeting point of three low mountain streams. It is nestled in the forest-covered hills of the Franconian Forest and the Thuringian Forest.

Historical buildings with slate facades provide a unique impression. Ludwigsstadt offers numerous accommodation possibilities. Points of interest apart from the Church of St. Mary and the slate museum of the Lauenstin Caslte are the dance square in Ebersdorf as well as the Evangelic Church of St. Elisabeth an der Haide.

From Lauenstein/Ludwigsstadt to Blankenstein | 39 km

26 To continue on the German-German border trail, turn left at the **B 85** and pass the **Fischbachsmühle** where you will find the main "Confiserie Burg Lauenstein", home to world-famous handmade chocolates which are even sold in the fancy department store "KaDeWe" in Berlin.

Turn right, cross over the railroad bridge and follow the Loquitz cycle trail, which you leave again after Falkenstein.

At Falkenstein it is worth taking a small detour to the left to Probstzella to the largest Bauhaus memorial in Thuringia.

"House of the People"

The "House of the People", opened in 1927 in Probstzella, was designed and built by the Bauhaus architect Alfred Arndt. The industrial pioneer, Franz Littig, gave it to the public as a site for culture and education. After being vacant for several years, the complex was extensively reconstructed in 2003. Today you will find bicycle friendly accommodation and restaurants in the Bauhaus style as well as a permanent exhibition concerning the "Green Belt of Germany and Europe".

Border station Probstzella

The last of formerly nine existing inner-German border stations between the Baltic Sea and the Bavarian Forest was in Probstzella. The village, with 1,500 inhabitants, was situated in the restricted zone, where people were only allowed to live there if they had a special stamp in their passport. Previously, in 1961, almost 50 "unreliable elements" had to leave the village and were forced to live somewhere else. The remaining inhabitants had to lock their fences and ladders. They rarely had visitors, as even relatives had to get permission before they could sit down for a cup of tea with their family.

The authors Erich Loest and Roman Grafe were two of a few supporters who pushed for keeping this old border station and turning it into a German-German memorial site. However, neither the government of Thuringia nor the federal government was willing to fund the project. Equally, the parish council of Probstzella did not want to finance it.

However, eventually the building was preserved and converted into the GDR Border Station Museum in 2010, which provides information about life in the border region and the controlling regime.

Continue straight ahead on the main route on Terrstraße. Turn half left in a sharp right bend after about 100 metres into a dirt road towards **Lichtentanne**.

After another left and right bend in the valley, the road leads towards Heckenbruch on the left after the shelter. Continue past the shelter to the right towards Lichtentanne and you will reach the **Steinbach mill**.

Steinbach mill

The Steinbach mill was first mentioned in 1487. It was operated with water power until 1970. During the German division, the path of the inner German border determined

the fate of the Steinbach mill. The property was divided, as the Steinbach was the border river between east and west. The basement and forest were then separated by the border. The basement was destroyed by the GDR border troops. Today, only the foundation walls can be seen.

After the Steinbach mill, a steep stretch of 1.5 kilometres follows, which cannot be avoided with an alternative route. **27** At the end of this, you will come to a shelter by a street which is where you turn right. The hill ends after about 500 m towards **Schmiedebach**.

There is a memorial at the next crossing on the left commemorating the victims of World War I and II and a little later, at the beginning of Schmiedebach, the "Laura" concentration camp memorial can be found. The foundations of houses can still be seen on the grounds as can the large kitchen that was used for the prisoners. The memorial stone is unfortunately fenced in so the inscription cannot be read. Around the Slate Mountain one can recognise the mining dumps.

The road to the right leads to the mountain and the slate city of Lehesten.

Lehesten
prefix: 036653

ℹ️ **Tourist-Information**, Obere Marktstr. 1, ✆ 2600, @ xlh835

🏛️🏞️ **Thüringer Schieferpark (Thuringian slate park)**, Am Staatsbruch 1, ✆ 26270, 🕐 nature park information site, Opening hours: April-Oct., 9:00-17:00, technical memorial, guided tours: Tu-Th 10:00 and 13:00, Fr 10:00, Sa 10:30 and 14:00, Su 14:00. Follow the tracks of the miners to a depth of 80 m, and view the former roof slate mine. @ gpf242

🛐 **St. Aegidien**, Kirchg., ✆ 2600. 250 years old, Biedermeier. Here you will find the largest slate board cut from one piece. It is over 3 m high and 2.5 m wide and serves as a memorial plaque dedicated to the war victims.

🛐 **Altvaterturm auf dem Wetzstein (Altvaterturm on the Wetzstein)**. The Wetzstein is the highest mountain in the south eastern Thuringian Forest with Altvaterturm as observation tower.

From Lehesten, the German-German border trail follows the **Rennsteig cycle trail** until you reach Blankenstein (cyclist with green "R").

On the road towards Brennersgrün you will pass through Lehesten. Shortly before the end of town, the cycle trail leads to the south around the **Wetzstein** in a big arc. There, at the so-called "rondel", you will find a special shelter. It is a steel bunker which stood on the summit of the Wetz-

stein until 1989 and served as the GDR National Security command centre.

Historical border stones at Rennsteig

This stretch has long been known as the Schönwappen-weg. Here you will find numerous artistic coats of arms from various centuries. The course of the German-German border is also oriented on the historical border stones. The course was merely measured and checked. The tradition of setting border stones was continued on November 11, 1994. Next to the connection road, Lehesten-Ziegelhütte, on the border between Bavaria and Thuringia, a coat of arms made of sandstone was erected instead of a simple border stone. The inscription reads: "Free State of Thuringia" and "Free State of Bavaria". Apart from this new coat of arms stone of sandstone, you can admire border stones from the 16th, 17th and 18th centuries. Several of these coat of arms stones have been restored.

Continue straight ahead on the main route through **Brennersgrün**. **28** At the end of the town, keep to the left and pass through the Buchbachtal.

At the corner where you turn left towards Grumbach and Rodacherbrunn, you will find the "Zum grünen Wald" restaurant where you can also spend the night for a reasonable price. After Brennersgrün, continue down the hill with an 8 percent grade. Continue past fields and meadows and you will soon reach the edge of the forest. Once in the forest, continue again uphill towards **Grumbach** and after

Historic border-stone at the Rennsteig

this town, continue parallel to the street on an unpaved road to Rodacherbrunn. In **Rodacherbrunn**, turn left and follow the road towards Neundorf and Moorbad Lobenstein. **29** ⚠ Watch out: Some distance after Rodacherbrunn, you will see two signs for the hiking trail - the Rennsteig route for cyclists goes off to the right and is a wide and generous gravel road. A black cyclist is depicted on a green "R" with white background on the sign.

Jürgen Lange – a successful escape

On May 30, 1969, Jürgen Lange and Rudi H. successfully escaped to Bavaria. The soldier, serving his military duty with the National People's Army, was appointed, together with the sergeant Rudi H., to protect an unmined alley during the night while border marking work was performed between Rodacherbrunn and Nordhalben. The accompanying sergeant was determined to flee and was prepared. When the soldier, Jürgen Lange, saw that his sergeant had jumped over the Cheval de frise around 6:30 and was heading towards the opposite border, he had to make a decision. Either shoot his comrade or take advantage of the opportunity. He contemplated for ten minutes, which seemed like an eternity to him. Since he did not want to shoot, he also decided to flee, which was not discovered until the first planned changing of the guard at 7:30.

When Jürgen Lange arrived in the West after fleeing, he discovered that the sergeant had rendered Lange's handgun useless by removing the lock.

After the escape, the Stasi looked into Jürgen Lange's life and even attempted to convince his father to cooperate with

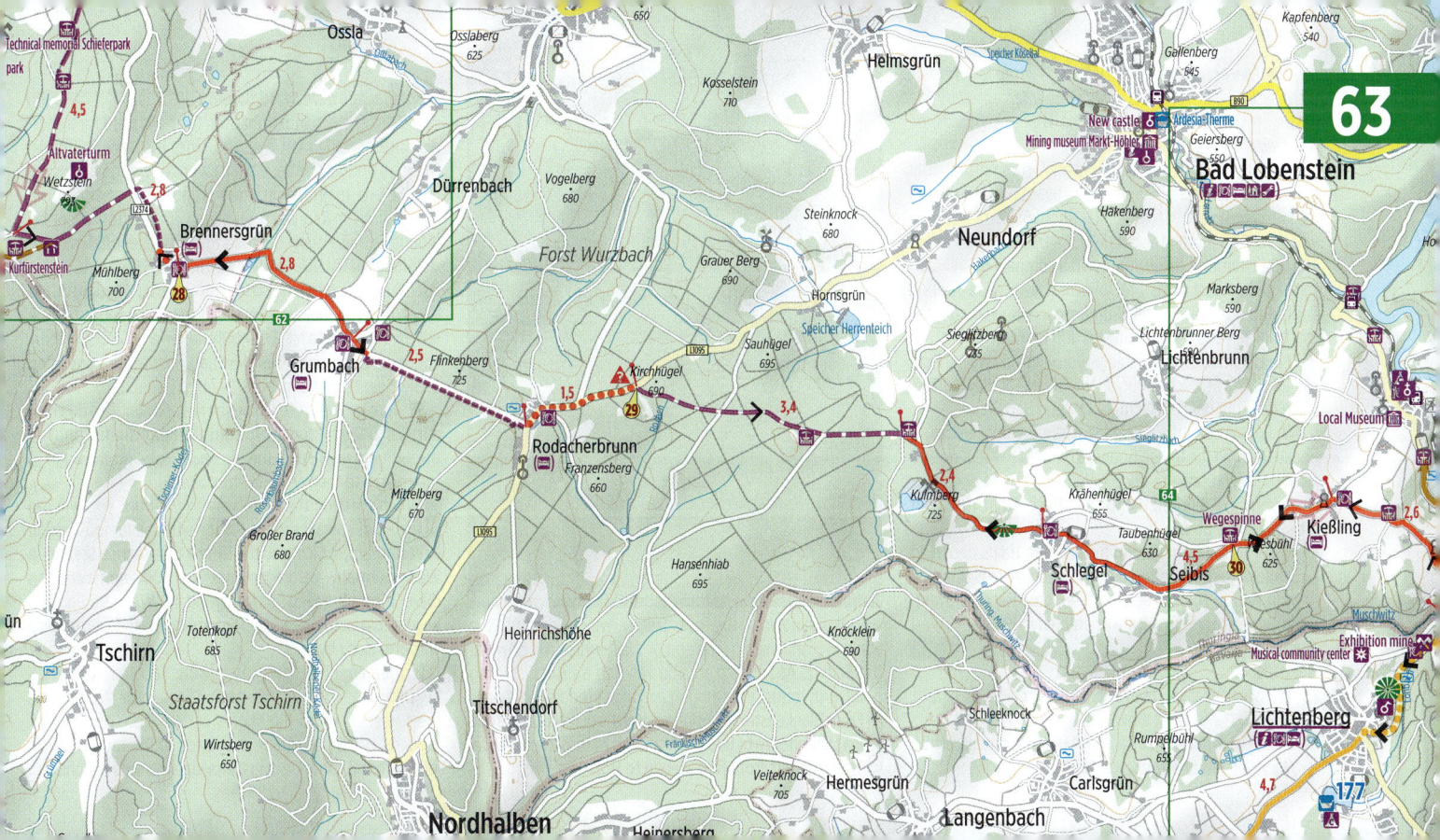

them but without success. The letters he wrote to his family were sadly never received. They were intercepted by the Stasi and stored until the fall of the Wall. Afterwards, he received the originals back.

Follow the course of the "Rennsteig" summit trail until you reach Blankenstein. Some very beautiful scenery and a comfortable section follows. It is about 6 kilometres until you reach Schlegel and about 13 kilometres to Blankenstein. The first kilometre takes you down a compact gravel road through the forest and is later followed by a section through fields and meadows. After **Kulmberg**, continue on a quiet road which leads you to **Schlegel** and Blankenstein.

TIPP Three kilometres after Schlegel you will find a walkers' car park with a protective hut, on the left side at the crossing. To the right leads to Lichtenberg and Bad Steben.

30 Follow the road which leads slightly uphill, straight ahead through the forest. Soon you will reach **Kießling** and from there you can already see Blankenstein an der Saale. Once you have reached the town at the bottom, turn right into **Bayrische Straße**.

ZUM BAHNHOF To get to the train station from where trains depart to Saalfeld, take the main road to the left. Across from the train station you can see the "Steinerne Rennsteigwanderer" stone carving which was erected in 1903.

Blankenstein
prefix: 036642

- **ℹ** Tourist-Information (Tourist information office), Selbitzpl. 1, ☎ 29533, ☎ 296026, @ dxg423
- **⊠** Rennsteig-Denkmal „Der Wanderer" (Rennsteig memorial "Der Wanderer"/the hiker), Absanger Str.

View of border fence and watchtower in Blankenstein, 1988

Continue down to the River Selbitz, which flows into the Saale in Blankenstein. The end of the Rennsteig is down at the Selbitz. At Selbitzplatz you will find a hikers' starting point with tourist information and a fast food snack bar.

AUSSTIEG From Blankenstein, continue along the quiet country road via Lichtenberg to Bad Steben some 7 km in the distance. Trains depart from Bad Steben to Hof.

From Blankenstein to Mödlareuth   19 km

In Blankenstein, turn right onto the main road for a short distance and then left again to cross the river Selbitz on the road bridge. Continue past a wooden bridge across the river Selbitz. In **Wolfstein**, you will find information plaques concerning the Rennsteig, Frankenweg and the Franconian Mountain trail. Follow the road towards **Eisenbühl** and **Rudolphstein**. First the road follows the Saale, then it distances itself from the river and continues towards **Kemlas** upon a hill. When you look back, you can see **Blankenberg** which lies on the side of a hill. Eisenbühl lies on a hill and you must conquer several metres of elevation. Follow the signposted Saale-Selbitz tour and cross through Eisenbühl.

31 Turn left before reaching the A 9 and continue downhill parallel to the motorway towards **Rudolphstein**. Continue through the town, past the big Saale Hotel on the edge of the town and then cross the motorway.

TIPP When crossing the motorway to the right you will see the Frankenwald service station with the famous bridge restaurant, which was the last or first service station in West Germany before or after the 300-kilometre-long drive through the GDR from and to West Berlin. The border crossing between Rudolphstein and Hirschberg was also close by.

Turn left after the motorway towards Sachsen-Vorwerk, a beautiful stretch of the sign-posted Saale cycle trail through the forest down to the shores of the Saale and further towards Hirschberg until you reach **"Kühnmühle"**. Turn left there and continue over the bridge towards Hirschberg.

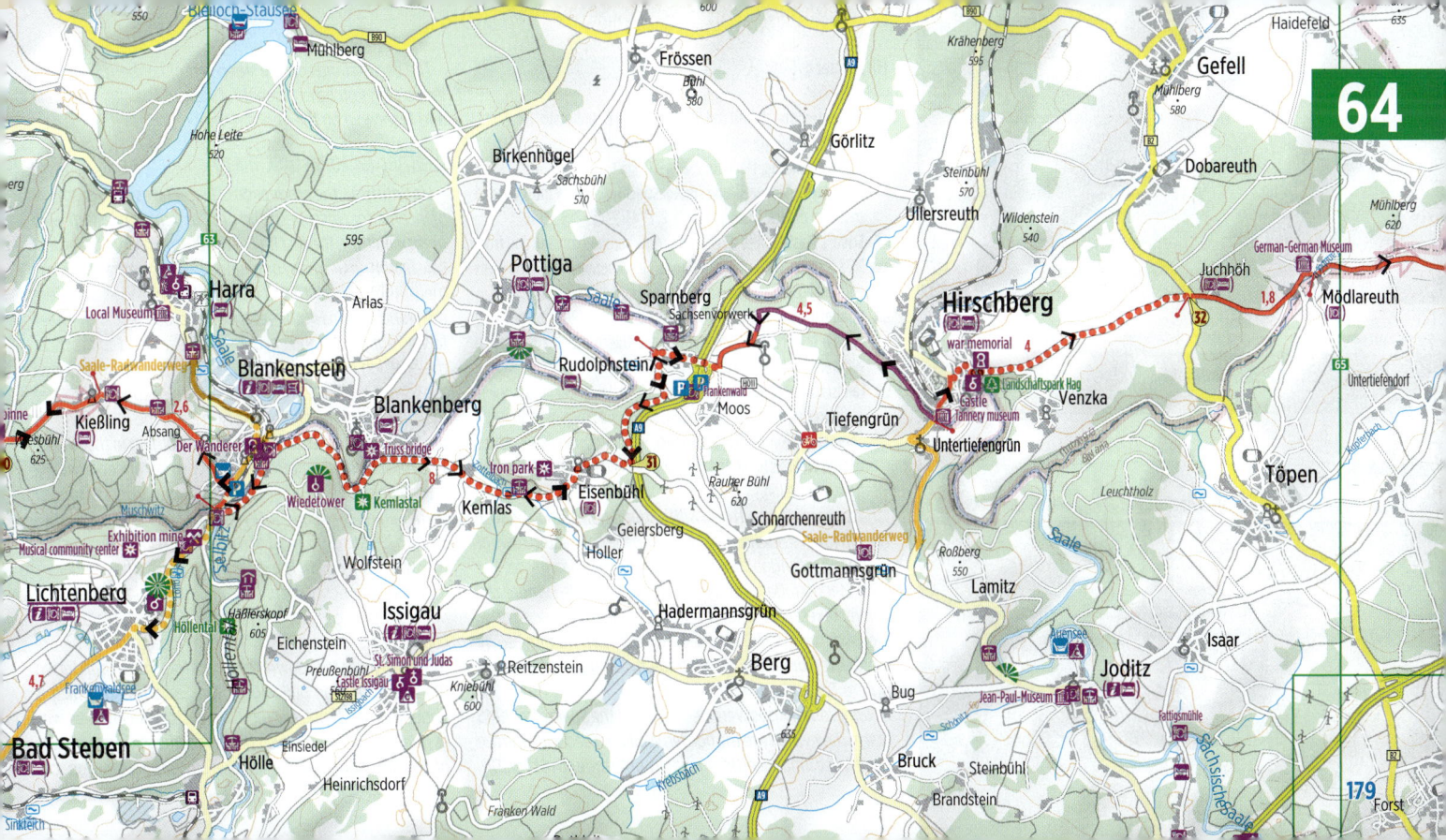

Blankenstein (1984/2006)

Hirschberg

prefix: 036644

- **Ferienregion Selbitztal-Döbraberg**, Bahnhofspl. 1, Naila, ☎ 09282/6829, @ nja758
- **Stadtverwaltung**, Marktstr. 2, ☎ 4300, @ sid847
- **Museum für Gerberei- und Stadtgeschichte (Tannery museum and museum of local history)**, Saalg. 2, ☎ 43139 ☺, @ iew721
- **Schloss (Castle)**, Alte Allee. The simple baroque construction from 1678 is situated on a high cliff from "Hirschberger Gneis" and gives you a spectacular view over Saaletal, Frankenwald and Altstadt.
- **Gondelstation (Gondel station)**, Hängesteg. Rowin boat and paddle boat rental. View the city and the former border from a different angle on the dammed Saale.
- **Landschaftspark Hag (Nature park Hag)**, Saaleufer. Numerous points of interest within the compound, which was reopened after the "border measures" were removed, with nice hiking trails. Check out the Wenzels höhle and the "longest bench in the world" carved from a single log.

Hirschberg is a small town with a population of about 2,300. The old town stretches from between the connected rows of houses near Ginggäßlein all the way down to Saalgasse. The wide Marktstraße is not only a street but is also where the market takes place. The current Kirchplatz was created after the great fire of 1835. The medieval old town was limited by the Obere Tor on the Marktstraße by Ginggäßlein and the Untere Tor at the stream.

Numerous houses were destroyed on the Saale after 1945 due to their vicinity to the border. Walls, barbed wire and the death zone influenced life in the city until the end of the GDR.

The castle stands on the steep cliff of Lohberg. From the castle cliff, you have a beautiful view of the city, the Saale and Franconia on the opposite side.

Leather factory Hirschberg

Up until 1992, the production of leather was a major source of income for Hirschberg and provided the Saalestadt with great wealth. In the first half of the 20th century, the largest sole factory in Germany originated from a small tannery, namely the leather factory of Heinrich Maximilian Knoch. Here the world known HK sole leather was produced. The leather factory supported and encouraged the railroad connection, the erection of residential houses, the new construction of the school, the Saale bridge and the local outdoor pool. After the nationalization of the factory in 1946, the transition was made to upper leather for shoes and clothing in the 1960's. Two million square metres of leather were tanned annually in Hirschberg. The leather factory was the largest employer in the region for nearly 100 years.

From 1993 to 1996, most of the buildings in the leather factory were torn down. The villas belonging to the company's founder, Heinrich Knoch, the office building (which now houses a museum), a horse stall and 16 hectares of clean construction land are all that remains today. Shortly before the factory was torn down, the city of Hirschberg purchased the administration building on the Saale bridge which is under memorial preservation, the factory archives as well as numerous objects which document the 250-year history of the Hirschberg leather factory. Since 1997, three special

exhibitions are presented every year and the museum on the Saale bridge has regular opening hours.

Keep to the right in Hirschberg, follow the narrow road which leads between the houses with a 20 percent (!) gradient. After exiting the town, continue towards **Juchhöh** and Mödlareuth.

TIPP Once you have nearly reached the top, you will see a war memorial in the ned which is dedicated to the victims of World War II.

Once you have reached the forest, the worst of the climb overcome. Travel through the forest, later on a level street past some meadows and fields. **32** In Juchhöh, cross the B 2.

TIPP Directly on the corner you will find a restaurant called Juchhöh (✆ 036649/80007) where you can stop for a meal and spend the night.

The road winds through a forest from Juchhöh to Mödlareuth, past an old cross border company, and soon you will see part of the border strip with car traps, convoy roads and a meshed, metal fence on the right.

Mödlareuth (Gefell)

🏛 **Deutsch-Deutsches Museum Mödlareuth (German-German museum Mödlareuth)**, Mödlareuth 13, ✆ 09295/1334 ⊜ In the once divided village, a part of the recent history of the German-German relationships is presented in an outdoor area with border facilities. ⓐ xts637

On Thuringian ground, you will first reach Mödlareuth, which belongs to the town of Gefell. On the other side of the Tannbach lies the Bavarian part, which belongs to Töpen. There are many things to look at in the town.

Mödlareuth – the divided village

The German-German border ran right through the village and remains of this division have been maintained over the years: a piece of concrete wall, two observation towers, GDR border columns and border stones, warning signs, spotlights and foundations of demolished buildings. The Americans called this village "Little Berlin".

The reason for the division of the village goes back to the year 1810 when the border stones were set which still remain today. The Kingdom of Bavaria was on one side, the Princedom Reuß on the other. After World War I, half of the village belonged to the Free State of Thuringia and the other half to the Free State of Bavaria.

After World War II, the demarcation lines mainly ran along the old borders defined in 1937. The border between the Soviet and American occupation zone ran along the small Tannbach in Mödlareuth. After 1949, this stream could only be crossed with a permit. As of 1952, the final division of the village was performed. A high wooden fence was built and due to compulsory security measures along the border strip, the "Obere Mühle" was the first to be torn down. The residents of this mill fled to the Bavarian side at the very last moment.

The village was separated be a 700-metre-long and 3.30-metre-high border wall from 1966 onwards.

Hundreds of metres of the original are maintained. Outside of the town you can still view 500 metres of border facilities along a four-kilometre-long education trail. In June 1994, the outdoor area of the museum was opened. Further exhibition

Hirschberg (1984/2006)

rooms, a museum shop and a movie theatre were built and made accessible to the public.

Mödlareuth and its 50 residents are still a curiosity. There are two mayors, one for the Bavarian said and one for the Thuringian side. There are also different postcodes, telephone prefixes and licence plates.

From Mödlareuth to the border triangle   30 km

From Mödlareuth follow the quiet country road slightly uphill to **Münchenreuth**, turn left into the **Kirchhofweg** and turn left again at the end towards **Gebersreuth**. Cross over the former border at the **"border triangle stone"** where the free states of Bavarian, Thuringia and Saxony meet and turn right towards **Grobau**. **33** Turn right again at the restaurant before the train station.

Border fence and watchtower in Mödlareuth

Rough pastures

The rough pastures in the Vogtland have become so rare that they have been put under natural protection along the former German-German border. In an intact pasture, 30-40 plant species can usually be found. The insects in these fields are even more numerous, which helps protected bird species such as the brown robin, a common bird in the Green Belt. The former death strip has developed into a refuge for more than 60 highly endangered bird species, which are on the "red list".

Continue along the railroad tracks on the **Gutenfürster Straße**, which you will later cross, to **Gutenfürst**.

Gutenfürst

The manor was first officially mentioned in 1418. The first railroad line between Plauen and Gutenfürst (34 km) was opened in 1848 and the entire stretch from Leipzig to Hof in 1851.

After the war, many of the tracks were removed in the Soviet occupation zone as part of the reparation. Now, over 20 years after the fall of the Wall, the stretch between Hof and Reichenbach can once again be travelled on two tracks and is electrified.

During the division, interzonal trains operated, which were not accessible for passengers from the GDR, from Berlin to Munich via Hof. Checks were performed on the train. The customs officials exited at the train station in Gutenfürst.

Barrier and border post in Mödlareuth

Special trains with GDR refugees from the German embassy in Prague stopped at the Bavarian train station of Feilitzsch in 1989.

Continue through Gutenfürst, straight ahead on the quiet main road, cross the A 72 where you will still find a GDR observation tower used by border troops and you will reach **Heinersgrün**. **34** Turn right onto a dirt road, which leads directly to **Blosenberg**. Cross the B 173 and you will reach **Sachsgrün** via **Wiedersberg** and **Loddenreuth**.

Continue to **Gassenreuth** and turn left onto the **S 307**. At the next possibility, branch off to the right and continue on the **Poststraße** to Posseck. Turn right onto the **S 309** before reaching **Posseck**, cross the border between Saxony and Bavaria, pass a GDR border column and a memorial stone. Turn left at the next possibility and you will reach **Nentschau**.

Keep to the left, follow the small road towards **Wieden** and turn right at the end. Follow the signs to the **border triangle** and turn left at the end of the road in **Oberzech**. A small paved forest trail turns left from the street a short distance later, which leads directly to the border triangle on a small meadow on the German-Czech border **36**.

Border triangle

On the right side you will find a memorial cross for the unknown soldier of World War II. Straight ahead you will see the border signs on the German and Czech side.

After 1,400 kilometres of German-German border, which begins on the peninsula of

Three-Freestates-Stone, near Münchenreuth

Priwall by Travemünde, you have reached the border triangle by Prex.

TIPP | **AUSSTIEG**
At the border triangle you can cross the German-Czech border on a small bridge and begin the next stage to As and Scheb. If you would like to continue to Hof from the border triangle, where many train connections are available, return to the intersection in Oberzech.

Leaving Hof

At the intersection in Oberzech, continue straight ahead towards Prex, then turn right towards Regnitzlosau and continue for 13 kilometres along the Vogtland cycle trail via Tauperlitz along the southern Regnitz and then on the Saale cycle trail to Hof and to the main train station. The route follows numerous paved cycle trails adjacent to the street and at times, partially along streets with some heavy traffic.

Hof
prefix: 09281

ℹ **Tourist-Information**, Ludwigstr. 24, ✆ 8157777, @ qsb365

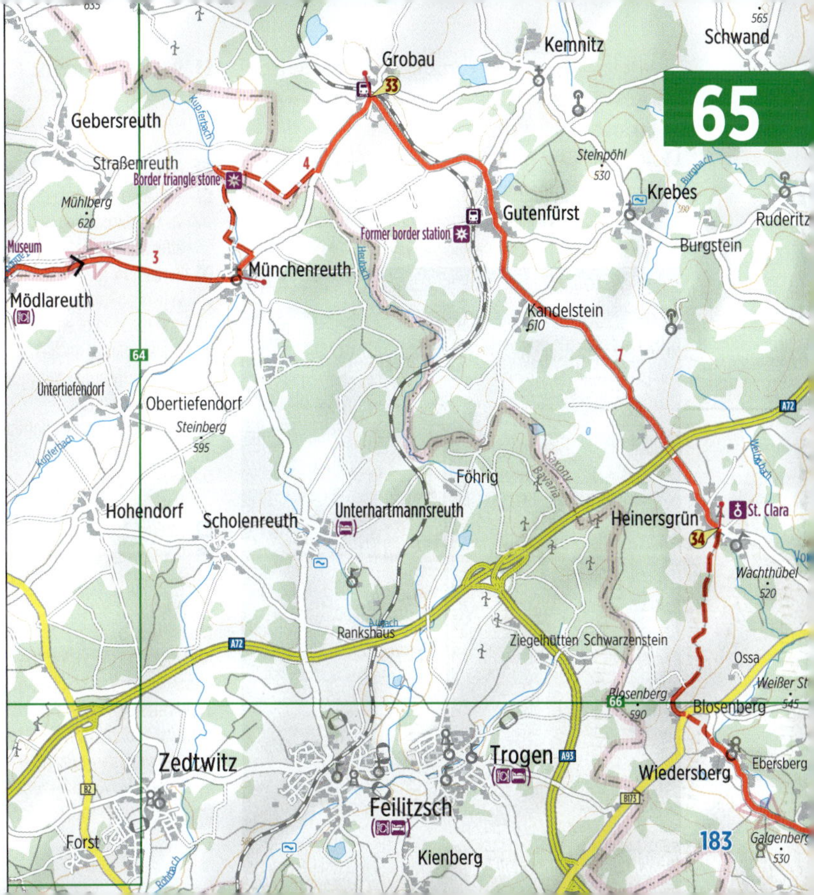

🏛 **Museum Bayerisches Vogtland (Museum Bavarian Vogtland)**, Unteres Tor 5a/5b, ✆ 815-2700 ☞ The main focus of the collections is the corporate and industrial history of the city. Two sections of natural history comprise nearly the

entire animal population of Europe. You can find a special exhibition on the topic of "Escape and Displacement" in the new annex. @ hhx/55

🜨 **St.-Lorenz-Kirche (St. Lorenz-Church)**, Lorenzstr. The St. Lorenz-Church, built in the 12th century, is the oldest church in the city of Hof. Inside you will find the famous Hertnid-von-Stein altar, probably from workshops in Bamberg around 1480. @ ttc273

🜨 **St.-Michaelis-Kirche (St. Michaelis Church)**, Kirchpl. The church is originally from the year 1230. After the big fire in 1823 it was rebuilt combining neo Gothic, classical and Biedermeier elements into a harmonic sacral construction. @ cmt424

🜨 **Hofer Wärschtlamo**, Sonnenpl.

✳ **Rathaus (City hall)**, Ludwigstr., corner Klosterstraße. The palace-like style of the building was originally built in 1563-66 and then rebuilt after fires and is definitely worth visiting.

🜨 **Bürgerpark Theresienstein.** The park is the oldest community park in Germany and is located in the north of the city. The nature park is in the style of an old English garden and represents over 200 years of garden architecture. It includes a zoological, botanical and geological garden and was voted Germany's most beautiful park in 2003. @ njv825

🜨 **Naherholungsgebiet Untreusee (The recreational area of Untreusee).** The area with over 60 hectares of water surface is only 3 kilometres from the Saale cycle trail and is located to the south of Hof. @ pid531

✉ **FreiBad**, Ascher Str. 32, ☎ 812450, @ ort673

✉ **HofBad**, Oberer Anger 4, ☎ 812440, @ kad623

The old town of Hof developed from the settlement of Rekkenze around Lorenzkirche (Church of St Lorenz), which was built in 1080. In 1230, Otto I, count of Andechs and Merania, founded the new town, which still retains the name Hof today. In 1373, the castle viscounts of Nuremberg acquired Regnitzland including the city of Hof. Consequently, the city at first belonged to the Nuremberg region, later to the margravate of Brandenburg-Bayreuth, finally to Prussia in 1792 and in 1806 it went to the French. It was only in 1810 that Emperor Napoleon I of France gave Regnitzland and the

The author at the Dreiländereck

city of Hof to the kingdom of Bavaria and in doing so ended the 400-year-long reign of the Hohenzollern in this region.

In 1823, a big fire destroyed nearly all the buildings in the new town. They were rebuilt in the classic architectural style, which makes the city look more modern than it actually is. The opening of the train line in 1848 allowed Hof and its many textile businesses to develop its economy and industry.

Hof has a population of 45,000 and is a popular destination for day trips. The city has an exceptionally high number of bakeries and butcher's shops, which makes it a culinary highlight on the trip: There is a great variety of Bratwurst, ham and sausages as well as good, homemade, regional dishes on offer in the city's many restaurants. Apart from these culinary delights, the city's great cultural attractions continuously draw in visitors.

Border-tower in the Dreiländereck

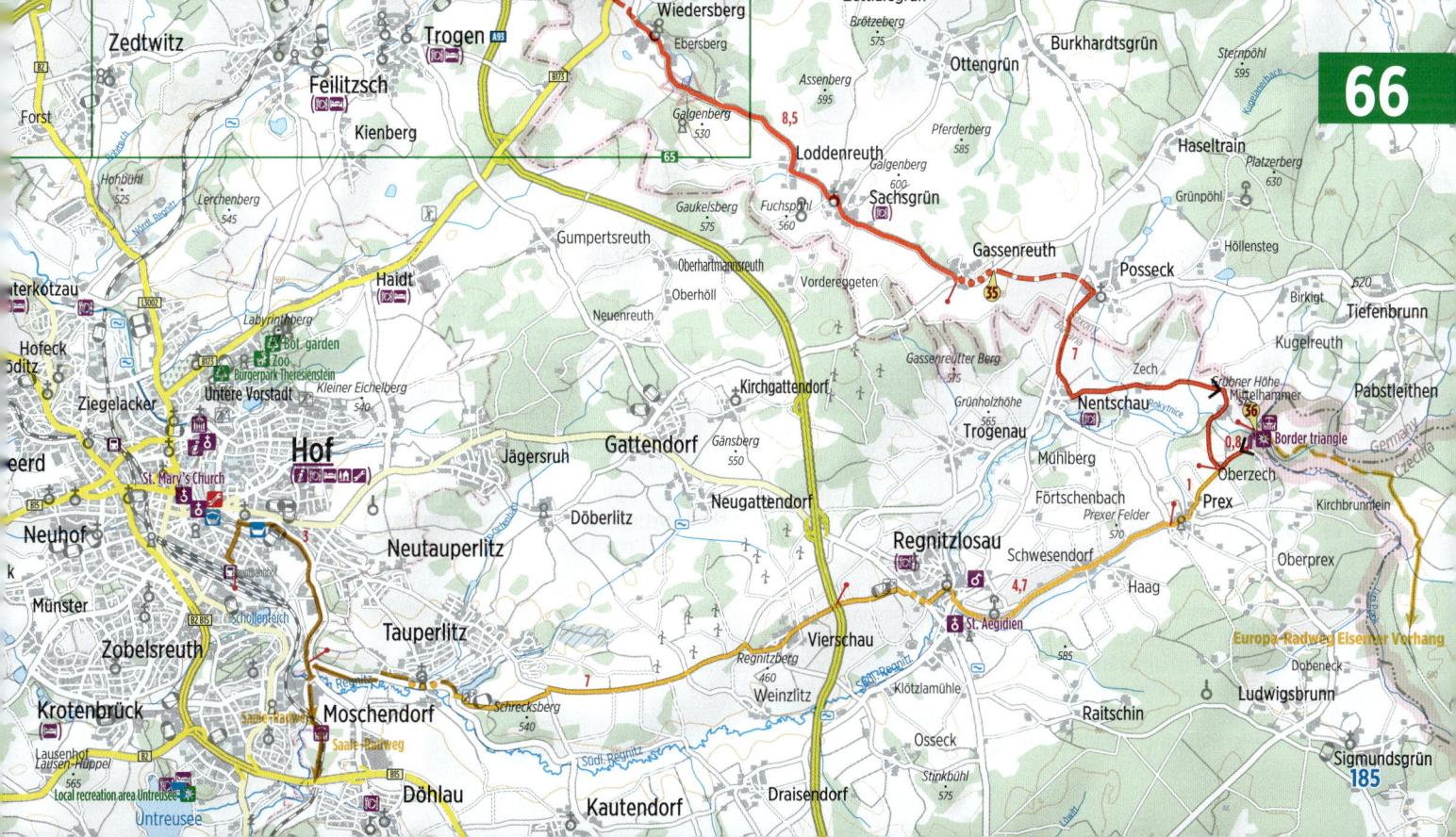

66

Overnight accommodation and bike service list

Accommodation addresses

The following list includes accommodation in the following categories:

Categories

- **i** Tourist-Information
- **H** Hotel, Inn
- **Hg** Hotel garni
- **BnB** Bed and Breakfast, Boarding House, Farm
- **Ho** Hostel
- **Mo** Motel
- **AH** Aparthotel, Holiday Flat (selection)
- **B** Bungalow
- **Hh** Hay hotel
- **S** Other
- **JH** Youth hostel
- **A** Camp ground
- **A** Tent site (nature tent site)

We have not attempted to list every possible place where visitors can spend the night, and listings should not be construed as any kind of recommendation. Because we wish to expand this list and keep it up-to-date, we welcome any comments, additions or corrections you may have. There is no charge for a single-line entry, for lack of space we cannot guarantee one.

Identification

I	Price Range less than € 25,–
II	Price Range € 25,– to € 35,–
III	Price Range € 35,– to € 50,–
IV	Price Range € 50,– to € 70,–
V	Price Range € 70,– to € 100,–
VI	Price Range over € 100,–
o.F.	no breakfast
HP	with breakfast and dinner
✗	only room with shared bathroom
☺	Bed+Bike Acommodation
2.5	distance to the route in kilometres

Prices

These categories are based on the price per person in a double room equipped with shower or bath, with breakfast. The indicated price categories correspond to the status of the survey or revision period and may differ from the actual prices. Price fluctuations are possible, especially during trade fairs, due to different room types and not least due to seasonal factors.

Bike Workshops and Rental

- Bike workshop
- Bike rental
- E-Bike charging station
- E-Bike rental
- lockable parking facilities

Distance

The blue number (2.5) at every accommodation shows the distance to the route in kilometres. Please note that this number refers to the linear distance, the difference in altitude and the actual distance covered is not included.

Updates

For further corrections concerning the overnight accommodation list see the LiveUpdate at www.esterbauer.com

Hansestadt Lübeck

Area Code: 0451

🛈 Tourist-Information, Holstentorpl. 1, ✆ 8899700 ⓪

Ⓗ Am Mühlenteich, Mühlenbrücke 6, ✆ 77171, III-IV ⓪⁵

Ⓗ Anno 1216, Alfstr. 38, ✆ 4008210, V ⓪⁵

Ⓗ Atlantic, Schmiedestr. 9-15, ✆ 384790, V ⓪

Ⓗ Klassik Altstadt Hotel, Fischergrube 52, ✆ 702980, IV-V ☺ ⓪⁵

Ⓗ Park Inn, Willy-Brandt-Allee 1-5, ✆ 15040, III-IV ⓪

Ⓗ Phönix Hotel Alter Speicher, Beckergrube 91-93, ✆ 71045, III ⓪⁵

Ⓗ Radisson Blu Senator Hotel, Willy-Brandt-Allee 6, ✆ 1420, IV-VI ⓪

Ⓗ Ringhotel Jensen, An der Obertrave 4-5, ✆ 702490, III-IV ⓪

Ⓗ Rucksack-Hotel Lübeck, Kanalstr. 70, ✆ 706892, OB, I ⓪⁵

Ⓗ Zur Alten Stadtmauer, An der Mauer 57, ✆ 73702, III-IV ⓪⁵

Ⓗg Altstadthotel Zum Goldenen Anker, Große Burgstr. 9, ✆ 71692, II Ⓘ

Ⓗ An der Marienkirche, Schüsselbuden 4, ✆ 799410, III-IV ☺ ⓪⁵

Ⓗg CVJM Hotel am Dom, Dankwartsgrube 43, ✆ 3999410, III ⓪⁵

🏠 Jugendherberge (DJH)Lübeck „Altstadt", Mengstr. 33, ✆ 7020399, II-III ⓪⁵

🚲 Die Fahrradwerkstatt, Hüxtertorallee 8, ✆ 7074335 ⓪⁵

🚲 Drahtesel Fahrräder, Schwartauerlandstr. 114, ✆ 4812590 ④

🚲 Falko Ellwitz Fahrradservice, Krähenstr. 25-27, ✆ 48971664 ⓪

🚲🚴 Laufrad Lübeck, Beckergrube 29, ✆ 72792 ⓪⁵

🚲🚴 Rückenwind, Krähenstr. 32, ✆ 2037067 ⓪

🚲 at Fahrräder, Beckergrube 63, ✆ 7982268 ⓪⁵

🚴 Mie Mie - Mietrad Mielke, Hüxterdamm 2, ✆ 0176/27280353 ⓪

🚴 Zweirad Wöltjen, Kanalstr. 54-56, ✆ 77351 Ⓘ

St. Jürgen (Hansestadt Lübeck)

Area Code: 0451

Ⓗ Centro Hotel Kaiserhof Deluxe, Kronsforder Allee 11-13, ✆ 703301, VI Ⓘ

Ⓗ Traveller Hotel, St.-Jürgen-Ring 60, ✆ 2967610, II-III Ⓘ

Ⓗ Wakenitzblick, Augustenstr. 30, ✆ 702630, IV ⓪

Ⓑ&Ⓑ Naturkostpension Grabau, Hohenstaufenstr. 8, ✆ 621160, III ⓪

Ⓑ Addicks, Bismarckstr. 8, ✆ 791847, I-II ⓪⁵

🚲🚴 Bike & Tour, Geniner Str. 2, ✆ 5041440 Ⓘ

🚲🚴 MTB-Market, Welsbachstr. 3-5, ✆ 51538 ⅠⱺⱢ

St. Lorenz Nord (Hansestadt Lübeck)

Area Code: 0451

Ⓗ Hanseatischer Hof, Wisbystr. 7-9, ✆ 300200, V-VI ⓪⁵

Ⓗ Herrenhof, Herrendamm 8, ✆ 46027, III ⅠⱺⱢ

Ⓗ Zum Ratsherrn, Herrendamm 2-4, ✆ 4077110, III ⅠⱺⱢ

Ⓗ Zum Scheibenstand, Fackenburger Allee 76, ✆ 473382, I 🚲 Ⓘ

Ⓗ ibis Lübeck City, Fackenburger Allee 54, ✆ 40040, III Ⓘ

Ⓗg Das Hotelchen, Schönböcker Str. 64, ✆ 41013, III ⅠⱺⱢ

🚲 MEGA Bike - Lübeck, St.-Jürgen-Ring 62, ✆ 4792175 Ⓘ

🚲 Zweirad Martens, Ziegelstr. 1, ✆ 41769 ⓪⁵

🚴 Call a Bike, Hauptbahnhof/Steinrader Weg ⓪⁵

St. Lorenz Süd (Hansestadt Lübeck)

Area Code: 0451

Ⓗ Excelsior, Hansestr. 3, ✆ 88090, IV ⓪

Ⓗ Hanseatic, Hansestr. 19, ✆ 83328, II-III ⓪⁵

Ⓗ Lindenhof, Lindenstr. 1a, ✆ 872100, IV-V ⓪

Ⓗ Park Hotel, Lindenpl. 2, ✆ 871970, IV ⓪

Ⓗ Tryp by Wyndham Aquamarin, Dr.-Luise-Klinsmann-Str. 1-3, ✆ 88020, ✆ 08001010880, II-IV ②

Ⓗg Baltic Hotel, Hansestr. 11, ✆ 85575, III-IV ☺ ⓪⁵

Ⓗg Stadt Lübeck, Am Bahnhof 21, ✆ 881880, ✆ 83883, II-III ☺ ⓪

Ⓑ 🏠 Claßen-Röder, Hansestr. 28a, ✆ 85251, II ⓪⁵

Ⓑ&Ⓑ B&B Hotel Lübeck, Konrad-Adenauer-Str. 7, ✆ 490500, II-III ⓪⁵

Genin (Hansestadt Lübeck)

Area Code: 0451

Ⓗ Trave, Geniner Dorfstr. 28, ✆ 807256, III ③

Schönböcken (Hansestadt Lübeck)

Area Code: 0451

Ⓗ Pache's Gasthof, Steinrader Damm 42, ✆ 23556, OB, II-III ☺ ③

🏕 Campingplatz, Steinrader Damm 12, ✆ 893090 ③

🚲 B.O.C. Lübeck, Herrenholz 14, ✆ 809008-0 ③

Bäk

Area Code: 04541

Ⓗg Jagdhaus am Soot, Am Soot 5, ✆ 89900-0, III ⓪

Ratzeburg

Area Code: 04541

🛈 Tourist-Information, Unter den Linden 1, im Rathaus, ✆ 8000886 ⓪⁵

Ⓗ Der Seehof, Lüneburger Damm 1-3, ✆ 860101, IV-V Ⓘ

Ⓗ Hansa-Hotel, Schrangenstr. 25-27, ✆ 8641-00, IV ☺ ⓪⁵

Ⓗ Heckendorf, Gustav-Peters-Pl. 1, ✆ 88980, II-III Ⓘ

Ⓗ Wittler's Hotel mit Gästehaus Cäcilie, Große Kreuzstr. 11, ✆ 3204, III-IV ☺ ⓪⁵

Ⓑ Drenckhahn, Am Mühlengraben 5, ✆ 83805, I ⓪⁵

Ⓑ Haß, Große Kreuzstr. 20, ✆ 4322, I ⓪⁵

Ⓑ Morgenroth, Am Jägerdenkmal 1, ✆ 83200 ⓪

Ⓑ Nath, Dermin 9, ✆ 83445, I Ⓘ

Ⓑ Reimers, Dermin 11, ✆ 83103, I Ⓘ

Ⓑ Scheele, Am Kaninchenberg 15, ✆ 801795, I ⅠⱺⱢ

🏠 Ferienwohnung am Biotop, Georg-Heinemann-Str. 15, ✆ 8949091, ✆ 0176/48375689, II ☺ ②

🏠 Jugendherberge (JH) Ratzeburg, Reeperbahn 6-14, ✆ 8409504, II ☺ ⓪⁵

🏕 Römnitz „Schwalkenberg", Dorfstr. 32, ✆ 80586 Ⓘ

🏕 Römnitz „Schöne Aussicht", Dorfstr. 3, ✆ 3348 Ⓘ

Schlagsdorf

Area Code: 038875

AH Grollmuß, Neubauernweg 18, ☎ 20037, II 0.5

AH Kofahl, Hauptstr. 14, ☎ 20358, I 0

Kneese
Area Code: 038876

H Forsthof Kneese, Hauptstr. 15, ☎ 31376, IV 1

Kittlitz (Lauenburg)
Area Code: 04546

AH Birkenhof, Dorfstr. 23, ☎ 326, I-II 0.5

Mustin
Area Code: 04546

B&B Auszeit, Dorfstr. 57, ☎ 808383, III 2.5

Dargow (Salem (Lauenburg))
Area Code: 04545

AH Schoppenhof, Schaalseeufer 1, ☎ 1377, I-V 0

Hh Schaalseehof, Alte Dorfstr. 1, ☎ 791100 0

Seedorf (Lauenburg)
Area Code: 04545

H Gasthof am See, Dorfstr. 10, ☎ 218, II-III 0

Groß Zecher (Seedorf (Lauenburg))
Area Code: 04545

B&B Zur Kutscherscheune, Lindenallee 15, ☎ 801 0.5

Zarrentin
Area Code: 038851

i Tourismus-Information, Hauptstr. 15, ☎ 333435 0

H Fischhaus, Amtsstr. 11, ☎ 55990, IV 0

H Landhaus am Schaalsee, Wittenburger Chaussee 11, ☎ 80538, III 0

AH Villa am Schaalsee, Bahnhofstr. 11, ☎ 32930, III 0.5

Zweiradservice Dietz, Hauptstr. 28, ☎ 25461 0

Valluhn
Area Code: 038851

AH Zum Trakehnerhof, Am Reiterhof 1, ☎ 80707, II 0.5

Büchen
Area Code: 04155

i Gemeinde, Amtspl. 1, ☎ 80090 0.5

H Ohlrogges Gasthof, Leuenburger Str. 28, ☎ 3315 1

AH Grunwald, Pracherbusch 38, ☎ 3833, ☎ 0160/7788789 1.5

A Campingplatz Am Waldschwimmbad, Am Waldschwimmbad 2, ☎ 5360 2

Zweirad Sandmann Büchen, Möllner Str. 15, ☎ 808150 1

Fitzen
Area Code: 04155

B Schönes vom Dorf, Dorfstr. 12, ☎ 2109, II 2

A Naturcamping Kiefernhütte, Auf der Claasen, ☎ 498187 2.5

A Zur Fähre, Zur Fähre 10, ☎ 8081865, II 3.5

Witzeeze
Area Code: 04155

A Forellensee, Forellensee 1, ☎ 2420 0

Lauenburg/Elbe
Area Code: 04153

i Tourist-Information, Elbstr. 59, ☎ 5909220 1

H Bellevue, Blumenstr. 29, ☎ 2318, III 1.5

H Lauenburger Mühle, Bergstr. 17, ☎ 5890, IV-V 0.5

H Zum Alten Schifferhaus, Elbstr. 114, ☎ 58650, III 0.5

B&B Von Herzen, Elbstr. 46, ☎ 5715123, OB, III 1

B Freidank, Großer Sandberg 5, ☎ 3836, I 0.5

B Gnasteiner's, Bei der Palmschleuse 4, ☎ 5729420, III 0

AH Lazy-Elbfish, Elbstr. 101, ☎ 01722/443226 0.5

Jugendherberge (JH) Lauenburg, Am Sportpl. 7, ☎ 2598 2

Jugendherberge (JH) Lauenburg „Zündholzfabrik", Elbstr. 2, ☎ 598880, II-III

Zweirad Sandmann, Hamburger Str. 39, ☎ 582000 1

Boizenburg/Elbe
Area Code: 038847

i Stadtinformation, Markt 14, ☎ 62667 0.5

H Boizenburger Hof, Weidestr. 2, ☎ 50093, III 2

H Stadt Boizenburg, Vor dem Mühlentor 14, ☎ 52302, II 0

B&B Am Hafen, Hamburger Str. 13, ☎ 53091, ☎ 0152/09684814 0

B&B Am Schäferbrink, Schäferbrink 16, ☎ 8115, II 0.5

B&B Herberge Froschkasten, Altendorf 11, ☎ 52655, I 0.5

B&B Yogazentrum Boizenburg, Baustr. 21, ☎ 33675, ☎ 0176/49379492 0.5

B Villa Luise, Hamburger Str. 50, ☎ 579544, ☎ 0162/4398552, II 0

Both-Motor, Berliner Str. 2, ☎ 52447

M. Strauß, Am Mühlenteich, ☎ 53016 0.5

Bleckede
Area Code: 05852

i Tourist-Information, Schlossstr. 10, Schloss Bleckede, ☎ 951414 0.5

H Elbhotel Bleckede, Elbstr. 5, ☎ 4089533, ☎ 0176/41659910, III 0

H Waldfrieden, Dahlenburger Str. 30, ☎ 97990, III 1.5

B&B Elbhof Harnisch, Wendischthuner Str. 15, ☎ 2945, ☎ 0171 1679947, I-III 0

B&B Soetbeer, Lauenburger Str. 3, ☎ 9519080, ☎ 2870, I-II 0

B Gästehaus Christa, Dahlenburger Str. 6, ☎ 615, ☎ 0170/9323720, III 0

B Haus Elbtalaue, Von-Estorffs-Weg 25, ☎ 1221, II 0.5

B Auf der Kleinburg, Lauenburger Str. 23, ☎ 1297, II 1

AH Casa Creativa, Fritz-von-dem-Berge-Str. 27, ☎ 390202, II 0

AH Rosenhaus, Zollstr. 32, ☎ 0162/2300461, II 0

AH Strathusen, Sannemannweg 1, ☎ 3322, ☎ 0171/1423193, II 0.5

Weber Fahrradshop, Breite Str. 6, ☎ 1272 0

Alt Garge (Bleckede)
Area Code: 05854

B Privatpension Kley, Göddinger Str. 22, ☎ 1685, I 1

A Campingpark Elbtalaue, Am Waldbad 23, ☎ 311 0.5

Walmsburg (Bleckede)
Area Code: 05853

AH Mackowski, Kateminer Str. 54, ☎ 608, I 0

A Mutter Grün, Bruchdorferstr. 30, ☎ 310 0.5

Radegast (Bleckede)

Area Code: 05857

🏠 Elbeling, Am Deich 9, 📞 555 `1.5`

Göddingen (Bleckede)

Area Code: 05854

🏠 Jugendherberge und Pension, Landstr. 12, Göddingen, 📞 1681, II `3`

Neu Wendischthun (Bleckede)

Area Code: 038844

🅱️🏠 Radlerherberge Alte Schule, Neu Bleckeder Str. 6, 📞 21840, I-II ⊙ `2`

Darchau (Amt Neuhaus)

Area Code: 038841

🅱️ Café Zur Elbe, Hauptstr. 9, 📞 20781, II `0`

🔧 Fahrrad Göldner, Hauptstr. 9, 📞 20781 `0`

Neu Darchau

Area Code: 05853

🅱️ Elb Nest, Hauptstr. 9a, 📞 0171/5116441, III
⊙ 🚲 `0`

🅱️ Vieregge, Elbuferstr. 21, 📞 1585 `0.5`

🏠 Schramm, Am Ring 6, 📞 1613 `0`

Katemin (Neu Darchau)

Area Code: 05853

🅱️🅱️ Auszeit an der Elbe, Hauptstr. 119,
📞 1766, 📞 0170/2294609, II ⊙ `0`

🅱️ Elvers, Nedderste Weg 6, 📞 422, I ⊙

Klein Kühren (Neu Darchau)

Area Code: 05853

🏠 Elbufer, Elbuferstr. 141, 📞 256, I `1`

Stapel (Amt Neuhaus)

Area Code: 038841

🅱️🅱️ Landhaus Stapel, Wallberg 8, 📞 61344,
📞 0174/8753156, II 🚲 `3.5`

Stixe (Amt Neuhaus)

Area Code: 038845

🅱️🅱️ Ferienhof Mayer, Landweg 3, 📞 41549,
📞 0174 474 4334, II-III ⊙ `2.5`

Bitter (Amt Neuhaus)

Area Code: 038855

🏠 Ferienappartements Lau, Elbstr. 5,
📞 51405, 📞 0170 2469160, II ⊙ `0`

🏠 Scheibner, Elbstr. 24, 📞 038845/40395,
I `0`

Hitzacker

Area Code: 05862

ℹ️ Kur- & Touristinformation Hitzacker, Am
Markt 7, 📞 96970 `0`

🏠 Bürgerstube, Marschtorstr. 5, 📞 6439,
📞 0175/5934867, III `0`

🏠 Parkhotel Hitzacker, Am Kurpark 3,
📞 9770, III-IV ⊙ `0`

🏠 Scholz, Prof.-Borchling-Str. 2, 📞 959100,
III-IV ⊙ `1`

🏠 Waldfrieden, Weinbergsweg 25,
📞 96720, III `0.5`

🏠 Zur Linde, Drawehnertorstr. 22-24,
📞 347, III 🚲 `0`

🏠 Schiller's, Drawehnertorstr. 14, 📞 987777,
📞 0152/53950167, III `0`

🅱️ Radke, Von-Oeynhausen-Str. 4, 📞 7350,
📞 0171/1944939, I 🐾 `1.5`

🅱️ Villa Romantika, Elbstr. 12, 📞 1407,
📞 0170/5509700, I 🚲 `0`

🏠 Freizeitanlage Meudelfitz, Bleckeder
Landstr., 📞 05841/7497, 📞 0163/9712703,
I. Auskunft bei: Kreisjugendpfleger des
Landkreis Lüchow-Dannenberg `2.5`

🏠 Jugendherberge Hitzacker, An der
Wolfsschlucht 2, 📞 244, II `1.5`

🔧 Die Fahrradwerft, Drawehnertorstr. 10, 📞 9875765, 📞 0170/1933989 `0`

🚲 Fahrradstation am Archäologischen
Zentrum. Mit WC, Duschen, Gepäckauf-
bewahrung und Caféterrasse. `0.5`

Wehningen (Amt Neuhaus)

Area Code: 038845

🏠 Holm, Hauptstr. 18, 📞 40939,
📞 0157/31640939, II `0`

🅱️ Sommerhaus Alte Tischlerei, Hauptstr. 33a, 📞 44544, 📞 01520/9413377, II
🐾 `0.5`

🏠 Drei Eichen, Feldstr. 6, 📞 70058, I `0.5`

Rüterberg (Dömitz)

Area Code: 038758

🏠 Wohnmobilstellplatz, Ringstr. 2,
📞 35826, 📞 0171/1583559 `0`

Dömitz

Area Code: 038758

ℹ️ Tourist-Information, Rathauspl. 1,
📞 22112 `1.5`

🏠 Dömitzer Hafen Hotel, Hafenpl. 3,
📞 364290, III-IV 🚲 `1.5`

🏠 ma maison Boutique Hotel, Friedrich-
Franz-Str. 6, 📞 36 96 96, 📞 0162133 84
34 `1.5`

🅱️🅱️ Radlerpension Steffen, Elbstr. 1, 📞 24484,
📞 0160/2496509, II 🚲 `1.5`

🅱️🅱️ Zur Festung, Goethestr. 15, 📞 368789,
📞 0162/5836316, II `1.5`

🅱️ Fam. Fähnrich, Marienstr. 5, 📞 22626, I-II
🚲 `1.5`

🅱️ Großmann, Schwarzer Weg 1, 📞 22296,
I-II ⊙ `2.5`

🅱️ Märchen-Pension im Scheunen-Café am
Deich, Elbstr. 26, 📞 22032, II 🐾 `1`

🏨 Herberge Alte Brauerei, Fritz-Reuter-
Str. 20, 📞 0174/4806232, II 🐾 `1.5`

🏠 Radlerpension zum Wartezimmer, Lud-
wigsluster Str. 24, 📞 0171/5659030,
📞 0171/5659030, II ⊙ `0.5`

🏠 Simone Schult, Roggenfelder Str. 16,
📞 22278, 📞 0173/7586366, I `2`

🏠 WasserWanderZentrum Dömitz, An der
Schleuse, 📞 01515/2019020, I `2`

🔧 Fahrrad Behncke, Friedrich-Franz-
Str. 21, 📞 22543 `1.5`

Heidhof (Dömitz)

Area Code: 038758

🅱️ Haus Seutter, Dömitzer Chaussee 7,
📞 351495, 📞 0152/08884964, II 🚲 `2.5`

Quickborn (Gusborn)

Area Code: 05865

🏠 Quickborner Jägerhof, Hauptstr. 9,
📞 247, I-II `4`

Grippel (Langendorf (Elbe))

Area Code: 05882

🅱️🅱️ Lechner, Dannenberger Str. 8, 📞 630,
I `0.5`

🏠 Elbhof Zipoll, Dannenberger Str. 15,
📞 439, II `0`

Gorleben

Area Code: 05882

🏠 Hotel Das Deichhaus & Barrel-Hostel,
Burgstr. 5, 📞 987484, 📞 0152/28700528,
II-III ⊙ `0`

🏠 Kaminstube, Hauptstr. 11, 📞 987560, I-II
⊙ 🚲 `0`

Brünkendorf (Höhbeck)

Area Code: 05846

🅱️ Holm, Ringstr. 8, 📞 1659, I `1.5`

🏠 Weber, Ringstr. 12, 📞 379, I `1.5`

Pevestorf (Höhbeck)

Area Code: 05846

🏠 🅷 Zum Lindenkrug, Fährstr. 30, 📞 1505,
II `1.5`

189

Vietze (Höhbeck)

Area Code: 05846

- ℹ️ Tourist-Information Gartow, Springstr. 14, Gartow, ✆ 333 5
- 🏨 Hütten-Hotel-Elbhöhe, Am Elbufer 9, ✆ 1707, II ☺ 0
- 🏨 Kastanienhof Vietze, Bergstr. 36, ✆ 9804662, ✆ 0160/5750452, II ☺ 🚲 0

Lenzen (Elbe)

Area Code: 038792

- ℹ️ Tourist-Information, Berliner Str. 7, Stumpfer Turm, ✆ 7302 1.5
- 🏨 Alte Wassermühle, Mühlenweg 33, ✆ 889991, ✆ 0162/2467982, III 🚲 2.5
- 🏨 Burghotel Lenzen, Burgstr. 3, ✆ 5078300, III-IV ☺ 1.5
- 🏨 Schützenhaus, Am Volkspl. 2, ✆ 9200, ✆ 0171/5405730, III ☺ 2
- 🛏️ Haus Lenzen e. V., Leuengarten 2, ✆ 9870, III 6
- 🛏️ Hof Janisch, Leuengarten 1, ✆ 7488, III 6
- 🅱️ Hennig, Hauptwache 1, ✆ 524244, ✆ 01590/2249910, OB, I 🍴 1.5
- 🏨 Cafe am Markt, Hamburger Str. 38, ✆ 7378, ✆ 0172/9511267, II 1.5
- 🏨 Hof Rademacher, Ausbau 1, ✆ 1400, ✆ 0172/5703394, II 1
- 🏕️ Lenzen am Rudower See, Leuengarten 9, ✆ 7588, ✆ 80075, ✆ 0152/22103105 6

190

Breetz (Lenzen (Elbe))

Area Code: 038792

- 🏨 Breetzer Herrenhaus, Kastanienallee 12, ✆ 50832, ✆ 0160/97913931, I 🚲 4.5

Lütkenwisch (Lanz)

Area Code: 038780

- 🛏️ Jaap, Elbstr. 5, ✆ 70693, II 🚲 0

Bernheide (Lanz)

Area Code: 038780

- 🏨 Unter den Linden, Dorfpl. 6, ✆ 7301, II

Cumlosen

Area Code: 038794

- 🏨 Schmidt, Lenzener Str. 25, ✆ 30214, ✆ 0170/9830085, II 🍴 0.5
- 🅱️ Bertelt, Seeviertel 22, ✆ 30242, II 🍴 0
- 🅱️ Grüning, Seeviertel 20, ✆ 30442, ✆ 0162/7305484, II 🍴 0

Wittenberge

Area Code: 03877

- ℹ️ Tourist-Information, Paul-Lincke-Pl. 1, im Kultur- und Festspielhaus, ✆ 929181, ✆ 929182 0
- 🏨 Alte Ölmühle, Bad Wilsnacker Str. 52, ✆ 567994600, IV 🚲 0.5
- 🏨 Am Stern, Turmstr. 14, ✆ 9890, III-IV 0
- 🏨 Germania, Bahnstr. 53a, ✆ 95590, III 🚲 0
- 🏨 Prignitz, Bismarckpl. 1, ✆ 92870, III 0.5

- 🏨 Zur Elbaue, Bahnstr. 107, ✆ 904118, III 🚲 0
- 🛏️ Am Festspielhaus, Friedrich-Ebert-Str. 9, ✆ 56799445, ✆ 01520/9080850, II 🚲 0.5
- 🛏️ Pension König, Tivolistr. 26, ✆ 69200, II 🍴 ☺ ℹ️
- 🛏️ Tollhaus, Perleberger Str. 155, ✆ 71491, II 🍴 0.5
- 🛏️ Zur Möwe, Elbstr. 22b, ✆ 403855, ✆ 0172/8744233, III ☺ 0
- 🅱️ Kuhn, Elbstr. 9, ✆ 69603, ✆ 0160/3102874, II 🍴 0
- 🅱️ Mnich & Paul, Tivolistr. 35, ✆ 79331, ✆ 0151/11959049, II 🍴 0.5
- 🅱️ Schwesig, Lenzener Chaussee 19a, ✆ 66445, ✆ 0174/4254037, II 🍴 1.5
- 🅱️ Zum Tivoli, Tivolistr. 36, ✆ 75768, ✆ 0174/3849295, III 🍴 0.5
- 🏨 Elbblick Wittenberge, Elbstr. 13, ✆ 69635, ✆ 0152/2907351, II 🍴 0
- 🏨 Haus am Festspielhaus, Müllerstr. 5, ✆ 9579525, ✆ 0152/09495660, II 🍴 0.5
- 🏨 Le Petit Jardin, Gartenstr. 20, ✆ 0157/72177559, III 🍴 0.5
- 🏨 Wüsten-Oase, Wüstenweg 4a, ✆ 904061, III 2
- 🏨 Zum Schlafwandler, Bürgerstr. 31, ✆ 66369, II 0
- 🏨 Jugendgästehaus, Perleberger Str. 64, ✆ 5627140, ✆ 79195, I 1

- 🏨 Strandbad Friedensteich, Gehrenweg 81, ✆ 5627140, I ☺. Übernachtung auch in Blockhütten möglich. 1.5
- 🚴 Fahrrad Raugsch, Am Stern 3, ✆ 9574826 0
- 🚴 Fahrrad Schukat, Rathausstr. 55, ✆ 61153 0
- 🚴 Zweirad-Center Berger, Bahnstr. 18, ✆ 60244 0

Lindenberg (Wittenberge)

Area Code: 03877

- 🅱️ Rumsch, Feldstr. 33, ✆ 403201, ✆ 0162/7822491, OB, III 3.5

Schnackenburg

Area Code: 05840

- ℹ️ Tourist-Information Gartow, Springstr. 14, Gartow, ✆ 05846/333 5
- 🏨 Hafencafé Felicitas, Alandstr. 9, ✆ 9897060, ✆ 0171/4420571, II 0
- 🛏️ Deichgraf, Elbstr. 7, ✆ 989367, ✆ 0173/5812920, II 0

Gartow

Area Code: 05846

- ℹ️ Tourist-Information Gartow, Springstr. 14, Gartow, ✆ 333 5
- 🏨 Seeblick, Roseng. 6, ✆ 9600, III-IV 🚲 5
- 🛏️ Ferienhof Kunzog, Am Ortfeld 6, ✆ 356, II 5

- 🏨 Familienferiendorf Gartow, Hahnberger Str. 76, ✆ 1613, ✆ 0171/1787003, II ☺ 🚲 5
- 🏨 Meyer, Elsebusch 89, ✆ 2466, II 5
- 🏨 Schwudke, Am Reiterpl. 21, ✆ 733, II 5
- 🚴 Freizeit- und Campingpark Gartow, Am Helk 3, ✆ 979060, ✆ 979060 ☺ 🚲 4.5
- 🚴 FDNF Fahrradtouristik, Hauptstr. 19, ✆ 9310. Auch E-Bike-Verleih. 5
- 🚴 Steffen Walter, Hahnenberger Str. 70, ✆ 2132 5

Laasche (Gartow)

Area Code: 05846

- 🏕️ Campingplatz Laascher See, Laasche 13, ✆ 980093 2.5

Deutsch (Zehrental)

Area Code: 039395

- 🏨 Baum & Blume, Deutscher Dorfstr. 20, ✆ 81554, III-III 2.5

Bömenzien (Zehrental)

Area Code: 039395

- 🏨 Werner, Dorfstr. 10, ✆ 81802, II 0

Ziemendorf

Area Code: 039384

- 🛏️ Pferde- und Freizeitparadies, Dorfstr. 49 g, ✆ 97295 0

Arendsee (Altmark)

Area Code: 039384

- 🛈 Tourist-Information, Töbelmannstr. 1, ✆ 27164 0.5
- 🏠 Deuschle, Salzwedelerstr. 52, ✆ 27139, III 0.5
- 🏠 Deutsches Haus, Friedenstr. 91, ✆ 2500, 9730, III-IV ⊙ 0.5
- 🏠 Ferienland Arendsee, Am Lindenpark 12, ✆ 0162/7561169, II 0.5
- 🏠 Haus am See, Lindenstr. 28, ✆ 9890, IV 0.5
- 🅱 Asia Oase, Friedenstr. 54, ✆ 983966, II 0.5
- 🅱 Riediger, Töbelmannstr. 19, ✆ 27396, I 0
- AH Goyer, Friedenstr. 85, ✆ 21012, ✆ 0172/9307437, II 0.5
- AH Hennings, Bungalowsiedlung 38-39, ✆ 02302/9786897, II
- AH Holz, Friedenstr. 12, ✆ 27379, I-II 0
- AH Schilling, Breitenstein 22, ✆ 986230 0.5
- 🏕 Campingplatz Arendsee, Harper Weg 1, ✆ 2587 0.5
- 🏕 Im kleinen Elsebusch, Lüchower Str. 6a, ✆ 27363 0.5

Schrampe (Arendsee (Altmark))
Area Code: 039384
- AH Winterling, Am Mühlengraben, ✆ 0521/140678, I-II 0.5

Zießau (Arendsee (Altmark))
Area Code: 039384

- 🏠 Zur Wildgans, Dorfstr. 8, ✆ 973895, ✆ 0171/3025917, II-III 0.5
- AH Pinnecke, Lindenweg 11, ✆ 03931/716166 0.5

Hansestadt Salzwedel
Area Code: 03901
- 🛈 Tourist-Information, Neuperverstr. 29, ✆ 422438 0.5
- 🏠 Kastanienhof, An der Warthe 4, ✆ 38883, III 3.5
- 🏠 Katharinenhöfchen, An der Katharinenkirche 5, ✆ 471262, III 0.5
- 🏠 Reitstadion, Gerstedter Weg 6, ✆ 0171/2326800, II 1.5
- 🏠 Siebeneichen, Kastanienweg 3, ✆ 35030, II-III ⊙ 1.5
- 🏠 Union Salzwedel, Goethestr. 11, ✆ 422097, III-IV 0.5
- 🏠 Zur Post, Breite Str. 39, ✆ 422034, III 0.5
- Hg Königsbrücke, Altperverstr. 10, ✆ 471262, III 1
- 🏠 Zum Bartelskamp, Am Bartelskamp 3, ✆ 32946, ✆ 0172/8799557, I-II 1.5
- 🅱 Altstadtpension, Südbockhorn 12, ✆ 3938853, II 0.5
- 🅱 Kruse Baumkuchen, Holzmarktstr. 4-6, ✆ 422107 1
- 🅱 Müller, Neuperver Tor 50, ✆ 33479, ✆ 0151/10326885, OB, I-II 1

- B&B Ritters-Hof, Arendsee Str. 65, ✆ 32520, I 1.5
- AH Weißbach, Wallstr. 10, ✆ 25803, II 0.5
- AH Zaunick, Amtsstr. 19, ✆ 3059907, ✆ 0160/96205244 1
- 🔧 Fahrrad-Rossi, Altperverstr. 56, ✆ 473311 1
- 🔧 Toma Bike Shop, Burgstr. 12, ✆ 422395 0.5

Güstritz (Wustrow (Wendland))
Area Code: 05843
- B&B Villa Wendland, Schwarzer Weg 2, ✆ 6309822, ✆ 0170/9951777, III 0

Bergen (Dumme)
Area Code: 05845
- 🛈 Gemeindeverwaltung, Breite Str. 35, ✆ 969885 2.5
- 🏠 Nigel, Breite Str. 9, ✆ 9600, III 2.5
- 🅱 Antik-Café E. Stamm, Hindenburgpl. 1, ✆ 1280, II 2.5
- 🏕 Campingpark - Fuhrenkamp, Am Fuhrenkamp 1, ✆ 348 ⊙ 1.5

Flecken Diesdorf
Area Code: 03902
- 🛈 Gemeinde Flecken Diesdorf, Himmelreichstr. 1, ✆ 276 0.5
- B&B Schlundt, Bergstr. 10, ✆ 273, II 0
- AH Ortwinkel, MTS-Siedlung 8, ✆ 60346 0.5

- 🔧 Technik-Center-Diesdorf, Am Klingenbusch 12, ✆ 305 0

Abbendorf (Flecken Diesdorf)
Area Code: 03902
- B&B Niemann, Dorfstr. 7, ✆ 381 1.5

Brome
Area Code: 05833
- B&B Haus Jürgens, Zu den Ohreauen 2, ✆ 234, III 0.5
- B&B Hintz, Taubenweg 8, ✆ 1076 1.5
- B&B Rauschenbach, Lindenstr. 19, ✆ 1305, OB 1
- B&B Templin, Vogelweg 9, ✆ 1548 1

Zicherie (Brome)
Area Code: 05833
- 🏠 Hubertus, Am Wildgehege 3, ✆ 4279975, III 0.5

Kunrau (Klötze)
Area Code: 039008
- B&B Schulze, Hauptstr. 21, ✆ 246 0
- 🅱 Heimann, Alte Bahnhofstr. 16, ✆ 410 0.5
- 🅱 Jürges, Alte Bahnhofstr. 11, ✆ 485 0.5
- 🅱 Schulz, Alte Bahnhofstr. 7, ✆ 310 0.5

Breitenrode (Oebisfelde-Weferlingen)
Area Code: 039002
- 🏠 Hildebrandt, Bauernerde 12, ✆ 42595, II 0
- B&B Schöndube, Im Balken 7, ✆ 43115, I 0

Wolfsburg
Area Code: 05361
- 🛈 Tourist-Information Wolfsburg, Willy-Brandt-Pl. 3, (direkt am Hauptbahnhof), ✆ 05362/899930 0
- 🏠 Alter Wolf, Schlossstr. 21, ✆ 05362/86560, III 1
- 🏠 Centro Hotel Goya, Poststr. 34, ✆ 05362/26600, III 0.5
- 🏠 Courtyard by Marriott Wolfsburg, Allerpark 8, ✆ 3066-0, IV-VI 0.5
- 🏠 Jäger, Stellfelder Str. 42, ✆ 05362/39090, IV-V 3
- 🏠 Penthouse-Hotel, Schachtweg 22, ✆ 05362/2710, III 0.5
- 🏠 Porschehotel, Porschestr. 64b, ✆ 05362/26620, III 1
- Hg Hotel am Klieversberg, Röntgenstr. 5, ✆ 8913417, III-IV ⊙ 2
- 🏠 Jugendherberge Wolfsburg, Kleiststr. 18-20, ✆ 13337 ⊙ 0.5
- 🏕 Campingplatz am Allersee, In den Allerwiesen 5, ✆ 63395 0
- 🔧 Fahrradwerkstatt Netzwerk Wolfsburg GmbH, Poststr. 33, ✆ 35860 0.5
- 🔧 Zweirad Schael, Kleiststr. 5, ✆ 14064 0.5
- 🔧 Zweirad Vogel, Weidenkamp 1a, ✆ 05362/62616 5

Oebisfelde-Weferlingen
Area Code: 039002

H Stadt Oebisfelde-Weferlingen, Lange Str. 12, ✆ 8310 0.5

H Am Markt, Marktpl. 3, ✆ 815730, III 0.5

B&B Im Royal, Gardelegener Str. 16, ✆ 43666, I 0.5

B Peters, Lindenstr. 46, ✆ 42363, II 0.5

Weferlingen (Oebisfelde-Weferlingen)
Area Code: 039061

H Zur Sonne, Bergstr. 16, ✆ 2385, II 0

Grasleben
Area Code: 05356

H Erbprinz, Vorsfelder Str. 1, ✆ 216 2

Walbeck
Area Code: 039061

H Barriere Rehm, Barriere 167, ✆ 2502, III 0

AH Lattermann, Marienthaler Str. 97a, ✆ 988744, ✆ 0151/15523491, I 0

Beendorf
Area Code: 039050

H Landhaus Beendorf, Schulpl. 3, ✆ 2378 0.5

Bad Helmstedt (Helmstedt)
Area Code: 05351

H Quellenhof, Brunnenweg 19, ✆ 1240 0

Helmstedt
Area Code: 05351

i Touristinfo im Bürgerbüro, Markt 1, Eingang Holzberg, ✆ 171717 0

192

H Best Western Hotel Helmstedt, Chardstr. 2, ✆ 1280 0.5

H Knigge, Leuckartstr. 54, ✆ 33066, III 1

H Parkhotel, Albrechtstr. 1, ✆ 544880, III 0.5

H Petzold, Schöninger Str. 1, ✆ 6001 0

Hg Frisco, Walbecker Str. 11, ✆ 55750, III 1.5

B Haus EWA, Vorsfelder Str. 27, ✆ 32784, ✆ 0177/9228423, OB, I 1.5

B Haus Haas, Meibomstr. 29, ✆ 537744 1

B Haus Meerkatz, Conringstr. 5, ✆ 32670, ✆ 01573/9439811, I 1

B Haus Schulz, Carlstr. 5, ✆ 33173 1

🚲 Karsten Vetter Fahrräder, Leipziger Str. 12a, ✆ 539893 0

Hötensleben

i Gemeindeverwaltung, Zimmermannpl. 2, ✆ 039409/9160 0.5

Schöningen
Area Code: 05352

H Schlafschöningen, Niedernstr. 39, ✆ 9084641, III 1

H Schloss Schöningen, Burgpl. 1a, ✆ 907590, III-IV 1.5

H Zeitreise, Am Wallgarten 12, ✆ 9099165, III 1

B&B Schäferstübchen, Schäferbreite 31a, ✆ 2242, II 2

▲ Jugendherberge Schöningen, Richard-Schirmann-Str. 6a, ✆ 3898, I 2.5

🚲 Schließer Bike, Wilhelmstr. 10, ✆ 8866 1.5

Hornburg
Area Code: 05334

i Stadtmarketing Hornburg, Pfarrhofstr. 5, ✆ 94910

H Schützenhof, Vor dem Vorwerkstor 3, ✆ 1211, III 0

B Villa Reischel, Vor dem Dammtor 2, ✆ 92990, II 0

AH Am Markt, Marktstr. 5, ✆ 948962, I 0

AH Hagenmühle, Hagenstr. 31, ✆ 1080, I 0.5

▲ Relax Campingpark, Am Stadtbad 2, ✆ 948964 0.5

🚲 Bike and Barbecue, Vor dem Braunschweiger Tor 7, ✆ 7218396 0.5

Bad Harzburg
Area Code: 05322

i Tourist-Information, Nordhäuserstr. 4, ✆ 75330 2

H Braunschweiger Hof, Herzog-Wilhelm-Str. 54, ✆ 7880, V 0.5

H Haus Bismarck, Bismarckstr. 39, ✆ 6227, III 0.5

H Parkhotel Bad Harzburg, Hindenburgring 12A, ✆ 9569070, III-V 1

H **AH** Plumbohms Bio-Suiten - Hotel, Herzog-Wilhelm-Str. 97, ✆ 3277, III-V 1

H Seela, Nordhäuser Str. 5, ✆ 7960, IV 2

H Tannenhof, Nordhäuser Str. 6, ✆ 96880, IV-V 2

H Vitalhotel am Stadtpark, Am Stadtpark 2, ✆ 78090, III-IV 1

H Winterberg, Nordhäuser Str. 8, ✆ 96880, IV-V 2

Hg Harzblick, Bohlweg 12, ✆ 83656, I-III 2

Hg Stadtparkhotel Alexandra, Am Stadtpark 43, ✆ 9875414, III 1.5

B&B Haus Roswita, Am Vorwerk 7a, ✆ 52656, ✆ 0162/1011145, II 0.5

B&B Villa Irene, Am Kurpark 1-2, ✆ 96250, II-III 1.5

NF NFH Bündheim, Waldstr. 5, ✆ 8788610, II-III 2

▲ Wolfstein, Ilsenburgerstr. 111, ✆ 3585, ✆ 01575/3647553 0.5

H Haus in der Sonne, Amsbergstr. 31, ✆ 96040, IV 1.5

🚲 Bike Store, Am Bahnhofspl. 2-8, ✆ 784190 0

Ilsenburg (Harz)
Area Code: 039452

i 🚲 Tourismus GmbH mit R1-Service- und Infostelle, Marktpl. 1, ✆ 19433 0.5

H Altstadthotel, Wernieröder Str. 1, ✆ 48990, III 0.5

H Berghotel Ilsenburg, Suental 5, ✆ 900, IV 0.5

H Ilsenburger Hof, Faktoreistr. 5, ✆ 9510, III 0.5

H Kurpark-Hotel, Ilsetal 16, ✆ 9560, III-IV 0

H Landhaus Zu den Rothen Forellen, Marktpl. 2, ✆ 9393, VI 0

H Waldhotel am Ilsenstein, Ilsetal 9, ✆ 9520, III 0

H Vogelmühle, Vogelsang 1, ✆ 99230, III 0

B&B Heinrich Heine, Marienhöfer Str. 9f, ✆ 209916, ✆ 0175/9303919, II 0.5

B&B Stadt Hamburg, Karl-Marx-Str. 16, ✆ 2211, II 0.5

B Aulich, Uferstr. 1, ✆ 86968, ✆ 0151/14255015, II 0.5

B Gresens, Grüne Str. 27, ✆ 86569, I 0.5

B Ruhe, Uferstr. 7, ✆ 80455, III 0.5

B Schließer, Schickendamm 5, ✆ 99193, OB, I 0.5

AH Ahorn, Ahornweg 2, ✆ 0171 7578348, III 4.5

AH Kirschberg, Kirschberg 13, ✆ 03943/603629, II 3.5

AH Klinger, Auf der See 20, ✆ 0171/3863333 0

AH Scarlett, Rudolf-Breitscheid-Str. 8, ✆ 486583, III 0

AH Schirbel, Ilsetal 15, ✆ 86894, II 0

🚲 Touren Harz, Marienhöfer Str. 2, ✆ 0151/20135900 0.5

Elend
Area Code: 039454

i Tourist-Information, Hauptstr. 19, ✆ 039455/375 0

H Waldmühle, Braunlager Str. 15, ✆ 039455/51222, III-IV ⓞ

B&B Bodetal, Hauptstr. 28, ✆ 039455/381, I ⓞ.5

B&B Harzhaus, Heinrich-Heine-Weg 1, ✆ 039455/386, II ⓞ

B&B „Eli Lenti", Hauptstr. 24, ✆ 039455/58970, III ⓞ

Schierke (Wernigerode)
Area Code: 039455

i Tourist-Information, Brockenstr. 10, ✆ 8680 ⓞ

H Brockenhotel, Brockenplateau, Brocken- plateau (Wernigerode), ✆ 120, IV-V ⓞ

H Brockenscheideck, Brockenstr. 49, ✆ 268 ⓞ

H Brockenstübchen, Brockenstr. 39, ✆ 252, II-III ⓞ

H Villa Bodeblick, Barenberg 1, ✆ 825550, IV ⓞ.5

H AH Villa Fichtenhof, Hagenstr. 3, ✆ 88888, II ⓞ

B&B Barbara, Brückenstr. 1, ✆ 8690, II ⓞ

B&B Mühlhahn, Brockenstr. 27a, ✆ 51529, II-III ⓞ

B&B Schmidt, Brockenstr. 13, ✆ 333, III ⓞ

B&B Zum Wildbach, Barenberg 15f, ✆ 589970, II ⓞ

AH Das Schierke, Alte Dorfstr. 1, ✆ 825550, VI ⓞ

AH Haus Walpurga, Alte Wenigeröder Str. 4, ✆ 51100, II ⓞ

M Jugendherberge Schierke, Brocken- str. 48, ✆ 51066, I-II ⓞ ⓞ

Sorge
Area Code: 039457

H Zum Sonnenhof, Benneckensteiner Str. 10a, ✆ 2426, II-III ⓞ.5

R Raststübl, Köhlerbergstr. 3, ✆ 3273, II-III ⓞ

Hohegeiß (Braunlage)
Area Code: 05583

i Tourist-Information, Kirchstr. 15a, ✆ 241 ⓞ

AH Aparthotel Panoramic Hohegeiß, Am Kurpark 3, ✆ 9392373, II-III ①

A Am Bärenbache, Bärenbachweg 10, ✆ 1306 ⓞ.5

Zorge
Area Code: 05586

H Altes Forsthaus, Im Förstergarten 12, ✆ 402, II ⓞ

H Kunzental, Im Förstergarten 7, ✆ 1261, III ⓞ

H Wolfsbach, Hohegeißer Str. 25, ✆ 9627610, III ⓞ

B&B Haus Birgit, Im Förstergarten 6, ✆ 1025, II ⓞ

Walkenried
Area Code: 05525

H Jagdschloss, Schlossstr. 15, ✆ 638, IV ⓞ

H Klosterschänke, Harzstr. 5, ✆ 209847, II ⓞ.5

A KNAUS Campingpark Walkenried, Ellri- cher Str. 7, ✆ 778 ①

Brochthausen (Duderstadt)
Area Code: 05529

H Zur Erholung, Brochthäuser Str. 65, ✆ 96200, II-III ⓞ

H Zur Endstation, Deichstr. 2, ✆ 919283, II ⓞ

AH Ballhausen, Hirtenklimp 8, ✆ 1380, I ⓞ.5

Fuhrbach (Duderstadt)
Area Code: 05529

H Zum Kronprinzen, Fuhrbacher Str. 31-33, ✆ 05527/9100, III-IV ⓞ

Gerblingerode (Duderstadt)
Area Code: 05529

H Hahletal, Teistunger Str. 43, ✆ 05527/1478, ✆ 05527/73055, III ⓞ

B&B Ferienparadies Pferdeberg, Bischof- Janssen-Str. 1, ✆ 05527/5733, III ①

B Weller, Restanger 26, ✆ 05527/9440398, OB, I ①.5

Duderstadt
Area Code: 05529

i Tourist-Information, Marktstr. 66, im hist. Rathaus, ✆ 05527/841200 ⓞ.5

H Budapest, Marktstr. 99, ✆ 05527/98630, III ⓞ

H Kurmainzer Eck, Am Sulberg 2-6, ✆ 05527/5046, II ①

H Zum Löwen, Marktstr. 30, ✆ 05527/849000, IV-V ⓞ.5

Hg Zum Halben Mond, Haberstr. 17-19, ✆ 05527/2698, II ⓞ.5

AH Block, Börseng. 1, ✆ 05527/2806, II ⓞ.5

M Jugendgästehaus, Adenauerring 23, ✆ 05527/98470 ⓞ.5

✦ Fahrrad Beckmann, Markstr. 4, ✆ 05527/941693 ⓞ.5

Teistungen
Area Code: 036071

H Victors Residenz-Hotel, Klosterweg 6-7, ✆ 03607/1840, III-IV ⓞ

Heilbad Heiligenstadt
Area Code: 03606

i Tourist-Information, Marktpl. 15, Rat- haus, ✆ 677903, ✆ 677142 ⓞ

H Am Jüdenhof, Am Jüdenhof 5-7, ✆ 663888, III ⓞ.5

H Am Vitalpark, In der Leineaue 2, ✆ 66370, IV-V ①

H Kurparkklinik, Felgentor 4, ✆ 6630, II ⓞ.5

H Norddeutscher Bund, Göttinger Str. 25, ✆ 55300, III ⓞ.5

H Stadthotel, Dingelstädter Str. 43, ✆ 6660, III ①.5

H Traube, Bahnhofstr. 2, ✆ 612253, III ⓞ

H Zum Dün, Dünstr. 40, ✆ 614414, I ①.5

H Schwarzer Adler, Wilhelmstr. 2, ✆ 612250, II ⊙ ⓞ.5

B&B Kruse, Lessingstr. 1, ✆ 612575, II ①

B&B Kur-Pension Hohes Rott, Nelkenweg 10, ✆ 619399, II ⓞ.5

B&B Perriello, Lindenallee 18, ✆ 6528870, ✆ 0176/63491885 ⓞ.5

B Flucke, Klausberg 3, ✆ 613186, I ⓞ.5

B Hartung, Margarethenweg 17, ✆ 608531 ⓞ.5

B Herwig, Heimenstein 27/29, ✆ 613286, ✆ 0151/15700274, I ⓞ.5

B Jutta Roth, Fichtenweg 4, ✆ 603588, I ①.5

B Kreuzburg, Dingelstädter Str. 59, ✆ 613174, I ②.5

B Köhler + Zirpel, Geschwister-Scholl-Str. 1, ✆ 613271 ①

B Schönstatt-Zentrum Kleines Paradies, Pater-Kentenich-Weg 3, ✆ 619790 ①.5

✦ Bode, Stubenstr. 17, ✆ 600410 ⓞ.5

✦ Maschinenkönig-Fahrradgeschäft, Wil- helmstr. 64, ✆ 553720 ⓞ.5

Arenshausen
Area Code: 036081

B Seeliger, Thomas-Müntzer-Str. 4, ✆ 8167985, I ⓞ

Bornhagen
Area Code: 036081

i Gemeinde Bornhagen, Am Kulturzent- rum 11, ✆ 61311 ⓞ

H Zweiburgenblick, Hansteinstr. 2, ✆ 0172/3600545, IV **i**

H Hh Klausenhof - Das alte Wirtshaus, Friedensstr. 28, ✆ 61422, I-V **0.5**

Werleshausen (Witzenhausen)
Area Code: 05542

Ma Z Jugendburg Ludwigstein, Burg Ludwigstein, ✆ 501710, I-II **0.5**

Lindewerra
Area Code: 036087

BuB Alte Brücke, Str. zur Einheit 5, ✆ 98398, I **o**

Wahlhausen
Area Code: 036087

BuB Pias Radlerrast, Kreisstr. 16, ✆ 979917 **0.5**

AH Gastrockscher Hof, Kreisstr. 35, ✆ 90160, I **o**

Z Camping-Oase, Kreisstr. 32, ✆ 98671, I **o**

Bad Sooden-Allendorf
Area Code: 05652

i Tourist-Information, Landgraf-Philipp-Pl. 1-2, ✆ 95870 **i**

H Central, Am Haintor 3, ✆ 958870, III **i**

H Haus Hilgenfeld, Freiherr-vom-Stein-Str. 23, ✆ 2324, III **i**

H Kurpark-Hotel, Brunnenpl. 1, ✆ 58764000, IV **i**

H LR6, Lange Reihe 6, ✆ 589434, II-III **i**

H Martina, Westerburgstr. 1, ✆ 2080, ✆ 95290, III **i**

H Parkhotel am Schwanenteich, Rosenstr. 4, ✆ 6000, III **0.5**

H Waldhotel Soodener Hof, Hardtstr. 7, ✆ 91930, III-IV **i**

H Deutsches Haus, Ackerstr. 56, ✆ 2481, II **o o o**

H Klosterschänke, Am Tor 3, ✆ 2388, II-III **0.5**

BuB Café Pension Feldmann, Landgrafenstr. 5+6, ✆ 917878, II-III **0.5**

BuB Gästehaus Reins, Wilhelm-Büchner-Str. 11, ✆ 3265, I **0.5**

BuB Haus DEA, Berliner Str. 1, ✆ 918060, ✆ 3377, III **0.5**

BuB Haus Erika, Am Haintor 22, ✆ 919061, ✆ 0152/22978291, II **0.5**

BuB Haus Johanna, Bismarckstr. 6, ✆ 2332, III **0.5**

BuB Meine Sonne, Hardtstr. 22, ✆ 4919, III **i**

B Gästehaus Axt, Königsberger Str. 15, ✆ 4800, ✆ 919706, ✆ 0172/5602654, I **o o**

B Gästehaus Dietrich, Weinreihe 8, ✆ 3481, I **i**

✍ Schülbe, Eschweger Landstr. 5, ✆ 928977, ✆ 0174/3152148 **0.5**

oto Eichenberg GmbH, Am Haintor 12, ✆ 2900 **i**

Stadtwerke Stadtwerke Bad Sooden-Allendorf, Werrastr. 24, ✆ 958550

Asbach-Sickenberg
Area Code: 036087

BuB Hof Sickenberg, Sickenberg 9, ✆ 97696, III **i**

Ahrenberg (Bad Sooden-Allendorf)
Area Code: 05652

H Berggasthof Ahrenberg, Auf dem Ahrenberg 5, ✆ 95730, III-IV **1.5**

BuB Simone's Landhaus, Auf dem Ahrenberg 4, ✆ 2538, II **1.5**

Ellershausen (Bad Sooden-Allendorf)
Area Code: 05652

AH Sonnenhaus Hüller, Am Ahrenbach 4, ✆ 0172/5603731, III **i**

Kleinvach (Bad Sooden-Allendorf)
Area Code: 05652

H Zur Linde, Brückenstr. 7, ✆ 2875, III **o**

Hh ✍ Radler u. Kanu-Rast Kleinvach - Heuhotel, Fährg. 6, ✆ 91210, ✆ 0171/3697446, II **o**

Albungen (Eschwege)
Area Code: 05652

H Werraside Inn, Burgstr. 5, ✆ 5875575, II **o**

Jestädt (Meinhard)
Area Code: 05651

BuB Villa Velo, Hauptstr. 18, ✆ 20675, II **o**

AH Apel, Am Kirchrain 4, ✆ 10090 **o**

Grebendorf (Meinhard)
Area Code: 05651

i Gemeindeverwaltung, Sandstr. 15, ✆ 74800 **0.5**

BuB Kochsberg Integrationshotel, Kochsberg 1, ✆ 3394060, III **o**

BuB Gimpel, Eschweger Str. 14, ✆ 32800, I **o**

Z Meinhardsee, Freizeitzentrum 2, ✆ 6200, ✆ 22272, I **0.5**

Schwebda (Meinhard)
Area Code: 05651

H Schloss Hotel Wolfsbrunnen, Am Berg 1, ✆ 335790, V **2.5**

BuB Magda's Pension, Jahnstr. 6b, ✆ 60271, ✆ 0160/96071791, II **i**

Z Werratalsee-Naturcamping, Am Seepark 1, ✆ 9926210, ✆ 0160/4309897, I **o**

Eschwege
Area Code: 05651

i Tourist-Information Eschwege, Hospitalpl. 16, ✆ 331985 **o**

H Deutsches Haus, Schlosspl. 7, ✆ 31180, III **o**

H Hotel-Altstadtgasthof Krone, Stad 9, ✆ 30066, III **o**

H Stadthalle Eschwege, Wiesenstr. 9, ✆ 951210, III **o**

H Zur Struth, Struthstr. 7a, ✆ 922813, III **✍**

Hg Villa Ponte Wisera, Brückenstr. 33-35, ✆ 2282048, IV **o**

H Schubarts Höhe, Schützenweg 4, ✆ 74810, III **i**

BuB Frankfurter Hof, Alter Steinweg 34, ✆ 5516, ✆ 0151/29110504, III **0.5**

AH Konny's Ferienwohnungen, Brühl 19, ✆ 6147, ✆ 0172/3613209, II **o**

JH Jugendherberge Eschwege, Jardin-de-Saint-Mandé 1, ✆ 60099 **o**

Z Eschweger Kanu Club, Torwiese 4-5, ✆ 0152/52817910, I. Bitte um Voranmeldung. **o**

Z Knaus Campingpark Eschwege, Am Werratalsee 2, ✆ 338883, I **0.5**

Z Velo Mangold, Hinter der Mauer 2, ✆ 754020 **o**

Z Zweiradhaus Ebert, Forstg. 2a, ✆ 50590 **o o o**

Mobil Mobilitätszentrale am Bahnhof, Am Bahnhof 1, ✆ 0800/8090688 **1.5**

Niederdünzebach (Eschwege)
Area Code: 05651

BuB Rad- und Raststation Alte Schule, Auerstr. 15, III. Es findet ein Betreiberwechsel statt, näheres bei der Tourist-Information. **✍**

Aue (Wanfried)
Area Code: 05651

AH Scharf-Polte, Rasenstr. 6, ☏ 31741, 0178/3080159, I 0̄

AH Trierweiler, Zum Schilbengrund 8, ☏ 335127, 0175/4020706, I ⛺ 🚲 0.5

Wanfried
Area Code: 05655

🚩 Stadtverwaltung, Marktstr. 18, ☏ 98940 0̄

H Zum Schwan, Marktstr.20, ☏ 924900, III 🚲 0.5

AH Lerchengrund, Celler Str. 18, ☏ 320395, II 0.5

AH Rittergut Wanfried, Kalkhof, ☏ 8534, III 2̄

🚵 2-Rad Rabe, In der Werraaue 2, ☏ 612 0.5

Völkershausen (Wanfried)
Area Code: 05655

H Die Schenke, Dorfstr. 37, ☏ 923441, I-II 🍴 ☺ 🚵 ℹ̄

Altenburschla (Wanfried)
Area Code: 05655

H Landhotel Gemeindeschänke, Am Anger 1, ☏ 92340, III-IV ☺ 0̄

B Balzhäuser, Lilienstr. 10, ☏ 1216, ☏ 0170/1057697, II-III 0.5

AH Heim-Diegel, Insel 5, ☏ 93177, II 0̄

AH R. Meyer, Schlierbachstr. 12, ☏ 1215 🚲 🚵

A An der Werra, Am Rasen 3, ☏ 0152/38767045, I 0.5

Großburschla (Treffurt)
Area Code: 036923

B&B Am Kamin, Langer Weg 11, ☏ 51112, OB, II 1.5

AH Höckel, Auf der Höhle 3e, ☏ 88164, ☏ 03302/801510, II 🚲 1.5

Heldra (Wanfried)
Area Code: 05655

H Wanderherberge im Kleegarten, Vor der Lücke 1, ☏ 923444, I-II 0̄

AH Steube, Hinterg. 14, ☏ 8259, I 🚲 0.5

AH Zum Heldrastein, Feldmühle 2, ☏ 1302, I 🚲 0.5

A Biwakplatz Heldra, Werrastr. 8, ☏ 1090, ☏ 0151/59432509, I 0176/51581269, I 0̄

Treffurt
Area Code: 036923

ℹ Tourist-Information, Puschkinstr. 3, ☏ 51542. Mit Informationsstelle zum Naturpark Eichsfeld-Hainich-Werratal. 🚲 0̄

H Waldblick, Heidewickchen 14, ☏ 80488, III-IV 0.5

B&B Weiherstraße, Weiherstr. 4, ☏ 50747, ☏ 0160/5503652, I 🚲 0̄

AH Meißner, Gartenstr. 10, ☏ 50252, ☏ 0171/1618402, I 0̄

AH Seelig, Hessische Str. 40, ☏ 0170/1480832, I-II 0̄

🚵 bikemaik, Ziddelstr. 6, ☏ 80377 0̄

Falken (Treffurt)
Area Code: 036923

ℹ Tourist-Information, Puschkinstr. 3, Treffurt, ☏ 51542. Mit Informationsstelle zum Naturpark Eichsfeld-Hainich-Werratal. 🚲 0̄

B&B Veronika's, Flutgraben 1, ☏ 80356, II 🚲 0̄

Frankenroda
Area Code: 036924

B Marx, Flurscheide 19, ☏ 30946, ☏ 0162/5934002, I 0̄

AH Rosengarth, Carl-Grübel-Str. 2b, ☏ 42049, I 0̄

Ebenshausen
Area Code: 036924

A Naturzeltplatz, Neue Str. 19, ☏ 47324, ☏ 0173/8519585, I 0.5

Mihla
Area Code: 036924

ℹ Tourist-Information, Marktstr. 18, ☏ 489830 ℹ̄

H Graues Schloss, Thomas-Müntzer-Str. 4, ☏ 42272, II-III 0.5

H Sandgut, Auf dem Sand 3, ☏ 42501, ☏ 42074, II 0̄

AH A Wassersportfreunde e.V., Bahnhofstr. 36, ☏ 42113, OB, I 0.5

AH Nr. 18, Maßholderweg 18, ☏ 30341, ☏ 0160/5538754, I 1.5

A Freibad Mihla, Am Schwimmbad 1, ☏ 42485, I 0̄

🚵 Fratscher, Am Anger 11, ☏ 42083 0.5

Buchenau (Mihla)
Area Code: 036924

B&B Gutshof, Werrastr. 3a, ☏ 42907, ☏ 42251, I 🚲 0̄

Creuzburg
Area Code: 036926

ℹ Tourist-Information Creuzburg, In der Burg Creuzburg, ☏ 98047 0.5

H Alte Posthalterei, Plan 1, ☏ 6014, III 0̄

H Auf der Creuzburg, Burgberg 1, ☏ 71304, III 0̄

H Torklause, Bahnhofstr. 8, ☏ 82286, II 0.5

B&B Klostergarten, Klosterstr. 34, ☏ 90300, II 0̄

B Haus Böttger, Plan 8, ☏ 82374, ☏ 71806, ☏ 0162/7946247 🚲 0̄

B Haus Reinhardt, Burgstr. 3, ☏ 90658, ☏ 0174/3359067, OB 🚲 0̄

B Heinemann, Bahnhofstr. 35, ☏ 82368, ☏ 82320, ☏ 0171/4646230, I 🚲 0.5

B Kühmstädt, Michael-Praetorius-Pl. 5, ☏ 82334, ☏ 0173/7579465, III 0̄

B Zimmervermietung Schwanz, Kasseler Str. 4, ☏ 90240, OB, II 🚲 0̄

A Kanubasis/Biwakplatz, Am alten Sportpl., ☏ 72679, I 0̄

Wilhelmsglücksbrunn (Creuzburg)
Area Code: 036926

H Biohotel Stiftsgut Wilhelmsglücksbrunn, ☏ 7100320, III 0̄

Hörschel (Eisenach)
Area Code: 036928

H Tor zum Rennsteig, Unterstr. 2-4, ☏ 90605, ☏ 90605, ☏ 0175/4824387, II 0̄

B Christel Bindel, Mühlstr. 34, ☏ 90276, ☏ 0173/6902807, II 0.5

Neuenhof (Eisenach)
Area Code: 036928

H Zur Guten Quelle, Hörscheler Str. 14, ☏ 90375, III 0̄

B&B Am Rennsteig, Eisenacher Weg 19, ☏ 90455, ☏ 0171/6767715, II 0̄

B&B Leischnerhof, Hörschelerstr. 6a, ☏ 98002, ☏ 0176/5620154, OB, II 0̄

Göringen (Eisenach)
Area Code: 036928

B Zur alten Schule, Lauchröder Str. 9, ☏ 90284 0.5

B&B Wagner, Brückengraben 2, ☏ 90361, II 🍴 0.5

Herleshausen
Area Code: 05654

195

ℹ Gemeindeverwaltung, Bahnhofstr. 15, ☎ 98950 [0]

H Gutschänke, Karl-Fehr-Str. 2, ☎ 9248363, II [0]

H Landhotel & Fleischerei Schneider, Am Anger 7, ☎ 6428, II ☺ [0]

H Schöne Aussicht, Bahnhofstr. 19, ☎ 923025, ☎ 0176/92635601, II [0]

B&B Gästehaus Bornscheuer, Sackg. 8, ☎ 6537, II [0]

🚲 bike Bike-Station Herleshausen, Waldstr. 2, ☎ 8894354, ☎ 0171/1441056 [0]

Sallmannshausen (Gerstungen)
Area Code: 036922

ℹ Gemeindeverwaltung, Wilhelmstr. 53, Gerstungen, ☎ 2450 [0]

AH Ferienanlage Kirchhof, Am Rain 13, ☎ 20352, ☎ 0172/4014058, III [0]

Gerstungen
Area Code: 036922

ℹ Gemeindeverwaltung, Wilhelmstr. 53, ☎ 2450 [0]

B&B Hofmeisters Landhaus, Karlstr. 9, ☎ 30062, ☎ 0171/3848191 [0]

Berka/Werra
Area Code: 036922

ℹ Verwaltungsgemeinschaft Berka, Kirchstr. 9, ☎ 330 [0.5]

H Zur Post, Lutherstr. 46, ☎ 28842, ☎ 0177/2599234, II [0.5]

B&B Erna, Lutherstr. 42-43, ☎ 42643, II [0.5]

B Daut, Friedhofstr. 6, ☎ 036992/42309, ☎ 0176/25263361, OB, I [0.5]

AH Freizeitcamp Kanu-Verleih Werra, Mühlweg 9a, ☎ 28220, ☎ 0173/2958531, II ☺ [0.5]

Dankmarshausen
Area Code: 036922

H Waldschlösschen, Waldstr. 31, ☎ 437200, III ☺ **bike** [0.5]

B&B Bürgerhaus d. Gemeinde, Kirchpl. 3, ☎ 0174/4717587, OB, I [0]

Widdershausen (Heringen (Werra))
Area Code: 06624

B&B Mäder, Hersfelder Str. 13, ☎ 423 [0]

B Heger, Festpl. 3, ☎ 8062 [0]

Heringen (Werra)
Area Code: 06624

ℹ Tourist-Information, Dickestr. 1, ☎ 919413, ☎ 5127 [0]

H Gunkel, Wagnersg. 6, ☎ 390, II ☺ [0]

B&B Alt Heringen, Fuldische Aue 7, ☎ 919330 [0]

B&B Am Werraufer, Apothekerstr. 13, ☎ 543787, II ☺ [0.5]

B&B Blüthgen, Oberland 3, ☎ 403, ☎ 0171/3623514 [0.5]

Werratal Camping, Am Steinberg 7
⛺ Werratal Camping, Am Steinberg 7, ☎ 542022, ☎ 0151/15957427 [1]

Vacha
Area Code: 036962

ℹ Stadt Vacha, Markt 4, ☎ 2610 [0.5]

H Adler, Markt 1, ☎ 2650, III [0.5]

H Zum Oechsetal, Jahnweg 15, ☎ 24370, ☎ 0170/2440123, II [1]

B Kasmierz, Burgwall 4, ☎ 24896, ☎ 0151/52972635, II-III [0.5]

AH Kanzler, Jahnweg 1a, ☎ 53896, III [1]

AH Scharfe Ecke, August-Bebel-Str. 24, ☎ 22786, ☎ 0151/67514314, II [1]

🚲 bike Fahrrad Eyring, Widemarkter Str. 17, ☎ 21260 [0.5]

Philippsthal (Werra)
Area Code: 06620

ℹ Gemeindeverwaltung, Schloss 1, ☎ 92100 [0]

H Rhönblick, Vachaerstr. 2a, ☎ 469, II [0]

B&B Helke, Südstr. 18, ☎ 8560, ☎ 0160/96917631, OB, I [0.5]

B Kliem, Mittelstr. 31, ☎ 0178/9384731, I [0]

B Zum Öchsenberg, Ufflanger Weg 29, ☎ 454, ☎ 0152/06681813, II [0.5]

AH Clute-Simon, Weidenhain 5, ☎ 8979, I [1]

Unterbreizbach
Area Code: 036962

AH Lapp, Sommerliete 1, ☎ 20613 [1]

Buttlar
Area Code: 036967

H Gästehaus Napoleons Rast, Frankfurter Str. 11, ☎ 59666, II [1]

H Zum Dorfkrug, Heug. 6, ☎ 71536, III [1.5]

AH Schloss Buttlar, Schlossgarten 2, ☎ 59666, ☎ 0171/9906660, III [1.5]

Mieswarz (Buttlar)
Area Code: 036967

B&B Zimmermann, Hauptstr. 1, ☎ 71522, I ☺ [5]

Borsch (Geisa)
Area Code: 036967

H Zum weißen Roß, Am Dorfbach 92, ☎ 75426, III [2]

Geisa
Area Code: 036967

ℹ Stadtverwaltung Geisa, Marktpl. 27, ☎ 690 [0]

H Fürstliches Schloss, Schlosspl. 4, ☎ 593550, III-IV [0]

H Geisschänke, An der Geis 27, ☎ 70651, I [0]

B&B Kött, Meritzer Weg 6, ☎ 51126, ☎ 0175/3515702, II [4.5]

B Heim, Röderweg 3, ☎ 75346, I [0]

🚲 Abel'S Fahrradladen, Borscher Str. 18, ☎ 75913 [0.5]

Schleid
Area Code: 036967

H Zur Pferdetränke, Schleider Hauptstr. 59, ☎ 70184, III [0]

AH Zum Ulsterblick, Ulsterweg 7, ☎ 6575, ☎ 0157/38916770, I-II [0]

Spahl (Geisa)
Area Code: 036967

H Heile Schern, Zum Geisaer Berg 1, ☎ 51088 [4.5]

Ketten (Geisa)
Area Code: 036967

H B. Stehling, Rößbergstr. 28, ☎ 52056 [5]

Günthers (Tann)
H Ulsterbrücke, Brückenstr. 1, ☎ 06682/9704046, II [0.5]

Schlitzenhausen (Tann)
Area Code: 06682

B&B Mihm, Schilfweg 13, ☎ 1399, II-III [0.5]

Tann
Area Code: 06682

ℹ Tourist-Information Tann, Marktpl., im Rathaus, ☎ 961111 [0.5]

H Am Rathaus, Am Marktpl. 16, ☎ 96220, III [0.5]

H Zur Krone, Am Stadttor 2, ☎ 213, II-III [0.5]

H Zur schönen Aussicht, Rhönbergstr. 17, ☎ 216, I [2.5]

B&B Ditzel, Rockenstuhlstr. 12, ☎ 8178, I [0.5]

Lahrbach (Tann)

H Landhaus Kehl, Eisenacher Str. 15, ☎ 06682/387, III 0.5

BB Haus am Felsenkeller, Ringweg 2, ☎ 06682/8515, II 0.5

Eckweisbach (Hilders)

Area Code: 06681

H Kühler Grund, Hauptstr. 21, ☎ 290, II 0

H Zum Rosenbachschen Löwen, Hauptstr. 24, ☎ 258, II–III 0

AH Landhaus Will, Von-Guttenberg-Str. 14, ☎ 318, II–III 😊 0.5

Hilders

Area Code: 06681

i Tourist-Information Hilders, Kirchstr. 2-6, ☎ 960815 0.5

H Landhotel Hohmann, Obertor 2, ☎ 296, III 0.5

BB Haus Winterberg, Am Mühlrain 2a, ☎ 1292, I 0.5

BB Rhön Hotel, Battensteinstr. 17, ☎ 1388, I–II 1

B Haus Hartung, Am Pfarracker 8, ☎ 1288, I 0.5

B Haus Weber, Am Winterberg 27, ☎ 7231, I–II 0

B Haus Wingenfeld, Birkenweg 6, ☎ 1205, I 0

B Haus am Kurpark, Oskar-Seifert-Str. 15, ☎ 7125, II 0.5

🚲 Fa. Spiegel, Bahnhofstr. 10, ☎ 8372, ☎ 0173/3120814 0

Findlos (Hilders)

BB Georgshof, Waldweg 2, ☎ 06681/8664, III 😊 0

Batten (Hilders)

Area Code: 06681

AH Spiegel, Hilderser Str. 11, ☎ 8616, I 0.5

Frankenheim

Area Code: 036946

H Thüringer Rhönhaus, Rhönhausstr. 1, ☎ 32060, II 1.5

H Debertshäuser, Dr.-Wuttig-Str. 18, ☎ 32141 0.5

B Rauch, Doktor-Wuttig-Str. 9, ☎ 32133 0.5

Fladungen

Area Code: 09778

i Tourist-Information, Marktpl. 1, ☎ 919111 0

H Sennhütte, Sennhütte 1, Hochrhönstraße beim Schwarzen Moor, ☎ 91010, III 2

H Sonnentau, Wurmberg 1-3, ☎ 91220, III–IV 0

H Haus Jutta, Flurstr. 6, ☎ 7141, II 0.5

H Sonne, Mußmächerstr. 1, ☎ 1484, II 0.5

BB Weihersmühle, Weihersweg 25+27, ☎ 356, II 😊 1

Weimarsschmieden (Fladungen)

H Zur Weimarschmiede, Gustav-Heß-Str. 4, ☎ 09778/1605, II 0

Hermannsfeld (Rhönblick)

Area Code: 036945

H Jägerstube, Fasanerie, ☎ 0171/6352007 0.5

Henneberg

Area Code: 036945

BB Altes Forsthaus, Hauptstr. 76, ☎ 519799, ☎ 0160/2106859 0

Behrungen

BB Gestüt Eschenhof, Hauptstr. 76, ☎ 036944/54856 0

Irmelshausen (Höchheim)

Area Code: 09764

H Zur Linde, Kirchpl. 1, ☎ 8150, II 0.5

A Badesee Irmelshausen, ☎ 655, ☎ 602 0

Bad Königshofen im Grabfeld

Area Code: 09761

i Kurbetriebs GmbH, Am Kurzentrum 1, ☎ 91200 0.5

H Ebner, Zeughausstr./Schottstr. 36, ☎ 91190, III 😊 0.5

H Landhotel Vierjahreszeiten, Bamberger Str. 18-20, ☎ 395660, III 😊 1

H Schlundhaus, Marktpl. 25, ☎ 1562, II 0.5

BB Haus Sankt Michael, Wallstr. 49, ☎ 910610, I–III 😊 0.5

B Edeltraud Schlosser, An der Gipsmühle 5, ☎ 0160/1815227 0.5

B Kleines Seehaus, Am Kneuerskeller 5, ☎ 1347, II 0

🚲 Fahrrad Burger, Keßlerstr. 2, ☎ 9273 0

Zimmerau (Sulzdorf an der Lederhecke)

H Berggasthof Bayernturm, Turmstr. 53, ☎ 09763/265, I 0.5

Lindenau (Bad Colberg-Heldburg)

Area Code: 036871

H Lindenau, Schulg. 17, ☎ 21147, I 0

Ummerstadt

Area Code: 036871

BB Neubert, Colberger Str. 2, ☎ 21812, I 0

B Mausolf, Coburger Str. 157, ☎ 21802, I 0.5

AH Treubig, Coburger Str. 239, ☎ 21950, I 0.5

Bad Colberg (Bad Colberg-Heldburg)

Area Code: 036871

i Tourist-Information, Hauptstr. 4, ☎ 20159 0

H Seysingshof, Reusseng. 20, ☎ 01577/2600555, II 0

BB Kaffeestübchen, Hauptstr. 36, ☎ 309383, II 0

B Rangerhof, Hauptstr. 34, ☎ 21711, I–II 0

Heldburg (Bad Colberg-Heldburg)

Area Code: 036871

H Altes Schützenhaus, Ziegelhütte 183, ☎ 317388, II 0.5

BB Unteres Tor, Schuhmarkt 92, ☎ 21341, I 0

Einöd (Bad Colberg-Heldburg)

Area Code: 036871

H Zum Rittergut, Hauptstr. 241, ☎ 21931, ☎ 21933, I 1.5

B Country Scheune, Einöd 385, ☎ 30490, II 1.5

Streufdorf (Straufhain)

BB Café im Hof, Roßfelder Str. 10, ☎ 036875/50103, II 😊 0

Bad Rodach

Area Code: 09564

i Gästeinformation, Schlosspl. 5, Haus des Gastes / im ehem. Jagdschloss von 1749, ☎ 1550 0

H Flair- und Kurhotel am Thermalbad, Kurring 2, ☎ 92300, IV–V 1.5

BB Hirschmühle, Hirschmüllersweg 1, ☎ 80155 1

Gauerstadt (Bad Rodach)

Area Code: 09564

H Landgasthof Wacker, Billmuthäuser Str. 1, ☎ 92384, III 😊 2.5

Heldritt (Bad Rodach)

Area Code: 09564

AH Alte Mühle, Zur Schwaige 9, ☎ 3842, ☎ 0177/9104185, II 2

Grattstadt (Bad Rodach)

Area Code: 09564

Ⓐ Edelgard, Brnnnwiesenweg 3, ☎ 720, III ⓪

Oberwohlsbach (Rödental)
Area Code: 09563

Ⓗ Alte Mühle, Mühlgarten 5, ☎ 72380, IV ⓪

Rödental
Area Code: 09563

Ⓗ Grosch, Oeslauerstr. 115, ☎ 7500, IV ☺ ⓪

Ⓗ Sauerteig, Oeslauer Str. 100, ☎ 1220, III ⓪.5

Lützelbuch (Coburg)
Area Code: 09561

Ⓗ Landhaus Fink, Lützelbucher Str. 25, ☎ 24940, III ⓪.5

Ⓗ Fink, Lützelbucher Str. 22, ☎ 24940, II ⓪.5

Coburg
Area Code: 09561

ⓘ Tourist-Information, Herrng. 4, ☎ 898000 ⓪

Ⓗ Best Western Blankenburg Hotel, Rosenauer Str. 30, ☎ 6440, IV ☺ ①

Ⓗ Bärenturm Hotelpension, Untere Anlage 2, ☎ 318401, IV ⓪

Ⓗ Gerberhof, Gerberg. 1, ☎ 871187, III-IV ⓪.5

Ⓗ Goldene Traube, Am Viktoriabrunnen 2, ☎ 8760, IV-V ⓪

Ⓗ Goldener Anker, Roseng. 14, ☎ 55700, IV ⓪

Ⓗ Hahnmühle, Steinweg 68, ☎ 354905, III-IV ⓪.5

Ⓗ Stadt Coburg, Lossaustr. 12, ☎ 8740, IV-V ⓪

Ⓗg Haus Gemmer, Rosenauer Str. 10, ☎ 55510, III ①

Ⓗg Stadtvilla, Seifartshofstr. 10, ☎ 2399370, IV-V ⓪.5

Ⓗg Vienna House Easy Coburg, Ketschendorfer Str. 86, ☎ 8210, IV ①

Ⓗ Münchener Hofbräu, Kleine Johannisg. 8, ☎ 234923, III ⓪

Ⓑ Gästehaus Heimrich, Humboldtweg 4, ☎ 420312, II ☺ ①

Ⓐ Leise am Markt, Herrng. 2, ☎ 7951735, II-III ⓪

Ⓐ Zürl, Gartenstr. 3, ☎ 643794, 0160/4900196, II ⓪.5

🚲 Bike Shop Coburg, Judeng. 20, ☎ 55220 ⓪.5

🚲 Radhaus Coburg, Rodacher Str. 10, ☎ 5966588 ①

Mönchröden (Rödental)
Area Code: 09563

Ⓑ Hochstädter Fremdenzimmer, Lange Wiesen 2, ☎ 5093172, ☎ 0176/61217212 ⓪

Neustadt bei Coburg
Area Code: 09568

ⓘ Stadtverwaltung, Georg-Langbein-Str. 1, ☎ 81133 ⓪

Ⓗg Am Markt, Markt 3, ☎ 920220, III ⓪

🚲 Zweirad Martin, Wittkenstr. 8, ☎ 94090 ⓪

Hönbach (Sonneberg)
Area Code: 03675

Ⓗ Zum Grünen Baum, Neustadter Str. 195, ☎ 802949, II ⓪.5

Bächlein (Mitwitz)
Area Code: 09266

Ⓗ Waldhotel Bächleinp, Bächlein 12, ☎ 9600, III-IV ⓪

Haig (Stockheim (Oberfranken))
Area Code: 09261

Ⓗ Landgasthof Detsch, Coburger Str. 9, ☎ 62490, III ☺ ⓪

Kronach
Area Code: 09261

ⓘ Tourismus- und Veranstaltungsbetrieb der Lucas-Cranach-Stadt Kronach, Marktpl. 5, ☎ 97236 ⓪.5

Ⓗ City-Hotel Sonne, Bahnhofstr. 2, ☎ 60970, III ⓪.5

Ⓗ Kronacher Stadthotels, Amtsgerichtsstr. 12, ☎ 504590, IV-V ⓪.5

Ⓗg Bauer's Bed & Breakfast, Kulmbacher Str. 7, ☎ 94058, III ⓪.5

Ⓗg Försterhof, Paul-Keller-Str. 3, ☎ 962364, III-IV ☺ ⓪

Ⓗ Klosterkeller, Amtsgerichtsstr. 33, ☎ 3086560, III ⓪.5

Ⓑ Galerie Ambiente, Stadtgraben 15, ☎ 51361, OB, II ⓪.5

Ⓑ&Ⓑ Ferienhof Barnickel-Thierauf, Alte Ludwigsstädter Str. 22, ☎ 2199, I-II ⓪

🏰 Festungsherberge Kronach, Festung 1, ☎ 94412, I ⓪.5

🚲 Radsport Dressel, Fröschbrunn 8, ☎ 3406 ①.5

Stockheim (Oberfranken)
Area Code: 09265

Ⓐ Mei Dehamm, Maximilianstr. 2a, ☎ 09261/53353, III ⓪

🚲 Mich's Fahrradschmiede, Bergwerksstr. 20, ☎ 1484, ☎ 0151/12889571 ①

Neukenroth (Stockheim (Oberfranken))
Area Code: 09265

Ⓗ Rebhan's Business and Wellness Hotel, Ludwigstädter Str. 95-97, ☎ 9556000, III ⓪.5

Ⓗ Fillweber, Ludwigsstädter Str. 25, ☎ 381, II ⓪

Spechtsbrunn (Sonneberg)
Area Code: 036703

ⓘ Naturparkinformationszentrum, Am Rennsteig 1, ☎ 70812 ⓪

Ⓗ Peterhänsel, Obere Sonneberger Str. 21, ☎ 81191, ☎ 0173/6113737, II ①

Ⓑ&Ⓑ Am Rennsteig, Obere Sonneberger Str. 2, ☎ 80389, III ☺ ①

Ⓐ Ferienwohnung am Rennsteig, Am Winterberg 11, ☎ 80555, II ☺ ①

Lauenstein (Ludwigsstadt)
Area Code: 09263

Ⓗ Posthotel, Orlamünder Str. 2, ☎ 99130, III ⓪

Ludwigsstadt
Area Code: 09263

ⓘ Tourist-Information, Lauensteiner Str. 44, ☎ 974541 ⓪

Ⓗ Zum Torpeter, Roseng. 10, ☎ 974037, I ⓪.5

Ⓐ Conrad, Waldleite 11, ☎ 1243, II ⓪.5

Probstzella
Area Code: 036735

Ⓗ Haus des Volkes, Bahnhofstr. 25, ☎ 46057, III ①.5

Lehesten
Area Code: 036653

ⓘ Tourist-Information, Obere Marktstr. 1, ☎ 2600 ⓪

Ⓗ Schieferpark, Staatsbruch 1, ☎ 26050, II-III ⓪

Ⓗ Glück Auf, Markt 1, ☎ 22216, II ⓪

Ⓗ Zur Linde, Schmiedebach Nr. 41, ☎ 22252, II ①

Ⓑ Wirth, Bergg. 2, ☎ 22790, II ⓪

Brennersgrün (Lehesten)
Area Code: 036653

B Rennsteighaus Brennersgrün, Brennersgrün 55, ☎ 036652/169816, ☎ 0152/53572544, II-III ⓞ

AH Rennsteig 48, Brennersgrün 48, ☎ 036652/22835, ☎ 0172/3465445, II ⓞ

Grumbach (Wurzbach)
Area Code: 036652

H Zum Frankenwald, Grumbach 40, ☎ 22832 ⓞ

B&B Pension und Pizzeria La Familigia, Grumbach 27, ☎ 169816, ☎ 0152/53572544 ⓞ

AH Alte Kegelbahn, Grumbach 15, ☎ 35386, ☎ 0174/2166890, I ⓞ

Rodacherbrunn (Wurzbach)
Area Code: 036652

B Taudt, Rodacherbrunn 5, ☎ 22012 ⓞ

Schlegel
Area Code: 036642

ℹ Tourist-Information, Selbitzpl. 1, Blankenstein, ☎ 29533, ☎ 296026 ⓞ

B Korn, Ortsstr. 10, ☎ 23002, I ⓞ

Kießling (Harra)
Area Code: 036642

B Schmidt, Rennsteig 4, ☎ 28110, I ⓞ

AH Brettschneider, Kießling 19, ☎ 29448, I-II ⓞ

Harra
Area Code: 036642

B Hrdina, Gartenwiese 2, ☎ 23727, II ①

A B Am Trepplesfelsen, Schlossberg, ☎ 22038, ☎ 0171/6112134 ①.⑤

Blankenstein
Area Code: 036642

ℹ Tourist-Information, Selbitzpl. 1, ☎ 29533, ☎ 296026 ⓞ

H Rennsteig, Lobensteiner Str. 3, ☎ 22230, ☎ 25886, II-III ⓞ

B&B Am Rennsteig, Rennsteig 3, ☎ 23207, ☎ 0172/4565520, II ☺ ⓞ

B&B Langheinrich, August-Bebel-Str. 3, ☎ 22595, II ⓞ

Blankenberg
Area Code: 036642

H Blankenberg, Schlossberg 9, ☎ 23913, II ⓞ.⑤

Rudolphstein (Berg)
Area Code: 09293

H Meister Bär Hotel Frankenwald, Panoramastr. 2, ☎ 9410, III-IV ⓞ

Pottiga
Area Code: 036642

H Hotel-Gasthof-Rüdiger, Anger 4, ☎ 3010, III ②

Berg
Area Code: 09293

ℹ Gemeindeamt Berg, Kirchpl. 2, ☎ 9430 ①

Hirschberg
Area Code: 036644

ℹ Ferienregion Selbitztal-Döbraberg, Bahnhofspl. 1, Naila, ☎ 09282/6829 ⑥

ℹ Stadtverwaltung, Marktstr. 2, ☎ 4300 ⓞ.⑤

H Kleeblatt, Gartenstr. 1, ☎ 434870, II-III ⓞ.⑤

H An der Lohmühle, Bahnhofstr. 21a, ☎ 21424, I ⓞ.⑤

B Weitermann, August-Bebel-Str. 4, ☎ 21428, I ⓞ.⑤

AH Söllner, Schulweg 5, ☎ 21964, ☎ 0152/53493233, I ⓞ.⑤

Juchhöh (Hirschberg)
Area Code: 036649

H Juchhöh, Juchhöh 61, ☎ 80007 ⓞ

Hof
Area Code: 09281

ℹ Tourist-Information, Ludwigstr. 24, ☎ 8157777 ①

H Akropolis, Sedanstr. 1 1/2, ☎ 87185, II ⓞ

H Am Kuhbogen, Marienstr. 88, ☎ 72030, III ①

H Burghof, Bahnhofstr. 53, ☎ 819350, III ⓞ.⑤

H Central, Kulmbacher Str. 4, ☎ 6050, III ②

H Hotel am Untreusee, Wilhelm-Löhe-Str. 3, ☎ 540653, III ②

H Munzert, Eppenreuther Str. 100, ☎ 783400, II ②.⑤

H Posthorn, Sedanstr. 8, ☎ 3324, II-III ⓞ

H Strauss, Bismarckstr. 31, ☎ 9720630, II-III ☺ ①

Hg Am Maxplatz, Ludwigstr. 15, ☎ 1739, IV ①

Hg Deutsches Haus, Marienstr. 33, ☎ 1048, ☎ 1049, II-III ①

H Deutsche Flotte, Plauener Str. 50, ☎ 92443, ☎ 0152/08690148, III ②

H Taverna Kostas, Pfarr 17, ☎ 87008, II ⓞ.⑤

B&B AH HOFZimmer, Friedrichstr. 8, ☎ 0176/39876220, II ①

B Baumgärtner, Friedrichstr. 1, ☎ 5939193, II ①

B Scholl, Brunhildweg 8, ☎ 86384, ☎ 0152/01776459, I-II ②.⑤

AH Jadehaus, Bismarckstr. 3, ☎ 160560, ☎ 0170/2911994, II ①

AH Park & See, Gartenstr. 35, ☎ 735337, II ②.⑤

AH Shashkin, Yorckstr. 1, ☎ 5919809, ☎ 0152/29516961, I ①.⑤

M Jugendherberge, Beethovenstr. 44, ☎ 93277 ①

🚲 Bike Station, Ernst-Reuter-Str. 64, ☎ 141444 ①.⑤

🚲 Radhaus Hensel&Koller, Wunsiedler Str. 16, ☎ 5402730 ⓞ.⑤

Thanks

Thank you to everyone who supported us so enthusiastically in the creation of this book. In particular, my thanks to: K. u. L. Janz; A. Weger; B. Bach; F. Korrmann; G. Rüthemann; K. Knolle; J. Klotz; U. Rosenbaum; S. u. R. Trepke; F. Gehrold, Hannover; ; A. Wauer; H. Schmitt u. H. Schmitt-Thomas; J. Hansen, Hamburg; M. Drewes; H. Scheinpflug, Roßtal; Christel & Annelene; M. Mayer, Donauwörth; R. Morr; C. Ludwig, Schöningen; W. Dubiel, Aurich; D. Dechau; K. Langer; A. Reikowski; L. Kossmann-Schulz, G. Schulz; J. Tetzlaff; M Schwanig, Oberursel; G. Herbermann, Georgsmarienhütte; U. Siebert, Espenau; U. Nitzbon, Reinbek-Ohe; K. Reiff, Bad Honnef; K.-H. Kupzick; A. Brodt-Zabka, J. Zabka, S. Kempfle, F. Messow, A. Bojunga, U. Homfeld, D. u. W. May; C. Pointner, Geretsried; D. Behrens, Frankfurt/Main; Chr. Otte, Porta Westfalica; J. Rohde; P. B. u. Chr. Dähler, CH-Küttingen; H. u. P. Schlüter; R. Guske; J. Starck, Arendsee/Altmark; F. u. L. Gohr; H. J. u. E. Friedrich; U. Hasenbein; K. S. u.R. Elmiger, CH-Konolfingen; B. Willasch; J.-W. Karl, Ammerbuch; H. Gertraud, München.

Geographical Index

The page numbers from p.186 refer to the list of accomodations.

A

Abbendorf	191
Abbenrode	96
Ahrenberg	194
Albungen	194
Altenburschla	128, 195
Alt Garge	44, 188
Arendsee	
Arendsee (Altmark)	65, 190
Arenshausen	121, 193
Asbach-Sickenberg	194
Aue	194
Aulosen	

B

Bächlein	198
Bad Colberg	154, 197
Bad Harzburg	192
Bad Helmstedt	192
Bad Königshofen im Grabfeld	151, 197
Bad Rodach	158, 197
Bad Sooden-Allendorf	124, 194
Bäk	32, 187
Batten	197

Beendorf	85, 192
Behrungen	150, 197
Berg	199
Bergen (Dumme)	191
Berkach	150
Berka/Werra	133, 196
Bernheide	190
Bitter	45, 189
Blankenberg	178, 199
Blankenstein	178, 199
Bleckede	43, 188
Böckwitz	77
Bohnenburg	48
Boizenburg	
Boizenburg/Elbe	42, 188
Bömenzien	64, 190
Borderland museum Eichsfeld	117
Bornhagen	121, 193
Bornsen	
Borsch	196
Breetz	190
Breitenrode	191
Brennersgrün	198
Brochthausen	112, 193
Brome	76, 191
Brünkendorf	189
Büchen	38, 188

Buchenau	130, 195
Büchen-Dorf	37
Buttlar	196

C

Campow	30
Coburg	162, 198
Creuzburg	130, 195
Cumlosen	60, 190

D

Dankmarshausen	133, 196
Darchau	189
Dargow	34, 188
Deutsch	190
Diesdorf	
Dömitz	50, 189
Duderstadt	113, 193

E

Ebenshausen	130, 195
Eckertal	97
Eckweisbach	197
Einöd	197
Elend	102, 192
Ellershausen	194
Ellrich	108
Eschwege	126, 194

F

Falken	195
Findlos	197
Fitzen	188
Fladungen	144, 197
Flecken Diesdorf	74, 191
Frankenheim	144, 197
Frankenroda	130, 195
Fuhrbach	193

G

Gartow	190
Gauerstadt	197
Geisa	138, 140, 196
Genin	187
Gerblingerode	193
Gerstungen	132, 196
Gladdenstedt	76
Göddingen	189
Göhr	72
Göringen	195
Gorleben	54, 189
Grasleben	192
Grattstadt	197
Grebendorf	125, 194
Grenzlandmuseum Eichsfeld	
Grippel	189